Compendium

Volume Six

to

Commentary

on

The Book of Mormon

Philip M. Hudson

Because
words are the
fire of God, every
element of mortality can
be a lyrical experience. To help
us to intellectually, emotionally,
and spiritually process the perceptions
that bombard our self-awareness, we have
been provided by Him with a banquet of truth
that was composed of the 22 mystical letters in the
Hebrew alphabet, and presumably also the "reformed
Egyptian". Each one flavors our conception of His
kingdom, as we engage a progressive curriculum
that nurtures us by teaching us about our own
world. Each one quietly and subtly shapes
our appreciation of the efforts of those who
created the record with blood, sweat, toil
and tears, as we embark upon our
own pilgrimage that will prove
to be transformative.

Copyright 2024 by Philip M. Hudson.
Published 2024.
Printed in the United States of America.
All rights reserved.

No portion of this book may be reproduced,
stored in a retrieval system, or transmitted
in any form or by any means, mechanical,
electronic, photocopy, recording, scanning,
or other, except for brief quotations in
critical reviews or articles, without
the prior written permission
of the author.

ISBN 978-1-957077-78-9
Illustrations - Google Images.

This book may be ordered from
online bookstores.

Publishing Services
by BookCrafters, Parker, Colorado.
www.bookcrafters.net

Nothing short of the plain
and most precious teachings of
the Lord and Savior Jesus Christ can
explain the special covenant relationship
that Israel has always enjoyed with its God.
(See 1 Nephi 13:26). These truths are even more
clearly understood in The Book of Mormon than
they are in the Bible, "wherefore they shall both be
established in one." (1 Nephi 13:41). Thru the Law
of Witnesses, these two books confirm the divinity of
the Lord and Savior. "That which shall be written" in
the Bible and The Book of Mormon will "grow together,
unto the confounding of false doctrines and laying
down of contentions," and establishing an era of
peace among the tribes of the House of Israel,
by "bringing them to a knowledge of my
covenants, saith the Lord," for He has
always been, and forever will be,
their one and only God.
(2 Nephi 3:12).

Index to Compendia Volumes 3-7

Before we commit to any significant course of action, such as accepting The Book of Mormon as Another Testament of Jesus Christ, we turn to the Lord and make the issue a matter of prayer so that we may experience the confirming witness of the Spirit. With fire for the deed, we cannot fail.

Volume 3 Essays

- Abstinence in a Permissive World
- Additional Scripture
- Addressing Deity
- Agency
- Agency and Opposition
- Agency and Youth
- Age of Accountability
- Alma's Discourse on Faith
- And it Came to Pass
- And Thus We See
- Angels
- Are Mormons Christian?
- Are We Alone in The Universe?
- (The) Atonement
- Bah Humbug!
- Baptism
- Batteries are Not Included
- Become as Little Children
- Before a Wound Can Heal
- Behold
- Being Well Grounded
- (The) Bible
- (The) Biggest Loser
- Blood, Covenant, and Land Israel
- (The) Book of Mormon as History
- Book of Mormon Strengths
- (The) Book of Mormon was Preserved for our Day
- Born Again Christians
- Brevity)
- Buddy Can You Spare a Dime?
- Caesar
- (A) Change of Heart
- (The) Character of God
- Choose the Harder Right
- Choose ye This Day
- Christians
- (A) Christmas Miracle
- Christ's Church is Restored
- (The) Church
- (The) Church of Jesus Christ in Former Times
- Circle of Knowledge
- Citizenship in The Church and Kingdom
- Civil Liberties
- (A) Coat of Many Colors
- Cogito Ergo Sum
- Cognates in The Book of Mormon
- Combatting Evil
- Commitment
- Conditional Sentences in The Book of Mormon
- Connections
- Construction Zone: Proceed with Caution
- Conversion

In response
to the direction
of a benevolent God,
angels have been sent from
heaven to administer the oil of
gladness. It is like having spiritual
angioplasty, facilitating the free flow
of communication between us and God.
It is inspired treatment for sclerosis of the
spirit. Mormon recounted that Ammon, one
of the 4 Sons of Mosiah, had reason to rejoice,
for he had been given a second chance to fulfill
his life's potential, after he had been born again.
He must have considered himself very fortunate
that God had looked beyond the behavior of his
rebellious youth, and had been able to see into
his heart. His rough exterior, as it turned out,
had been nothing more than a façade. His
true character was only revealed when
the Atonement released him from the
awful bondage of sin, and in the
miracle of a spiritual rebirth,
he became a new creature
in the Lord and Savior
Jesus Christ.

Volume 4 Essays

- Courage
- Covenant Consciousness
- Covenants
- (The) Creation of The World
- Dancing With the Stars
- (The) Desert Shall Rejoice
- Diversity
- Doctrine – The Meaning of
- (The) Door Swings Both Ways
- Dry Humor in The Book of Mormon
- (The) Dust of The Earth
- (The) Duty of The Priest
- Education
- (The Best) Education
- Enduring to The End
- Entropy in The Physical and Eternal Worlds
- Environmental Concerns: An Eternal Perspective
- Establishing the Word
- (Our) Eternal Nature
- Eternal Progression in a Dynamic Universe
- Everyone Wants to Go to Heaven
- Evidences of God
- Faith and Knowledge
- Faith Building
- Faith is a Principle of Power
- (The) Fall
- Fasting
- Fate
- Father Forgive Them
- Finding Balance in Our Lives
- Friendship
- Focus
- Follow the Prophet
- Forgiveness
- For Unto Us a Child is Born
- (The Importance of) Friends
- Friendship
- Gathering of Israel
- General Conference
- (The) Germination of our Faith
- Gifts of The Spirit
- God is NowHere
- Godly Qualities
- God's Tactical Flashlight
- Gold – The Appearance of
- Grace
- Gratitude

The Book of Mormon will expose us to opportunities to bear each other's burdens. It does not debate the merits of the petitions of the weak and impoverished who need our aid and it turns a blind eye to our prejudices that threaten to influence the depth and breadth of our compassion.

Volume 5 Essays

Happiness
Happiness and Sharing the Gospel
Happiness / Wickedness
Having Been Commissioned of Jesus Christ
Heaven Can Wait
Heavenly Father Knows Us
(The) Heavens Were Opened
Higher Dimensional Realities
(The) Holy Ghost
(The) Holy Grail of Religious Doctrine
Honesty
(The) Hourglass of Life
How Does God Get Things Done?
Huckleberries and Chokeberries
Humility
Hypocrisy
I am a Child of God
I Have Fought a Good Fight
I Have Overcome the World
Isaiah in The Book of Mormon
Is Heaven Hotter Than Hell?
It's Our Book
Joseph Smith: A Rough Stone Rolling
Joseph Smith History
Joseph Smith's World

Jumping Out of Our Skin
Just Get Back on The Bike
Justice
Justice and Mercy
Keep Smiling
Labels
Lamanites by The Waters of Sebus
(The) Last Judgment
Life is a Three Act Play
Life or Death?
Life's Greatest Questions
Life's Important Decisions
Light
Light and Darkness
Light and Truth
(The) Light of Christ
(The) Light of The World
Limiting Beliefs
Living Water
Look Who's Coming to Town
Lost Books of The Bible
(The) Lost Manuscript
(The) Lost Ten Tribes
Lucifer

It was in the Fifth Century
A.D., at the commencement of the
Middle Ages, that the White Martyrs
of Christian Ireland clothed themselves
in distinctive white wool robes and fanned
out all across Europe. In dozens of locations,
they founded monasteries. Their influence is
incalculable. They re-established literacy, and
breathed new life into the exhausted cultures
of Europe. "And that is how the Irish saved
civilization." (Thomas Cahill). P.S. And
that is also how the Sons of Mosiah
saved the Anti-Nephi-Lehies.
(See Alma 23:5-8).

Volume 6 Essays

- (A) Mailbox Marked With an "X"
- Management by The Spirit
- (The) Manifestation of Spirits
- May the 4th Be With You
- (The) Millennium
- (The) Mind of God
- Missing Scripture
- Missionary Work
- Moral Discipline
- Mothers
- Multi-tasking
- (The) Name of Christ in The Book of Mormon
- (The) Nature of God and Our Covenants
- (Our) Neighbors
- No Greater Call
- (The) Number of Disciples Was Multiplied
- Obedience
- One Lord, One Faith, One Baptism
- Persecution
- Personal Revelation
- (The) Plan of Salvation
- (The) Plan of Salvation 15 Names
- (A) Positive Mental Attitude
- Power: The Ultimate Test of Character
- Pragmatism in The Book of Mormon
- Premortal Life
- Preparation
- Pride
- (The) Priests of Baal in Our Lives
- (The) Prime Directive
- Professors
- Proper Prior Preparation
- (The) Prophet Joseph Smith
- Prophet, Seer, and
- (The) Q Continuum
- Quorum Sensing
- Receiving Revelation
- Recognizing the Church of Christ
- Removing the Barnacles of Life
- Restoration – The Early Days
- Revelation
- Reverence
- (The) Sabbath
- (The) Sacrament
- Sacramental Waters
- Satan
- (The) Scope of Our Decisions
- (The) Second Mile
- Service
- Set Apart
- Sharing the Gospel
- Sharper Than a Two-edged Sword
- (The) Sons of Mosiah
- Speak Kind Words to Each Other
- (The) Spirit of Revelation

It is the gospel of Jesus Christ as it has been revealed in The Book of Mormon that inspires us to enthusiasm. After all, it is the good news that practically begs us to experience the feeling of being possessed by a god, to have supernatural inspiration, and enjoy prophetic frenzy. The definition found in the dictionary is unmistakable. If we are suffused with enthusiasm, our actions are no longer ours; for it is God Who has taken control of our destiny, with kindness and benevolence.

Volume 7 Essays

Spiritual Calisthenics
Spiritual Gifts
Spiritual Identity Theft
(A) Standard of Excellence
Strangers in The Land
Strengths and Weaknesses
Studying the Scriptures
Success Strategies
Symbols
Talents
Teaching in The Church
Teaching Key Doctrine
Technological Traps
(A) Testimony of Christ
(A) Thirty Day Spiritual Fitness Program
Thou Hast Done Wonderful Things
(The) Thrill of Victory / Agony of DeFeet
Tithing
Too Good to Be True
(The) Tools of The Trade

Touching His Garment
Tough Questions
Travel at The Speed of Thought
(The) Twelve Tribes of Israel
Types, Rites, Ceremonies, and Symbols (Alma Unity
Updates are Ready
Walk in The Light of The Lord
(Our) Weaknesses
Were There Two Cumorahs?
What Think Ye of Christ?
Wherefore and Therefore in The Book of Mormon
(A) Whirlwind into Heaven
Who is Packing Your Parachute?
Why We Laugh
Words of Mormon
Work and Personal Responsibility
Worship in Music
Writing on Metal Plates Was a Pain
Zion

Gleaming jaws epitomize the gateway to hell. (See 2 Nephi Chapter 9). They are dripping with the sickening slurry of the saliva of Satan, that has been saturated with sin. They menacingly portray the entrance to the inhospitable spirit prison of the unjust. The way to avoid this awful portal is to offer the Lord the required sacrifice which is to be broken in our hearts with sorrow for sin, and in the spirit of contrition to come to Him in an attitude of sincere and purposeful repentance, that we might obtain forgiveness through His tender mercies.

Compendium Volume 3-7 Scriptures

Introduction - Look Who's Coming to Town
1 Nephi 1:20 - Follow the Prophet
2 Nephi 1:30 - Friendship
1 Nephi 2:1-3 - Life's Important Decisions
1 Nephi 3:7 - Obedience
1 Nephi 3:15-16 - Just Get Back on The Bike
1 Nephi 8:2 - Cognates in The Book of Mormon
1 Nephi 8:20 – (The) Hourglass of Life
1 Nephi 8:24 & 11:25 - Being Well Grounded
1 Nephi 9:5-6 - (The) Lost Manuscript
1 Nephi 11:6 & 8 - Jumping Out of Our Skin
1 Nephi 11:25 - Living Water
1 Nephi 13:26 – (The) Lost Books of The Bible
1 Nephi 14:7 - Book of Mormon Strengths
1 Nephi 14:10 – (The) Church
1 Nephi 15:14 - Teaching Key Doctrine
1 Nephi 15:20 - Gathering of Israel
1 Nephi 15:30 - God's Tactical Flashlight
1 Nephi 17:22 - Speak Kind Words
1 Nephi 17:50-51 - Multi-tasking
1 Nephi 19:12 - Environmental Concerns
1 Nephi 20:6 - Circle of Knowledge
1 Nephi 21:25 - Combatting Evil
2 Nephi 1:30 - Friendship
2 Nephi 2:4 – (The) Fall
2 Nephi 2:11 - Entropy
2 Nephi 2:15-16) - Work & Responsibility
2 Nephi 2:16 & 27 - Agency
2 Nephi 2:2 &, Alma 42:8 - Why We Laugh
2 Nephi 2:27 - Fate
2 Nephi 2:28 - Cogito Ergo Sum
2 Nephi 3:7 - Joseph Smith: A Rough Stone
2 Nephi 3:7 & 15 – (The)Prophet Joseph Smith
2 Nephi 31:16 & 18, & Moroni 10:5 - Joseph Smith

2 Nephi 4:35 - Life's Greatest Questions
2 Nephi 9:13 - Plan of Salvation Names
2 Nephi 9:13 - Holy Grail of Religious Doctrine
2 Nephi 9:18 – (The) Church in Former Times
2 Nephi 9:29 - Agency and Opposition
2 Nephi 9:29 - Education
2 Nephi 11:7 – (The) Creation of The World
2 Nephi 12:5 - Walk in The Light
2 Nephi 15:20 - Light and Darkness
2 Nephi 21:6-9 – (The) Millennium
2 Nephi 21:22-23 – (The) Desert Shall Rejoice
2 Nephi 21:31 - Quorum Sensing
2 Nephi 21:31 – (The Meaning of) Doctrine
2 Nephi 24:1 - Strangers in The Land
2 Nephi 24:12 - Lucifer
2 Nephi 25:23 - Grace
2 Nephi 25:1 - Are Mormons Christian?
2 Nephi 26:14 – (The) Church in The Last Days
2 Nephi 26:16 - Book of Mormon Preserved
2 Nephi 26:16 - Establishing the Word
2 Nephi 26:29 – (The) Priests of Baal
2 Nephi 27:10-11 - Receiving Revelation
2 Nephi 27:26 – Wonderful Things
2 Nephi 28:3-4 – (The Best) Education
2 Nephi 28:12 - Pride
2 Nephi 28:20 - God is NowHere
2 Nephi 28:26 - Power: Ultimate Test of Character
2 Nephi 28:30 - Christ's Church is Restored
2 Nephi 28:30-32 - Updates are Ready
2 Nephi 29:3 – (The) Bible
2 Nephi 29:6 - For Unto Us a Child is Born
2 Nephi 29:7-8 - Additional Scripture
2 Nephi 30:2 & 2 Nephi 24:1-2 - Blood, Covenant, and Land Israel

In an address to his people who lived in Zarahemla, King Benjamin explained a revelatory truth: "Because of the covenant which you have made, you shall be called the children of Christ, his sons, and his daughters, for behold, this day he hath spiritually begotten you; for you say that your hearts are changed through faith on his name; therefore, you are born of him." (Mosiah 5:7).

2 Nephi 31:16 & 18, & Moroni 10:5 - Joseph Smith History
2 Nephi 31:17-18 - Eternal Progression
2 Nephi 31:19-20 - (The) Prime Directive
2 Nephi 31:20 - Spiritual Calisthenics
2 Nephi 32:5-6 - Faith and Knowledge
2 Nephi 33:4 – (The) Second Mile
Jacob 1:6 - Revelation
Jacob 1:13-14 – (Our) Neighbors
Jacob 2:31 - Abstinence in a Permissive World
Jacob 4:6 – (The Spirit of) Revelation
Jacob 4:8 – (The) Mind of God
Jacob 4:11 - Faith Building
Jacob 4:13 - Too Good to Be True
Jacob 5:10 - Is Heaven Hotter Than Hell?
Enos 1:27 - Spiritual Identity Theft
Jarom 1:4 - Godly Qualities
Jarom 1:5 – (The) Sabbath
Jarom 1:20 - Plan of Salvation
Omni 1:26 - Fasting
Words of Mormon 1:3 - Words of Mormon
Words of Mormon 1:5 - Brevity
Mosiah 2:1 - General Conference
Mosiah 2:17 - Service
Mosiah 2:25 – (The) Dust of The Earth
Mosiah 3:12-13 - Proper Prior Preparation
Mosiah 3:15 - Symbols
Mosiah 3:19 – (The) Atonement
Mosiah 4:9 - Are We Alone in The Universe?
Mosiah 4:19 - Buddy Can You Spare a Dime?)
Mosiah 4:20-21 - Batteries are Not Included
Mosiah 4:27 - Finding Balance in Our Lives
Mosiah 5:7 - I am a Child of God
Mosiah 5:7 - Born Again Christians
Mosiah 5:7 - A Change of Heart
Mosiah 5:8-10 - Huckleberries and Chokeberries
Mosiah 8:13 & 16-17 – Heavens Were Opened
Mosiah 8:16 - Prophet, Seer, and
Mosiah 15:14-18 – (The) Thrill of Victory &
  The Agony of DeFeet
Mosiah 18:20 - Before a Wound Can Heal
Mosiah 18:21 – (A) Positive Mental Attitude
Mosiah 23:16-17 & 25:29 - Having Been
  Commissioned of Jesus Christ
Mosiah 25:19-20 – (The) Duty of The Priest

Mosiah 26:22 - Father Forgive Them
Mosiah 27:3 - Teaching in The Church
Mosiah 27:8-9 - Agency and Youth
Mosiah 27:11 - Angels
Mosiah 29:2 - Caesar
Mosiah 29:12-13 - Citizenship
Alma 5:7 - Set Apart
Alma 5:26 - Worship in Music
Alma 5:46 - Personal Revelation
Alma 7:20 - How Does God Get Things Done?
Alma 9:19-23 - Talents
Alma 11:43 – (The) Biggest Loser
Alma 12:27 – (The) Last Judgment
Alma 13:3 - Life is a Three Act Play
Alma 13:3 - Premortal Life
Alma 17:2-3 – (The) Sons of Mosiah
Alma 17:4 - Sharing the Gospel
Alma 17:34-36 – Lamanites by The Waters of Sebus
Alma 22:18 - Removing the Barnacles of Life
Alma 26:8 - Gratitude
Alma 27:27 - Honesty
Alma 26:23-24 – (The) Scope of Our Decisions
Alma 29:1 - Happiness and Sharing the Gospel
Alma 29:1-2 - No Greater Call
Alma 29:4 - Life or Death?
Alma 30:7-9 - Choose Ye This Day
Alma 30:13 - Everyone Wants to Go to Heaven
Alma 30:13 - Evidences of God
Alma 30:41 – (A) Testimony of Christ
Alma 30:44 - Dancing With the Stars
Alma 31:5 - Studying the Scriptures
Alma 31:5 - (Spiritual Fitness Program
Alma 32:5 - Limiting Beliefs
Alma 32:27 - Alma's Discourse on Faith
Alma 32:28 – (The) Germination of Our Faith
Alma 32:35 - Light
Alma 32:42-43 – (The) Tools of The Trade
Alma 34:32 - Preparation
Alma 36:12-14 - Bah Humbug!
Alma 36:19 - I Have Overcome the World
Alma 37:45 - Types, Rites, Ceremonies,
  and Symbols
Alma 40:20 - Construction Zone

The Nephites
risked relaxing, distorting, or
losing their firm grip on reality when
they crowded themselves into doctrinal dead
ends, religious roundabouts, and conceptual cul-
de-sacs from which there was no easy avenue of escape.
In their day and in ours, a one-dimensional person with
a narrow view of the world will perceive things not as they
really are, but only as their limited vision permits them to
see. The gospel perspective gives us a multi-dimensional
view of existence that provides a much more accurate
representation of our surroundings. In this sense,
the glory of God is intelligence, or the ability to
perceive and process information relating to
the physical and spiritual worlds around
us, even the multi-dimensional world
that is our native environment, in
spite of the fact that it cannot
be seen with our natural
eyes.

- Alma 40:23-24 – (Our) Eternal Nature
- Alma 41:10 - Happiness
- Alma 41:13 - Justice
- Alma 42:13-15 - Justice and Mercy
- Alma 42:26 – (The) Character of God
- Alma 46:12 - A Coat of Many Colors
- Alma 46:15 - Christians
- Alma 46:20 - May the 4th Be With You
- Alma 48:7 - Courage
- Alma 48:19 - Choose the Harder Right
- Alma 50:23 - Happiness / Wickedness
- Alma 51:5-6 - Civil Liberties
- Alma 56:47-48 - Mothers
- Alma 60:6-7 - Focus
- Helaman 3:25-28 - The Number of Disciples Was Multiplied
- Helaman 3:33 - Professors
- Helaman 3:35 - Touching His Garment
- Helaman 3:35 - Humility
- Helaman 5:12 - Covenant Consciousness
- Helaman 6:37 - Missionary Work
- Helaman 10:6 - Heavenly Father Knows Us
- Helaman 12:7-10 - Sharper Than a Two-edged Sword
- Helaman 16:23 - Satan
- Helaman 13:19-20 - Missing Scripture
- Helaman 13:38 - Heaven Can Wait
- 3 Nephi 1:12-13 - (A) Christmas Miracle
- 3 Nephi 9:33 - Conversion
- 3 Nephi 11:10-11 – (The) Light of the World
- 3 Nephi 12:2 - What Think Ye of Christ?
- 3 Nephi 12:10 - Persecution
- 3 Nephi 12:48 - Nature of God and Covenants
- 3 Nephi 13:9 - Addressing Deity
- 3 Nephi 13:14 - Forgiveness
- 3 Nephi 13:14-15 – Door Swings Both Ways
- 3 Nephi 13:22 – (The) Q Continuum
- 3 Nephi 14:5 - Hypocrisy
- 3 Nephi 14:11 - Spiritual Gifts
- 3 Nephi 14:22-23 – (A) Mailbox Marked With an "X"
- 3 Nephi 15:9 - Enduring to The End
- 3 Nephi 16:1-3 – (The) Twelve Tribes of Israel
- 3 Nephi 17:4 – (The) Lost Ten Tribes
- 3 Nephi 19:30 - Keep Smiling
- 3 Nephi 23:1 - Isaiah in The Book of Mormon
- 3 Nephi 24:8-10 - Tithing
- 3 Nephi 26:14 - Become as Little Children
- 3 Nephi 27:5 - (The) Name of Christ in The Book of Mormon
- 3 Nephi 27:8 - Recognizing the Church of Christ
- 3 Nephi 27:13-20 - Baptism
- 3 Nephi 27:22 - Restoration, The Early Days
- 3 Nephi 27:28-29 - Tough Questions
- 3 Nephi 28:6 - Travel at The Speed of Thought
- 3 Nephi 28:13-15 - Higher Dimensional Realities
- 3 Nephi 28:13-15 – (A) Whirlwind into Heaven
- 3 Nephi 29:3 - Covenants
- 4 Nephi 1:17 - Labels
- 4 Nephi 1:17-18 - Unity
- Mormon 1:3-4 – Book of Mormon as History
- Mormon 3:20-22 - It's Our Book
- Mormon 6:2 - Were There Two Cumorahs?
- Mormon 8:5 – (The Importance of) Friends
- Mormon 8:8 - Age of Accountability
- Mormon 8:35 - Connections
- Mormon 8:35 - Joseph Smith's World
- Mormon 8:38 – (Our) Neighbors
- Mormon 8:38 - Technological Traps
- Mormon 9:6 - Who is Packing Your Parachute?
- Mormon 9:32-33 - And it Came to Pass
- Ether 4:12 - Light and Truth
- Ether 12:24-25, Jacob 4:1 & Mormon 8:17 - Writing on Metal Plates Was a Pain
- Ether 12:26 – (Our) Weaknesses
- Ether 12:27 - Strengths and Weaknesses
- Ether 15:11 - Gold – The Appearance of
- Moroni 2:2 – (The) Holy Ghost
- Moroni 4:1 – (The) Sacrament
- Moroni 5:1-2 - Sacramental Waters
- Moroni 6:9 - Reverence
- Moroni 7:13 - Management by The Spirit
- Moroni 7:19 – (The) Light of Christ
- Moroni 7:24 - Diversity
- Moroni 7:33 - Moral Discipline
- Moroni 7:41 - Success Strategies
- Moroni 7:44 - Faith is a Principle of Power
- Moroni 8:8 - Commitment
- Moroni 8:25-26 - One Lord, One Faith, One Baptism

The Book of Mormon is in harmony with the principles of the gospel and the doctrine of Christ. When reviewing that doctrine, it is important to remember that God's work is progressive. It may change its appearance, but never its principles. Practices may change with circumstances, but doctrine remains constant. This doctrine draws attention to the issue of continuing revelation from God. "We believe all that God has revealed, all that he does now reveal, and we believe that he will yet reveal many great and important things pertaining to the Kingdom of God." (Ninth Article of Faith).

Moroni 10:8 - Gifts of The Spirit
Moroni 10:8 – (The) Manifestation of Spirits
Moroni 10:31 - Zion

Moroni 10:31 – (A) Standard of Excellence
Moroni 10:34 - I Have Fought a Good Fight

In the
symbolism
of the tree of life,
we see the reflection
of the love of God. Its fruit,
as expected, represents eternal
life, which is the greatest gift our
Father could give His children. There
are many who are actively, passionately,
and desperately fighting their way through
swirling mists of darkness as they make their
way to the tree of life and its precious fruit. In
Nephi's account, those who arrived at the tree
fell down at its base, completely spent as a
result of their efforts. A new meaning is
given to Alma's expression of being
"swallowed up in the joy of (our)
God, even to the exhausting
of (our) strength."
(Alma 27:17).

If you don't find what you are looking for in the Index of Volumes 3 – 7, check out this list of topics with related essay references.

Abstinence – Abstinence in a Permissive World
Accountability – Age of Accountability
Adaptivity – Updates are Ready
Apocrypha – Additional Scripture
Apocrypha – Lost Books of The Bible
Apocrypha – Missing Scripture
Apostolic Church – (The) Church of Jesus Christ in Former Times
Are We Alone in The Universe? – Dancing With the Stars
Attitude - Just Keep Smiling
Authority – Having Been Commissioned of Jesus Christ
Born Again – A Change of Heart
Ceremonies – Types, Rites, Ceremonies, and Symbols
Character – Our Eternal Nature
Charity – Buddy Can You Spare a Dime?
Charity – A Mailbox Marked With an X
Chastity – Abstinence in a Permissive World
Christians – Are Mormons Christians
Christ – What Think Ye of Christ?
Church – Recognizing The Church of Christ
Consequences – The Scope of Our Decisions
Corrections – Writing on Metal Plates Was a Pain
Covenants – Covenant Consciousness
Covenants – The Nature of God and Our Covenants
Cumorah – Were There Two Cumorahs?
Darkness – Light and Darkness
Death – Everyone Wants to Go to Heaven
Dependency – Who is Packing Your Parachute?
Devil – Lucifer
Discipline – Moral Discipline
Doctrine – Teaching Key Doctrine
Evangelicals – Born Again Christians
Evil – Combatting Evil
Excellence – A Standard of Excellence
Faith – Alma's Discourse on Faith
Faith – The Germination of our Faith
Faith – Alma's Discourse on Faith
Feet – The Thrill of Victory / The Agony of DeFeet

Forgiveness – The Door Swings Both Ways
Forgiveness – Father Forgive Them
Freedom of Choice - Agency
Free Will – Agency
Gathering of Israel – The Desert Shall Rejoice
Gifts of The Spirit – Spiritual Gifts
Government – Caesar
Government – Management by The Spirit
Great Apostasy – Apostasy
Heaven – Higher Dimensional Realities
Holy Ghost – Batteries are Not Included
Holy Ghost – God's Tactical Flashlight
Humility – The Dust of The Earth
I Am a Child of God – Spiritual Identity Theft
Immorality – Abstinence in a Permissive World
I Think, Therefore I Am – Cogito, Ergo Sum
Joseph's Technicolor Dream Coat – A Coat of Many Colors
Kindness – Speak Kind Words to Each Other
Knowledge – The Circle of Knowledge
Last Days – The Church in The Last Days
Laughter – Why We Laugh
Light – Walk in The Light
Mercy – Justice and Mercy
Missionary Work – Happiness and Sharing The Gospel
Missionary Work – No Greater Call
Missionary Work – The Number of Disciples Was Multiplied
Missionary Work – Sharing The Gospel
Missionary Work – The Sons of Mosiah
Missionary Work – Strangers in The Land
Music – Worship in Music
Non-members – Strangers in The Land
Omniscience – (The) Q Continuum
One Way – One Lord, One Faith, One Baptism
Opposition – Agency and Opposition
Opposition – Lamanites by The Waters of Sebus
Optimism – Huckleberries and Chokeberries

In language that is peculiar, or unique, to The Book of Mormon, the prophet-historian Mormon recorded that Jesus "smile(d) upon them and behold, they were as white as the countenance and also the garments of Jesus; and behold the whiteness thereof did exceed all the whiteness, yea, even there could be nothing upon earth so white as the whiteness thereof." (3 Nephi 19:25). They had been purified thru the redeeming blood of Christ, and by the grace of God they were saved. They enjoyed a relationship of the Second Comforter, and their faces reflected His light. To the Latter-day Saints, the Lord re-affirmed: "If your eye be single to my glory, your whole bodies shall be filled with light, and there shall be no darkness in you." (D&C 88:67).

Peer Pressure – (The) Priests of Baal in Our Lives
Permissiveness – Abstinence in a Permissive World
Perseverance – Just Get Back on The Bike
Personal Responsibility – Work and Personal Responsibility
Plan of Salvation – (The) Hourglass of Life
Plan of Salvation – Life is a Three Act Play
Plates – Writing on Metal Plates Was a Pain
Power – May the 4th Be With You
Preaching the Gospel – Establishing the Word
Preparedness – Spiritual Calisthenics
Priest's Duty – (The) Duty of The Priest
Primitive Church – (The) Church of Jesus Christ in Former Times
Pseudepigrapha – Additional Scripture
Repentance – Before a Wound Can Heal
Repentance – Removing the Barnacles of Life
Responsibility – Work and Personal Responsibility
Restoration – Christ's Church is Restored
Revelation – The Heavens Were Opened
Revelation – Personal Revelation
Revelation – (The) Spirit of Revelation
Revelation – Receiving Revelation
Rites – Types, Rites, Ceremonies, and Symbols
Satan – Lucifer
Scripture Not in The Bible – Additional Scripture

Scriptures – Studying the Scriptures
Speed of Light / Thought – Travel at The Speed of Thought
Spirits – (The) Manifestation of Spirits
Spiritual Fitness – (A) Thirty Day Spiritual Fitness Program
Spiritual Gifts – Gifts of The Spirit
Symbols – Types, Rites, Ceremonies, and Symbols
Technology – Technological Traps
Telestial / Celestial – Jumping Out of Our Skin
Ten Tribes – (The) Lost Ten Tribes
Translation – (A) Whirlwind into Heaven
Truth – Light and Truth
Types – Types, Rites, Ceremonies, and Symbols
Unity – Quorum Sensing
Weakness – Strengths and Weaknesses
Why Things Fall Apart – Entropy in The Physical and Eternal Worlds
Wickedness – Happiness and Wickedness
Wishful Thinking – Too Good to Be True
Word of God – Sharper Than a Two-edged Sword
Work in Progress – Construction Zone: Proceed With Caution
Worship – Worship in Music
Youth – Agency and Youth

In Book of Mormon doctrine, it's reaffirmed that the highest pinnacle of spirituality is not joy in the unbroken sunshine, but absolute and undoubting trust in the love of God. Every life must endure a soaking rain every now and again, together with the attendant mud that inevitably follows. Change will come "like a clap of thunder, and a flash of lightning. But after the storm, flowers will bloom."

(I Ching).

Table of Contents

"Scripture consists not in what we read,
but in what we understand."
(St. Hilary).

Adversity can behave as a diamond dust that polishes us to a high luster, or it can be an abrasive that wears us down and grinds us up. However, we cannot hope to successfully deal with our difficulties without having first centered our lives on Jesus Christ. He said: "And if men come unto me, I will show unto them their weakness. I give unto men weakness that they may be humble; and my grace is sufficient for all men that humble themselves before me; for if they humble themselves before me, and have faith in me, then will I make weak things strong unto them."
(Ether 12:27).

Author's Note...1

Introduction...3

Essays..11

It is in the congealed distillate of their life experiences, that
the thoughts and feelings of Book of Mormon prophet-historians that
were recorded over a course of a thousand years of Nephite and Lamanite
history relating to the Savior stand revealed as their innocent attempts to
yoke their emotions to language. From Nephi to Alma to Moroni, not to
mention the Jaredite record-keepers, they hoped that latter-day Israel
would find their expressions of faith refreshing, would use them
as food for thought, and would be motivated to act upon
their expanding awareness and appreciation of the
principles of the Plan that are explained
with refreshing clarity
in the book.

Observations

Observations..245

Commentary, Compendia, & Observations Index

Commentary, Compendia, & Observations Index..365

It will not take long
for you to see that the observations
that have been sprinkled throughout this
volume have been carefully crafted to represent a
variety of geometrical designs. It may be surprising to
learn that the construction of these patterns has helped me to
coherently organize my thoughts. In many cases, the outcome
almost seems to have been foreordained, as I moved words around
until, as if my magic, they dropped into their proper positions on the
page. Often, I had envisioned beforehand the particular framework that I
wanted to achieve, and when I had appropriately arranged the words, one
or two would stand out and grab my attention, because they still didn't
feel quite right. Frequently, it was not difficult to find an alternative
that would not only fit better physically, but also was etymologically
much better suited to the spiritual concept that I wished to convey.
As my work on the project continued, I was intrigued by the
natural evolution of the process. That made me consider
whether my success might have been stimulated
by unconventional thought processes that
are more commonly characterized as
inspiration or discernment.

Author's Note

These Compendia have taken on a life of their own, expanding into a collection of eight volumes of detailed information about The Book of Mormon that supplement my three volumes of Commentary. In essence, they are a distillation of my feelings that relate to The Book of Mormon. Their content is more visceral that that of the Commentary, and perhaps it more accurately reflects my personal feelings about the monumental themes that run throughout all of scripture. They summarize the more comprehensive body of work in my Commentary and showcase my feelings, in the hope that they might become living documents that not only reflect my present understanding of The Book of Mormon, but also the paradigms that expand with the utilization of new tools of discovery. It's a good bet that there is more to come. As the adage encourages, we need to "Think ourselves empty, read ourselves full, write ourselves clear, pray ourselves hot, and let ourselves go!"

When
we sink our roots
down into the earthy
loam of ordinances and
covenants, we find that they
have become intertwined with
the principles and doctrines
of The Book of Mormon.

Introduction

Mormon foresaw our day when secular Christianity would be abominable, and its mission would have become corrupted, because it would subtly lead the children of God away from the truth. Without their conscious realization, it would stop their progression by destroying the purpose of mortality in God's great Plan of Salvation. Insult would be added to injury as hypocrisy further perverted doctrine into humanized, spiritually impotent dogma, when Christians would not really believe, but only be professors of religion. Such have been labeled by the Lord as imposters, who "draw near to Him with their lips, but whose hearts are far from Him." Those who are substantively no more than 'professors of religion' are those who "teach for doctrines the commandments of men." They have "a form of godliness, but they deny the power thereof." (J.S.H. 1:19).

Cicero wrote: "The first law for the historian is that he shall never dare utter an untruth. The second is that he shall suppress nothing that is true. Moreover, there shall be no suspicion of partiality or of malice in his writing." The accounts in The Book of Mormon written by the prophets Nephi, Jacob, Alma, Mormon, Moroni, and others, and abridged by the prophet-historian Mormon, were true to the mandate given by Cicero. Although, as Washington Irving brooded: "It is the rule that history fades into fable; fact becomes clouded with doubt and controversy; the inscription moulders, and columns, arches, and pyramids are but heaps of sand, and their epitaphs, nothing but characters written in the dust," yet The Book of Mormon stands as a shining example of the divine model.

It "is the witness that testifies to the passing of time. It illuminates reality, vitalizes memory, provides guidance in daily life, and brings us tidings of antiquity." It is the "evidence of time, the light of truth, the life of memory, the directress of life, committed to immortality." (Cicero, "De Oratore," ii, 36). In its pages, "the centuries roll back to the ancient age of gold." (Horace, "Odes," IV, ii, 39).

In one of the beautiful simplicities of the gospel, we are taught that the Plan allows all of us to enjoy the same access to the simplest, and yet most powerful, witness to the truth. In an inarticulate voice softer than the faintest whisper of sweet breath on the cheek, the Holy Ghost gently testifies, or bears witness, of truth. As Moroni 10:5 teaches (in a verse that is often overlooked, in favor of the previous verse): "By the power of the Holy Ghost ye may know the truth of all things."

The Holy Ghost has revealed all that is true, and has illuminated every eternal principle that has guided the minds of men and women since the dawn of history. We constantly benefit from that which He reveals. In the Last Days, when the Spirit is "poured out upon all flesh, and when "young men see visions, and old men dream dreams," (Joel 2:28), it will be the Holy Ghost Who provides the creative drive. The irony is that many will fail to recognize the source of their inspiration. Job did not. He wrote: "For God speaketh once, yea twice, yet man perceiveth it not. In a dream, in a vision of the night, when deep sleep falleth upon men, in slumberings upon the bed; then he openeth the ears of men, and sealeth their instruction." (Job 33:14-16). We cannot help but think of the experience of Joseph Smith in his bedchamber, when we read Job's description of how, at certain times, Heavenly Father chooses to communicate with His children.

All who desire to have a sure personal witnesses must carefully and prayerfully read The Book of Mormon, and then ask in faith if what they have studied is true. They will then receive the testimony of the Holy Ghost to motivate them to seek out the Priesthood and to enter into sacred covenants with God. It will be as it was on the Day of Pentecost, when Peter and others were preaching to a multitude whose hearts and minds were open and receptive to the truth. The words of the Apostles carried the weight of authority, and penetrated the hearts of their listeners to the end that they asked: "Men and brethren, what shall we do? Then Peter said unto them, Repent, and be baptized every one of you in the name of Jesus Christ for the remission of sins, and ye shall receive the gift of the Holy Ghost." (Acts 2:37-38). And on that day, there were about 3,000 souls added to the kingdom of God on earth. (See Commentary Reference to 3 Nephi 15:21-24).

A similar scenario exists today. Since the restoration of the gospel, there has been a Pentecostal outpouring of the Spirit, and those with a sincere desire to understand the will of God bring the same humble petition to the doorstep of the missionaries: "Now that we have heard your message, have put it to the test of prayerful inquiry, and have received a witness of the Spirit, what shall we do?" The response of the servants of the Lord is unequivocal: "You must exercise saving faith that leads to the waters of baptism and to continuing commitment, dedicated discipleship, selfless service, and sustained spirituality."

Shakespeare wrote: "The past is prologue." ("The Tempest," Act 2, Scene 1). The phrase was intended to imply that our

Always looking for the easy
way out condemns us to negotiate
the instability of the shaky ground
of telestial turf, as opposed to the
solid foundation that The Book
of Mormon offers to those
who put their trust in
the Holy Ghost.

past is merely a prologue, or an introduction, to the great adventure upon which we will embark if we follow through on our plans. This original interpretation teaches that what has come before on our journey through life doesn't matter in the grand scheme of things, because a new future lies before us, subject to the choices we will yet make. The human condition does not change much over time, which is one reason why the Lord has revealed The Book of Mormon in the Last Days, so that we might profit from the experiences of the Nephites who are distant from us in time and yet are so like us.

Hugh Nibley observed: "Men fool themselves, when they think for a moment that they can read scripture without ever adding something to the text or omitting something from it." Therein lies the power inherent in its study. We glean insight and understanding every time we investigate the word of God. I have learned to love the scriptures, and I often think of St. Hilary, who wrote: "Scripture consists not in what we read, but in what we understand." In these Compendia, I have consistently tried to anchor to the scriptures the ideas swirling around in my head.

Utilization of commentaries and compendia does not replace personal scripture study. The spiritual awakening that accompanies prayerful efforts to understand the mysteries of God through the study of His word cannot be achieved through another person's interpretation. Perhaps, though, my own perspectives on the eternal themes expressed within The Book of Mormon will be helpful to you as you read and seek your own guidance. It is my hope that you will use these compendia only to assist you in your own personal journey to Christ.

Our challenge is to enlist the aid of the Holy Ghost as we undertake that journey. Many years ago, Dallin Oaks wrote: "Latter-day Saints know that learned or authoritative commentaries (and compendia) can help us with scriptural interpretation, but we maintain that they must be used with caution. (They) are not substitutes for the scriptures any more than a good cookbook is a substitute for food. When I refer to "commentaries," I mean everything that interprets scripture, from the comprehensive book-length commentary to the brief interpretation embodied in a lesson or an article, such as this one."

"One trouble with commentaries," he continued, "is that their authors sometimes focus on only one meaning to the exclusion of others. As a result, commentaries, if not used with great care, may illuminate the author's chosen and correct meaning but close our eyes and restrict our horizons to other possible meanings. Sometimes, those other less obvious meanings can be the ones most valuable and useful to us as we seek to obtain answers to our own questions. This is why the teaching of the Holy Ghost is a better guide to scriptural interpretation than is even the best commentary." ("Ensign," 1/1985).

Harold B. Lee taught: "We are convinced that our members are hungry for the gospel undiluted, with its abundant truths and insights. There are those who have seemed to forget that the most powerful weapons the Lord has given us against all that is evil are His own declarations – the plain and simple doctrines of salvation as found in the scriptures." (Regional Representatives Seminar, 10/1/1970).

Bruce R. McConkie explained that "revelation is necessary because … each pronouncement in the holy scriptures is so written as to reveal little or much, depending on the spiritual capacity of the student." ("A New Witness for The Articles of Faith," p. 71).

And so, as President Oaks continued, "the scriptures are not the ultimate source of knowledge, but what precedes the ultimate source. The ultimate source comes by revelation. We encourage everyone to make careful study of the scriptures and of prophetic teachings … and to prayerfully seek personal revelation to know their meaning for themselves … If we seek and accept revelation and inspiration to enlarge our understanding, we will have the mysteries of God unfolded to us by the power of the Holy Ghost."

It is only after we have tried the virtue of the word of God, that can we know that he "doth grant unto (us) whatsoever (we) ask that is right, in faith, believing that (we) shall receive. O then, how (we) ought to impart of the substance that (we) have, one to another." (Mosiah 4:21). The church offers us wonderful opportunities for our practice of an active, meaningful brotherhood. An institutional welfare, on the other hand, generally offers only detached, disinterested, and disconnected paternalism, all with an economic baseline that either trivializes or ignores the intrinsic worth of souls.

Elder McConkie also said: "I sometimes think that one of the best kept secrets of the kingdom is that the scriptures open the door to the receipt of revelation." ("Doctrines of The Restoration," p. 243). And President Oaks reaffirmed: "We do not overstate the point when we say that the scriptures can be a Urim and Thummim to assist each of us to receive personal revelation."

President Oaks enlarged upon the perspective of the young prophet: "Joseph was, by his own admission, no writer. He felt imprisoned by what he called the 'total darkness of paper, pen, and ink." (Joseph Smith to William W. Phelps, 11/27/1832, B.Y.U. Press, 2002, p. 287). He thus considered it 'an awful responsibility to write in the name of the Lord'. (Joseph Smith Papers, 1:367).

He did not suppose that he could receive the revelations perfectly, nor did the Lord ever set that standard. Joseph and his appointed brethren edited the revelations (see D&C 70:1-4) based on (that) same premise ... namely, that he represented the voice of God as he spoke in what he characterized as his own 'crooked, broken, scattered, and imperfect language'. (Joseph Smith to William W. Phelps, 11/27/1832, quoted in "Making Sense of the Doctrine & Covenants, a Guided Tour Through Modern Revelation," Steven Harper. "Personal Writings of Joseph Smith," p. 186-187).

President Oaks concluded his own epistle by stating a simple truth: "Latter-day Saints know that true doctrine comes by revelation from God, and not by worldly wisdom." (See Moses 5:58). He was in good company, for the Apostle Paul wrote that we are not capable of thinking any thing of ourselves; but we look to God for our wisdom. (See 1 Corinthians 3:5).

I could not agree more heartily with these wise words of counsel. As a matter of fact, every time I proofed my compendium (and I did this many times) I found myself scribbling additional notes in the margins and thinking to myself, "Why didn't I see that before?." That is precisely what I hope will be the experience of everyone who takes the time to read my compendia. I trust the process will motivate you to search the scriptures more carefully and to be instructed by the Spirit, as you do so, that you might be led in directions that will prove to be personally illuminating.

I would expect that my older grandchildren who read this compendium will be impacted in ways that are different from my adult children or my contemporaries. I hope that my observations will touch you differently each time you read them. When I am long-gone, perhaps the considerable thought that went into its production will generate a palpable bond that will span the years separating us. Maybe, the gulf that then divides us will not be as great, and our shared energies will pave the way to an eventual joyous reunion.

As the seasons of our lives unfold before us, we realize just how much we need the influence of The Book of Mormon, as we engage the Plan of Salvation. "For life is a sheet of paper white, where each of us may write a line or two, and then comes night. Greatly begin! If thou hast time for but a line, make that sublime. Not failure, but low aim, is crime." (James Lowell).

Essays

My own
weak attempts to
unlock the mysteries
of The Book of Mormon
in this volume remind me
of the Amish, who make some
of the finest quilts in the world.
On purpose, they build mistakes into
their projects, because they believe that
any attempt on their part to design
and produce a flawless creation
would be a mockery of God,
Who alone is perfect.

(A) Mailbox marked with an "X"

"Many will say
to me in that day: Lord,
Lord, have we not prophesied
in thy name, and in thy name have
cast out devils, and in thy name done
many wonderful works? And then
will I profess unto them: I never
knew you; depart from me."
(3 Nephi 14:22-23).

When I was a boy, I remember hearing my mother talk about her childhood experiences growing up during The Great Depression. She lived in rural Pennsylvania, along the Penn Central line about 50 miles south of Philadelphia. Although unemployment was running above 25%, my grandfather had been lucky enough to keep his job. There was always food on their table; nevertheless, she was not unfamiliar with soup kitchens and bread lines. The Depression spawned the familiar line: "Buddy, can you spare a dime?" It was a time of terrible want for too many Americans.

My grandmother was a good cook who prepared delicious and nutritious meals. In the warm months of spring and summer, their kitchen windows would be thrown wide-open to let in fresh air. At the same time, they also let the smell of bread fresh out of the oven or stew simmering on the stove escape into the outside air.

These tempting aromas often acted as a homing-beacon for "hobos" who rode the rails in search of greener pastures. Today, these homeless men are found huddled around gratings on sidewalks and near steam vents in most of our large cities and even in small towns, back then, this "flotsam and jetsam on the sea of life" Congregated in hobo camps near the railroad lines that crisscrossed America.

If my grandmother spotted a hobo loitering about near her house, she invariably called out to him with an invitation to sit in the shade of her front stoop. She would pour him a glass of cold milk or fresh-squeezed lemonade, give him a bowl of stew and a slice of bread, and cut him a piece of hot apple pie. These gestures were always accompanied by profuse thanks on the part of the grateful recipient of her kindness, who would leave with a full belly, a slightly more positive outlook on life, and the energy to carry on for one more day in the face of indescribable despair.

My grandfather was not a horticulturalist, but he did take great pride in his garden, and he kept his front yard in immaculate condition. If you can picture a quaint country cottage with whitewashed clapboard siding, black shutters, red brick chimney, window boxes full of flowers, and a white picket fence surrounding a green lawn bordered by shrubs, you will have a pretty good idea of what their home looked like. They lived in Moylan-Rose Valley, and the name fit perfectly. When I think of their community, visions of Brigadoon come to my mind.

One feature along the road that will forever be etched in my mind's eye is the mailbox perched on a post set in the grass alongside the road. After the crash of the stock market sent our economy into a free-fall, one of the hobos befriended by my grandmother had marked their mailbox with an "X." This simple scratch endured the wind, rain, sleet, and snow of a dozen winters during the Depression, and it spoke volumes. It was a hobo sign, universally recognized across the vast expanse of the country, alerting other riders of the rails that a hot meal and a piece of pie would always be waiting for them at the far end of a front walkway. The "X" acknowledged that someone recognized them, cared about them, and was prepared to help them in a tangible way.

My grandmother may not have thought of herself as a disciple of Christ. She didn't have a well-worn Bible, and was not well-acquainted with the Savior's life and teachings, but she intuitively followed His example. She committed His admonition to life, if not to memory: "Inasmuch as ye have done it unto one of the least of these my brethren, ye have done it unto me." (Matthew 25.40).

"There are no ordinary people," wrote C.S. Lewis. "You have never talked to a mere mortal. It is immortals with whom we joke, work, marry, snub and exploit. Our charity must be a real and costly love. Next to the blessed sacrament itself, your neighbor," and the homeless person with a cardboard sign, "is the holiest object presented to your senses." The perception of C.S. Lewis was clear and accurate. He could see the autobiographical thread of his neighbors leading backward to Deity. He understood that even the most hardened soul has within him "the acorn of a potential oak, the unsculpted image of a glorified personality." (Truman Madsen, "Eternal Man", p. 17).

Meanwhile, "little people, like you and me, if our prayers are sometimes granted beyond all hope and probability, had better not draw hasty conclusions to our own advantage. If we were stronger, we might be less tenderly treated. If we were braver, we might be sent, with far less help, to defend far more desperate posts in the great battle." (C.S. Lewis, "The World's Last Night, p. 10-11).

As true disciples, we actively practice our religion. John Taylor observed: "There are some Christian people in this world who, if a man were poor or hungry, would say, let us pray for him. I would suggest a little different regimen for a person in this condition; rather take him a bag of flour and a little beef or pork. A few such comforts will do him more good than your prayers." When a person is down and out, "an ounce of help is better than a pound of preaching." (Anonymous). Socrates said, "Know thyself." Cicero said, "Control Thyself." But Jesus said, "Give of thyself." We establish our commitment to actively embrace the demands of discipleship by following the example of Jesus.

Giving ourselves requires a revision of commonly accepted standards of qualification. In the Kingdom of God, it is not ability, or inability, but availability that is important. Brigham Young once said something to the effect that he never counted the cost of anything. He just found out what the Lord wanted him to do, and he did it. It is this kind of discipleship, no matter what our circumstances, that establishes our commitment and dedication.

Late in his life, Thomas Jefferson mused: "If, in my retirement to the humble station of a private citizen, I am accompanied with the esteem and approbation of my fellow citizens, trophies obtained by the blood-stained steel, or the tattered flags of the tented field, will never be envied. The care of human life and happiness, and not their destruction, is the first and only legitimate object of good government and was my only objective." ("The Writings of Thomas Jefferson," 8:165).

"But you were always a good man of business, Jacob." said Scrooge. "Business!" Cried the ghost, wringing its hands again. "Mankind was my business. The common welfare was my business; charity, mercy, forbearance, and benevolence were all my business. The dealings of my trade were but a drop of water in the comprehensive ocean of my business.

At this time of the rolling year," the spectre said, "I suffer most. Why did I walk through crowds of fellow-beings with my eyes turned down, and never raise them to that blessed Star which led the Wise Men to a poor abode? Where there no poor homes to which its light would have conducted me?" (Charles Dickens, "A Christmas Carol")

Our "mailboxes" are marked with an "X" when we treat others kindly through both conscious and unconscious acts of service and charity. Elder William R. Bradford of the Seventy once spoke with the bishop of a ward whose youth had worked to earn money for an activity. The bishop asked Elder Bradford if he would help the youth get some recognition for what they had done. To the bishop's surprise, Elder Bradford said he would not. He said that he was glad that the young people had worked hard, but that it was not important that they receive public recognition for their work.

When the youth then decided to donate their money to the Church's general missionary fund instead of using it for the activity, they wanted to have their picture taken with Elder Bradford as they made the donation, and they wanted to have the picture and an article put into the newspaper. Again, Elder Bradford surprised them by saying "no." He told the bishop: "You might consider helping your young people learn a higher law of recognition. Recognition from on high is silent. It is carefully and quietly recorded there. Let them feel the joy and gain the treasure in their heart and soul that come from silent, selfless service."

The Savior said: "Take heed that ye do not your alms before men, to be seen of them: otherwise ye have no reward of your Father which is in heaven." (Matthew 6:1). Jesus referred to these people as hypocrites, those who only pretend to have certain qualities and who try to appear righteous but are not. The Savior said of them: "They have their reward." (Matthew 6:2). "For where your treasure is, there will your heart be also." (Matthew 6:21).

The Savior "gave all he had to those in need for ones so meek and small like me; and in return I too will give all that I have, for I will live according to his perfect plan designed for woman, child and man; determined to return someday into his open arms and say: "My life, dear Lord, I lived for you, and through the trials I had, I grew. I served with all my heart and soul. Each day I strived to reach my goal to become like you in every way, putting faith in you as I knelt and prayed. My love for you cannot be told; as strong as that of prophets old. Oh Lord, my God, to you I gave all that I had each day I lived." (Anonymous).

Every day of our lives, as we strive to improve, the "X" on our mailbox will be brought into focus. However, we are all a little like the man who prayed: "Dear God, So far today I've done all right. I haven't gossiped. I haven't lost my temper. I haven't lied or cheated. I haven't been greedy, grumpy, nasty, selfish, or overindulgent. I'm very thankful for that. But, in a few minutes, Lord I'm going to get out of bed, and from then on, I'm probably going to need a lot more help." (Anonymous).

The assistance He will give us is greater sensitivity to those around us who stand in need, for real "poverty is never being curious about the world around you, and never wanting to explore it or the people in it. It is untested potential resulting from self-imposed limitations. It is having so many clothes you haven't got a thing to wear. It is eating so well you have to think about going on a diet. It is being loaded down with toys at birthdays and Christmas, and then being bored silly because there's nothing to do. It is having three degrees and feeling unfulfilled in your job. It is never stopping to see the beauty of the world. It is being white, healthy, middle class and unhappy." (Anonymous).

It is having a beautiful home in a fashionable section of town, with a yard maintained by a hired gardener and a mailbox that stands out by the conspicuous absence of an "X."

The teaching in Matthew 7:12 is often called the Golden Rule. "Therefore all things whatsoever ye would that men should do to you, do ye even so to them: for this is the law and the prophets." (Matthew 7:12). A group of Church members considered the question: "How can you tell if someone is converted to Jesus Christ?" For fifteen minutes those in attendance made numerous suggestions in response to the question, and the discussion leader carefully wrote down each answer on a large chalkboard. All of the comments were thoughtful and appropriate, but after a time, this great teacher erased everything he had written. Then, acknowledging that all of the comments had been worthwhile and appreciated, he taught a vital principle: 'The best barometer of our spiritual progress is the way we treat other people.' That simple indicator is always quietly evidenced by our mailbox marked with an "X."

Management by The Spirit

"Everything which inviteth
and enticeth to do good and to
love God, and to serve him,
is inspired of God."
(Moroni 7:13).

Love is the characteristic that underlies the quest for perfection in all things. It brings to mind friends, family, the teachings of the scriptures and the prophets, missionary work, the Savior, and our Father in Heaven. Its opposite is cunning, cruelty, and insensitivity. The contrasts deal with healing versus wounding, nurturing versus destroying, and encouragement versus disparagement.

There are many characteristics that need the softening influence of love before they become celestial qualities, for it is like an ether that allows us to catch a glimpse of heaven. It allows us to bridge the gulf between the world of everyday, and the land unpromised and unearned.

When energies are properly focused, to be zealous can be an admirable quality. One who is zealous attends to duties and responsibilities passionately, with ardent feeling and with fervor. When we are overzealous, however, we shoot the arrow blindly, and then move the target so that we can score what we mistakenly think is a bullseye. When we thus distort the doctrine, we play right into the hands of Satan, who caresses our neck with flaxen cords until we find ourselves bound with his strong chains. When we abandon our core values, we strain our eyes, lose our focus, and consequently look beyond the mark.

Obedience without love is hypocrisy. The characteristics of a Zion society are simply the result of a spiritual transformation in the lives of people that comes about as men and women live the Celestial Law of the Lord, not because they are compelled to do so, but because they want to do so.

Likewise, reverence without love is rigid and intolerable. Reverence embraces regard, deference, honor, and esteem. Without some degree of it, therefore, there would be no courtesy, no gentility, no consideration of others' feelings or of others' rights. "It is the fundamental virtue in religion. If there were more reverence in human hearts, there would be less room for sin and sorrow, and increased capacity for joy and gladness. Reverence for God and sacred things is the chief characteristic of a great soul." (David O. McKay).

Honesty is a virtue, but without love it is cruel. When we back people into a corner, the only way they can come out is fighting. The quality of honesty coupled with love, however, can instill in a person a sense of integrity that shines like a light through the eyes. George Washington wrote: "I hope I shall always possess firmness and virtue enough to maintain what I consider the most enviable of all titles, the character of an honest man."

Knowledge without love leads to misunderstanding, and knowledge without understanding is dogmatism. Within the gospel framework, our lives are dynamic and changing. As knowledge increases, so does our responsibility and commitment to obedience. As our testimony of Christ swells, faith intensifies our desire to repent. In this sense, when our lives are in harmony with gospel principles, we are in a constant state of improvement leading to perfection. Becoming Christ-like is the ultimate, incredible journey. It is the road less traveled, but the rewards make completing the trip worth the effort.

Humility can be a celestial quality, but without love it is a charade. The best way to come to a knowledge of the truth is to love the Lord through meekness, lowliness of heart, and humility. Meekness is a good word for the humility that comes through voluntary effort rather than as the result of pressure from external constraints.

Tolerance without love leads to neglect. On the telestial turf of secular humanism, Satan has home court advantage, and when we venture onto it, we risk losing our way. The quicksand of a false liberal ideology that accepts everything and risks nothing lies ready to suck the unwary into the underworld of the adversary.

Humor without love is tasteless, and leads to embarrassment, that quickly leads to humiliation. Humor can be a poor excuse for joy, that "none receive save it be the truly penitent and humble seeker of happiness." (Alma 27:18). Too often, humor is a poor excuse for the despair that comes because of iniquity. When our lives are lived in obedience to law, a blessing is given that results in happiness, or joy. When that law is disobeyed, punishment is given that results in unhappiness, or misery. Despair is the feeling of hopelessness that accompanies disobedience. Tasteless humor and sin often go hand in hand. In the words of Samuel the Lamanite: "Ye have sought all the days of your lives for that which ye could not obtain; and ye have sought for happiness in doing iniquity, which thing is contrary to the nature of that righteousness which is in our great and Eternal Head." (Helaman 13:38).

When we are in the service of our fellow beings, we are in God's service, but without love it is insincere and is often unappreciated or even resented. "God does notice us, and He watches over us. But it is usually through another person that He meets our needs. Therefore, it is vital that we serve each other. The abundant life is achieved as we magnify our view of life and expand our view of others and our own possibilities. Thus, the more we follow the teachings of the Master, the more enlarged our perspective becomes. We see many more possibilities for service that we would have seen without this magnification. There is great security in spirituality, and we cannot have spirituality without service." (President Spencer W. Kimball, "Ensign," 10/1985).

There is no greater call than to be a teacher, but teaching without love violates the mandate given by the Master Himself. As a matter of fact, without the Spirit, one cannot teach, for the Savior said, "if ye receive not the Spirit ye shall not teach." (D&C 42:14). The power to convey gospel principles comes through the Spirit. It must reside in both the one who delivers the word and the one who receives it. This is the beauty of gospel instruction. It is a foolproof method for disseminating information of eternal worth, and it cannot be mishandled or misrepresented. The responsibility is so great that it is no wonder that the Savior warned: "Be ye clean that bear the vessels of the Lord." (D&C 38:42).

Ministering to others without love insults the spirit of the program, and is a dereliction of our duty to God. The Lord has reminded the Saints: "There has been a day of calling, but the time has come for a day of choosing; and let those be chosen that are worthy." (D&C 105:35).

Missionary work without love is a contradiction in terms. It is ineffective at best, and inoperative at worst. Feeding the flock of the Good Shepherd with the nourishing bread of life will eventually bring His missionary army into complete harmony with the attributes of our Father in Heaven. "And ye shall be even as I am, and I am even as the Father, and the Father and I are one," said the Savior to the Three Nephite missionaries. (3 Nephi 28:37).

Before Fiorello La Guardia became mayor of New York City, he was a magistrate. One day there appeared before him a man accused of stealing a loaf of bread. Upon questioning, the man explained that he'd committed the crime to feed his family, for they were starving. Whereupon, La Guardia dismissed the case, and sentenced all present in the courtroom to pay a fine for living in a city where a man must steal to feed his family.

The Lord illustrated the gospel principle of concern for the welfare of others, when He said unto them, "I am the bread of life: He that cometh to me shall never hunger; and he that believeth on me shall never thirst." (John 6:35). In the Eternal Court of Justice, what will be the penalty for failure to provide others with the Bread of Life, or for feeding them stale, or moldy, or otherwise unwholesome bread?

Lyman Abbott said: "The brotherhood of man is an integral part of Christianity no less than the Fatherhood of God; and to deny the one is no less infidel than to deny the other." Truly, there is no brotherhood of man without the fatherhood of God. "The mystic bond of brotherhood makes all men one." (Thomas Carlyle). "The universe is but one great city, full of beloved ones, divine and human, by nature endeared to each other." (Epictetus).

Discipline without love is a bitter rebuke. Disciplined actions motivated by love, however, will swell the chorus of voices shouting "Hallelujah," and may significantly hasten the millennial reign of the Lord. B.H. Roberts once said that "the Latter-day Saints are the white-hot sparks struck off the Divine Anvil of God," destined to kindle a fire that will burn so brightly that it will celestialize the earth so that it might receive its rightful King.

True disciples commit the Thirteen Articles of Faith to life as well as to memory, and actively practice their religion. John Taylor observed that "there are some Christian people in this world who, if a man were poor or hungry, would say, let us pray for him. I would suggest a little different regimen for a person in this condition; rather take him a bag of flour and a little beef or pork. A few such comforts will do him more good than your prayers." ("Companion to The Old Testament," p. 192). An ounce of help is almost always better than a pound of preaching. Those who establish the church are committed to actively embrace the demands of discipleship in just this way.

Criticism without love is like a dagger in the heart. Those who have been in bondage need our sustaining support in order to experience sunbursts of awakening comprehension. As Joseph Smith exhorted the Saints: "Brethren, shall we not go on in so great a cause?. Go forward and not backward. Courage, brethren; and on, on to the victory! Let your hearts rejoice, and be exceedingly glad." (D&C 128:22). Now, he knew how to motivate people!

Temple work without love can sabotages our spiritual reservoirs. The pure in heart go to the temple to get their bearings on eternity. It is there that they receive an endowment of spiritual and priesthood power. But we must approach the altar of sacrifice with a broken heart and contrite spirit in an attitude of love unfeigned for our Savior.

Gifts without love are like the Trojan Horse of antiquity, rather than like the tokens of friendship they ought to be. Socrates had said: "Know thyself," Cicero admonished, "Control thyself" and Jesus taught by the greatest example of all, saying, "Give thyself" Completely, and without reservation.

"But you were always a good man of business, Jacob." said Scrooge. "Business!" Cried the ghost, wringing its hands again. "Mankind was my business. The common welfare was my business; charity, mercy, forbearance, and benevolence were all my business. The dealings of my trade were but a drop of water in the comprehensive ocean of my business."

"At this time of the rolling year," the spectre said, "I suffer most. Why did I walk through crowds of fellow-beings with my eyes turned down, and never raise them to that blessed Star which led the Wise Men to a poor abode? Were there no poor homes to which its light would have conducted me?" (Dickens, "A Christmas Carol").

Pride without love is an abomination, and is the sin responsible for the downfall of nations as well as of individuals. But it can be a warm appreciation for our God given gifts and talents. The scriptures warn us repeatedly and in unmistakable language that a threat to our temporal and spiritual welfare exists. It is hidden in a time bomb called pride, ready to explode and scatter its lethal contents among all the people who call themselves the disciples of Christ. The warning is relevant especially to all who have taken upon them the name of Christ, and live securely within the Fold. It applies especially to our own day, for those who have moved beyond a law of carnal commandments to a Celestial Standard.

When we live in thanksgiving daily, and love ourselves, our fellowmen, and our Savior, we tend to see the glass as half full. No matter what life may throw at us, we put a positive spin on our experiences. Then, our love and its companion attitudes overpower our carnal nature, with its jealousies, hatred, and prejudices, and carry us upward into the rarified atmosphere of heaven on earth.

(The) Manifestation of Spirits

(D&C 50)

> "I exhort you, brethren, that ye deny not the gifts of God, for they are many; and they come from the same God. And there are different ways that these gives are administered; but it is the same God who worketh all in all; and they are given by the manifestations of the Spirit of God unto all men, to profit them."
> (Moroni 10:8).

When Joseph Smith received this revelation, "some of the elders did not understand the manifestations of different spirits abroad in the earth." Therefore, the Lord gave specific instruction "in response to his special inquiry on the matter. So-called spiritual phenomena were not uncommon among the members, some of whom claimed to be receiving visions and manifestations." (Superscript).

If the Saints are not to be led astray, they must "give ear to the voice of the living God" that is the voice of safety and the sure way. (V. 1). Those in the Church believe in the spiritual manifestations of "the gift of tongues, prophecy, revelation, visions, healing, interpretation of tongues, and so forth," through intimate association with such phenomena. (Eighth Article of Faith). In stark contrast are those who seem to "have chosen up sides to see who can articulate the most sophisticated despair, who are not describing the broad spectrum of life, but only life without God." (Truman Madsen, "Are Mormons Christians?"). These are the cynics among us who "do not really like religion in its living forms, but find terribly interesting religion in its dead ones.

That is why an old Christian text, one from the first century for example, is deemed a worthy subject of scholarship. But a fresh Christian expression is available principally for ridicule, but never for study. Religious experience in the third century is fascinating. Religious experience in the Twentieth Century is frightening or absurd." (Jacob Neusner, "Bulletin of the Council on The Study of Religion," 12/1977).

This is so, because Satan has unleashed "many spirits which are false spirits, which have gone forth in the earth, deceiving the world." (V. 2). Mormon warned us of the dangerous consequences that are the inevitable result of faithlessness. He said that when miracles cease, then "wo be unto the children of men, for it is because of unbelief, and all is in vain." (Moroni 7:37). All around him, after all, "there were sorceries, and witchcrafts, and magics, and the power of the evil one was wrought upon all the face of the land" because of the lack of faith of the people. (Mormon 1:19). The same manifestations are pandemic today. Faith is the only spiritual strong searchlight powerful enough to supplant darkness, expose the enemies of Christ, and illuminate saving principles.

The Lord provided His people with a simple formula to discern evil spirits. He counseled: "If you behold a spirit manifested that you cannot understand, and you receive not that spirit, ye shall ask of the Father in the name of Jesus; and if he give not unto you that spirit, then you may know that it is not of God. And it shall be given unto you, power over that spirit; and you shall proclaim against that spirit with a loud voice that it is not of God." (V. 2, 31-32). This instruction seems more practical than does the "grand key by which the correct nature of ministering angels and spirits may be distinguished." (Superscript to D&C 129).

On a continuing basis, members of the church ask searching questions of themselves that help to define and make purposeful their faith: "How can I know of a surety? Can I withstand the sayings of the prophets? Just how powerful is the voice of the Spirit? Do I trample the Holy One under my feet? Would I make a mockery of my own Savior? How can I be so puffed up in the pride of my heart? Will temporal concerns, and my seemingly insatiable desire for worldly goods, forever cloud my vision? Will I continue to set my heart upon the vain things of the world, and upon its riches? Do I not yet understand that all is vanity? Will I persist in supposing that I am better than other people? Do I think that my accumulation of telestial trinkets establishes superiority over others of less substantial means? Do I persecute my brethren who humble themselves and walk after the Holy Order of God? Will I turn my back upon the poor? Will I withhold my substance from them?"

Satisfying answers to these and other questions are found when we conduct our lives in conformity to the commandments. Then, the windows of heaven will be opened unto us, and the blessings of the Lord will be poured out to the end "that (we) may not be seduced by evil spirits, or doctrines of devils, or the commandments of men." (D&C 46:7). For "Satan hath sought to deceive you," warned the Lord, "that he might overthrow you." (V. 3). He uses every stratagem, that he might stir up "their hearts to anger against this work." (D&C 10:24). He says to the weak-willed: "Deceive and lie in wait to catch, that ye may destroy; behold, this is no harm. And thus, he flattereth them, and telleth them that it is no sin to lie ... And thus he ... leadeth them along until he draggeth their souls down to hell; and thus, he causeth them to catch themselves in their own snare. And thus, he goeth up and down, to and fro in the earth, seeking to destroy the souls of men." (D&C 10:25-27). In this way, "Satan thinketh to overpower your testimony," the Lord told Joseph, "that the work may not come forth in this generation." (D&C 10:33). But, He continued, "I will not suffer that they shall destroy my work; yea, I will show unto them that my wisdom is greater than the cunning of the devil." (D&C 10:43).

The Lord and His prophets have repeatedly cautioned the Saints to keep oil in their vessels and their lamps trimmed. For "at that day, when I shall come in my glory," said the Lord, "shall the parable be fulfilled which I spake concerning the ten virgins." (D&C 45:56). Of that parable, the Lord cautioned: "Until that hour (when I should come) there will be foolish virgins among the wise; and at that hour cometh an entire separation of the righteous and the wicked." (D&C 63:54). Clearly, this parable speaks of members of the church who lack the necessary oil in their lamps to receive the bridegroom. At the conclusion of the parable, when the foolish virgins came unto him "saying, Lord, Lord, open to us. He answered, and said, Verily I say unto you, Ye know me not." (J.S.T. Matthew 25:10-11). Of the virgins, the Lord said that those who will abide the day of His coming are they who "are wise and have received the truth, and have taken the Holy Spirit for their guide, and have not been deceived." (D&C 45:57).

The Lord has provided a multitude of means for us to endure the day of His Coming. "That ye may not be deceived," He counseled, "seek ye earnestly the best gifts, always remembering for what they are given." (D&C 46:8). God will continue the ministry and work miracles among the children of men as "long as time shall last, or the earth shall stand, or there shall be one man upon the face thereof to be saved." (Words of Mormon 1:36).

When the gifts of the Spirit are absent, however, we must declare, as did Mormon, that "faith (has) ceased also; and awful is the state of man, for they are as though there had been no redemption made." (Words of Mormon 1:38). In Alma's view: "If ye have procrastinated the day of your repentance even until death," or if you have waited to develop saving faith until you were spiritually dead to the Light of Christ, "behold, ye have become subjected to the spirit of the devil, and he doth seal you his," because you can no longer make the vital distinctions between good and evil, truth and error, or light and darkness. "Therefore, the Spirit of the Lord hath withdrawn from you, and hath no place in you, and the devil hath all power over you," for you have voluntarily surrendered your agency to act independently, "and this is the final state of the wicked," for there is no recovery, and it will be as if there had been no redemption made." (Alma 34:35).

Mormon addressed the Latter-day Saints and challenged them to rise to the occasion. He said: "I judge better things of you, for I judge that ye have faith in Christ because of your meekness; for if ye have not faith in him then ye are not fit to be numbered among the people of his church." (Moroni 7:39). He was like wise old Tevya, who gave his daughters counsel that echoes across time: "In Anatevka, God knows who you are, and what you may become." (Joseph Stein, "Fiddler on The Roof").

Gifts of the Spirit "are given for the benefit of those who love me," said the Lord, and for those who "keep all my commandments, and him that seeketh so to do; that all may be benefited that seek or that ask of me. (D&C 46:9). These gifts are sufficient to guide us to make behavioral choices that are consistent with celestial principles. God wants each of us to satisfy the entrance requirements for admittance to the Celestial Kingdom. With what greater gifts could He bless us than those that help us to pass our individual tests of mortality?

The Lord desires to fortify us with His power; therefore, He said: "I will give unto you a pattern in all things, that ye may not be deceived." (D&C 52:14). This pattern allows us to choose our own destiny and to be responsible for the consequences of our actions. His Plan of Happiness preserves free will and allows truth to prevail even as error is exposed in the sunlight of the application of correct principles under the scrutiny of applied gospel doctrine. The Plan is perfect and is designed to provide self-diagnosis, positive feedback, and course correction. Those who embrace its program are strengthened when damaging data is identified and filtered out and gentle suggestions for improvement are offered.

"I teach people correct principles and they govern themselves," declared Joseph Smith. (First cited by John Taylor, 11/1851 in the Millennial Star 13:22 page 339). This is not the course of safety, but it is the best way to allows us to progress as fast as our desire will allow. God declared to Adam in the Garden of Eden: "Thou mayest choose for thyself, for it is given unto thee." (Moses 3:17). If we use our agency incorrectly, it may be forfeit. While we have our birthright, we may choose to give it away, but once it is gone, it is lost. The consequence of the unrighteous use of agency is the loss of real freedom and power. In fact, there are two freedoms - the false, where we are free to do what we like; and the true, where we are free to do what we ought. The Lord wants to teach us to use our free will to do what we should do, following the pattern that defines celestial character.

The implementation of the Plan counteracts the negative influence of Satan, who "is abroad in the land, and (who) goeth forth deceiving the nations." (D&C 52:14). Before the resurrected Lord visited the Saints in Zarahemla, the Nephites there "were much disturbed, for Satan did stir them up to do iniquity continually; yea, he did go about spreading rumors and contentions upon all the face of the land, that he might harden the hearts of the people against that which was good and against that which should come." (Helaman 16:20-22). This technique can be very effective in blinding our eyes. It is a strategy that is even today employed by Satan to great effect. When he gets "hold upon the hearts of the people," the fate of nations hangs in the balance. (Helaman 16:23). "For there are many yet on the earth among all sects, parties, and denominations, who are blinded by the subtle craftiness of men, whereby they lie in wait to deceive, and who are only kept from the truth because they know not where to find it." (D&C 123:12).

In this revelation, we learn that even the congregation of the Saints is at risk. "I, the Lord, have looked upon you, and have seen abominations in the church." (V. 4). As Satan attempts to thwart our progression, he will "rage in the hearts of the children of men, and stir them up to anger against that which is good. And others will he pacify, and lull them away into carnal security, and thus the devil cheateth their souls, and leadeth them away carefully down to hell. And behold, others he flattereth away, and telleth them there is no hell, and thus he whispereth in their ears until he grasps them with his awful chains from whence there is no deliverance." (2 Nephi 28:20-22). He is the master of techniques whereby unsuspecting but weak-willed individuals are led "by the neck with a flaxen cord, until he bindeth them with his strong cords forever." (2 Nephi 26:22). He is able to accomplish this because he seeks out those whose "hearts are corrupt, and full of wickedness and abominations; (who) love darkness rather than light, because their deeds are evil." (D&C 10:21). Rather than seeking the guidance and direction that the Lord is anxious to provide, they are left in a state of vulnerability to be stirred up by Satan and led "to destruction" or spiritual death. (D&C 10:22).

Paul wrote to the Thessalonian Saints that they should "pray without ceasing." (1 Thessalonians 5:17). Amulek enlarged upon this principle, and counseled the Zoramites: "After ye have done all these things, if ye turn away the needy, and the naked, and visit not the sick and afflicted, and impart of your substance, if ye have, to those who stand in need, behold your prayer is vain and availeth you nothing, and ye are as hypocrites who do deny the faith. (Alma 34:28). The Savior warned against meaningless prayer, devoid of substance, and helped His disciples to understand how to avoid such a practice. "But when ye pray," he cautioned, "use not vain repetitions, as the heathen do: for they think that they shall be heard for their much speaking." (Matthew 6:7).

Prayer is "in vain" when it is reduced to the status of an academic exercise, when it is an empty and meaningless ritual, performed without effect, or without the desired or intended result. To "try in vain" is to try without success. Meaningless prayer is blasphemous because it uses the Lord's name improperly and without authority. Those who do so are imposters, invoking the name of Deity in a false, misleading, and counterfeit way. We blaspheme the name of God when we invoke His Holy name unsuccessfully because of our unworthiness.

There are isolated instances of abomination in the church when, through uninspired or misguided leadership or followership, the Saints are led to practices that draw them away from the binding ordinances. The Lord confirmed that Joseph Smith was given the "power to lay the foundation of this church, and to bring it forth out of obscurity and out of darkness, the only true and living church upon the face of the whole earth, with which I, the Lord, am well pleased, speaking unto the church collectively and not individually." (D&C 1:30). The church has been perfectly organized in the sense that keys have been vested in its leaders giving them the authority and power to shepherd the flock back into the presence of God.

The reality of the apostasy and the subsequent restoration of priesthood authority was foretold in the scriptures, has been documented in secular history, and is confirmed in the records of the church. No other church has the authority of the priesthood to bind and ratify the covenants we make with God, the power to break the death grip of Satan, or the full and unabridged support of "the only living and true God." (D&C 20:19).

"Of the other churches, we do not say they are wrong, so much as we say they are incomplete." (Boyd K. Packer, C.R., 10/1964). All the branches of the House of Israel, as well as the Gentiles who were grafted in, had become corrupted by the time the gospel was restored in 1830. With prophetic vision, Zenos had foreseen that "notwithstanding all the care with which we have taken of my vineyard, the trees thereof have become corrupted, that they bring forth no good fruit." (Jacob 5:46).

There is always the "possibility that man may fall from grace" or from good standing in the sight of Deity, "and depart from the living God" previous service or righteousness notwithstanding. (D&C 20:32). In our day, Babylon has become firmly entrenched in the world, and her polluting influence even encroaches upon the fortifications of the church and threatens to undermine, corrupt, or compromise the Kingdom. She is "the great whore that sitteth upon many waters, with whom the kings of the earth have committed fornication." (Revelation 17:1-2). To some extent, all who have entered into a wicked and idolatrous relationship with the world have been intimate with the whore.

Two of the terrible consequences of a fascination with Babylon are spiritual insensitivity and inconsistency. Isaiah foresaw the Last Days when he wrote: "Stay yourselves, and wonder; cry ye out, and cry: they are drunken, but not with wine; they stagger, but not with strong drink. For the Lord hath poured out upon you the spirit of deep sleep, and hath closed your eyes: the prophets, and your rulers, and seers hath he covered." (Isaiah 29:9-11).

In contrast, the ideal is expressed in the Ninth Article of Faith and in the action verb "to believe." "We believe all that God has revealed, all that He does now reveal, and we believe that He will yet reveal many great and important things pertaining to the Kingdom of God." The church needs a listening ear, for there is no revelation where there is no student.

Many people in the world deny themselves the blessings of heaven simply because they do not ask for them. The Savior explained how anxious He is to grant the righteous requests of His children. Comparing His benevolence to that of our earthly fathers, His Son declared: "How much more shall your Father who is in heaven give good things to them that ask him?" (3 Nephi 14:11). It is critical to the welfare of members of the church that they "take heed and pray always, lest they fall into temptation." (D&C 20:33). Prayer is a way to exercise faith and is a powerful weapon against the devil. Joseph Fielding Smith, Jr. taught: "No man can retain the spirit of the Lord unless he prays." (C.R., 10/1919).

The Lord is mindful of His covenant relationship with the members of His church, and so He requires extraordinary performance of those "who profess (His) name." (D&C 50:4). Professors represent themselves as independent witnesses. Memorable professors back up their words with deeds, and give vitality, or life to desire. Good intentions, after all, are only dreams. As Harold B. Lee observed: "Vision without work is dreamery. Work without vision is drudgery. But work with vision is destiny!"

Professors are persevering and stay focused on the tasks at hand. They begin with the end in mind and settle for more, and not for less. They are purposeful, determined, disciplined, focused, and are not easily distracted or persuaded. Their foundation is on bedrock. They have depth and breadth, and have made regular deposits to their spiritual bank accounts, from which they may take timely, strategic, and significant withdrawals.

Professors are guided by the Spirit, and teach by example. They are leaders, and not just managers. They help others to clarify their own feelings, and their teachings are founded on principles rather than values. Professors are not easily swayed by conventional wisdom or politically correct ideology and are uninfluenced by situational ethics or expediency. If the testimony of Jesus is the spirit of prophecy, then every professor of the name of Christ, every member of His church who carries the burden of a testimony of His divinity, is a facilitator who helps to bring others of Heavenly Father's children into the light. Thus, professors are light bearers who carry the torch of truth as a beacon to guide others who are having difficulty finding their own way. The best among them wear the heavy robes of responsibility of God's true priesthood or operate under its influence and by its direction.

Professors "are faithful and endure, whether in life or in death, for they shall inherit eternal life." (V. 5). They endure to the end and lay claim to the promise of the Lord, Who said He would disperse the powers of darkness from before them, and cause the heavens to shake for their good. (D&C 21:6). The doors to the spirit prison of the unjust shrink in significance, (see D&C 76:13, 23, & 73, 138:8 & 28, Isaiah 61:1, 1 Peter 3:19, & Moses 7:57) and, as the Lord has promised, their confidence will wax strong in the presence of God; and the doctrine of the priesthood will distill upon their souls as the dews from heaven. The Holy Ghost will be their constant companion, and their scepter will be an unchanging scepter of righteousness and truth; and their dominion will be an everlasting dominion, and without compulsory means it will flow unto them forever. (D&C 121:45-46).

The real tragedy in life is not that we set our sights too high, and then fail to achieve our goals. Rather, it is that those who have not participated in the curriculum of the gospel aim too low, easily reaching their objectives but having little to show for their consistently timid efforts. Professors do not accept mediocrity in their lives; instead, their behavior is in harmony with the nature of God, Who dwells in perfection in the Celestial Kingdom. What He has, He could easily give to us, if He chose to do so. But we would likely squander the inheritance, failing to recognize its value. Instead, God has provided a mortal experience for us, and complimented it with moral testing, so that we can learn to be what He is. These are the conditions under which His grace may be granted, and this is the only way we may claim the reward that is intricately interwoven within the elements of the Plan.

Professors "hunger and thirst after righteousness," and are "filled with the Holy Ghost." (3 Nephi 12:6). Nephi encouraged professors, saying: "If ye shall press forward" with complete dedication, "feasting upon the word of Christ" or receiving physical and spiritual strength and nourishment, "and endure to the end" with continuing responsibility and accountability, "behold, thus saith the Father: Ye shall have eternal life," which is the greatest of God's gifts. (2 Nephi 31:20).

For professors, endurance is positive and pleasant. Their faith motivates them to be spiritually fit, for the exalting principles of the gospel bestow upon them gifts that to be earned require effort. Consequently, they are sometimes admonished: "Behold, you have not understood; you have supposed that I would give it unto you, when you took no thought save it was to ask me. But, behold, I say unto you, that you must study it out in your mind." (D&C 9:7-8). One noted professor named Lorenzo Snow declared: "It is impossible to advance in the principles of truth, to increase in heavenly knowledge, except we exercise our reasoning faculties and exert ourselves." (J.D., 18:371). Agency is not free, but is purchased at a substantial price. "For all who will have a blessing at my hands," explained the Lord, "shall abide the law which was appointed for that blessing, and the conditions thereof, as were instituted from before the foundation of the world" when the Plan was ratified by its future participants. (D&C 132:5).

The Lord said that professors should press forward, not with the crowd who jostles for position in the circus of telestial trivialities, but rather with the Saints who seek "wisdom; and…the mysteries of God" that are those truths that can only be known by revelation from the Holy Ghost. (D&C 11:7).

"But wo unto them that (in contrast to professors) are deceivers and hypocrites." (D&C 50:6). The word "hypocrite" is from the Greek, where it describes the mask used by actors. A hypocrite, the is someone who professes to be one thing, when actually it is a charade; he is an entirely different person behind his mask. Satan exults in hypocrisy and is a master of the techniques whereby we are methodically moved by subtraction from brilliant, dazzling white, through every shade of grey, to a fathomless black that is the absence of every good thought, word, deed, or worthy principle. His flattery and subtle suggestions that he does not exist leads us to judge ourselves to be deserving of peace and plenty without having earned the reward. (2 Nephi 30:22). We seek to subvert the curriculum as if it were possible to hack into the system that records our grades and give ourselves undeserved high marks. Meanwhile, as C.S. Lewis wrote: "Little people, like you and me, if our prayers are sometimes granted beyond all hope and probability, had better not draw hasty conclusions to our own advantage. If we were stronger, we might be less tender treated. If we were braver, we might be sent, with far less help, to defend far more desperate posts in the great battle." ("The World's Last Night," p. 10-11).

"Wherefore, let every (professor) beware lest he do that which is not in truth and righteousness before me." (D&C 50:9). "That ye may not be deceived," Joseph was counseled, "seek ye earnestly the best gifts, always remembering for what they are given." (D&C 46:8). God will continue the ministry, and work miracles among us, as "long as time shall last, or the earth shall stand, or there shall be one (professor) upon the face thereof to be saved." (Words of Mormon 1:36).

"And now come ... and let us reason together, that ye may understand; Let us reason even as a man reasoneth one with another face to face ... Even so will I, the Lord, reason with you that you may understand." (V. 10-12). In His Preface to The Book of Commandments, the Lord explained: "These commandments are of me, and were given unto my servants in their weakness, after the manner of their language, that they might come to understanding. And inasmuch as they erred, it might be made known; And inasmuch as they sought wisdom they might be instructed; And inasmuch as they sinned they might be chastened, that they might repent; And inasmuch as they were humble they might be made strong, and blessed from on high, and receive knowledge from time to time." (D&C 1:24-28).

A typical strategy of those who wear the academic robes of the false priesthood is to lead people astray by attacking the fundamental revealed doctrine of Christ. They do this in a perverted way by wresting the scriptures and misrepresenting their meaning away from their true or proper signification, and by perverting, misinterpreting, misapplying, or turning them from their right application. When self-appointed prophets and teachers wrest the scriptures, and especially when they twist their meaning to their own material advantage, we can be sure that reasonable dialogue, insight, mutual understanding, and the welfare of Zion are far from their thoughts. Those who break windows are more interested in the sound of tinkling glass than in letting in fresh air.

Stephen Robinson has written: "Time and again Latter-day Saints are denied the privilege of defining and interpreting their own doctrines. Quite frequently one attempting to explain the tenets of his or her faith to non-Mormons will be interrupted by some self-styled expert who says, 'No, that's not what you believe; this is what you believe.' There generally follows a recital of some hocus-pocus that is certainly not taught by the L.D.S. church. The resulting fictions generally fall into one of three categories: outright fabrications, distortions of genuine L.D.S. doctrines into unrecognizable forms, or the representation of anomalies within the L.D.S. tradition as mainline or official L.D.S. teachings." ("Are Mormons Christians," in the chapter entitled "The Exclusion by Misrepresentation," p. 9-10).

Those who are all form and no substance contribute nothing, and church members risk falling into transgression in consequence of a shallow understanding of principles and doctrines. As Alma declared to the inhabitants of Ammonihah: "Behold, the scriptures are before you; if ye will wrest them it shall be to your own destruction." (Alma 13:20). Picking apart the scriptures can distort dogma into fruitless fragments without any coherent connection. Those who decline the Lord's invitation to establish a discernible dialogue through the scriptures deny themselves the opportunity to embrace celestial principles and to prosper through enlightenment. In 1820, the Lord characterized such individuals as those who "draw near to me with their lips, but (whose) hearts are far from me. They teach for doctrines the commandments of men, having a form of godliness, but they deny the power thereof." (Joseph Smith History 2:19). They are all form and no substance, because they do not have anything to contribute to our welfare. Madison Avenue, and not the Holy Ghost, is the driving force and power that propels their message. As a result, they often meet with success among those who have itching ears. "Unto what were ye ordained?" asked the Lord. (V. 13). In the judgment, the question will not be: "What did you do?" or "Where did you serve?" but rather: "Did you put me first?" and "Did you serve me with all your heart?" We are, after all, ordained to preach the "gospel by the Spirit, even the Comforter which was sent forth to teach the truth." (V. 14). Therefore, we must gird up our loins to prepare for the journey to Christ along the difficult road that leads to Gethsemane, and we must go to work with real determination so that the Atonement will not have been in vain. In the years since the Lord delivered this revelation to Joseph Smith, significant changes have taken place in the world, and his prophetic vision has been validated as the gospel is being taken to every nation, kindred, tongue, and people. The stone cut out of the mountain is rolling over the whole earth and cannot be stopped. (See Daniel 2:34). What a thrill it is for members of the restored church of Jesus Christ to march in the ranks of Christian soldiers who take the battle for truth directly into the camp of the willfully or ignorantly disobedient.

"He that is ordained of me and sent forth to preach the word of truth by the Comforter, in the Spirit of truth, doth he preach it by the Spirit of truth," whose influence has probably been responsible for more real conversions than in all other ages of the world combined. (V. 17). As Joseph Fielding Smith, Jr. said: "The impressions on the soul that come from the Holy Ghost are far more significant than a vision. It is where spirit speaks to spirit, and the imprint upon the soul is far more difficult to erase." ("Ensign," 6/1971).

On another occasion, he wrote that because of the Holy Ghost, "there should be no laymen in The Church of Jesus Christ of Latter-day Saints. If there are any such, then they have neglected their responsibilities and obligations which the Lord has placed upon them." ("Melchizedek Priesthood Personal Study Guide," 1972-73, p. 190). It will be through the instrumentality of the Holy Ghost that, in the Last Days, "they shall teach no more every man his neighbor, and every man his brother, Saying, Know the Lord: for they shall all know me, from the least of them unto the greatest of them." (Jeremiah 31:34).

In our day, the Holy Ghost is being poured out in rich abundance. The Lord has promised: "God shall give unto you knowledge by his Holy Spirit, yea, by the unspeakable gift of the Holy Ghost, that has not been revealed since the world was until now." This is a time when "nothing shall be withheld ... All thrones and dominions, principalities and powers, shall be revealed ... And also, if there be bounds set to the heavens or to the seas, or to the dry land, or to the sun, moon, or stars, (all this) shall be revealed in the days of the dispensation of the fulness of times." (D&C 121:26-31).

Members of the church should strive to be the agents through whom this knowledge comes. The Prophet Joseph Smith wrote: "As the dews of Carmel, so shall the knowledge of God descend upon" the Latter-day Saints. (D&C 128:19). There is more to the gospel than obedience and covenants. Our knowledge of God's active concern for us, and the application of the principles of the gospel for our benefit is progress too. As Joseph Smith taught: "In one sense of the word, the keys of the kingdom ... consist in the key of knowledge" which comes through the Holy Ghost. (D&C 128:14).

In the church today, there are many striking evidences of the sanctifying and unifying power of the Holy Ghost. For example, in spite of the many translations of the scriptures used by members worldwide, there is remarkably little disagreement as to their meaning. In church organization and Church government, ecclesiastical leaders enjoy virtual harmony in spite of cultural, social, political, and economic differences. The ordinances from baptism to the endowment in the temple are universally understood and faithfully administered.

Every six months, Saints from all over the world gather at church headquarters to hear the word of the Lord from His authorized servants. As Harold B. Lee once explained: "If you want to know what the Lord has for this people at the present time, I would admonish you to get and read the discourses that have been delivered at this conference, for what these brethren have spoken by the power of the Holy Ghost is the mind of the Lord, the will of the Lord, the word of the Lord, and the power of God unto salvation." (C.R., 4/1973).

If we preach without the Spirit, that is to say, "if it be by some other way it is not of God." (V. 18). For "the Spirit shall be given unto you by the prayer of faith; and if ye receive not the Spirit ye shall not teach." (D&C 42:14). This verse is both a commandment and a statement of fact for it is impossible to communicate the doctrines of the kingdom without the companionship of the Holy Ghost. "The great objective of all our work," declared Spencer W. Kimball, "is to build character and increase faith in the lives of those whom we serve. If one cannot accept and teach the programs of the church in an orthodox way, without reservation," submitting to the will of the Spirit that gives utterance, "he should not teach." (C.R., 4/1948). Alma helped to establish the precedent, when in the church in the wilderness, he saw to it that only just men were consecrated under his own hands to be faithful priests and teachers, and this, only after he had received a personal witness from the Lord confirming the proposed action. (Mosiah 25:21).

Before any attempt to teach is undertaken, we must obtain the Spirit through prayer. As Brigham Young observed: "It matters not whether you or I feel like praying, when the time comes to pray, pray. If we do not feel like it, we should pray 'til we do. You will find that those who wait 'til the Spirit bids them to pray will never pray much on the earth." ("Discourses of Brigham Young," p. 44). Without prayer, the fountain of living water that is the wellspring of the Spirit, will remain just beyond our reach.

"He that receiveth the word of truth, doth he receive it by the Spirit of truth or some other way?" (V. 19). "As often as thou hast inquired," of me, said the Lord, "thou hast received instruction of my Spirit." (D&C 6:14). In a variety of ways, Heavenly Father has always provided direction for His children. The Nephites were given the Rod of Iron, or the word of God, which would lead them along a strait and narrow path directly to the tree of life. (1 Nephi 19-20, & 30).

Soon thereafter, they were given the "Liahona," which is an old word from the language of the fathers, needing to be interpreted by Alma as "a compass." (Alma 37:38). He taught: "It is as easy to give heed to the word of Christ (our compass) which will point you to a straight course to eternal bliss, as it was for our fathers to give heed to this compass, which would point unto them a straight course to the promised land. Do not let us be slothful (or move slowly) because of the easiness of the way. Look to God, and live." (Alma 37:38-47).

From the beginning, God has raised up prophets to testify of His existence, of the Redeemer of the World, and of the Plan of Happiness. "Surely the Lord God will do nothing, but he revealeth his secret unto his servants the prophets." (Amos 3:7). Yes, "there is a God in heaven that revealeth secrets, and maketh known ... what shall be in the latter days." (Daniel 2:28). As the Lord said of Joseph Smith and Sidney Rigdon: "For by my Spirit will I enlighten them, and by my power will I make known unto them the secrets of my will - yea, even those things which eye has not seen, nor ear heard, nor yet entered into the heart of man." (D&C 76:10). The Latter-day Saints believe "all that God has revealed, all that He does now reveal, and (they) believe that He will yet reveal many great and important things pertaining to the Kingdom." (Ninth Article of Faith).

The way is easy. For the Israelites in the Wilderness of Sinai, it was only necessary that they look upon the staff of Moses, the Brazen Serpent that typified Christ. "And as many as should look upon that serpent should live, even so as many as should look upon the Son of God, with faith, having a contrite spirit, might live, even unto that life which is eternal. (Helaman 8:13-16). Today, our trials are no more sophisticated. Noah preached of the flood. Ezra Taft Benson warned of a food of pornography that is inundating the world. Moses wrote of the bondage of Israel in Egypt, and Gordon B. Hinckley of the temporal bondage of financial indebtedness, and of the spiritual bondage that comes from sacrificing our free will to the popular idols of the day.

Elijah rebuked those who worshiped Baal. Our leaders caution us against spiritual death that comes from the worship of contemporary gods of wood and of stone. Joseph endured seven years of famine in Egypt. The First Presidency has counseled us since 1936 to gather our year's supply. The Nephites endured the depravations of the Band of Gadianton. We strain against "the evils and designs which do and will exist in the hearts of conspiring men in the last days." (D&C 89:4). The Old Testament condemned murder; we face the deception and damnable heresy of "pro-choice." The dietary code of the Law of Moses set the Israelites apart from their neighbors, as does our Word of Wisdom. The Apostles warned of unnatural affection, while our prophets condemn "alternative lifestyles" as deviant behavior of an abominable nature. The message is the same. "We talk of Christ, we rejoice in Christ, we preach of Christ, we prophesy of Christ, and we write according to our prophecies, that our children may know to what source they may look for a remission of their sins." (2 Nephi 25:26). Christ was, is, and shall ever be the light and life of the world.

Even if we receive the truth, if it does not come by the Spirit, "if it be (by) some other way it is not of God." (V. 20). But if we make the requisite effort, we shall "lift up (our) voices by the (we) have heard, and verily believe, and know to be true." (D&C 80:4). For the Holy Ghost is an unimpeachable witness and "knoweth all things, and beareth record of the Father, and of the Son." (D&C 42:17). The Spirit shapes and defines gospel instruction, is the power that gives it substance, and is the conveyor of understanding.

When asked what set the church apart, Joseph Smith replied: "We have the Holy Ghost." ("The Wentworth Letter"). During the Renaissance, Western Europe enjoyed a rebirth of ideas whose stimulus was the Holy Ghost. The Reformation set the stage for an Age of Enlightenment and the Restoration. Today we enjoy an Age of Inspiration by the Spirit. There has been a measured, steady, quantifiable, hierarchal progression defining our ascent.

The Holy Ghost lifts us upward toward God the Father and Jesus Christ and is the wind beneath our wings. It is He Who inspired the poet to declare: "Oh, I have slipped the surly bonds of earth and danced the skies on laughter-silvered wings. Sunward I've climbed, and joined the tumbling mirth of sun-split clouds, and done a hundred things you have not dreamed of; Wheeled and soared and swung high in the sunlit silence. Hovering there, I've chased the shouting wind along, and flung my eager craft through footless halls of air. Up, up the long, delirious, burning blue I've topped the windswept heights with easy grace, where never lark, or even eagle flew. And, while with silent, lifting mind I've trod the high untrespassed sanctity of space, I put out my hand, and touched the face of God." (John G. Magee, Jr., "High Flight"). "Wherefore, he that preacheth and he that receiveth, understand one another, and both are edified and rejoice together." (V. 22).

Teaching is the priesthood's main function. "This is the order after which I am called," declared Alma, "to preach unto my beloved brethren, yea, and every one that dwelleth in the land." (Alma 5:49). Alma did not define his responsibilities only in terms of what he could do to reclaim those who had neglected their baptismal covenant. He also understood that the Oath and Covenant of the Melchizedek Priesthood included standing as a witness of God to those who lived in the Land of Zarahemla who were not yet members of the Church.

The efforts of the early church priesthood leaders were directed toward rediscovering the power of God. With one united voice, they sought to vitalize the church with His authority. They might have agreed with Martin Luther, who said: "I have sought nothing beyond reforming the church in conformity with the Holy Scriptures. The spiritual powers have been not only corrupted by sin, but also absolutely destroyed, so that there is now nothing in them but a depraved reason and a will that is the enemy and opponent of God. I simply say that Christianity has ceased to exist among those who should have preserved it." (Ernest Schweibert, "Luther and His Times," p. 188).

As the Savior declared: "That which doth not edify is not of God, and is darkness." (V. 23). He called His disciples to a higher plane of spirituality and to a commitment to selfless consecration of effort with this counsel: "Lay not up for yourselves treasures upon earth, where moth and rust doth corrupt, and thieves break through and steal; But lay up for yourselves treasures in heaven, where neither moth nor rust doth corrupt, and where thieves do not break through nor steal." (3 Nephi 13:19-20). To the Latter-day Saints, He promised: "If your eye be single to my glory, your whole bodies shall be filled with light, and there shall be no darkness in you, and that body which is filled with light comprehendeth all things." (D&C 88:67).

But He also cautioned: "If thine eye be evil, thy whole body shall be full of darkness." (3 Nephi 13:23). The influence of Satan that gripped Joseph in the Sacred Grove before his heavenly deliverance illustrates just how overwhelming that intense darkness can be. Joseph wrote: "I was seized upon by some power which entirely overcame me, and had such an astonishing influence over me as to bind my tongue so that I could not speak. Thick darkness gathered around me, and…I was ready to sink into despair and abandon myself to destruction - not to an imaginary ruin, but to the power of some actual being from the unseen world." (J.S.H. 1:15-16). We are reminded of those who lost their way in mists of spiritual darkness in Lehi's Vision of The Tree of Life. (See 1 Nephi 8:23).

"That which is of God is light; and he that receiveth light, and continueth in God, receiveth more light; and that light groweth brighter and brighter until the perfect day." (V. 24). Jesus Christ is the Creator, Who acted under the direction of the Father to form the earth. The Savior's words echo from the pages of The Book of Mormon: "Behold, I am Jesus Christ the Son of God, I created the heavens and the earth, and all things that in them are." (3 Nephi 9:15). To the Nephites who heard His voice in the midst of the darkness then enveloping the land, the words of Christ must have been like a penetrating searchlight as He declared: "I am the light and the life of the world." (3 Nephi 9:18). "I have sent mine everlasting covenant into the world," He reiterated to the Latter-day Saints, "to be a light to the world." (D&C 45:9). Today, His words are a beacon that guides the faithful with unerring accuracy to the safe harbor of the gospel. Brigham Young warned that if we ignore His counsel, however, our "land will eventually become desolate, forlorn, and forsaken," as nature withholds her bounties. If we alienate ourselves from God, all nature becomes our enemy. In the days of Enoch, because of the wickedness of the people, when he spoke the word of the Lord by the power of the rivers of water were turned out of their course; and the roar of the lions was heard out of the wilderness." (Moses 7:13).

Joseph Fielding Smith cautioned the Saints: "We should wake up to the realization that it is because of the breaking of covenants, especially the new and everlasting covenant, which is the fulness of the gospel as it has been revealed, that the world is to be consumed by fire and few men left. Since this punishment is to come at the time of the cleansing of the earth when Christ comes again, should not Latter-day Saints take heed unto themselves? We have been given the new and everlasting covenant, and many among us have broken it, and many are now breaking it; therefore, all who are guilty of this offense will aid in bringing to pass the destruction in which they will find themselves swept from the earth when the great and dreadful day of the Lord shall come." ("Deseret News," 10/17/1936, p. 7).

The Light and the Life is "Jesus Christ, the Son of God, who was crucified for the sins of the world." (D&C 35:2). His influence spans the eternities from that time when we were uncreate intelligence, through our development as spiritual children of our Heavenly Father, on into mortality, and finally to our reunion with Him in the resurrection. As far as we are concerned, He has always existed. His attributes define His flawless and perfected character. If we were to model our behavior after anyone, it would be Him. As the mortal expression of His Divine Parents, Mormon taught: "In Christ there should come every good thing." (Moroni 7:22).

His light is a type of the physical and spiritual rapport that exists between Him and the Father, and between them and true believers. This completeness is facilitated by the Holy Ghost, allowing us to become one in the spiritual sense. The Priesthood further enhances this unity by administering gospel ordinances that lead to the temple, where we enter into the patriarchal order of Celestial Marriage and are organized into eternal family units. There, we learn principles of spiritual and temporal government and make covenants to consecrate our time and talents to the church and kingdom, and to lend our efforts to the preparation of the earth for the millennial reign of the light of the world, our Savior Jesus Christ.

Without the temple, civilization is an empty shell and a structure of custom and convenience only. When we qualify to enjoy the blessings reserved for the obedient, however, we are freed from the bondage of sin that binds us to Babylon. Our character, molded by obedience to gospel principles, is simply the result of a spiritual transformation in our lives that comes about as we live the Celestial Law of the Lord.

To make sure that we would be able to "chase darkness from among (us)," the Lord reiterated: "He that is ordained of God and sent forth, the same is appointed to be the greatest, notwithstanding he is the least and the servant of all." (V. 25-26). "Woe shall come unto the inhabitants of the earth," said the Lord, "if they will not hearken unto my words." (D&C 5:5). "Wo" is a condition of deep suffering that is the result of misfortune and affliction, or grief and calamity. Our lives are days of probation, a time of testing or of putting to the proof our declared values. The gospel of "repentance is (always available) unto them that are under condemnation and under the curse of a broken law." (Moroni 8:24). If we successfully complete our probationary trial, we will escape the ordained consequences of disobedience. Therefore, the Lord told Joseph Smith that it would be critical that "hereafter (he should) be ordained and go forth and deliver (His) words unto the children of men," that the gospel might be written in their hearts. (D&C 5:6).

He would be "possessor of all things; for all things (would be) subject unto him, both in heaven and on the earth, the life and the light, the Spirit and the power, sent forth by the will of the Father through Jesus Christ, his Son." (V. 27). He would have all things in his hands in the sense that the elements of the earth would be subject to Him. He would be given "dominion, and glory, and a kingdom, that all people, nations, and languages, should serve him." (Daniel 7:14).

But neither Joseph nor any other person could ever hope to attain the spiritual stature of Christ, "except he be purified and cleansed from all sin. And if ye are purified and cleansed from all sin, ye shall ask whatsoever you will in the name of Jesus, and it shall be done. But know this, that it shall be given you what you shall ask." (V. 29-30). If we set the stylus of our compass on the purification process, within the circle thus scribed will be the Sacrament, the Endowment, and the other ordinances driven by the engine of the priesthood. Within these ordinances the power of godliness is manifest, and our active involvement initiates a cleansing and purification process wherein we may ask God in complete confidence for our desired blessings. From the perspective of such a state of innocence and holiness, the nature of the spirits abroad on the earth will be plainly manifest so we may be given "power over that spirit." (V. 32). We may receive the means to lay bare the true nature of such spirits, "not with railing accusation ... neither with boasting nor rejoicing," but with the measured response expected of the Lord's anointed. (V. 33).

"Giving heed and doing these things" will bring us into harmony with the powers of Heaven. When that happens, the omnipotent Lord promises: "The kingdom is given you of the Father, and power to overcome all things ... for your sins are forgiven you." (V. 35-36). With such a foundation, at the conclusion of this revelation the Lord commanded Parley P. Pratt: "Go forth among the churches and strengthen them by the word of exhortation." (V. 37). By the authority of the priesthood, he was to preach the gospel to introduce the principles, truths, and concepts pertaining to the Plan of Salvation. Afterward, he was to teach the principles, or bring them into sharp focus, and illustrate them in meaningful ways. Then, he was to expound or enlarge upon the principles, in order to expand the understanding of the listeners. Next, he was to offer exhortation, to help them to want to incorporate the principles into their own lives, to encourage ownership, and through personal witness or testimony to validate the worth of the principles being taught.

The Lord had marshaled a priesthood army of recent converts were also to "labor in the vineyard." (V. 38). The church was just 13 months old at the time this revelation was given. Consequently, the Lord cautioned: "Ye are little children and ye cannot bear all things now; ye must grow in grace and in the knowledge of the truth." (V. 40). "For (the church) cannot bear meat now, but milk they must receive." (D&C 19:22). It was important in the days of the infancy of the restored church that the Saints focus their attention on the first principles and ordinances of the gospel and strive to keep the faith whatever trials might come, for as Joseph Smith said: "As far as we degenerate from God, we descend to the devil and lose knowledge, and without knowledge we cannot be saved." ("Teachings," p. 217).

"Fear not," the Lord told His "little children, for you are mine, and I have overcome the world, and you are of them that my Father hath given me." (V. 41). They had good reason to have confidence, for the Lord extended in the closing verses of this revelation a number of very reassuring promises: None of those whom the Father had given His Son would be lost. (V. 42). The Saints would be one with the Father, just as the Son is one with the Father. (V. 43). The Stone of Israel would be in the midst of the church. (V. 44, See Genesis 49:24). The day would come when the Saints would hear the voice of the Lord and see His face. (V. 45). Those who were prepared would be ready to face any challenge with which they might be confronted. (V. 46).

By reading The Book
of Mormon, we learn to bear our stripes
for the Savior with patience, and it is for Him
that we turn the other cheek. Fueled by the power of
His example, we love our brethren as ourselves. Because
He awakens us to re-commitment, we are alive to our
responsibilities, minister to the weak, the sick and
infirm, wash the wounds of the injured, and
we go about in humility, performing
acts of quiet Christianity.

May the 4ᵗʰ Be with You

"Behold, whosoever will
maintain this title (of liberty)
upon the land, let them come forth
in the strength of the Lord, and enter
into a covenant that they will maintain
their rights, and their religion, that
the Lord God may bless them."
(Alma 46:20).

Jedi Knights both serve and utilize a mystical power called the Force to assist them as the guardians of peace and justice in the galaxy. Their philosophy of self-denial stands in contrast to that of their archenemies, the Sith, who use the dark side of the Force, that they might control others.

"May the Force be with you!" declared General Dodonna before the Death Star battle in Episode 4 of the Star Wars saga. Obi-Wan Kenobe described the Force as "what gives a Jedi his power. It's an energy field created by all living things. It surrounds us and penetrates us. It binds the galaxy together." Duct tape, something with which we are all familiar, is like the Force. It has a light side, and a dark side, and it, too, binds the universe together.

The Master Teacher Yoda explained to young Luke Skywalker: "A Jedi's strength flows from the Force. But beware of the dark side: Anger, fear, and aggression. The dark side are they. Easily they flow, quick to join you in a fight. If once you start down the dark path, forever will it dominate your destiny, consume you it will." We must resist the temptation to yield to the dark side, or to the baser elements of our nature.

The universal Force for good is the hope of the galaxy. Isaiah described it in these words: "For unto us a child is born, unto us a son is given, and the government shall be upon his shoulder: and his name shall be called Wonderful, Counsellor, The mighty God, The everlasting Father, The Prince of Peace." (Isaiah 9:6). Dominus vobiscum is a Latin phrase meaning "The Lord be with you." It is an ancient salutation and blessing traditionally used by the clergy in the Roman Catholic Mass. In other words, "May the Force be with you." Yoda explained: "My ally is the Force, and a powerful ally it is. Its energy surrounds us and binds us. Luminous beings are we, not this crude matter. You must feel the force around you, everywhere."

The scriptures refer to the Force, albeit somewhat obliquely. Alma described the "strong force." (Alma 57:8). He also described how a Nephite city enjoyed the protection of "an exceedingly strong force." (Alma 55:26). On another occasion, to accomplish an objective, he said: "We were obliged to employ all our force." (Alma 57:13). Even under the most trying of circumstances, when there were significant demands upon his energies and resources, Alma "retained all his force." (Alma 59:10).

Jeremiah described "the forces that were with him," and how a group of his enemies "that fled stood under the shadow of Heshbon because of the force." (Jeremiah 41:11 & 38:45). Mormon wrote that his armies fought "with all (their) force." (Mormon 3:6). Job revealed that his "force (was) is in the navel of his belly." (Job 40:16). Joseph Smith described his experience with the Force, when he wrote: "Never did any passage of scripture come with more power to the heart of man than this did at this time to mine. It seemed to enter with great force into every feeling of my heart." (J.S.H. 1:12).

When the Force is used righteously, it is almost always associated with peace. Luke asked the Jedi Master Yoda: "How am I to know the good side from the bad?" Yoda explained to his apprentice: "You will know. When you are calm, at peace, passive. A Jedi uses the Force for knowledge and defense, never for attack." In "Star Wars: The Return of The Jedi," when Luke was engaged in personal combat with Darth Vader and threw his lightsaber away instead of making a killing blow, we see what Yoda meant. In that moment, Luke understood the power of the Force and became a true Jedi Knight.

The scriptures also describe the dark side of the Force: "And there went out another horse that was red: and power was given to him that sat thereon to take peace from the earth, and that they should kill one another: and there was given unto him a great sword," reminiscent of a lightsaber. (Revelation 6:4). "When you look at the dark side, careful you must be," cautioned Yoda, "for the dark side looks back." Be careful of the company you keep.

We think of the light side of the Force when we consider these scriptures. "Peace be both to thee, and peace be to thine house, and peace be unto all that thou hast. (1 Samuel 25:6). The Force is associated with the Holy Spirit of God. Hence, Jesus said: "Peace be unto you." (Luke 24:36). Early on, Joseph Smith was taught about the guidance of the Force. He was told by the Savior: It will "be signalized unto you by the peace and power of my Spirit, that shall flow unto you." (D&C 111:8).

Even when engaged in mortal combat, Jedi consciously calm their spirits and exercise discipline when focusing their minds, in order to be at one with the Force. But it is not enough to simply be at peace when engaging its power. A Jedi Knight must move beyond simple tranquility; he must publish peace. The Sons of Mosiah, for example, were as Jedi, for they "did publish peace; they did publish good tidings of good; and they did declare unto the people that the Lord reigneth." (Mosiah 27:37).

The Force goes hand-in-hand with faith. Jesus said to one young woman: "Daughter, be of good comfort: thy faith," or thy ability to allow the Force to heal thee, "hath made thee whole; go in peace." (Luke 8:48). For true Jedi, faith and fear are incompatible. Those who have faith are never in fear of loss, for that "is a path to the Dark Side." (Yoda).

In essence, Pater taught that "grace and peace (are) multiplied (by the Force) through the knowledge of God." (2 Peter 1:2). In other words, the power of the Force is magnified as we become more familiar with, and the more we emulate, the mission of the Savior. The Force is strong in those who give heed and diligence to the word of God. For example, "there was continual peace among (the people of Nephi), and exceedingly great prosperity in the church because of their heed and diligence which they gave" to the Force. (Alma 49:30).

The Force bears fruit because faith buttressed by works support its principles. "And it came to pass that Nephi went forth among the people, and also many others, baptizing unto repentance, in the which there was a great remission of sins. And thus, the people began again" to feel the power of the Force, and "to have peace in the land." (3 Nephi 1:23).

Sometimes the Force is manifest by a tangible and palpable "covenant of peace" that moves out in concentric waves through the galaxy. (Numbers 25:12). Isaiah exclaimed: "How beautiful upon the mountains are the feet of him that bringeth good tidings, that publisheth peace;" that embraceth the Force, "that publisheth salvation; that saith unto Zion, Thy God reigneth!" (Isaiah 52:7).

But, for those who turn to the dark side, "there is no peace," whatsoever, "saith the Lord." (1 Nephi 20:22). Sometimes the righteous need to call upon all of their energies to apply the power of the Force in support of "their liberty, their lands, their wives, and their children, and their peace, and that they might live unto the Lord their God, and that they might maintain that which was called by their enemies the cause of Christians." (Alma 48:10).

The Force is associated with truth, as well. "I will … reveal unto (the Jedi) an abundance of peace and truth," said Jeremiah. (Jeremiah 33:6). While the lightsaber is the weapon of choice of the Jedi Knights, they are nevertheless counseled to "stand, therefore, having (their) loins girt about with truth, having on the breastplate of righteousness, and (their) feet shod with the preparation of the gospel of peace." (D&C 27:16).

The Jedi do not employ the Force with pomp, ostentation, or for purposes of self-aggrandizement. It is used quietly. "I will give peace and quietness unto Israel," promised the Lord to those who embrace the Force. (1 Chronicles 22:9). It speaks hope to the soul, emboldens our faith, and encourages those who feel its power with the confidence of deliverance out of the hands of their enemies. (See Alma 58:11).

The light side of the Force locks horns with the Dark Side. The Jedi know that there are only two options: "Do. Or do not. There is no try." (Yoda). Through an angel, the Lamb of God declared that He would use the Force to "work a great and a marvelous work among the children of men; a work which shall be everlasting, either on the one hand or on the other—either to the convincing of them unto peace and life eternal, or unto the deliverance of them to the hardness of their hearts and the blindness of their minds unto their being brought down into captivity, and also into destruction, both temporally and spiritually, according to the captivity of the devil." (1 Nephi 14:7). "If you end your training now," Yoda cautioned young Luke Skywalker, "if you choose the quick and easy path as Vader did, you will become an agent of evil. Once you start down the dark path, forever will it dominate your destiny."

The Jedi understand that the righteous application of the Force does not guarantee freedom from tribulation. "These things I have spoken unto you, that in me ye might have peace. In the world ye shall have tribulation: but be of good cheer," for the Force shall be with you, and with it, "I have overcome the world." (John 16:33). Yoda would have us remember that "fear is the path to the dark side. Fear leads to anger. Anger leads to hate. Hate leads to suffering."

Those who fight to maintain the influence of the Force recognize the righteousness of their cause. When "the spirit came upon Amasai, who was chief of the captains" of the armies of Israel, "he said, Thine are we, David, and on thy side, thou son of Jesse: peace, peace be unto thee, and peace be to thine helpers; for thy God helpeth thee." (1 Chronicles 12:18). This Israelite warrior, this Jedi Knight, understood the power of the Force.

Those who learn to use the Force for righteous purposes in the protection of the Galactic Republic are sanctified by the Spirit. Paul besought the Saints: "And the very God of peace sanctify you wholly; and I pray God your whole spirit and soul and body be preserved blameless" by the power of the Force "unto the coming of our Lord Jesus Christ." (1 Thessalonians 5:23). The scriptures promise every Jedi apprentice: "Peace be multiplied unto you." (Daniel 4:1).

Those who mature in their instruction in the application of the Force will find that it gives them power over the elements. Just as Yoda used the Force to lift Luke's T-65 X-Wing out of the swamp at Dagobah, so too Jesus "arose, and rebuked the wind, and said unto the sea, Peace, be still. And the wind ceased, and there was a great calm." (Mark

4:39). On the other hand, "The dark side clouds everything." (Yoda). "Remember," however, "that it is not the work of God that is frustrated, but the work of men." (D&C 3:3).

When modern-day Jedi Knights apply the Force, they acquaint themselves with the Author of peace. Yoda explained: "To be Jedi is to face the truth, and choose. Give off light; be a candle." Job's equivalent exhortation was: "Acquaint now thyself with him, and be at peace: thereby good shall come unto thee." (Job 22:21). Jedi of all ages, and throughout the galaxy, recognize the source of their strength, that is given by grace "from God our Father, and from the Lord Jesus Christ." (Philippians 1:2). It was given, Paul wrote, "unto Timothy, my own son in the faith: Grace, mercy, and peace." All three are equal manifestations of the Force, "from God our Father and Jesus Christ our Lord." (1 Timothy 1:2).

"In the end," explained Yoda, "cowards are those who follow the dark side." The Jedi have "strong minds, great hearts, true faith and ready hands." They are "men whom the lust of office does not kill; men whom the spoils of office cannot buy; men who possess opinions and a will; men who have honor; men who will not lie; men who can stand before a demagogue and damn his treacherous flatteries without winking! Tall men, sun-crowned, who live above the fog in public duty and in private thinking. For while the rabble, with their thumb worn creeds, their large professions, and their little deeds, mingle in selfish strife, Lo! Freedom weeps, Wrong rules the land, and Justice sleeps." (Josiah Gilbert Holland, who is rumored to have been a Jedi Knight in disguise).

(The) Millennium

"The wolf also shall dwell
with the lamb, and the leopard
shall lie down with the kid, and the
calf and the young lion and fatling
together; and a little child shall lead them.
And the cow and the bear shall feed; their young
ones shall lie down together; and the lion shall eat
straw like the ox. And the suckling child shall play on
the hole of the ask, and the weaned child shall put his hand
on the cockatrice's den. They shall not hurt nor destroy in
all my holy mountain, for the earth shall be full of the
knowledge of the Lord, as the waters cover
the sea. (2 Nephi 21:6-9).

"The Millennium consists in this - every heart in the church and Kingdom of God being united in one; the Kingdom increasing to the overcoming of everything opposed to the economy of heaven, and Satan being bound, and having a seal set upon him. All things else will be as they are now." (Brigham Young, "Discourses of Brigham Young," p. 115). Isaiah foresaw such a millennial society, prophesying: "They shall build houses, and inhabit them, and they shall plant vineyards, and eat the fruit of them." (Isaiah 65:21). But only the righteous who have lived virtuous and honest lives will live on the earth during the Millennium. Such individuals "shall not hurt nor destroy in all my holy mountain, saith the Lord." (Isaiah 65:25).

He taught that when righteousness dictates the behavior of societies, "the earth under their feet will be holy." When they are "filled with the Spirit of God ... every animal and creeping thing will be filled with peace; the soil of the earth will bring forth in its strength, and the fruits thereof will be meat for man. The more purity that exists, the less is the strife; the more kind we are to our animals, the more will peace increase, and the savage nature of the brute creation vanish away. If the people will not serve the Devil another moment whilst they live, if this congregation is possessed of that spirit and resolution, here in this house is the Millennium. Let the inhabitants of this city be possessed of that spirit, let the people of the territory be possessed of that spirit, and here is the Millennium. Let the whole people be possessed of that spirit and here is the Millennium, and so will it spread over all the world." ("Discourses of Brigham Young," p. 115-116).

Temple work will occupy much of the time of those who live during the Millennium. "Resurrected beings will help us correct the mistakes we have made in doing research concerning our dead ancestors. They will also help us find the information we need to complete our records" so that we may forge links in our family history all the way back to Father Adam and Mother Eve. (Gospel Principles Lesson Manual). "Children will be sealed to parents until the chain is made perfect back to Adam, so that there will be a perfect chain of Priesthood from Adam to the winding up scene." (Brigham Young, "Discourses of Brigham Young," p. 116).

The gospel will be taught with great power to all people. Eventually, there will be no need to teach others the first principles because they shall all know the Lord. "Then the heathen that are left round about you shall know that I the Lord build the ruined places," and refresh the desolate earth with the bounty of the gospel. (Ezekiel 36:36).

The earth will be as it was when Adam and Eve lived in the Garden of Eden. Our 10th Article of Faith affirms: "We believe … that the earth will be renewed and receive its paradisiacal glory." "For behold, I create new heavens and a new earth: and the former shall not be remembered, nor come to mind" (Isaiah 65:17). "For the Lord shall comfort Zion; he will comfort all her waste places; and he will make her wilderness like Eden, and her desert like the garden of the Lord." (Isaiah 51:3). "This land that was desolate (shall) become like the garden of Eden." (Ezekiel 36:35). Satan shall be bound, for "in that day (he) shall not have power to tempt any man." (D&C 101:28).

In the millennial day, "the earth shall be given unto (the righteous) for an inheritance; and they shall multiply and wax strong, and their children shall grow up without sin unto salvation." (D&C 45:58). Isaiah saw that peace would prevail, when he declared: "The whole earth is at rest, and is quiet." (Isaiah 14:7). "For the Lord shall be in their midst, and his glory shall be upon them, and he will be their king and their lawgiver." (D&C 45:59). There will be no strife between men when "Babylon is fallen … and all the graven images of her gods (have been) broken unto the ground." (Isaiah 21:9).

Peace on earth will prevail, with neither ideological strife nor physical violence. Every tool of technology that has been used for warfare will be turned to productive purposes. The wealth created by honest toil will be put to good use. "They shall beat their swords into plowshares, and their spears into pruning hooks; nation shall not lift up sword against nation, neither shall they learn war any more." (Isaiah 2:4).

Nephi wrote that, during the Millennium, "because of the righteousness of his people, Satan … hath no power over the hearts of the people." (1 Nephi 22:26). This suggests that Satan will be present to tempt men during the thousand years of peace, but their righteousness will prevent him from exerting the influence he craves. In that day of enlightenment, every man, woman, and child will burn with faith as "white hot sparks struck off the divine anvil of God." (B. H. Roberts). Darkness will be banished from the minds of men.

In our day, "the light shineth in darkness, and the darkness comprehendeth it not; nevertheless, the day shall come when (we) shall comprehend even God, being quickened in him and by him." (D&C 88:49). As Bagheera, the powerfully built black panther in "The Jungle Book," confided to Mowgli the man-cub: "I had never seen the jungle. They fed me behind bars from an iron pan till one night I felt that I was Bagheera the Panther, and no man's plaything, and I broke the lock with one blow of my paw and came away." (Rudyard Kipling, "The Jungle Book," p. 26).

So too, those holding the priesthood with its keys of authority, power, and blessing will become kings and priests of the Most High God. Even now, "that priesthood is a perfect law of theocracy, and stands as God to give laws to the people, administered in endless lives to the sons and daughters of Adam." (Joseph Smith, "Teachings," p. 322).

The Millennium will restore faith in righteous government, as the word of the Lord flows from two great capitals: "For out of Zion shall go forth the law, and the word of the Lord from Jerusalem." (Isaiah 2:3).

"Millennial man will live in a state akin to translation. His body will be changed so that it is no longer subject to disease or death, as we know it, although he will be changed in the twinkling of an eye to full immortality when he is a hundred years of age." (Bruce R. McConkie, "The Millennial Messiah," p. 644). "And he that liveth when the Lord shall come, and hath kept the faith, blessed is he; nevertheless, it is appointed to him to die at the age of man. Wherefore, children shall grow up until they become old; old men shall die; but they shall not sleep in the dust, but they shall be changed in the twinkling of an eye" to await the resurrection. (D&C 63:50-51).

All things shall be revealed, "things which have passed, and hidden things which no man knew, things of the earth, by which it was made, and the purpose and the end thereof - things most precious, things that are above, and things that are beneath, things that are in the earth, and upon the earth, and in heaven." (D&C 101:32-34). Those who live during the Millennium will lend a listening ear and will understand with greater clarity and through direct experience the words of the Psalmist, who long ago wrote "Be still, and know that I am God." (Psalms 46:10). When we are no longer busy or preoccupied with trivial affairs, the still small voice of the Spirit will speak with eloquence.

There will be changes in the animal kingdom, as well. In poetic metaphor, both Isaiah and Nephi described the Millennium, when "the wolf also shall lie down with the lamb, and the leopard shall lie down with the kid, and the calf and the young lion and fatling together; and a little child shall lead them. And the cow and the bear shall feed; their young ones shall lie down together; and the lion shall eat straw like the ox. And the suckling child shall play on the hole of the asp, and the weaned child shall put his hand on the cockatrice's den." (Isaiah 11:6-8, & 2 Nephi 21:6-9). However far we carry these figures of speech, these verses paint a portrait of a new God-centered earth that is "full of the knowledge of the Lord, as the waters cover the sea." (Isaiah 11:9). There will be one final struggle at the end of the Millennium. Some people will lose their "covenant consciousness," that will allow Satan to gather his armies together one last time. But Michael (Adam) will vanquish him, and he will be cast out forever.

Then in the final judgment, "the wicked shall go away into unquenchable fire, and their end no man knoweth on earth, nor ever shall know, until they come before me in judgment," while those who have lived on the earth will receive the glory that they deserve. (D&C 43:33). "Treasure these things up in your hearts," the Lord told the new members of the church who were flooding in to Kirtland, Ohio, "and let the solemnities of eternity," that are our covenants, "rest upon your minds." (D&C 43:34).

As we approach the Millennium, the Savior's expectations are much higher for members of the church than they are for the world. "For of him unto whom much is given much is required; and he who sins against the greater light shall receive the greater condemnation." (D&C 82:3). Since all will be judged by the law to which they were responsible while on the earth, accountability will vary for the deeds done in the body. The power of the gospel is to give us an eternal perspective to see beyond the horizon of our physical limitations. One of our temptations is to confuse dreams with reality, but a defeat of cosmic proportion comes when those dreams are surrendered to the narrow and confining reality of the carnal and sensual pre-millennial world.

"Life is a sheet of paper white," wrote the poet, "where each of us may write a line or two, and then comes night. Greatly begin. If thou hast time but for a line, make that sublime. Not failure, but low aim is crime." (James Russell Lowell). Bruce R. McConkie was once asked "How can we reach the Celestial Kingdom." His answer: "Set your course, and move along it."

In our dependence upon the Millennial Christ, we acknowledge His leadership and emulate His example. He sets the course, and we follow the established guidelines. He gives the commands, and we yield to His will. He requires obedience, and we accept His guidance without hesitation or question, because we love Him and He has proven in the past that He loves us. He has promised reward for following through, and cautions that the inevitable consequence of willful neglect of our responsibilities is unhappiness. What makes the Plan fair is continual feedback from the Master. We accepted the risks attendant to mortality because we believed in the Plan, and we knew He would never leave us. Our trust in Him can be complete and total and unflinching. When we leave Him, though, we are vulnerable. When His Presence, or that of His servants, is dominant in our lives, and when our foundation is grounded on the bedrock of the gospel, we can be sure of our ultimate success, because it was ordained in the heavens before the world was, that, with God's help, we might fulfil the measure of our creation. After all, it is the Plan of Redemption and the Plan of Happiness. It is the key to our salvation, and will be the means of our joy in the millennial day.

(The) Mind of God

"Great and marvelous are the works of the Lord. How unsearchable are the depths of the mysteries of him; and it is impossible that man should find out all his ways. And no man knoweth of his ways save it be revealed unto him; wherefore, brethren, despise not the revelations of God."
(Jacob 4:8).

The ordinances of the gospel teach us that there exists a second order of mind. The experiences of the temple, for example, repetitively reinforce the shadow of otherworld experiences that are only spiritually discerned. Hugh Nibley introduced an interesting twist on perspective when he wrote: "As to taking a calm and deliberate look at more than one thing at a time, that is a gift denied us at present. I cannot imagine what such a view of the world would be like, but it would be more real and correct than the one we have now. Once we can see the possibilities that lie in being able to see more than one thing at a time, the universe takes on new dimensions and God takes over.

Let us remember," he continued, "that quite peculiar to the genius of Mormonism is the doctrine of a God who could preoccupy Himself with countless numbers of things. 'The heavens they are many, and they cannot be numbered unto man; but they are numbered unto me, for they are mine," said the Lord. (Moses 1:37). Plainly, we are dealing with higher level thinking. 'For my thoughts are not your thoughts, neither are your ways my ways, saith the Lord. For as the heavens are higher than the earth, so are ... my thoughts than your thoughts.' (Isaiah 55:8-9)." ("Nibley on The Timely & Timeless," p. 263-264).

Orson Pratt spoke of the ability to obtain and consider many different ideas at the same time, instead of thinking unilaterally by following only one course of reasoning at any given time. If God were to give us a sixth, a seventh, even a fiftieth sense, we would see the world in a new light that was arguably more real, inasmuch as each of these senses could potentially convey as much information as the sense of smell, or sight, or hearing do. If we accept the proposition that our five poor senses do not represent all the elements of nature, a much broader panorama of new ways of "looking" at the world appears.

Elder Pratt theorized that, in such a scenario, "knowledge (will) rush in from all quarters; it will come in like light which flows from the sun, penetrating every part, informing the Spirit, and giving understanding concerning ten thousand things at the same time; and the mind will be capable of receiving and retaining all. Not one object at a time, but a vast multitude of objects rush before his vision (the vision of a celestialized soul), and are present before his mind, filling him in a moment with the knowledge of worlds more numerous than the sands of the seashore. Will he be able to bear it? Yes, his mind is strengthened in proportion to the amount of information imparted. It is this tabernacle, in its present condition, that prevents us from a more enlarged understanding." (J.D., 2:238-248). With greatly expanded powers of observation, we would be able to look in every direction at once in order to receive a more accurate appreciation of the creations of God. After all, it was under such inspiration that Moses looked, and "beheld the world and the ends thereof, and all the children of men which are, and which were created." (Moses 1:8).

We would receive knowledge forever barred from us as long as we remain imprisoned within the narrow confines of our mortal bodies. Recall the experience of Moses, who, left to himself, "fell to the earth," so completely overcome "that it was for the space of many hours before (he) did again receive his natural strength like unto man." (Moses 1:9-10).

Elder Pratt reasoned: "There must be some faculty or power natural to God and to superior beings, that man, in this life, is not in possession of in any great part, by which they can look at a great variety of objects at once." It was only under the influence of the Spirit, for example, that "the Brother of Jared could look upon past, present, and future generations; they all came before him, and there was not a soul that he did not behold. (Mormon 8:35). Here, then, is a new faculty of knowledge, very extended in its nature, that is calculated to throw a vast amount of information upon our minds, almost in the twinkling of an eye.

Elder Pratt continued by explaining that celestial beings have the ability to perceive with all parts of their bodies. "The spirit, like the eye, is inherently capable of experiencing the sensations of light. I think we could then see in different directions at once, instead of looking in one particular direction; we could then look all around us at the same instant." This sheds understanding on the explanation of the Prophet Joseph Smith who said after receiving revelation: "My whole body was full of light, and I could see even out at the ends of my fingers and toes." (N.B. Lundwall, "The Vision," p. 11). Perhaps this is why the angel Moroni hovered in the air when he was visiting Joseph. He wanted to see more clearly, for he too could see even out of his toes. As the Lord explained: "If your eye be single to my glory, your whole bodies shall be filled with light, and there shall be no darkness in you; and that body which is filled with light comprehendeth all things." (D&C 88:67).

Brigham Young once declared: "I long for the time that a point of my finger or motion of the hand will express every idea without utterance. When a man is full of the light of eternity, then the eye is not the only medium through which he sees, nor the brain the only means by which he understands. When the whole body is full of the Holy Ghost, he can see behind him with as much ease, without turning his head, as he can see before him. If you have not had that experience, you ought to have. It is not the optic nerve alone that gives the knowledge of surrounding objects to the mind." (J.D., 1:70-71).

Parley P. Pratt believed that we could even move from one place to another without the passage of time, by willing ourselves to be there. "There is no apparent limit," he reasoned, "to the speed attainable by the body, when unchained, set free from the elements which now enslave it, and dictated by the will." ("Key to The Science of Theology," p. 162).

A concurrent belief of Brigham Young stated: "The brightness and glory of the next apartment is inexpressible. (Beings in that realm shall) move with ease and like lightning. If we want to visit Jerusalem, or this, or that, or the other place, there we are. If we want to behold Jerusalem as it was in the days of the Savior, or if we want to see the Garden of Eden as it was when created, there we are. We may behold the earth as at the dawn of creation." (J.D., 14:231). Note that Brigham Young described movement through both space and time, or the spacetime continuum, (a concept only articulated much later by physicists utilizing a discipline of theoretical science that did not exist in his day).

When the Saints dwell with God, what will their state of existence be? Since "the glory of God is intelligence, or in other words, light and truth" (D&C 93:36), it must be that the righteous will dwell amidst the fire and smoke that are symbolic of the presence of God. The wicked, on the other hand, will be consumed as stubble by the brightness of His Coming. What will our resurrected bodies be like? What will our capabilities be? What powers will we command? We can only guess, but the Lord has intrigued us with the promise that His Spirit will enlighten us to behold His glory. He said: "By my power will I make known ... the secrets of my will - yea, even those things which eye has not seen, nor ear heard, nor yet entered into the heart of man." (D&C 76:10). Our "wisdom shall be great, and (our) understanding reach to heaven; and before (us) the wisdom of the wise shall perish, and the understanding of the prudent shall come to naught." (D&C 76:9).

From among many spiritual manifestations, Joseph Smith had one in particular that caused him to recall: "The veil was taken from our minds, and the eyes of our understanding were opened." In other words, he enjoyed an extra-sensory experience so profound that it almost defied description. "We saw the Lord," He said, "standing upon the breastwork of the pulpit, before us; and under his feet was a paved work of pure gold, in color like amber. His eyes were as a flame of fire; the hair of his head was white like the pure snow; his countenance shone above the brightness of the sun; and his voice was as the sound of the rushing of great waters." (D&C 110:1-3)

The Apostle Paul, who had his share of similar experiences, wrote that now we "see through a glass darkly," but then, if our eye be single to His glory, we shall look upon Him who is eternal "face to face." (1 Corinthians 13:12). We can only imagine what it will be like to look upon the wide expanse of eternity as a boundless perspective floods our minds with comprehension. Perhaps only then will its solemnity rest upon our minds, as it should. Perhaps only when the Lord reveals its wonders to our expanded capacity will we see things as they really are, and will we have a fulness of joy.

What will it be like when we dwell
with God? Since His glory "is intelligence, or
in other words, light and truth" (D&C 93:36), it must
be that the righteous will dwell amidst the fire and smoke
that are symbolic of His presence. The Apostle Paul, who had
his share of similar experiences, wrote that now we "see through
a glass darkly," but then, if our eyes are single to His glory, we
shall look upon Him Who is eternal "face to face." (1 Corinthians
13:12). We can only imagine what it will be like to look across
the wide expanse of eternity as a boundless perspective floods
our minds with comprehension. Perhaps only then will its
solemnity rest upon our minds, as it should. Perhaps
only when the Lord reveals His wonders to our
expanded capacity will we see things as
they really are, and will we receive
a fulness of joy.

Missing Scripture

"Behold, the prophet Zenos,
did testify boldly; for the which
he was slain. And behold, also
Zenock, and also Ezias."
(Helaman 8:19-20).

"A true servant of God will never teach a false doctrine. He will never deny new revelation. He never will tell you that the canon of scripture is full, or that the New Testament is the last revelation ever intended to be given to man." (Orson Pratt).

Latter-day Saints recognize that many ancient scriptures are missing from the canon texts. Fragments of these sacred records have survived, but much remains obscure. Latter-day Saints look forward to a time when all things revealed from God will be restored and made known again. The Bible is of inestimable worth; nevertheless, it testifies to its own incompleteness, mentioning sacred works that have been lost to history. For example: The Book of The Covenant (Exodus 24:7), the Book of The Wars of the Lord (Numbers 21:14), the Book of Jasher (Joshua 10:13), the Book of The Acts of Solomon (1 Kings 11:41), the Books of Nathan and Gad (1 Chronicles 29:29), the Prophecy of Ahijah and Visions of Iddo (2 Chronicles 9:29), the Book of Shemaiah (2 Chronicles 12:15), the Book of Jehu (2 Chronicles 20:34), the Acts of Uzziah (2 Chronicles 26:22), the Sayings of The Seers (2 Chronicles 33:19), an earlier Epistle of Paul to the Ephesians (Ephesians 3:3), an epistle of Paul from Loadicea (Colossians 4:16), a former Epistle of Jude (Jude 3), and prophecies of Enoch (Jude 14).

Likewise, The Book of Mormon identifies several prophetic writings absent from the Bible, such as words of Zenos, Zenock, Neum, Ezias, and Joseph of Egypt that were found on the plates of brass. (H.C. 2:236). Their prophecies dealt with the future of Israel and the coming of Jesus Christ. Nephi's brother Jacob stated that all the prophets had testified of Jesus Christ (Jacob 4:4-6; 7:9-11; See John 5:39), a fact not readily apparent in our Old Testament. The Prophet Joseph Smith wrote in 1832, "From sundry revelations which had been received, it was apparent that many important points touching the salvation of man, had been taken from the Bible, or lost before it was compiled." (HC 1:245; See 1 Nephi 13:26- 42). Remedying this, in part, was one of the purposes of the publication of the Joseph Smith Translation of the Bible.

The Doctrine and Covenants speaks of lost writings of John (D&C 7:1-8 & 93:5-18) and refers to a law of dealing with enemies given by God to Abraham, Isaac, Jacob, and Joseph, that is not found in the Bible (D&C 98:28-37). The Pearl of Great Price has restored a portion of the writings of Abraham, Moses, Enoch, and Adam, especially those dealing with the Creation and early history of God's dealings with man. Enoch mentioned an ancient book of remembrance and a genealogy of Adam (Moses 6:5-8, 46), along with now missing blessings and prophecies uttered by Adam and his descendants at the valley of Adam-ondi-Ahman before Adam's death. (D&C 107:53-57).

Many Book of Mormon source materials are not currently accessible. The plates given to Joseph Smith in 1827 mention a record of Lehi (1 Nephi 1:16-17) and other writings of Nephi (1 Nephi 9:1-6). Jacob, Mormon, and Moroni note that they could scarcely include "the hundredth part" of what could have been written. (Jacob 3:13; 3 Nephi 5:8 & Ether 15:33). The Lord often commanded the Nephite record keepers not to write about certain events. (See 1 Nephi 14:25-28; 3 Nephi 26:11-12), and Joseph Smith was similarly commanded by the Lord not to translate a large, sealed portion of the plates. (D&C 17:6; See Ether 4:1-7 & 5:1-6)

In a broader sense, a vast quantity of "scripture" was never written down at all, for whatever God's authorized servants say "when moved upon by the Holy Ghost" is scripture. (D&C 68:1-6). If all the acts and words of the Savior had been recorded, for example, "the world itself could not contain the books that should be written." (John 20:30-31 & 21:25). Myriad inspired utterances of prophets and apostles and of other men and women who were filled with the Holy Ghost were never recorded but are not lost to God. "All things are written by the Father," Jesus said, and testimonies spoken on earth are recorded in heaven for the angels to look upon and will be recalled at some future day. (3 Nephi 27:26 & D&C 62:3).

Missionary Work

"Some wish to live within sight
of a chapel, while others wish to serve
a mission within a yard of hell."
(Anonymous).

"And it came to pass
that the Lamanites did hunt
the band of robbers of Gadianton;
and they did preach the word of God
among the more wicked part of them,
insomuch that this band of robbers
was utterly destroyed from
among the Lamanites."
(Helaman 6:37).

"This is our first interest as a church - to save and exalt the souls of the children of men." (Ezra Taft Benson, C.R., 4/1974). "Proclaim my gospel from land to land, and from city to city. Bear testimony in every place, unto every people." (D&C 66:5 & 7). "Go ye into all the world, and preach the gospel to every creature." (Mark 16:15). "And this gospel shall be preached unto every nation, and kindred, and tongue, and people." (D&C 133:37). The scriptures attest that the Lord's church is a missionary church: "And thus the gospel began to be preached, from the beginning." (Moses 5:58).

The First Presidency, Quorum of the Twelve Apostles, and the Seventy are called to be "special witnesses of the name of Christ in all the world." (D&C 107:22-25). For example, Bruce R. McConkie, in his last General Conference address, testified: "In a coming day I shall feel the nail marks in his hands and in his feet and shall wet his feet with my tears. But I shall not know any better then than I know now that he is God's Almighty Son, that he is our Savior and Redeemer, and that salvation comes in and through his atoning blood and in no other way." (C.R., 4/1985).

Every member of the church needs to be a missionary, because many of Heavenly Father's children are blinded by false teachings and "are only kept from the truth because they know not where to find it." (D&C 112:12). Studies have found that 5% of the church membership prays for guidance in doing missionary work. Interestingly, about 5% of the members of the church have reported that they regularly have missionary experiences. Consequently, Spencer W. Kimball urged: "Make no small plans, for they have no magic to stir men's souls." (Attr. Daniel Burnham).

In the moving words of Tom Paine: "These (Last Days) are the times that try men's souls. The summer soldier and the sunshine patriot will, in this crisis, shrink from their service (in the church); but he that stands it now, deserves the love and thanks of man and woman. (Ignorance,) like hell, is not easily conquered; yet we have this consolation with us, that the harder the conflict, the more glorious the triumph. What we obtain too cheap, we esteem too lightly. 'Tis dearness only that gives everything its value. Heaven knows how to put a proper price upon its goods; and it would be strange, indeed, if so celestial an article as (a knowledge of the Plan of Salvation) should not be highly rated. ("The Political Works of Thomas Paine," p. 55, see "The Crisis," 12/23/1776).

All who "have desires to serve God" are called to the work. (D&C 4:3). "My understanding," declared George Albert Smith, "is that the most important mission that I have in this life is first, to keep the commandments of God, and second, to teach them to my Father's children who do not understand them." (C.R., 10/1916). As those enlisted in the missionary army of Jesus Christ continue to focus their attention on their less fortunate brethren, they will eventually be brought into complete harmony with the attributes of our Father in Heaven. "And ye shall be even as I am, and I am even as the Father, and the Father and I are one," said the Savior to the Three Nephites. (3 Nephi 28:10).

To the Latter-day Saints, He promised: "If it be so that you should labor all your days in crying repentance unto this people, and bring, save it be one soul unto me, how great shall be your joy with him in the kingdom of my father." (D&C 18:15). In a very real and urgent sense, "it becometh every man who hath been warned to warn his neighbor." (D&C 88:81). The Lord will assist us in this work as the message is spread "unto the uttermost parts of the earth." (D&C 58:64). In the process, our minds will be inspired "to create inventions that further the work of the Lord in ways this world has never known." (Russell M. Nelson, "Ensign", 4/1988, p. 73).

Each of us can share the gospel by being a light to the world and by living gospel principles. We can show kindness to others. We can demonstrate by our behavior the principles of the gospel to our friends. We can invite them into our homes. We can prepare our children to serve missions. We can pay our tithing and contribute to the missionary fund. We can assist others who are financially unable to support themselves on missions. We can do family history research and temple work to support the three-fold mission of the church. We can support ward activities that promote missionary work.

We can "serve him with all (our) heart, might, mind and strength, that (we) may stand blameless before God at the last day." (D&C 4:2). Because the Master requires that we be unreservedly committed to the work, He calls us to higher planes of spirituality and to commitments to selfless consecration of effort. He urges us to lose ourselves in service and to let our lights shine before others. In the process, we will lay up for ourselves "treasures in heaven, where neither moth nor rust doth corrupt, and where thieves do not break through nor steal." (3 Nephi 13:19-20).

"Faith, hope, charity and love, with an eye single to the glory of God," qualify us for the work. (D&C 4:5). The standard of the world is: "Seeing is believing." But seeing is irrelevant to the acquisition of faith. Harold B. Lee taught: "You must learn to walk to the edge of the light, and then a few steps into the darkness. Then the light will appear and show the way before you." ("B.Y.U. Today," 3/1991). This is the way saving faith is developed and strengthened.

We can have hope in Christ, an assurance of peace and a confirmation that our lives' direction is on course. Our hope, rather than a high stakes gamble, becomes the inevitable result of well-founded faith. We will have the feeling of encouragement that comes when we are "meek and lowly of heart" and have given control of our desires and emotions to the Lord. (Moroni 7:43).

Charity follows the qualities of hope and faith and is the supreme characteristic of member missionaries. "And charity suffereth long" or is the quality of patience, "and is kind" or is characterized by sensitivity toward others, and is empathic, "and envieth not" or is less concerned with telestial trinkets and is more focused on celestial sureties, "and is not puffed up" or is humble, "seeketh not her own" or is selfless, "is not easily provoked" but reflects poise under provocation, "thinketh no evil" or has no secret agenda to follow, " rejoiceth not in iniquity" but is repulsed by sin, "but rejoiceth in the truth, beareth all things, believeth all things, hopeth all things, endureth all things" or is drawn toward the light, and is continually open to that which is good. (Moroni 7:45).

Without these qualities, we cannot be effective missionaries. Our efforts will be in vain, and our own progression will stop along with that of those we might have saved had we done our duty. Without charity, we are "nothing, for charity never faileth. Wherefore, (we must) cleave unto charity, which is the greatest of all" the spiritual gifts, "for all things must fail" without it." (Moroni 7:46). Charity is the greatest of all the qualities we may cultivate as we seek to emulate the character of our Father.

It "is the pure love of Christ, and it endureth forever, and whoso is found possessed of it at the last day, it shall be well with him." (Moroni 7:47). As it motivates us to Christian service, it also prepares us to be like God so that we will feel comfortable when we regain His Presence. It is a gift bestowed upon the faithful by the grace of God.

The Lord specifically reminded his missionaries to "remember faith, virtue, knowledge, temperance, patience, brotherly kindness, godliness, charity, humility, (and) diligence." (D&C 4:6). We do this, Peter wrote, "that we might be partakers of the divine nature." (2 Peter 1:4). When God said: "Let us make man in our image, after our likeness," He meant not only that we should have not only the physical characteristics as our Parents, but also their spiritual characteristics. (Moses 2:26). When we are finally "like" God, we will have matured to reach the stature of our divine potential.

"For this end was the law given," to prepare us to believe in Christ and to emulate Him. Then "we are made alive in Christ because of our faith." (2 Nephi 25:25). The virtue of the word is its incredible power to touch our hearts with the pixie dust that frees us to spread our wings and fly. The light and knowledge we receive of God is given by revelation that is a principle that speaks to the very core of our being. As Hugh B. Brown said: "Sometimes, during solitude, I hear truth spoken with clarity and freshness; uncolored and untranslated it speaks from within myself in a language original but inarticulate, heard only with the soul." ("Eternal Quest," p. 435).

Wo unto those, however, who are enslaved by selfish indulgence. Such people are blinded to that which is before their very eyes. "They regard not the work of the Lord, neither consider the operation of his hands." (2 Nephi 15:12). They are captive precisely because they have no knowledge of God, even as they proclaim their independence. "Their honorable men are famished, and their multitude dried up with thirst." (2 Nephi 15:13).

Their condition is contrasted to God's exalted state. "Therefore, hell hath enlarged herself, and opened her mouth without measure; and their glory, and their multitude, and their pomp, and he that rejoiceth, shall descend into it. And the mean (or common) man shall be brought down, and the mighty man shall be humbled, and the eyes of the lofty shall be humbled. But the Lord of Hosts will be exalted in judgment, and God that is holy shall be sanctified in righteousness." (2 Nephi 15:14-16).

The Lord is patient and long-suffering, and extends His arm of mercy long after the faint-hearted would have given up. Elijah complained to the Lord: "The children of Israel have forsaken thy covenant, thrown down thine altars, and slain thy prophets with the sword; and I, even I only, am left; and they seek my life to take it away." To this grievance, the Lord responded: "Yet I have left me seven thousand in Israel, all the knees which have not bowed unto Baal, and every mouth which hath not kissed him." (1 Kings 19:14 & 18).

Joseph Fielding Smith, Jr. declared: "The greatest crime in all this world is to lead men and women away from the true principles." (C.R., 4/1951). The Lord illustrated the gospel principle of concern for the welfare of others when He said: "I am the bread of life: He that cometh to me shall never hunger; and he that believeth on me shall never thirst." (John 6:35). In the Eternal Court of Justice, there will be stiff penalties for failure to have provided for others the Bread of Life, or for having fed them stale, or moldy, or otherwise unwholesome bread.

Lyman Abbott said: "The brotherhood of man is an integral part of Christianity no less than the Fatherhood of God; and to deny the one is no less infidel than to deny the other." Its "mystic bond makes all men one." (Thomas Carlyle). "The universe is but one great city, full of beloved ones, divine and human, by nature endeared to each other." (Epictetus).

The only motive strong enough to encourage us to exercise the self-control required by the gospel of Jesus Christ is our love of God and man, and so there is a contrast between those who are stiff-necked and those who have charity. The former are prevented from looking up to Heavenly Father for guidance, over to priesthood leaders for counsel, around to seek out those in need, or down in an attitude of humility. The latter enjoy the companionship of the Holy Spirit or Holy Ghost, "which maketh manifest unto the children of men, according to their faith." (Jarom 1:4).

Those who have embraced the gospel and made covenants have softened their telestial tendencies. They become as pliable clay in the hands of the Master Potter. It should come as no surprise that the covenants we make with God reflect His attributes. He is moral, so He gives us the Covenant of Chastity. He has charity, so He commands us to love Him and each other. He is disciplined, so He gives us the Law of Obedience. Because He is a righteous steward, He gives us the Law of Consecration. Out of His love for His less fortunate children emerges the Law of the Fast. Since He has a perfected, resurrected body, we are given the Word of Wisdom. Because He is omniscient, we receive the commandment to seek knowledge. In consequence of the Gift of His Son, He gives us the Law of Sacrifice. Because He rested from His labors on the seventh day, He gives us the Law of the Sabbath.

God our Father is perfect in every way. He could give us everything He has, but what He is we must earn for ourselves as we struggle to overcome adversity and gain self-mastery. Missionary work is necessary because it is within our eternal reach to become as God is. We are engaged in the work not to make the lives of our friends and neighbors better, but to expose them to the Plan of Salvation that extends the promise of salvation and exaltation in the Celestial Kingdom to all.

Joseph F. Smith declared: "No man need fear in his heart when he is conscious of having lived up to the principles of truth and righteousness as God has required it at his hands, according to his best knowledge and understanding." (C.R., 4/1903). When we are diligent in our obedience, our agency enjoys its greatest expression. The perfect law of liberty is one of the hardest things for the unconverted to understand. But when we embrace missionary work, hearts are touched, lives are changed on both sides of the equation, and souls are added to the harvest. "Grace and peace (are) multiplied unto (us) through the knowledge of God, and of Jesus our Lord." (2 Peter 1:2).

Moral Discipline

"I count him
braver who overcomes his
desires than he who conquers his
enemies; for the hardest victory
is the victory over self."
(Aristotle).

As the
white-hot sparks
of faith are struck
off the Divine Anvil of
God, they ignite the flame
of our resolve, and we develop
the "power to do whatsoever thing
is expedient," or that is right to do,
under the circumstances.
(Moroni 7:33).

Moral discipline involves the consistent exercise of choice to ennoble eternal principles with action that may not be easy or convenient, but is simply the right thing to do. If we want to have positive outcomes, our God-given right to choose must be accompanied by the strength to exercise moral discipline manifest in righteous behavior.

Having good values is not enough. Our society has failed miserably to instill high standards in the rising generation. When a culture believes that truth is relative and that it is up to individuals to decide what is right or wrong, the stage is set for disaster. When "every man walketh in his own way, and after the image of his own god," the erosion of moral discipline followed by the chaotic crash of cultural stability is inevitable. (D&C 1:16).

When that happens, external controls are often implemented to manipulate behavior to regain a semblance of steadiness. Our increased reliance on laws to regulate moral discipline says something about our culture. The world seeks change by exerting external control, and fails miserably. The gospel seeks change by transforming the inner vessel, and succeeds brilliantly. It does this by calibrating our internal moral compass to orient us toward moral discipline.

Moral discipline involves the consistent exercise of choice to ennoble eternal principles with action that may not be easy or convenient, but is the right thing to do. If we want to have positive outcomes, our God-given ability to choose must be accompanied by strength to exercise moral discipline manifest in righteous behavior. Exhibiting good values is simply not enough. Our society has failed miserably to instill higher standards in the rising generation. When a culture believes that truth is relative and that it is up to individuals to decide what is right or wrong, the stage is set for disaster. When "every man walketh in his own way, and after the image of his own god," the erosion of moral discipline followed by the chaotic crash of cultural stability is inevitable.
(D&C 1:16).

Mothers

"Now they never had fought, yet the did not fear death; and they did think more upon the liberty of their fathers than they did upon their lives; yea, they had been taught by their mothers, that if they did not doubt, God would deliver them. And they rehearsed unto me the words of their mothers, saying: We do not doubt our mothers knew it." (Alma 56:47-48).

President Ezra Taft Benson once stated: "No more sacred word exists in secular or holy writ than that of mother." This seems like a particularly bold statement to make, especially in light of some other powerfully charged words like Savior, Celestial Kingdom, Atonement, Repentance, Priesthood, and so on. I think the reason he said that is because "mother" is the keystone of the gospel arch, and central to the Plan of Salvation. Without mothers there would be no one to participate in the Plan.

I believe that it was with this in mind that President David O. McKay taught: "Motherhood is the greatest potential influence either for good or ill in human life. The mother's image is the first that stamps itself on the unwritten page of the young child's mind. It is her caress that first awakens a sense of security; her kiss, the first realization of affection; her sympathy and tenderness, the first assurance that there is love in the world. This ability and willingness properly to rear children make motherhood the noblest office or calling in the world. She who rears successfully a family of healthy, beautiful sons and daughters deserves the highest honor that man can give, and the choicest blessings of God."

The world recognizes the sociological significance of the mother's role. The relationship that a mother develops with her children and the influence she has over them as they develop a value system is critical to their long-term success as functioning individuals in society. But Latter-day Saints are not just playing one key on the gospel piano. We appreciate the role of motherhood more than any other people because we view it from the wider perspective of the restored gospel.

First, we believe in God the Father and Mother. As early as 1839 the Prophet Joseph Smith taught the concept of an eternal mother, as reported in several accounts from that period. From that same era, Eliza R. Snow's poem "O My

Father" recognizes the role of divine parents in the Plan of Salvation, and President John Taylor declared that she wrote it under the inspiration of heaven and considered it a revelation from God.

In the heavens are parents single? No, the thought makes reason stare! Truth is reason; truth eternal, ells me I've a mother there. When I leave this frail existence, when I lay this mortal by, Father, Mother, may I meet you in your royal courts on high? (Hymn no. 292).

In 1909, the First Presidency of the church wrote that "man, as a spirit, was begotten and born of heavenly parents, and reared to maturity in the eternal mansions of the Father," as an "offspring of celestial parentage," and that "all men and women are in the similitude of the universal Father and Mother, and are literally the sons and daughters of Deity."

The Church of Jesus Christ of Latter-day Saints accepts literally Paul's teaching: "The Spirit itself beareth witness with our spirit, that we are the children of God. And if children, then heirs of God, and joint heirs with Christ." (Romans 8:16-17). We believe that all who come to the earth are actual spiritual offspring of God the Eternal Father. (See Numbers 16:22; Hebrews 12:9).

The title "Elohim" suggests the plural of the Canaanite El, and is accepted as the majestic title of deity. Genesis 1:27 reads, "So God created man in his own image, in the image of God created he him, male and female created he them." This suggests that Heavenly Parents, male and female, participated jointly in the creative process. The Temple Endowment is symbolic of that creative process, and supports this view.

As no other people, the Latter-day Saints recognize the responsibility of mortal parents to provide nurturing environments for the spirit children of our Heavenly Father. President Spencer W. Kimball said: "Mothers have a sacred role. They are partners with God. He has placed women at the very headwaters of the human stream."

Patricia Holland wrote, "The significance of motherhood continues undiminished following the birth of a child. The long-term stability, security, and peace of a human soul are built in large measure upon the foundation of love, and any individual's ability to give and receive love is rooted strongly in that person's earliest relationships. For most people, that earliest influence is the mother.

She who gives the child life is first and foremost the one to give it a way of life, teaching the child what it should or should not do. She encourages strong character formation as she teaches the child to impose limitations on some of its natural instincts. By her words and actions, she teaches her child the regard that should be shown other individuals if that child wishes to be included and loved as a member of the family circle, later as a member of society, and finally as a participating member of the kingdom of God.

The ultimate responsibility of a mother, then, is to lead her child lovingly through its personal development and toward its divine destiny. Latter-day Saints believe that if a mother is prayerful and totally committed to such a weighty responsibility, she will receive divine intuitions and spiritual whisperings to aid her in her mothering. Living as a conduit for divine instruction to her child, a mother can greatly enhance its opportunity for joy and exaltation. The child who has been mothered in this profound way usually develops a moral conscience, a respect for society, a desire to contribute to the well-being of humankind, and, most important, a love of God and a love for self that will bring everlasting joy and inner peace."

What really sets the Latter-day Saints apart from the rest of Christianity, and the world, is the doctrine that family relationships continue after death when they have been sealed by the authority of the Priesthood. Thus, is guaranteed to worthy parents the opportunity to enjoy in the eternities a family relationship founded on sacred covenants made with our Heavenly Father.

The Encyclopedia of Mormonism declares that "Every worthy woman who lives a virtuous life and who promotes righteousness in her family and in the church and her family is entitled both to the designation "mother in Israel" and to the promises given to Sarah and other biblical mothers in Israel. These promises are open to all faithful women who teach others to love the Lord and keep his commandments. The title designates intelligent and faithful support of the church and its leaders, and historically it has been applied most frequently to leaders among women. It is often found in patriarchal blessings and is a title and a promise with more than earthly significance. Motherhood is a God-given role vital to the exaltation of a woman and her family.

Mary Fielding Smith had only two children of her own, both young enough when she died that no claim could be made of their future significance, yet at her death, evidently in recognition of her character and commitment, she was called a mother in Israel. A son and a grandson later became Presidents of the church.

Currently the term "mother in Israel" may be found most frequently in patriarchal blessings. President Joseph Fielding Smith said, "To be a mother in Israel in the full gospel sense is the highest reward that can come into the life of a woman." It is a promise open to all faithful sisters who love and serve the Lord and keep his commandments, including those who do not have the opportunity to bear children in this life."

Our Latter-day Saint concept of the eternal family molds our people, as does no other doctrine. It is God's Plan, it is all encompassing, spanning the time when we were nurtured at our Parents' side in our pre-mortal life, through mortality, and on into the eternities. Is it any wonder, then, that stable and secure parental relationships founded on priesthood covenants and ordinances are central to the success of the Plan?

As no other people, the Latter-day Saints recognize the responsibility of parents to provide nurturing environments for the spirit children of our Heavenly Father. President Spencer W. Kimball said: "Mothers have a sacred role. They are partners with God, Who has placed women at the headwaters of the human stream."

Multi-Tasking

"If God had commanded me to do all things, I could do them. And now, if the Lord has such great power, and has wrought so many miracles among the children of men, how is it that he cannot instruct me?" (1 Nephi 17:50-51).

Multi-tasking is doing more than one thing at a time. A dentist can juggle 5 treatment rooms and a reception area full of patients thanks to multi-tasking. When a busy soccer mom gets one kid to practice, another to the orthodontist, and a third to music lessons, while thinking about her upcoming Sunday School lesson, her grocery store shopping list and what to make for dinner, she is multi-tasking. When she is changing the baby's diapers while applying band aids to skinned knees, running 4 loads of wash, sorting 16 pairs of socks, canning a bushel of peaches, and scheduling her visiting teaching, you can bet she is a skilled multi-tasker. When dad drives the kids to mutual while figuring out how to fit in mowing the lawn, repairing the washing machine, writing the missionaries, going home teaching, and taking mom out on a date, he is multi-tasking. When the kids write in their journals while thinking about scripture mastery, doing their homework, attending seminary, serving in their classes, and participating in intramural sports and extracurricular activities, they are multi-tasking.

Bishops are able to better magnify their callings because the Lord blesses them to be consummate multi-taskers. High Priest Group Leaders, Elder's Quorum Presidents, and auxiliary presidents delegate when they can, and the rest of the time they multi-task. We have long-since learned that when a house is divided against itself, it cannot stand. (See Matthew 12:25). We wear many hats and often pile them on, one after another. We are multi-faceted and have many layers. When we multi-task we are as the brilliant cut of a diamond whose 58 facets reflect light in a dazzling array, and whose breathtaking beauty confirms that its whole is somehow greater than the sum of its parts. Multi-tasking lifts us out of the ordinary to surge past the limitations of our poorly perceived potential.

We can even multi-task righteousness. At the beginning of each day, we wake up with a prayer in our hearts even as, in other ways, we prepare for the day. While attending to his responsibilities, Harold B. Lee was often asked difficult ecclesiastical questions. He often answered: "In the early hours of the morning, while I was pondering that very question." Multi-taskers seize every opportunity to ponder the important questions of life. While brushing our teeth at the break of day, we keep pads of paper and pencils on the counter, because thoughts pop into our minds relating to the complexities that lie before us. Whoever invented 3 M and computer sticky notes had multi-tasking in mind. When we multi-task, the capabilities of our minds are more breathtaking than the most sophisticated computer that can still "think" only in a linear fashion.

When we go out and face the day, conflicts begin to pile up, but using gospel principles as multi-tasking tools helps us to successfully cope as each challenge arises. At one and the same time, as we deal with issues that demand our conscious attention, there are underlying currents of honesty, benevolence, patience, courage, and virtue that define our behavior. How we comport ourselves is a witness of our faith and testimony. Our charity, compassion, and tolerance are silent evidences of our core values. The harmonic resonation within our being allows our character to run on cruise-control even as we multi-task.

Multi-tasking can help us to avoid the conceptual cul-de-sacs of those who having eyes cannot see and who having ears cannot hear. It can soften hardened hearts, ease the muscle spasms in stiff necks, and create pliancy and elasticity where once there had been obstinacy and rigidity. Multi-tasking righteousness moderates our appetites and suppresses our hunger pangs and cravings for the kinds of gaudy paraphernalia and telestial trappings that attract the curious but demand neither commitment nor dedication.

When we multi-task righteousness, we live abundantly, enjoy expanding opportunities, and experience a "consciousness of victory over self, and of communion with the infinite." (David O. McKay, C.R., 10/1969). As the circle of our interests expands like a balloon, so does the corresponding surface area of the unknown, but we optimistically face our futures with the expectation of even greater opportunities to multi-task.

Consummate multi-taskers are hopeful, cheerful, confident, positive, buoyant, and humble, and are like Sir Isaac Newton, who once reflected: "I was like a boy playing on the seashore, and diverting myself now and then finding a smoother pebble, or a prettier shell than ordinary, whilst the great ocean of truth lay all undiscovered before me." Multi-tasking allowed him to write Principia Mathematica, one of the most important books ever written. He lay the foundations for the scientific revolution, and defined classical mechanics, universal gravitation, and the laws of motion. He built the first reflecting telescope, and demonstrated the visible light spectrum, formulated the empirical law of cooling, and studied the speed of sound. He developed differential equations and integral calculus (while home from the university when it was closed during a plague epidemic). He demonstrated generalized binomial theorem, developed a method for approximating the roots of functions, and contributed to the understanding of power series. He was one of the most influential persons in history, who walked to the edge of the light, and took a few steps into the darkness. There he found that the light re-appeared and moved ahead of him, revealing multiple doors that stood ajar, just waiting for him to push through them to an even greater illumination of the mind.

Multi-taskers are as "the man who stood at the gate of the year, (who said) 'Give me a light that I may tread safely into the unknown.' And he replied, 'Go into the darkness and put your hand into the hand of God. That shall be to you better than light and safer than a known way!' So, I went forth and finding the Hand of God, trod gladly into the night. He led me towards the hills and the breaking of day in the lone east. So, heart be still! What need our human life to know if God hath comprehension in all the dizzy strife of things both high and low?" (Minnie Louise Haskins, "A Dialogue Between a Man, and The Keeper of The Gate of The Year").

Because multi-taskers have their fingers in many pots, they don't require instant gratification, but have learned to be realistic and to temper their expectations. They live not so much for the reward but for the experience. For them, it is the journey and not the destination that enriches life. Albert Einstein revealed something of the character of multi-taskers when he mused: "The years of searching in the dark for a truth that one feels, but cannot express; the intense desire and the alternations of confidence and misgiving, until one breaks through to clarity and understanding, are only known to him who has himself experienced them." (1933). His consummate understanding of classical mechanics, electromagnetism, mathematics, and physics, enabled him to conceive the most famous equation of them all: $E = MC^2$, and to devote the later years of his life to seeking an answer to the holy grail of multi-taskers: Is there a grand unifying theory of everything?

The gospel grooms us to be multi-taskers and teaches us to regard both the parts and sum of our experiences. It teaches us that if we are gliding smoothly and effortlessly through life, we are probably going downhill and have neglected our multi-tasking opportunities, because real progress and achievement take effort as we face and overcome myriad challenges. As the poet wrote: "My life is but a weaving between my Lord and me. I cannot choose the colors. He worketh steadily. Oft times He weaveth sorrow, and I, in foolish pride, forget He sees the upper, but I the underside. Not 'til the loom is silent, and the shuttles cease to fly, shall God unroll the canvas and explain the reason why. The dark threads are as needful in the Weaver's skillful hand, as threads of gold and silver in the pattern He has planned." (Benjamin Malachi Franklin).

Sometimes, we can be too focused on trivialities that hamper our ability to learn to be multi-taskers. Telestial trash traumatizes us, obstructs our perception of celestial sureties, and hinders our capacity to do more than one thing at a time, freezing the moment, as it were. These can be diversions that are as innocuous as social networking, text messaging, computer compulsions, television, music, the media, sleep, and leisure time. The opacity of these things can strangle our ability to distinguish reality from its caricatures and influence us to think and act in narrowly-defined and self-limiting linear dimensions.

Celestial certainties, on the other hand, enhance our ability to multi-task and are signposts that guide us through the minefields of mortality and the complexities of our multi-faceted lives. We consecrate a tenth to the Lord as we simultaneously learn to work hard and enjoy the fruits of our labors. We eat, drink, and are merry, even as the Word of Wisdom tempers our behavior and teaches us to consciously remember that our bodies are the temples of our spirits and the templates of our souls. The Law of Chastity generously permits us to enjoy the cornucopia of experience offered by life, while at the same time channeling our thoughts, words, and deeds within divinely defined boundaries. The Law of Consecration teaches us not only to work hard to earn a living, and to even store away a surplus, but also to dedicate our time, talents, and means, all that the Lord has blessed us with, and all that He may bless us with, to the building of the kingdom. Our God-given agency safeguards our ability to multi-task. But free will is a renewable resource that may slip between our fingers if we abandon our core values and our self-discipline, and it may be lost forever if it is carelessly squandered.

Heavenly Father wants us to learn to multi-task while Satan's efforts are focused on keeping us in ignorance of its benefits. If he can keep us in the dark, we might never see the summits that would otherwise have been within our reach. He whimpers: "You can't," while God stresses: "You can." He has a strong "won't" while God has a more powerful "Will." He snivels about inability while God emphasizes availability. His focus is single-minded and narrowly defined, while God's love is ecumenical and all-encompassing. He is the ultimate pessimist, while God's optimism gives us courage. He is anti-enemy, while God is pro-gospel. He promotes unfaithfulness, with an emphasis on the "un." If we follow his example, everything unravels, is undone, and our unbelief becomes a bottomless pit of unfulfilled dreams. God, on the other hand, encourages faithfulness, with an emphasis on the "full." In its abundance we find that we have more than enough, even a surplus, a surfeit, that is overflowing and brimming with possibilities, and when our cup runneth over, we multi-task our way right into the embrace of eternity.

Those who persist in stubbornly refusing the invitation of our Heavenly Father to come in out of the cold, will instead sometimes seek refuge in the drafty fortress of what is nothing but a perceived satisfaction in their superficial accomplishments. (See Alma 30:17). In order to maintain at least outward appearances, the fabrication of a façade is required that demands inordinate attention to trivial detail and to continual cosmetic reconstruction. But in the end, their efforts lack substance, and are nothing but smoke and mirrors.

(The) Name of Christ in The Book of Mormon

"Ye must
take upon you the name
of Christ, which is my name.
For by this name shall ye be
called at the last day."
(3 Nephi 27:5).

The first use of the name of Christ in The Book of Mormon occurs in 2 Nephi 10:3, that reads: "Wherefore, as I said unto you, it must needs be expedient that Christ - for in the last night the angel spake unto me that this should be his name - should come among the Jews."

This begs the question: Since Christ is the central figure in The Book of Mormon, why wasn't the name "Christ" used until its seventy-eighth page? The obvious answer is that it wasn't until then that an angel revealed His name to Jacob. But that simplistic explanation begs another question: Why, then, didn't the angel reveal His name earlier in the narrative, to Lehi, Nephi, and/or Jacob? The answer may seem surprising, at first, but it lends credence to the assertion that the book is authentic ancient scripture.

The word "Christ" is Greek. The same term in Hebrew is "Messiah" which Nephi used 28 times prior to 2 Nephi 10:13 (excluding quotations from Isaiah). Neither he nor his family knew Greek, coming as they did, from a culture that spoke Hebrew. Instead, they used a name that was familiar to them and that was drawn from their own language and culture. Consistent with this explanation, Nephi used the term "Messiah" until Jacob received revelation about the name Christ. After that time, "Messiah" fell out of favor. Nephi used it only 10 times subsequent to Jacob's revelation, and "Christ" became the primary term that thereafter was used to identify the Savior.

Between 2 Nephi 10:3 and 2 Nephi 33:15, Nephi used the term "Messiah" only 10 more times, and Jacob never used it. After Nephi's death, "Messiah" was used only 3 times in the remainder of The Book of Mormon. Looking at it another way, before Jacob's revelation, the term "Christ" was never used, but afterwards, it was used nearly 400 times, with the highest percentage attributed to Jacob, Mormon, and Moroni.

This suggests that Nephi had the humility to listen to his younger brother, and to learn from him. He wasn't blinded by his own position, authority, influence, experience, or even his access to revelation, and by characteristically and consistently using the title of Christ as Jacob had received it by revelation, he provided provocative evidence that The Book of Mormon is ancient scripture.

There are many sincere Christians who possess only a shallow understanding of the Great Plan of the Eternal God (see Alma 34:9), restricting them to shrink it down into a single finite point in time and space. Evangelicals will often employ the term "born again" when they are referring to the precise moment of their conversion. (See Alma 7:14). They frequently describe an epiphany that moved them to accept the Lord, and be 'saved." (See Alma 5:31-62). Sincere though their feelings might be, their experiences with the Spirit are only the first steps of a conversion process that was meant to continue until their last breath. The Plan of Redemption (see Alma 29:2) is found only in restored gospel of Jesus Christ, and more pointedly in The Book of Mormon, where God has provided us with an educational experience that was designed to engage us in the journey of a lifetime.

(The) Nature of God and Our Covenants

"I would that
ye should be perfect
even as I, or your Father
who is in heaven is perfect."
(3 Nephi 12:48).

Joseph Smith rightly stated: "There are but a very few beings in the world who understand rightly the nature of God, and if men do not understand the character of God they do not comprehend themselves." (H.C., 6:303). The purpose of our existence is to help us to develop qualities and character traits that are consistent with His divine nature.

Our Heavenly Father glories in the possibility that we might one day be like Him, and offers us His grace, consisting of the gifts and power by which we may be brought to His perfection and stature, so that we may enjoy not only what He has, but what He is. "If ye by the grace of God are perfect in Christ, and deny not his power, then are ye sanctified in Christ by the grace of God, through the shedding of the blood of Christ, which is in the covenant of the Father unto the remission of your sins, that ye become holy, without spot." (Moroni 10:33).

The priesthood energizes His grace by administering the ordinances of salvation that allow us to receive the blessings of the gospel by binding us to Him by means of covenants of action. These ordinances bring us to a greater understanding of His nature. They are binding contracts between ourselves and God and must come through revelation. No person enters into such covenants except on the basis of direct revelation from God. It follows that the only ones who can legitimately enter into covenants are members of The Church of Jesus Christ!

The covenants we make with God reflect His grace, as well as His attributes. He is moral, so He gives us the Covenant of Chastity. He has charity, so He commands us to love Him and each other. God is disciplined, so He gives us the Law of Obedience. Because He is a righteous steward, He gives us the Law of Consecration. Because He loves His less fortunate children, He gives us the Law of the Fast. Because His is a perfected, resurrected body, He gives us the Word of Wisdom. Because He is omniscient, He gives us the commandment to seek knowledge. In consequence of the Gift of His Son, He gives us the Law of Sacrifice. Because He rested from His labors on the seventh day, He gives us the Law of the Sabbath.

God could give us everything He has, but what He is, we must earn for ourselves, as we struggle to overcome adversity and gain self-mastery. The purpose of our covenants is to help us to focus our efforts to become as He is. If it were not possible to become as He is, covenants would be unnecessary. Keeping covenants puts us beyond the influence of the adversary and endows us with the priesthood and spiritual power necessary to overcome evil and obtain exaltation.

The Prophet Joseph Smith said that salvation consists of our being placed beyond the power of our enemies, meaning the enemies of our progression, such as dishonesty, greediness, lying, immorality, and other vices. Only by making covenants with God can we break the bands of death and are we made free to enjoy His grace. "There is no other name given whereby salvation cometh," said Benjamin; "therefore, I would that ye should take upon you the name of Christ, all you that have entered into the covenant with God." (Mosiah 5:8). No other organization has the power to break the death grip of Satan, who would drag our souls down to hell in an instant, if he were given the opportunity to do so. Is it any wonder that The Church of Jesus Christ of Latter-day Saints is a missionary oriented church, and that the Lord Himself proclaims that it "is the only true and living church upon the face of the whole earth, with which I, the Lord, am well pleased?" (D&C 1:30).

(Our) Neighbors

"Now the people which were not Lamanites were Nephites; nevertheless, they were called Nephites, Jacobites, Josephites, Zoramites, Lamanites, Lemuelites, and Ishmaelites. But I, Jacob, shall not hereafter distinguish them by these names, but I shall call them Lamanites that seek to destroy the people of Nephi, and those who are friendly to Nephi, I shall call Nephites, or the people of Nephi."
(Jacob 1:13-14).

"It's a beautiful day in the neighborhood, a beautiful day for a neighbor. Would you be mine? Could you be mine? I have always wanted to have a neighbor just like you. I've always wanted to live in a neighborhood with you. So, let's make the most of this beautiful day. Since we're together, we might as well say, would you be mine? Could you be mine? Won't you be my neighbor? Won't you please, please won't you be my neighbor?" (Fred Rogers).

Jesus taught us to love our neighbors as ourselves. (Matthew 19:19). This counsel is diametrically opposed to the world's philosophy, that is best articulated by Daddy Warbucks, who told Annie: "You don't have to be nice to those you climb over, or step on, on your way up the ladder of success, if you don't plan on coming back down again." We are constantly reminded: "It's not what you know; it's who you know. You don't get what you deserve; you get what you negotiate. He who has the gold makes the rules." But as Brigham Young declared: "If we go on lusting after the groveling things of this life which perish with the handling, we shall surely remain fixed with a very limited amount of knowledge and like a door upon its hinges, move to and fro from one year to another without any visible advancement or improvement." If we really want to get ahead in the world, we need to learn to prioritize the needs of our neighbors.

We love our neighbors as ourselves when we yield to the influence of the Holy Spirit, put off our telestial tendencies, begin to appreciate the scope of the Atonement of Christ, return to our childhood roots, and become meek, submissive, humble, patient, full of love, and willing to submit to all things. (See Mosiah 3:19). We become teachable, as we are guided by the peaceable things of the kingdom. We learn to see past our neighbors' shortcomings, and unconditionally and ceaselessly forgive every one of our "brothers their trespasses," until "seventy times seven." (Matthew 18:32 & 35).

We do this in the face of Satan's Golden Question, which seizes upon our telestial tendencies like a bulldog sinks its teeth into a postman's pants: "Do you have any money?" He has done a tremendous job of perverting the Lord's teaching by having us believe that we can have anything in this world for money, including the admiration and respect of our neighbors. Does a need exist? Solve the problem with a generous application of money, to be repeated in incrementally larger doses four times a day for life. This is the prescription upon which the world relies to cure our ills and those of our neighbors.

When the noise of the world gets in the way and we forget who our neighbors really are, it's time to get out the body bags, because the inevitable casualties of war will soon begin to stack up. No matter how much we have patronized them, we lose friends in a slow hemorrhage, as they defect to the enemy's camp. Our self-preoccupation wastes our energy with distractions we cannot control. Because of our shortsightedness, we damage ourselves in ways both subtle and unexpected. We cannot persist in self-centered behavior that relies on the corrosive elements of animosity, rancor, bitterness, hostility, acrimony, sullenness, anger, and vindictiveness toward others, without suffering self-inflicted wounds. All this can be avoided by following the simple admonition to love our neighbors as ourselves, which is one of the fundamental operational principles of the Plan of Salvation. Brigham Young declared: "All organized existence is in progress either to an endless advancement in eternal perfections, or back to dissolution. There is no period in all the eternities wherein organized existence will become stationary, that it cannot advance in knowledge, wisdom, power, and glory." (J.D., 1:349).

"Who are our neighbours?" asked the lawyer of Jesus. (See Luke 10:25-37). They are those who speak Aymara, Afrikaans, Fijian, Polish, Mandarin, and around 6,500 other languages. They live in 196 countries on 7 continents and on the isles of the sea. The color of their skin is red, yellow, brown, black, and white, and everything in between. They are equally comfortable wearing a sarong, a grass skirt, a lava lava, a burqa, or blue jeans. They find shelter in igloos, bamboo huts, thatch cottages, canvas tents, cardboard shanties, and condominiums. They eat kaeng khua, poi, muamba de galinha, raggmunk, hrútspungar, and hamburgers on sesame seed buns. Most importantly, and whether or not they recognize the feeling, each one carries a spark of divinity that is the gentle glow of the light of Christ.

It was with this "worldview" that the Savior embraced His neighbors. Giving them more than just "lip service," He practiced what He preached. His counsel encouraged substantive assistance rather than passive inattention. As John Taylor taught: "There are some Christian people in this world who, if a man were poor or hungry, would say, 'Let us pray for him.' I would suggest a little different regimen for a person in this condition: rather take him a bag of flour and a little beef or pork. A few such comforts will do him more good than your prayers." The Savior actively involved Himself in the lives and fortunes of His neighbors, and was non-discriminatory in His attention to their needs.

Mosiah also knew who his neighbors were, and how to treat them. The Savior was his mentor and the model for his behavior. He was ready to succor those that stood in need and provide for them of his own substantial means. He withheld judgment and assisted the poor, asking: "Are we not all beggars? Do we not all depend upon the same Being, even God, for all the substance which we have, for both food and raiment, and for gold, and for silver, and for all the riches which we have of every kind?" (Mosiah 4:16-19). His love of his neighbors cast a benevolently blind eye on their supposed faults or shortcomings. His example taught that good intentions and empathy are not enough, and that our love for others needs to be as wide as the encircling arms of the Lord Jesus Christ.

No Greater Call

"The intensity of our desire to share the gospel is a great indicator of the extent of our personal conversion." (Dallin Oaks).

Alma cried: "O that I were an angel, and could have the wish of mine heart, that I might go forth and speak with the trump of God, with a voice to shake the earth, and cry repentance unto every people! Yea, I would declare unto every soul, and with the voice of thunder, repentance and the plan of redemption, that they should repent and come unto our God, that there might not be more sorrow upon all the face of the earth." (Alma 29:1-2).

One of the best places to get a spiritual education is the Lord's University or the mission field. He has made it clear that there is no room for summer soldiers or sunshine patriots in His missionary army. "The thing which will be of the most worth unto you," He explained to His saints, "will be to declare repentance unto this people, that you may bring souls unto me, that you may rest with them in the kingdom of my Father." (D&C 15:6). On another occasion, He emphasized: "It becometh every man who hath been warned to warn his neighbor." (D&C 88:81).

"I will forgive you of your sins with this commandment," He promised, "that you remain steadfast in your minds in solemnity and the spirit of prayer, in bearing testimony to all the world of those things which are communicated unto you. (D&C 88:61). "For if you will that I give unto you a place in the celestial world, you must prepare yourselves by doing the things which I have commanded you and required of you." (D&C 78:7).

"Let your preaching be the warning voice," He taught, "every man to his neighbor, in mildness and meekness." (D&C 38:41). The message is clear. We cannot lengthen our stride while sitting down or resting on our laurels. "When Spencer W. Kimball urged members to lengthen their stride, he knew that their spirituality would be intensified. Christ urged those in bondage to go the second mile, to double their stride. The second mile is a gift of spiritual independence that removes the veil of insensitivity to a destiny." (Richard L. Gunn, "Sensitivity and Spirit," p. 197).

Abraham Lincoln said: "To sin by silence, when words should be spoken, makes cowards of men." (Original quotation by Ella Wheeler Wilcox). And so, the Lord cautioned: "With some I am not well pleased, for they will not open their mouths, but they hide the talent which I have given unto them, because of the fear of man. Wo unto such, for mine anger is kindled against them. And it shall come to pass, if they are not more faithful unto me, it shall be taken away, even that which they have." (D&C 60:2-3).

The Lord is in control of our destiny, but He generally uses His servants to promote the cause of Zion. Ultimately, our "finest hours are those when extraordinary challenge is met with extraordinary response." (Winston Churchill). Such was the case after Elisha lamented: "The children of Israel have forsaken thy covenant, thrown down thine altars, and slain thy prophets with the sword; and I, even I only, am left; and they seek my life, to take it away." Then, the Lord said: "Yet have I left me seven thousand in Israel, all the knees which have not bowed unto Baal." (1 Kings 19:14 & 18).

Before Fiorello La Guardia became mayor of New York City, he was a magistrate. One day there appeared before him a man accused of stealing. Upon questioning, the man explained that he'd committed the crime to feed his family for they were starving. Whereupon, La Guardia dismissed the charges, and instead sentenced all in the courtroom to pay a fine for living in a city where a man must steal to feed his family. "Jesus said unto them, I am the bread of life: He that cometh to me shall never hunger; and he that believeth on me shall never thirst." (John 6:35). In the Eternal Court of Justice, what do you suppose will be the penalty for failure to have fed others the bread of life?

"Faith, hope, charity, and love, with an eye single to the glory of God, qualify (us) for the work." (D&C 4:5). Therefore, we have been admonished to "strengthen (our) brethren in all (our) conversation, in all (our) prayers, in all (our) exhortations, and in all (our) doings." (D&C 108:7). When we take this responsibility seriously, we may measure up to Leo Tolstoy's assessment of the power of the restored gospel to "become the most powerful social influence in the world." (Reported to have been said to President Andrew White of Cornell University). But more than that, we may measure up our divine commission to share the gospel so that souls might be saved in the Celestial Kingdom of God.

(The) Number of the Disciples Was Multiplied

"And so great was the prosperity of the church," Mormon reported, "and so many the blessings which were poured out upon the people, that even the high priests and the teachers were themselves astonished beyond measure. And it came to pass that the work of the Lord did prosper unto the baptizing and uniting to the church of God, many souls, yea, even tens of thousands. Thus we may see that the Lord is merciful unto all who will, in the sincerity of their hearts, call upon his holy name. Yea, thus we see that the gate of heaven is open unto all, even to those who will believe on the name of Jesus Christ, who is the Son of God. (Helaman 3:25-28).

"For the body is not one member, but many. If the foot shall say, Because I am not the hand, I am not of the body; is it therefore not of the body? And if the ear shall say, Because I am not the eye, I am not of the body; is it therefore not of the body? If the whole body were an eye, where were the hearing? If the whole were hearing, where were the smelling? But now hath God set the members every one of them in the body, as it hath pleased him. And if they were all one member, where were the body? But now are they many members, yet but one body. And the eye cannot say unto the hand, I have no need of thee: nor again the head to the feet, I have no need of you." (1 Corinthians 12:14-21).

During the Apostolic ministry, the church grew rapidly. This was cause for great rejoicing, but it also created some challenges. As the church grew, the Apostles needed other members to help direct the church and build up the kingdom of God. "And in those days, when the number of the disciples was multiplied, there arose a murmuring of the Grecians against the Hebrews, because their widows were neglected in the daily ministration. Then the twelve called the multitude of the disciples unto them, and said, It is not reason that we should leave the word of God, and serve tables. Wherefore, brethren, look ye out among you seven men of honest report, full of the Holy Ghost and wisdom, whom we may appoint over this business. But we will give ourselves continually to prayer, and to the ministry of the word. And the saying pleased the whole multitude: and they chose Stephen, a man full of faith and of the Holy Ghost, and Philip, and Prochorus, and Nicanor, and Timon, and Parmenas, and Nicolas a proselyte of Antioch: Whom they set before the apostles: and when they had prayed, they lay their hands on them. And the word of God increased; and the number of the disciples multiplied in Jerusalem greatly; and a great company of the priests were obedient to the faith." (Acts 6:1-7).

Today, diversity within the church can be equally challenging, but it also enriches and strengthens its members. Zion comes in many different colors. It speaks Aymara, Dutch, Fijian, French, Mandarin, Russian, Slovene, and dozens of other languages. It lives in over 3,000 stakes in practically every country in the world, (1,579 in the United States, and 1,661 outside the United States as of 2016) from Argentina to Zimbabwe. It has over 17 million members (2022) who are red, yellow, brown, black, and white. Zion wears a sarong, a grass skirt, a blue collar, a tupeno, a kilt, and a business suit. It lives in igloos, bamboo huts, double-wides, townhomes, cardboard shacks, and high-rises. Most important of all, it shares a common testimony that Jesus is the Christ, and that His love, indeed, makes the world go round. Today it is more important than ever to remember that there is no United States of America in heaven. The great equalizer in the sight of God is obedience by His children to His will. Thus, we may be at-one with Christ.

It is remarkable that although members of the church differ from each other and live in strikingly different cultures, they are still unified. Coast redwoods are among the largest living things. The tallest known tree reaches a height of 368 feet, weighs hundreds of tons, and has been living for well over 2,000 years. But, curiously, while most other trees of massive size have deep roots to support their great weight, the root system of the redwood is very shallow. The key to its survival is the intertwining of the roots of one tree with those of several of its neighbors. Redwoods live in groves; they cannot stand alone. Interdependence is critical to the stability and longevity of each individual tree.

In our day, the Lord has initiated organizational changes as the church has grown, that are similar to the interdependence of the redwoods. These changes have helped meet the needs of church members throughout the world. The Quorums of the Seventy and Area Presidencies, for example, have created an interdependency that fosters strength and unity.

Snowflakes are at the other extreme from coast redwoods, and are one of nature's most fragile creations. Although delicate in structure, look at what these unique individuals can do when they stick together. As in the case of redwoods or snowflakes, so it is with the church, which "hath need of every member," that the whole may be kept in perfect working order, and so that each individual within the organization may perform to the level of his or her potential. (D&C 84:110).

Church members echo Paul, who declared from imprisonment in Rome: "We, being many, are one body in Christ." (Romans 12:5). Today, there are many striking evidences of the spiritual and intellectual unity of the church. For example, in spite of subtle textual variations within the many translations of the scriptures used by members worldwide, there is remarkably little disagreement as to their meaning. In church organization and church government, ecclesiastical leaders enjoy virtual harmony in spite of individual cultural, social, political, and economic differences. The ordinances of the gospel, from baptism to the endowment in the temple, are universally understood and faithfully administered by Latter-day Saints whose sense of community overshadows any perceived differences.

Stephen was one of the original Seventy who were called to help the Twelve Apostles. who testified before the Sanhedrin. He was arrested on false charges of blasphemy and brought to the Jewish council to testify before the Sanhedrin. (Acts 6:11-15). "When they heard these things, they were cut to the heart, and they gnashed on him with their teeth. But he, being full of the Holy Ghost, looked up steadfastly into heaven, and saw the glory of God, and Jesus standing on the right hand of God." (Acts 7:54-55).

Stephen's last words reveal the depth of his discipleship. As he was stoned, he called upon God, "saying, Lord Jesus, receive my spirit. And he kneeled down, and cried with a loud voice, Lord, lay not this sin to their charge. And when he had said this, he fell asleep." (Acts 7:59-60).

Philip, another of the original Seventy, preached and performed miracles in Samaria, but somehow had not been given the authority to bestow the gift of the Holy Ghost. "Now when the apostles which were at Jerusalem heard that Samaria had received the word of God, they sent unto them Peter and John: Who, when they were come down, prayed for them, that they might receive the Holy Ghost: (For as yet he was fallen upon none of them: only they were baptized in the name of the Lord Jesus). Then laid they their hands on them, and they received the Holy Ghost." (Acts 8:14-17).

"And when Simon (the sorcerer) saw that through laying on of the apostles' hands the Holy Ghost was given, he offered them money Saying, Give me also this power, that on whomsoever I lay hands, he may receive the Holy Ghost." (Acts 8:18-19). "But Peter said unto him, Thy money perish with thee, because thou hast thought that the gift of God may be purchased with money. Thou hast neither part nor lot in this matter: for thy heart is not right in the sight of God. Repent therefore of this thy wickedness, and pray God, if perhaps the thought of thine heart may be forgiven thee. For I perceive that thou art in the gall of bitterness, and in the bond of iniquity." (Acts 8:20-23).

James E. Faust said: "This greatest of all powers, the priesthood power, is not accessed the way power is used in the world. It cannot be bought or sold. Worldly power often is employed ruthlessly. However, priesthood power is invoked only through those principles of righteousness by which the priesthood is governed." (C.R., 4/1997). We can all hear the voice of the Lord. "What I the Lord have spoken, I have spoken, and I excuse not myself; and though the heavens and the earth pass away, my word shall not pass away, but shall all be fulfilled, whether by mine own voice or by the voice of my servants, it is the same." (D&C 1:38).

Many of us can relate to the experience of Oliver Cowdery, who was told: "Did I not speak peace to your mind concerning the matter? What greater witness can you have than from God?" (D&C 6:23). Later, Oliver was told: "I will tell you in your mind and in your heart, by the Holy Ghost, which shall come upon you, and which shall dwell in your heart." (D&C 8:2).

The counsel of the Lord has come to all of us, through Joseph Smith: "These words are not of men nor of man, but of me; wherefore, you shall testify they are of me and not of man; For it is my voice which speaketh them unto you; for they are given by my Spirit unto you, and by my power you can read them one to another; and save it were by my power you could not have them; Wherefore, you can testify that you have heard my voice, and know my words." (D&C 18:34-36).

Robert D. Hales said: "For the most part, conversion happens over a period of time as study, prayer, experience, and faith help us to grow in our testimony and conversion." (C.R., 4/1997). We, like the early Saints, are living in a time when the church is growing rapidly. The Lord wants each of us to serve in his kingdom as it grows. Each of us needs to recognize and appreciate the different qualities, talents, and experiences that members bring to the Lord's service, but at the same time, to be sensitive to the voice of the Spirit that speaks personally and privately to each of us at sundry times and in diverse places. (See D&C 128:21).

The phenomenon of "quorum sensing" has been described in both behavioral and natural science as a type of decision-making process used by decentralized groups to coordinate behavior. It functions as long as individuals within the group have a means of assessing the numbers of those with whom they interact, and as long as they are able to initiate a standard response once a threshold number of other individuals is detected. In its most esoteric form, quorum sensing finds its expression in the doctrine of Christ, which is "the only and true doctrine of the Father, and of the Son, and of the Holy Ghost, which is one God, without end." (2 Nephi 31:21).

Obedience
(D&C 39)

"I, Nephi, said unto my father: I will go and do the things which the Lord hath commanded, for I know that the Lord giveth no commandments unto the children of men, save he shall prepare a way for them that they may accomplish the thing which he commandeth them."
(1 Nephi 3:7).

This revelation is addressed to "James Covill, who had been a Baptist minister for about forty years, (and who had) covenanted with the Lord that he would obey any command that the Lord would give to him through Joseph the Prophet." (Superscript to Section 39).

"Hearken and listen to the voice of him who is from all eternity to all eternity, the Great I Am, even Jesus Christ." (V. 1). Perhaps there was a hidden message in this simple declaration. If James Covill were to have read between the lines, he would have realized that God exists in the present tense; He is the Great I AM. As Paul wrote: "Jesus Christ is the same yesterday, and today, and for ever." (Hebrews 13:8). The Lord Himself declared: "I appeared unto Abraham, unto Isaac, and unto Jacob, by the name of God Almighty, but by my name JEHOVAH was I not known to them." (Exodus 6:3).

When Jehovah spoke to Moses, He revealed: "I AM THAT I AM: and he said, Thus shalt thou say unto the children of Israel, I AM hath sent me unto you." (Exodus 3:14). Therefore, did Jesus say unto the unbelieving Jews of His day: "Verily, verily, I say unto you, Before Abraham was, I am." (John 8:58).

Christ is "the light and the life of the world; a light which shineth in darkness and the darkness comprehendeth it not." (V. 2). Is there another subliminal message here that was proffered to penetrate the heart of James Covill, who may have only been giving lip service to the Lord? The Savior taught: "The light of the body is the eye. If, therefore, thine eye be single, thy whole body shall be full of light." (3 Nephi 13:22). To the Latter-day Saints, He promised: "If your eye be single to my glory, your whole bodies shall be filled with light, and there shall be no darkness in you, and that body which is filled with light comprehendeth all things." (D&C 88:67).

He continued: "But if thine eye be evil, thy whole body shall be full of darkness. If, therefore, the light that is in thee be darkness, how great is that darkness!" (3 Nephi 13:23). The influence of Satan that gripped Joseph in the Sacred Grove before his deliverance illustrates the contrast between light and darkness and reveals just how overwhelming the latter can be. Joseph wrote: "I was seized upon by some power which entirely overcame me, and had such an astonishing influence over me as to bind my tongue so that I could not speak. Thick darkness gathered around me, and it seemed to me for a time as if I were doomed to sudden destruction ... I was ready to sink into despair and abandon myself to destruction - not to an imaginary ruin, but to the power of some actual being from the unseen world." (J.S.H. 1:15-16). One is reminded of those who lost their way in mists of darkness in Lehi's Vision of The Tree of Life. (See 1 Nephi 8:23). Truly, darkness does not comprehend the light of Christ, and is blinded by even the faintest glimmer of celestial brilliance. James Covill who was poised to slide into spiritual oblivion, should have recognized the urgency of the counsel to embrace light.

"The same which came in the meridian of time unto mine own, and mine own received me not." (V. 3). This is one of only three instances in the scriptures where the term "meridian of time" is used. (See Moses 5:57 and Moses 7:46).

"But to as many as received me, gave I power to become my sons." (V. 4). James Covill would have the opportunity to become a son of God. Christ has all power to grant unto men that they might become "the sons of God." (3 Nephi 9:17). His promise is to all who "shall believe on (His) name, for behold, by (Him) redemption cometh, and in (Him) is the law of Moses fulfilled." (3 Nephi 9:17).

King Benjamin told his people that because of their covenant with God, they would "be called the children of Christ, his sons and his daughters." (Mosiah 5:7). James Covill was at a pivotal time in his life when he could recognize that "Jesus Christ (is) the Son of God, the Father of heaven and earth, the Creator of all things." (Mosiah 3:8). He was being asked to proudly take upon himself His name.

Just as we are known by the name of our mortal parents, so too are we called by the name of Christ in a familial way. We are Christ's children in the sense that He united our body and spirit through the Resurrection: "For this day He hath spiritually begotten you," explained Benjamin. (Mosiah 5:7). There is a special family relationship reserved for the faithful that is in addition to the reality that we are all spirit children of the Father.

Those who enter into the Covenant "are born of him." (Mosiah 5:7). "Born Again Christians" are in covenant relationships with the Lord, and since only members of Christ's true church benefit from the authority of the priesthood, if follows that the only real Born-Again Christians are Latter-day Saints!

Only by making covenants with God and Christ could James Covill break the bands of death and be made free. "There is no other name given whereby salvation cometh," said Benjamin, "therefore, I would that ye should take upon you the name of Christ, all you that have entered into the covenant with God." (Mosiah 5:8). The church Joseph Smith helped to found was to be a missionary oriented church that the Lord Himself proclaimed was to be "the only true and living church upon the face of the whole earth." (D&C 1:30). James Covill had been a minister, but he must have realized that no other church had the authority of the priesthood necessary to bind and ratify the covenants made with God. The reality of the apostasy and the subsequent restoration of priesthood authority were well documented in the scriptures and in the unfolding history of the church. Through the Prophet Joseph Smith, the Lord wanted James Covill to know that no other organization had the power to break the death grip of Satan.

Through a spiritual rebirth, James Covill was poised to acquire the distinctive characteristics of Christ, become a partaker of His divine nature, and become His son. By the covenant of baptism, he had taken upon himself a new name, which is His name, and by his obedience to the principles of the gospel, he could have enjoyed the companionship of His Spirit. This spiritual rebirth would have permitted a mighty change in his nature.

"This is my gospel," the Savior taught, "repentance and baptism by water, and then cometh the baptism of fire and the Holy Ghost, even the Comforter, which showeth all things, and teacheth the peaceable things of the kingdom." (V. 6). "We live in a day and in a world full of doubts and confusion, where people do not know what to believe, where tensions are high, where the pace is frantic and progress in terms of righteousness is not a popular goal. Violence and crudity are everyday patterns all around us. What a blessing it is to know there is a haven, a place of rest from the turmoil of the world. The prophets and the Savior have called upon us to enter into the rest of the Lord, where life has purpose and direction, and where priesthood power is possible." ("Gospel Doctrine Manual," p. 79).

"My servant James, I have looked upon thy works and I know thee ... Thine heart is now right before me at this time." (V. 7-8). In The Book of Mormon, when Benjamin's subjects had repented of their sins, the King was able to say of them: "'Because of the covenant which ye have made ye shall be called the children of Christ, his sons, and his daughters; for behold, this day he hath spiritually begotten you; for ye say that your hearts are changed through faith on his name; therefore, ye are born of him and have become his sons and his daughters." (Mosiah 5:7). Thirty-five years later, Benjamin's first Chief Judge Alma found it necessary to go among these same people, "for the hearts of many were hardened, and their names were blotted out, that they were remembered no more among the people of God. And also, many withdrew themselves from among them." (Alma 1:24).

But "thou hast rejected me many times because of pride and the cares of the world." Now "the days of thy deliverance are come, if thou wilt hearken to my voice." (V. 9-10). Early in Nephite history, the Prophet Jacob gave his brethren the antidote for pride. The formula consisted of the Nephite version of the Golden Rule: "Think of your brethren like unto yourselves," and "before seeking for riches," seek the kingdom of God. (Jacob 2:17). This is the number one priority.

Pride is a character crippling personality trait that can prevent us from obtaining the kingdom. We can disqualify ourselves from obtaining the blessings associated with church membership, in large part because of pride. Pride is enmity toward man and God and can lead to all other transgressions. Ezra Taft Benson called pride "the universal sin (that) limits or stops progression and adversely affects all of our relationships." (C.R., 4/1989).

It leads to a distorted sense of self-importance that blinds us to the reality of our complete dependence on God and to our sense of responsibility to act as His stewards in the service of our fellowmen. It induces spiritual sclerosis, a hardening of our spiritual arteries, and manifests itself in the stagnation of our sensitivities. Bound in its rigidity, we tend to make "a mock of that which (is) sacred, denying the spirit of prophecy and of revelation." (Helaman 4:12). When pride prevents us from relating to things that we do not directly experience, we die as to things of the spirit and are prone to attack whatever we cannot physically understand, including the humble followers of Christ.

Our pride is manifest in selfishness, which is "much more than an ordinary problem because it activates all the cardinal sins. It is the detonator in the breaking of the Ten Commandments. The selfish individual seeks to please not God, but himself. He will even break a covenant in order to satisfy an appetite." (Neal A. Maxwell, C.R., 10/1990).

"By pride cometh contention," resulting in the power struggle that comes when we pit ourselves, our possessions, or our intellect, against others. (Proverbs 13:10). The proud are easily offended, hold grudges, withhold forgiveness, and will not receive counsel or correction. All these internal traits become a fertile seedbed for the external manifestations of contention." (Robert L. Millet, et. al, "Doctrinal Commentary on The Book of Mormon," p. 348).

Boasting is a manifestation of pride that is so common that it is almost overlooked. The treatment for this disease is to "pour out (our) souls in (our) closets, and (our) secret places, and in (our) wilderness. Yea, and when (we) do not cry unto the Lord, let (our) hearts be full, drawn out in prayer continually." (Alma 34:26-27). When we pray to the Father continually, we are not likely to lose sight of our utter dependence on Him for both our temporal and spiritual welfare, nor will we forget from Whom both talents and blessings come.

Whenever we turn to the arm of flesh for security, we will not prosper for long. The best course when we find ourselves doing so is to immediately repent. We would do well to remember the example of the Nephites, for "no matter how wicked and ferocious and depraved the Lamanites might have been," observed Hugh Nibley, "no matter how much they outnumbered the Nephites, darkly closing in on all sides, no matter how insidiously they spied and intrigued and infiltrated and hatched their diabolical plots and breathed their bloody threats and pushed their formidable preparations for all out war, they were not the Nephite problem. They were merely kept there to remind the Nephites of their real problem, which was (the difficulty with which they managed) to walk uprightly before the Lord." ("Since Cumorah," p. 376).

The Nephites "saw that they had become weak, like unto their brethren, the Lamanites, and that the Spirit of the Lord did no more preserve them; yea, it had withdrawn from them because the Spirit of the Lord doth not dwell in unholy temples. Therefore, the Lord did cease to preserve them by his miraculous and matchless power, for they had fallen into a state of unbelief and awful wickedness." (Helaman 4:24-25). This observation by Mormon is more than an editorial comment. It is a clarion call to those living in the Last Days to learn from the mistakes of his people and to turn to the Lord for the protection so vital in our own perilous times.

"And if thou do this, I have prepared thee for a greater work." (V. 11). We must not rest on our laurels or pause for too long on plateaus, when we need to be moving onward and upward. Eternal progression is a path, not a point. In New Testament times, there was to be no "Book of The Resolutions of The Apostles," but only the "Book of The Acts of The Apostles." Good intentions may be noble, but achievement is the hallmark of progress. Harold B. Lee was fond of saying: "Work without vision is drudgery, and vision without work is dreamery, but work with vision is destiny!"

Spencer W. Kimball told a group of mission presidents: "So much depends upon our willingness to make up our minds, both individually and collectively, that present levels of performance are not acceptable, either to ourselves or to the Lord. In saying that, I am not calling for flashy, temporary differences in our performance levels, but (for) a quiet resolve to lengthen our stride." ("Church News," 3/22/1975).

At another time, he said: "We have paused on some plateaus long enough. Let us resume our journey forward and upward. Let us quietly end our reluctance to reach out to others, whether in our own families, wards, or neighborhoods. We have been diverted, at times, from fundamentals on which we must now focus in order to move forward as a person or as a people." (C.R., 4/1979).

"Thou art called to labor in my vineyard, and to build up my church, and to bring forth Zion." (V. 13). The Dead Sea Covenanters of Qumran provide a parallel view of the unity of the faithful that the Lord described to James Covill through Joseph Smith. The writers of the Scrolls called their organization a "Yanad" or "church," and the name they gave themselves was "Latter-day Saints." Their emphasis on oneness is a reminder that these churches in the wilderness thought of themselves as scale models of Enoch's City of Zion.

"And the Lord called his people Zion, because they were of one heart and one mind, and dwelt in righteousness." (Moses 7:18). There is power in Zion to "break mountains, to divide the seas, to dry up waters, to turn them out of their course; to put at defiance the armies of nations, to divide the earth, to break every band, to stand in the presence of God." (J.S.T. Genesis 14:30-31).

"Wherefore, go forth, crying with a loud voice, saying: The kingdom of heaven is at hand; crying, Hosanna! blessed be the name of the Most High God." (V. 19). The power of the church rests in the vitality of its members. It rises and falls on the tide of their personal witnesses. Alvin R. Dyer warned: "We must not be caught in the bind of building a church and killing the articles of its faith, or permitting form to triumph over spirit. The church and kingdom of God is built by the ardor and conviction of its members. We must be alert to the expansion of its assets at the cost of lost conviction. When buildings or institutions grow bigger and bigger, let us be fearful lest the Spirit will thin out." ("A Foundation for Education").

As members of the church continue to witness for Christ, the foundation of the Kingdom of God is planted in bedrock as was the wall built by an Irishman around his farm. When asked why he built the wall five feet high and eight feet thick, he replied that if the wind ever blew so hard that it toppled the wall, it would still be five feet thick. The church is such an organization. There is a redundancy built into the covenants that makes embracing their principles akin to donning an impregnable shield of faith.

"Go forth baptizing with water, preparing the way before my face for the time of my coming." (V. 20). It is impossible to overestimate the power inherent in the ordinance. None of us can lift ourselves to celestial glory. Our growth depends on the light of Christ, guidance of the Holy Ghost, and the power of the priesthood that is given us by God and his Son. The religion of Jesus Christ is not just a philosophy of life; it is the generator of life itself. If we go it alone, we cannot succeed. If we receive His power, we will increase and make it. There is no other way." ("My Religion and Me," Sunday School Course Manual).

Alma compared the fountain at the waters of Mormon to the attitude of the righteous who contemplate the ordinance of baptism and its associated covenants. "These currents and many more are part of the flowing fountain of the church. If we do not drink, if we die of thirst while only inches from the fountain, the fault comes down to us. For the free, full, flowing, living water is there." (Truman Madsen, "Christ & The Inner Life," p. 31).

With this in mind, Alma urged his congregation to be baptized. "Now I say unto you," he asked, "if this be the desire of your hearts, what have you against being baptized in the name of the Lord, as a witness before him that ye have entered into a covenant with him, that ye will serve him and keep his commandments, that he may pour out his Spirit more abundantly upon you?" (Alma 18:10).

The Manual of Discipline from The Serek Scroll at Qumran vividly describes the rebirth that follows baptism: "His sin is forgiven him and in the humility of his soul he is for all the Laws of God; his flesh is cleansed shining bright in the waters of purification, even in the waters of baptism, and he shall be given a new name in due time to walk perfectly in all the ways of God." (Hugh Nibley, "An Approach to The Book of Mormon," p. 149).

"On as many as ye shall baptize with water, ye shall lay your hands, and they shall receive the gift of the Holy Ghost." (V. 23). There are different levels of testimony. By the power of separate and individual witnesses, "every member of the church is entitled to know that God our Heavenly Father lives. They are also entitled to know that our elder brother, Jesus Christ, is the Savior and Redeemer of the world, and that he has opened the door for us, that we, through our individual acts, may receive salvation and exaltation and dwell once again in the presence of our Heavenly Father." (Henry D. Taylor, "Ensign," 6/1971).

However, "seeing, even the Savior, does not leave as deep an impression in our minds as does the testimony of the Holy Ghost. The impression on our souls that comes from the Holy Ghost is far more significant than a vision. It is where spirit speaks to spirit, and the imprint is far more difficult to erase." (Joseph Fielding Smith, Jr., "Seek Ye Earnestly," p. 213).

James Covill received both a promise and a warning that those who will not believe in the power of God unto salvation and decline the invitation to baptism will not be able to continue their eternal progression and are therefore damned. The gospel is not like the arbitrary programs established by man, with corollaries, footnotes, and exceptions to the rule. The foundation covenant of baptism is central to the Plan of Salvation, and is the hinge upon which swings the gate opening the way to eternal life with Heavenly Father. It is His ordained Plan. It is a perfect Plan, and is all the more beautiful because of its simplicity. It is established in the Bible and is clarified in its companion scriptures. It is clearly defined in The Book of Mormon and in the Doctrine & Covenants so that there will be no disputations among the people concerning this vital point of doctrine, which is that all who have faith in Jesus Christ, and truly repent of their sins, entering into a baptismal covenant with the Lord, will receive the Holy Ghost Who will then direct their lives, showing them the things they must do, and the manner in which they must live, to achieve salvation. James Covill had been a Baptist minister for 40 years, and had only been a member of the church for a few months, but already he had received a personal revelation from God through His prophet. A line had been drawn in the sand, and it was time for him to decide whether or not he would stand with Joshua and be counted to serve the Lord.

One Lord, One Faith, One Baptism

"Once the game is over, the King and the
pawn go back in the same box."
(Italian Proverb).

"The first fruits of repentance is baptism;
and baptism cometh by faith unto the fulfilling the
commandments; and the fulfilling the commandments
bringeth remission of sins; and the remission of sins bringeth
meekness, and lowliness of heart; and because of meekness and
lowliness of heart cometh the visitation of the Holy Ghost,
which Comforter filleth with hope and perfect love,
which love endureth by diligence unto prayer,
until the end shall come, when all the
saints shall dwell with God."
(Moroni 8:25-26).

There will be many at the Judgment Bar of Christ who will argue that there are many paths leading to the Kingdom of God that are equally acceptable to God. They will ask if it matters so much whether they were Methodist, Quaker, or Lutheran. They will advocate the position that as long as they accepted Christ, invoked his Holy Name, and gave Him the credit for whatever accomplishment has resulted, their efforts could not have been in vain.

But Christ suggests otherwise. "Many will say to me in that day: Lord, Lord, have we not prophesied in thy name, and in thy name have cast out devils, and in thy name done many wonderful works?" (3 Nephi 14:22). At the Bar of Justice, He will declare the simple fact: "I never knew you; depart from me, ye that work iniquity." (3 Nephi 14:23). What a contrast this will be to those who come to the Lord with their sheaves of good works. (Psalms 126:6). These will be as Job, of whom the Lord said: "There is none like him in the earth, a perfect and an upright man, one that feareth God, and escheweth evil." (Job 1:8).

Interestingly, Mosiah 26:25 suggests: "They that never knew me (shall) come forth and shall stand before me." This is more in harmony with the next verse in 3 Nephi that binds discipleship to performance. "Therefore, whoso heareth these sayings of mine and doeth them, I will liken him unto a wise man." (3 Nephi 14:24). The key is spiritual consistency. Brigham Young once said something to the effect that he never counted the cost of anything. He just found out what the Lord wanted him to do, and he did it

When we are on the path leading to eternal life, it is important to move forward with purpose. It is not enough to have been baptized and to have received the Holy Ghost. We must not camp out on the path and comfortably settle into a trance-line passive or vegetative state. There is "one lord, one faith, one baptism." (Ephesians 4:5).

It must be remembered, though, that the Lord acknowledges and rewards the simple faith of those who are pressing forward with what light they have received, however dimly it may illuminate gospel principles. For example, in the springtime of the year 1820, a young boy approached God in a quiet grove of trees in upstate New York. He was not yet a member of The Church of Jesus Christ, nor did he have a clear conception of God. Nevertheless, his humble prayer was answered with spectacular results. That drama is replayed hundreds of thousands of times each year, as the Holy Ghost visits those who earnestly seek the truth.

For those who are already members of the church, however, the expectations of the Savior are much higher. "For of him unto whom much is given much is required; and he who sins against the greater light shall receive the greater condemnation." (D&C 82:3). Since we will be judged by the laws to which we were responsible, we will vary in our accountability. Therein lies the hidden power of the gospel to give us the eternal perspective to see beyond the limited horizon of our vision. One of our greatest temptations is to confuse dreams with reality, but a defeat of cosmic proportion comes when our dreams are surrendered to the narrow reality of our five limited senses.

Life begins as "a sheet of paper white, where each of us may write a line or two, and then comes night. Greatly begin. If thou hast time but for a line, make that sublime. Not failure, but low aim is crime." (James Russell Lowell). Bruce R. McConkie was asked: "How can we reach the Celestial Kingdom." His answer was "Set your course, and move along it." The restored gospel of Jesus Christ provides the way to do just that, as the church builds upon the rock of continuing instruction from God.

We acknowledge His leadership and emulate His example. He marks the way, and we follow the established guidelines. He gives us commandments, and we yield to His will. He requires obedience, and we accept the rewards for following through, as well as the consequences for willful neglect of our responsibilities. The Plan provides self-diagnostics with continual monitoring from the Master. We accepted the risks attendant to mortality because we believed in the Plan, and we knew He would never leave us. When we leave Him, though, we are vulnerable. When we feel His Presence, and when our foundation is grounded on the bedrock of the gospel, we can be sure of our ultimate success, because it was ordained in the heavens before the world was. The Plan of Happiness is our key to redemption and salvation and is our ticket home.

Persecution

"Blessed are all
they who are persecuted for
my name's sake, for theirs is
the kingdom of heaven."
(3 Nephi 12:10).

In the Twenty-First Century, it is sobering to reflect upon the sacrifices of our own forefathers, who shed their blood, that they might articulate and protect the freedoms of religious expression and free speech that were purchased so long ago, at the cost of the best blood of England; that of Wycliffe, Tyndale, Latimer, Ridley, and other martyrs. To safeguard the freedom of speech that we too frequently take for granted, today we often take our cases to impartial courts, but it was not always so. Every time we open our mouths to express our opinion, every time we read a controversial book, every time we post our thoughts of social media, every time we do a Google search on an interesting topic, we have men like Tyndale and his contemporaries to thank, who gave their lives to first establish, and then to protect, and finally to preserve our expressions and our desire for unhindered scholarship, that is all in the comfort of our native tongue. "If any man hear my voice and open the door, I will come in unto him and will sup with him, and he with me." ("Tyndale Bible", Revelation 3:20). So that a divine communication might freely flow, Tyndale opened that door by squarely addressing the question: "How can we whet God's Word our children and household, when we are violently kept from it and know it not?"

It must have been so painful for Tyndale to witness the persecution of true believers that he could not stand by as a silent witness to the martyrdom of parents who only wanted their children to become familiar with the Lord's Prayer or with the Ten Commandments. Therefore, he determined to make the scriptures within reach of even the illiterate ploughboys who dotted England's rural countryside. He wrote: "Here seest thou that it is God's gift, to suffer for Christ's sake. Happy are ye if ye suffer for the name of Christ; for the glorious Spirit of God resteth in you. Is it not an happy thing, to be sure that thou art sealed with God's Spirit to everlasting life? And, verily, thou art sure thereof, if thou suffer patiently for his sake.

Tribulation maketh feeling; or it maketh us feel the goodness of God, and his help, and the working of his Spirit. Lo, Christ is never strong in us till we be weak. As our strength abateth, so groweth the strength of Christ in us. Therefore, very gladly will I rejoice in my weakness, that the strength of Christ may dwell in me." Confronted with that quality of conviction, how could the authorities ever hope to successfully compete?

On another occasion, Tyndale wrote: "Behold, God setteth before us a blessing and also a curse: a blessing, if we suffer tribulation and adversity with our Lord and Savior Christ; and an everlasting curse, if, for a little pleasure's sake, we withdraw ourselves from the chastising and nurture of God, wherewith he teacheth all his sons, and fashioneth them after his godly will, and maketh them perfect, and maketh them apt and meet vessels to receive his grace and his Spirit, that they might perceive and feel the exceeding mercy which we have in Christ, and the innumerable blessings and the unspeakable inheritance, whereto we are called and chosen, and sealed in our Savior Jesus Christ, unto whom be praise for ever." There is no indication that Tyndale ever wavered in that determination or conviction during a relentless persecution that lasted for well over a decade.

When we study his translations and writings, we sense the portent of his own martyrdom, but more significantly, we are enveloped in the fire of his words that brim over with an enthusiastic expectation of unspeakable joy. He was as Jeremiah, who wrote: "But his word was in mine heart as a burning fire shut up in my bones, and I was weary with forbearing, and I could not stop." (K.J.V. Jeremiah 20:9). Or, as Tyndale wrote in his Old Testament translation: "But the word of the Lord was a very burning fire in my heart and in my bones, which when I would have stopped, I might not." ("Tyndale Bible," Jeremiah 20:9).

He made little or no distinction between the anticipation of eternal happiness in the resurrection and the realization of joy, or more properly, hope, during his sojourn through this vale of tears. His faith was firmly based on that hope, which gave him the ability to see things as they really are. Consequently, he enjoyed a confidence that was not dependent upon circumstances. "Forasmuch, then, as we must needs be baptized in tribulations, and through the Red sea, and a great and a fearful wilderness, and a land of cruel giants, into our natural country; yea, and inasmuch as it is a plain earnest that there is no other way into the kingdom of life than through persecution, and suffering of pain, and of very death, after the ensample of Christ; therefore, let us arm our souls with the comfort of the scriptures: how that God is ever ready a hand, in time of need, to help us; and how that such tyrants and persecutors are but God's scourge, and His rod to chastise us." Faced with that sense of determination, his tormenters could never gain the upper hand, for in his mind they were special friends sent from God to try him and to prove him, and to make sure that he was worthy of his hire.

He may have been something of a fatalist, but it cannot be disputed that he was somehow completely at ease with the memory of his former life and the purpose of his call, and that he never wavered in his zealous determination to fulfil a mission whose purpose was clearly defined in his own mind. He persevered because he was sure of his election as a servant of the Lord Jesus Christ, and it seems that, particularly in his darkest hours, his Master had already invited him to come and "sup with Him." ("Tyndale Bible," Revelation 3:20). The Savior had granted His faithful servant a peace that surpasses our understanding. "Let us receive all things of God," he encouraged, "whether it be good or bad: let us humble ourselves under his mighty hand, and submit ourselves unto his nurture and chastising, and not withdraw ourselves from his correction."

Before his martyrdom, Joseph Smith had said: "I am going like a lamb to the slaughter; but I am calm as a summer's morning; I have a conscience void of offense towards God, and towards all men. I shall die innocent, and it shall yet be said of me: he was murdered in cold blood." (D&C 135:4). The conduct of William Tyndale's life expressed a similar peace born of confident expectation. "He will not work until all be past remedy," Tyndale wrote, "and brought unto such a case, that men may see, how that his hand, his power, his mercy, his goodness and truth, hath wrought altogether. He will let no man be partaker with him of his praise and glory. His works are wonderful, and contrary unto man's works. Who ever, saving he, delivered his own Son, his only Son, his dear Son, unto the death, and that for his enemies' sake, to win his enemy, to overcome him with love, that he might see love, and love again, and of love do likewise to other men, and overcome them with well doing?" The Catholic Church in England did not stand a chance, in the face of such passionate logic, conviction, and determination.

Personal Revelation

These things
"are made known unto
me by the Holy Spirit of God.
..... I have fasted and prayed many
days that I might know these things of
myself. And now I do know of myself that
they are true; for the Lord God hath made
them manifest unto me by His Holy
Spirit; and this is the spirit of
revelation which is in me."
(Alma 5:46).

We take for granted that prophets, seers, and revelators receive revelation. But wouldn't it be wonderful if for each of us the sound of the voice of the Lord that is so familiar to them were for us "a continuous melody and a thunderous appeal?"

It is possible that one of the reasons the Lord provided us with the Doctrine & Covenants was that we might utilize it as a resource to fine-tune our revelatory capabilities. "Most of the revelations of the Prophet Joseph Smith in this holy record," observed Spencer W. Kimball, "came as deep impressions." ("The Teachings of Spencer W. Kimball," p. 455-456). In fact, "most recorded revelations in the Doctrine and Covenants were a consciousness of direction from above. This is the sort of revelation individuals often have for their own needs." (Spencer W. Kimball, "Faith Precedes the Miracle," p. 30). When we have similar impressions, we are experiencing revelation from above.

D&C 6:22-23 provides counsel to Oliver Cowdery that confirms President Kimball's guidance: "Did I not speak peace to your mind concerning the matter?" the Lord asked. "What greater witness can you have than from God?" Have we not all experienced peace to our minds concerning matters of great personal importance?

Members of the church do not have a monopoly on revelation. Millions believe there are "angels among us." (Lyrics by "Alabama"). Countless newlyweds believe that their match was made in heaven. Others believe that they have been "touched by an angel" in one way or another. Promptings and impressions influence "black and white, bond and free, male and female... both Jew and Gentile" to move in positive directions. (2 Nephi 26:3). Persons of conscience among all creeds believe their actions are guided and directed by the Spirit. Christopher Columbus said after his epic voyage of discovery: "The Lord was well disposed to my desire, and he bestowed upon me courage and understanding. Knowledge of seafaring he gave me in abundance, and of geometry and astronomy likewise. The Lord with provident hand unlocked my mind, sent me upon the sea, and gave me fire for the deed. Those who heard of my enterprise called it foolish, mocked me, and laughed. But who can doubt that the Holy Ghost inspired me?" (John Wasserman, quoted in "Columbus, the Don Quixote of the Seas," p. 19-20).

Before they commit to baptism, those who have seriously investigated the church receive the confirming witness of the Spirit that what they are studying is true. They may have the same intensity of experience as that reported by Lorenzo Snow, who recalled: "Previous to accepting the ordinance of baptism, in my investigations of the principles taught by the Latter-day Saints … I was thoroughly convinced that obedience to those principles would impart miraculous powers, manifestations and revelations. With sanguine expectations of this result, I received the baptism and ordinance of laying on of hands by one who professed to have divine authority; and, having thus yielded obedience to these ordinances, I was in constant expectation of the fulfillment of the promise of the reception of the Holy Ghost.

(Shortly thereafter), I heard a sound, just above my head, like the rustling of silken robes, and immediately the Spirit of God descended upon me, completely enveloping my whole person, filling me, from the crown of my head to the soles of my feet, and O, the joy and happiness I felt! No language can describe the almost instantaneous transition from a dense cloud of mental and spiritual darkness into a refulgence of light and knowledge. As it was at that time imparted to my understanding, I then received a perfect knowledge that God lives, that Jesus Christ is the Son of God, and of the restoration of the holy Priesthood, and the fulness of the gospel. It was a complete baptism - a tangible immersion in the heavenly principle or element, the Holy Ghost; and even more real and physical in its effects upon every part of my system than the immersion by water; dispelling forever, so long as reason and memory last, all possibility of doubt or fear in relation to the fact handed down to us historically, that the 'Babe of Bethlehem' is truly the Son of God; also the fact that He is now being revealed to the children of men, and communicating knowledge, the same as in the Apostolic times. I was perfectly satisfied, as well I might be, for my expectations were more than realized, I think I may safely say, in an infinite degree." ("Biography and Family Record of Lorenzo Snow," p. 7-9).

But why don't more people have such revelation? Why isn't it common to have "a tangible immersion in the heavenly principle or element?" President Kimball said: "We do not expect the people of the world to understand such things, for they will always be quick to assign their own reasons or to discount the divine process of revelation." ("New Era," 4/1980, p. 36). While revelation can only be recognized on God's terms, curiously, He waits on the initiative of His children in a process that they cannot summarily influence or amend.

The feeble efforts of the worldly to disparage its delivery in order to bring revelation into harmony with their views ring hollow against the thunder and lightning of Sinai. Their determination to synchronize its circulation with their expectations cannot marginalize its importance. Their attempts to meddle with its manifestation in order to satisfy prurient interest cannot amend His inevitable decrees. Though they tamper with its expression to indulge their wicked and adulterous cravings, the signs and tokens remain untarnished. They may reinvent its flow and rework its stream according to Satan's counterfeit coin of spurious currency, they may tinker with its phrasing to homogenize its powerful message and to assuage their consciences, they may modify its distribution to greedily capture greater market share among the masses, and they may demean its delivery in a weak attempt to hustle the heavens. But they will fail in their efforts to hush the host of angels who are only waiting for a confirmation of our faith, that they might sound the clarion call of their trumpets in our ears. The wicked cannot erase the simple fact that it is God in whom we trust.

As Joseph Smith taught: "Does it remain for a people who never had faith enough to call down one scrap of revelation from heaven, and for all they have now are indebted to the faith of another people who lived hundreds and thousands of years before them, does it remain for them to say how much God has spoken and how much He has not spoken?" ("Teachings," p. 61).

"How presumptuous and arrogant," declared President Kimball, "for any man to say God is unapproachable, unknowable, unseeable, or unhearable because he has not prepared himself for the experience? ("Church News," 6/4/1966). Even members of a church that embraces revelation as a tenet of faith run the risks associated with their neglect of preparation to receive streams of enlightenment from the heavens.

As the prophet Mormon warned: "Yea, wo unto him that shall deny the revelations of the Lord, and that shall say the Lord no longer worketh by revelation, or by prophecy, or by gifts, or by tongues, or by healings, or by the power of the Holy Ghost!" (3 Nephi 29:6). His warning extends to members of the church whose shallow understanding of the scriptures, or whose lack of commitment to follow the teachings the Lord's authorized servants, betrays their implicit denial of the revelations.

Even among the ranks of the righteous, perhaps the failure to recognize revelation constitutes a denial of sorts, as well. President Kimball observed: "Many people expect that if there be revelation it will come with awe-inspiring, earth-shaking display. For many it is hard to accept revelations as deep, unassailable impressions settling down on the mind and heart as dew from heaven or as the dawn dissipates the darkness of night. Expecting the spectacular, (they) may not be fully alerted to the constant flow of revealed communication."

He went on to explain: "When, after prayer and fasting, important decisions are made (by General Authorities), new missions and new stakes are created, new patterns and policies initiated, the news is taken for granted and possibly thought of as mere human calculation. But to those who sit in the intimate circles and hear the prayers of the prophet and the testimony of the man of God; to those who see the astuteness of his deliberations, to them he is verily a prophet. To hear him conclude important new developments with such solemn expressions as 'the Lord is pleased,' 'that move is right,' or 'our Heavenly Father has spoken,' is to know positively." ("Instructor," 8/1960, p. 257).

Should we not also be able to say, after prayerful inquiry: "The Lord is pleased, the move is right, our Heavenly Father has spoken?" We do not have to be ecclesiastical leaders of the church to receive revelation from the Lord. "God hath not revealed anything to Joseph, but what He will make known unto the Twelve, and even the least Saint may know all things as fast as he is able to bear them." (Joseph Smith, "Teachings," p. 149).

We need personal revelation, perhaps as never before. In 1991, at the dawn of the creation of the Internet (1990), and before the introduction of I Pads, smart phones, Snap-chat, Twitter, Facebook, HBO, and Netflix, Boyd K. Packer said: "No one of us can survive in the world of today, much less in what it soon will become, without personal inspiration" (C.R., 10/1991). His statement underscores an observation made long ago, by Helen Keller: "The only thing worse than being blind is having sight but no vision."

When honing our revelatory capabilities, we can build upon the experiences we have already had, that include our testimonies of Jesus Christ and of His gospel, of the divine authenticity of The Book of Mormon and of the mission of the prophet Joseph Smith, of divine truths including tithing, the law of the Fast, and the Word of Wisdom, and of our familiarity with personal revelation to receive guidance beyond our own limited understanding in answering life's questions, meeting challenges, and making decisions. How fitting when our testimony meetings consist of our discreet expressions relating to our familiarity with these revelatory experiences.

Each day, we spend roughly sixteen hours going about our daily business in confident expectation of an outpouring of the gifts of inspiration, or divine creativity, and discernment, or keenly selective judgment. Our anticipation is justified if we have first qualified for such guidance "by setting our lives in order and by becoming acquainted with the Lord through frequent and regular conversations with him." (Spencer W. Kimball, "Ensign," 6/1975). He "will not force himself upon people; and if they do not believe, they will receive no visitation. If they are content to depend upon their own limited calculations and interpretations, then, of course, the Lord will leave them to their chosen fate." (Spencer W. Kimball, C.R., 10/1966). As He counseled Oliver Cowdery through Joseph Smith, so it is with each of us: "You must study it out in your mind; then you must ask me if it be right, and if it is right I will cause that your bosom shall burn within you; therefore, you shall feel that it is right." (D&C 9:8).

The Prophet Joseph can be our example. What he did in preparation for his great theophany in the Sacred Grove can be our pattern, as well. His "mind was called up to serious reflection and great uneasiness." His "feelings were deep and often poignant," and he "attended…meetings as often as occasion would permit." His "mind at times was greatly excited" to understand the will of God." He wondered to himself: "How shall I know" and recognize the truth? (J.S.H. 1:8-10). His experience underscores several basic principles. As we study matters out in our own minds preparatory to receiving answers to our prayers, we become actively, rather than passively, involved in the processes of inquiry and discovery. We dust off our agency, and actually use it as it was envisioned. We expand our capabilities as we exercise the gifts, resources, and reserves provided by the principles of the Plan of Salvation. President Kimball promised: "If there be eyes to see, there will be visions to inspire. If there be ears to hear, there will be revelations to experience. If there be hearts which can understand, know this: that the exalting truths of Christ's gospel will no longer be hidden and mysterious, and all earnest seekers may know God and his program." (C.R., 10/1966).

The Doctrine & Covenants illustrates how studying and contemplating the scriptures can help us to grow spiritually. Joseph F. Smith recalled therein how he had sat in his room "pondering over the scriptures, and reflecting upon the great atoning sacrifice" of the Savior. He wrote that as he did so, he "was greatly impressed" by the scriptures, so much so that "the eyes of (his) understanding were opened, and the Spirit of the Lord rested" upon him. (D&C 138:1-11).

Joseph Smith's similar experience when reading James 1:5-6 speaks for itself. He recalled: "Never did any passage… come with more power to the heart of man than this did at this time to mine. It seemed to enter with great force into every feeling of my heart. I reflected on it again and again." (J.S.H. 1:11-12). As Dallin Oaks explained: "We do not overstate the point when we say that the scriptures can be a Urim and Thummim to assist each of us to receive personal revelation. Because we believe that scripture reading can help us receive revelation, we are encouraged to read the scriptures again and again." ("Ensign," 1/995). Boyd K. Packer pointed out: "No message appears in scripture more times, in more ways, than: 'Ask, and ye shall receive'." (C.R., 10/1991). In fact, most of the revelations in the Doctrine and Covenants came as answers to questions that the Prophet Joseph Smith had posed to the Lord.

When we act in faith, we will be blessed, as was Oliver Cowdery, with "a knowledge of whatsoever things (we) shall ask in faith, with an honest heart, believing that (we) shall receive." (D&C 8:1). But we must ask in earnest, with sincerity, and with genuine humility and meekness. "Do you offer a few trite words and worn-out phrases, or do you talk intimately to the Lord?" asked Spencer W. Kimball. "Do you pray occasionally when you should be praying regularly, often constantly? When you pray, do you just speak, or do you also listen? Do you give thanks or merely ask for favors?" ("New Era," 3/1978).

The example of Joseph Smith in the Sacred Grove teaches us how to pray with equal intensity, and with a power of concentration that unlocks and then cracks open the door to heaven, allowing shafts of celestial light to flood our minds and our spirits. He prayed vocally, knelt in humility, and offered up the desires of his heart, and when necessity required it, he exerted all of his powers to call upon God. (J.S.H. 1:13-16). Later, when the Lord spoke through him, the Savior said to those who followed his example: "Blessed art thou for what thou hast done; for thou hast inquired of me, and behold, as often as thou hast inquired thou hast received instruction of my Spirit." (D&C

6:14). As President Kimball promised: "The Lord is eager to see (our) first awakening desires and (our) beginning efforts to penetrate the darkness. Having granted freedom of decision, he must permit (us) to grope (our) way until (we) reach for the light. But when (we) begin to hunger, when (our) arms begin to reach, when (our) knees begin to bend and (our) voices becomes articulate, then and not till then does our Lord push back the horizons, draw back the veil, and make it possible for (us) to emerge from dim uncertain stumbling to sureness, in heavenly light." (Munich Germany Area Conference, 8/1973). He further counseled: "If (we) rise from (our) knees having merely said words, (we) should fall back on (our) knees and remain there until (we) have established communication with the Lord." ("The Teachings of Spencer W. Kimball", p. 124).

Dallin Oaks taught: "We cannot have the companionship of the Holy Ghost - the medium of individual revelation - if we are in transgression, or if we are angry, or if we are in rebellion against God's chosen authorities." ("Ensign," 3/1997). We must seek revelation from God in an attitude of deep humility, which is a character trait that does not come consciously or easily. David Whitmer recalled that one morning when Joseph Smith was getting ready to continue his translation of The Book of Mormon, "something went wrong about the house and he was put out about it. Something that Emma, his wife, had done. Oliver and I went upstairs, and Joseph came up soon after to continue the translation, but he could not do anything. He could not translate a single syllable. He went downstairs, out into the orchard, and made supplication to the Lord; was gone about an hour - came back to the house, and asked Emma's forgiveness and then came upstairs where we were, and then the translation went on all right. He could do nothing save he was humble and faithful." ("Comprehensive History of the Church," 1:131).

Boyd K. Packer taught (back in 1991): "Inspiration comes more easily in peaceful settings. The world grows increasingly noisy. Clothing and grooming and conduct are looser and sloppier and more disheveled. Raucous music, with obscene lyrics blasted through amplifiers while lights flash psychedelic colors, characterizes the drug culture. Variations of these things are gaining wide acceptance and influence over our youth. This trend to more noise, more excitement, more contention, less restraint, less dignity, less formality is not coincidental nor innocent nor harmless. The first order issued by a commander mounting a military invasion is the jamming of the channels of communication of those he intends to conquer. Irreverence suits the purposes of the adversary by obstructing the delicate channels of revelation in both mind and spirit." (C.R., 10/1991).

Revelation is at the foundation of the living gospel of Jesus Christ, and is a cornerstone of God's perfect Plan of Salvation. "There are those who would assume that the printing and binding of these sacred records would be the "end of the prophets." But again, we testify to the world that revelation continues and that the vaults and files of the church contain these revelations, which come month to month and day to day. Of all things, that for which we should be most grateful today is that the heavens are indeed open and that the restored church of Jesus Christ is founded upon the rock of revelation. Continuous revelation is, indeed, the very lifeblood of the gospel of the living Lord and Savior, Jesus Christ." (Spencer W. Kimball, C.R., 4/1977).

The Plan provides the loom upon which we are free to weave the complex tapestry of our lives, to create our own coat of many colors. But central to the vitalization and execution of our efforts is direct contact with our Father in Heaven. Our introduction and our active participation in the Plan presuppose the establishment of ongoing two-way communication with its Author.

Chauncy Riddle seriously accepted that challenge, and his expressions echo the similar experiences of countless members of The Church of Jesus Christ of Latter-day Saints. He wrote: "I felt I had received some revelation before. However, I saw that random revelation was not sufficient. To be a rock, a bastion of surety, revelation must be something on which one can count and receive on every occasion of real need. I began to seek it actively. I prayed, I fasted, and I lived the gospel as best I knew. I was faithful in my church duties. I tried to live up to every scruple that my conscience enjoined upon me. And dependable revelation did come. Intermittently, haltingly at first, then steadily, over some years it finally came to be a mighty stream of experience. I came to know that at any time of day or night, in any circumstance, for any real need, I could get help.

That help came in the form of feelings of encouragement when things seemed hopeless. It came in ideas to unravel puzzles that blocked my accomplishment. It came in priesthood blessings that were fully realized. It came in whisperings of prophecy that were fulfilled. It came in support and even anticipation of what the General Authorities of the church would say and do in general conference. It came in the gifts of the Spirit, as the wonders of eternity were opened to the eyes of my understanding. That stream of spiritual experience is today for me a river of living water that nourishes my soul in every situation. It is the most important factor of my life. If it were taken away, all that I have and am would be dust and ashes. It is the basis of my love, life, understanding, hope, and progress. My only regret is that though this river is so wonderful, I have not been able to take full advantage of it, as yet. My life does not yet conform to all that I know. But now I do know; I do not just believe." ("Sunstone," 5/1988).

(The) Plan of Salvation

*"What could I write
more than my fathers have
written? For have not they revealed
the plan of salvation? I say unto you,
Yea; and this sufficeth me."
(Jarom 1:2).*

The focus of this essay is simply to explore the genius behind the construction of the Plan of Salvation, consider its compelling capacity to influence change, and quantify the inherently positive influence of the three words of its name, whether it is Plan of Salvation, Plan de Salut, Gottes Einfacher Heilsplan, Plan De Dios, or Guds Enfle Frelsesplan.

I hope this essay does not oversimplify the elements of the Plan of Salvation. During my study, I have come to believe that many conscientious Christians have only a shallow understanding of God's Plan. This permits them to conveniently shrink it down and neatly package it into a single finite point in time and space. Evangelicals can often identify their precise moment of conversion, when they were "born again," and describe how an epiphany moved them to accept Christ and thus be "saved." Genuine though their feelings may be, their experience is only the first step of a refining and conversion process that should continue to their last breath. In contrast, the Plan of Salvation is found only in the restored gospel of Jesus Christ and provides an educational experience that has been carefully designed to engage each of us for a lifetime.

"Born again" and "saved" evangelical Christians would be surprised to learn that "Plan of Salvation" (count the words: Plan - 1, of - 2, Salvation – 3) may be the most etymologically connected three word phrase in the English language, inasmuch as it brings to mind "council in heaven," "agency and opposition," "justice and mercy," "apostasy and restoration," "modern day prophets," "latter day revelation," and "Jesus The Christ," all triads in their own right. When we invite the Spirit to guide us, we learn that God has a Plan that cannot be ignored, trivialized, or easily dismissed.

Joseph Smith's theophany in the Sacred Grove (another three-word blockbuster) is a powerful example that even a heavenly manifestation by Deity is not enough to save us. The intensity of Joseph's initial personal experience with the Godhead was necessarily followed by angelic instruction, personal revelation, diligent obedience, and repentance when required. Conversion follows testimony building, and is accompanied by an expanding awareness of principles and commitment to covenants that culminate in an endowment of power that makes sure our calling and election as children of promise.

The freely given Light of Christ (a three-word smash hit) is enough to kindle a spark of interest within us that motivates us to ponder the depths of eternity. But it would be wrong to leave it at that, underestimate the magnitude of the Plan, or define it in a way that demeans its overarching importance in every aspect of our lives. At the end of the day, the Plan of Salvation provides us with tools that allow us to monitor with precision our relationship with God. It is founded upon the very points of doctrine that focus on Salvation, and it is upon these elements that its correct understanding hinges. The "Plan of Salvation," as it turns out, is a very good choice of words when describing the intimacy that our Heavenly Father desires to have with each of us.

In the world, we find three-word headliners that shadow the Plan of Salvation. In physics, the Unified Field Theory explains almost everything. It falls short of the power inherent in the "Plan of Salvation," but in many ways these two concepts are reflections of each other. If the Unified Field Theory could be mathematically quantified, it would allow the fundamental forces and elementary particles of the physical world to be written in terms of a single field. In fact, this sounds a lot like the Plan of Salvation, which is really a working construct that allows us to reconcile our place in the cosmos with practical instruction relating to our divine potential. In science, the Unified Field Theory comes close to being a theory of everything, a single, coherent framework that explains all of the physical relationships within our universe. In a religious context, the Plan of Salvation does that and more. For the faithful, it establishes a link between the realities of our physical world and the promises of eternity, and seamlessly harmonizes the two in ways that provide us with a model within which we may hash out the details of our progression. The Plan of Salvation provides more than physical laws that permit the tides to rise and fall, cause the seasons to change, and make the sun to rise. It articulates commandments and covenants of a spiritual nature that allow God's children to expand their capacities in ways that would be otherwise impossible.

After Moses had been shown the visions of eternity, it was not for the space of many hours that he "did again receive his natural strength like unto man; and he said unto himself: Now, for this cause, I know that man is nothing, which thing I never had supposed." (Moses 1:10). Until the Spirit touched him, he had no idea how magnificent the Plan of Salvation was, and he could not appreciate its capacity to fit even one such as he into its grand design.

Later, God further revealed to Moses His Own binding association with the Plan of Salvation, when He declared: "This is my work and my glory - to bring to pass the immortality and eternal life of man." (Moses 1:39). This brings to mind Henri Bergson's expansive declaration: "The universe is a machine for the making of Gods."

There is also a powerful three-word theory of particle physics called "The Standard Model" that deals with the electromagnetic, weak, and strong nuclear interactions, all of which regulate the behavior of particles on a subatomic level. The Standard Model was developed during the latter half of the 20th century in a collaborative effort of scientists around the world. The discovery of quarks, tau neutrinos, and Higgs bosons has confirmed the validity of The Standard Model. It is called The Theory of Almost Everything because it doesn't adequately deal with gravity, describe the expansion of the universe, or explain the existence of dark matter. While its experimental predictions have been validated, its equations leave some phenomena unexplained. Perhaps we could compare The Standard Model to the imperfect doctrines of those "among all sects, parties, and denominations, who are blinded by the subtle craftiness of men, whereby they lie in wait to deceive." The Standard Model version of gospel doctrine only keeps us from the truth because we "know not where to find it." (D&C 1123:12).

In relation to the Unified Field Theory and The Standard Model with which we are becoming more familiar, the Plan of Salvation embraces questions that run the gamut from trivial to profound, and that may take a lifetime to comprehend. A shopping list may take only 5 minutes to compile and can be written on a scrap of paper; a daily task list can be completed in about 10 minutes, and assembling a Fisher Price toy (accompanied by pages of incomprehensible instructions written by a Chinese engineer with a rudimentary understanding of English grammar) might take 24 hours. Putting together a back-yard swing set using the enclosed plans may take 3 days, while building a house from blueprints may require the labor of a dozen subcontractors over a span of 6 months or more, even considering a dozen change-orders. The Empire State Building was erected in 1 year and 54 days. Planning and executing the construction of an entire city can require decades, while creating a new world order, beginning with the organization of the United Nations, on October 24, 1945, has taken generations.

While physicists have been toying with the Unified Field Theory, and now The Standard Model, for a hundred years or so, family planning is a never-ending process that is fundamental to the successful implementation of the Plan. As the Lord Jehovah promised Abraham: "I give unto thee a promise that … all the families of the earth (shall) be blessed, even with the blessings of the gospel (Plan), which are the blessings of salvation, even of life eternal." (Abraham 2:11).

The Plan of Salvation is also described in The Book of Mormon in just three words as the Plan of Mercy, Plan of Redemption, Plan of Deliverance, Plan of Restoration, and Plan of Happiness. Its objectives are mercy, deliverance, redemption, restoration, and happiness, to name a few. Its three-word antonyms include Plan of Gadianton, and Plan of Wickedness. "There is," after all, "an opposition in all things." (2 Nephi 2:11).

The three words of the Plan of Salvation keep secular company with The New Deal, Social Security Act, War on Poverty, Voter Registration Act, The New Frontier, The Great Society, Language, Culture, Borders, and I Like Ike. (However, bureaucratic plans can get wound up in verbosity. Consider, for example, The Health Insurance Portability and Privacy Act, and The Patient Protection and Affordable Care Act. In the private sector, convoluted language is also sometimes employed with no demonstrable benefit. For example, when announcing layoffs to save costs (how hard was that to say), Citigroup issued this press release: "Today a series of repositioning actions was initiated that will further reduce expenses and improve efficiency across the company while maintaining Citi's unique capabilities to serve clients, especially in the emerging markets. These actions will result in increased business efficiency, streamlined operations and an optimized consumer footprint across geographies." The observation of Polonius comes to mind: "Since brevity is the soul of wit, and tediousness the limbs and outward flourishes, I will be brief." ("Hamlet," Act 2, Scene 2).

Many of the most significant concepts in mankind's struggle for freedom have been articulated in three simple words that convey meanings of earth-shaking import: Rights of Man, Power and Responsibility, Declaration of Independence, Articles of Confederation, The Federalist Papers, United States Constitution, Bill of Rights, The Executive Branch, The Legislative Branch, and The Judicial Branch, not to mention Faster, Higher, Stronger (Citius, Altius, Fortius).

It is entirely appropriate that the Plan of Salvation is articulated in three words, because the sacred number three pops up throughout religious history and all over the world, and not just because of its obvious association with the Christian Holy Trinity. The ancient Greeks wrote of a divine triad, Theos (God), Logos (the Word), and Psyche (the Soul). The father, mother, and son gods of the Egyptians were Osiris, Isis, and Horus. In Norse mythology, Yggdrasil supported the world with three roots: one extended into Asgard, the abode of the Gods, one into Jotenheim, the home of the Giants, and the third into Nifleheim, the region of the Unknown. Three precious gifts were given to the Jews; the Law of Moses, the Land of Israel, and Paradise.

The number three points us to what is real, essential, perfect, substantial, complete, and divine. It is almost universally understood as a key to the integrity and interdependence of all existence. The triangle is the most perfect geometrical figure, inasmuch as it is the first form complete in itself. There are three spatial dimensions: width, depth, and height. Time has three categories: past, present, and future, and their related divisions are birth, life, and death. Three persons in grammar represent all of our relationships: I, You, and They. The simplest forms of argument are completed with a major premise, a minor premise, and a conclusion. Thought, word, and deed represent the sum of our capabilities. The three sister virtues are faith, hope, and charity. There are three states of matter: gas, solid, and liquid, and three kingdoms represent our understanding of its composition: animal, vegetable, and mineral, not to mention land, sky and water, or sun, moon, and stars. God has three attributes: omnipresence, omniscience, and omnipotence. The number three represents the unity of body, mind, and spirit. Oak, ash, and thorn are called the triad of trees, and it is said that when they are found together, fairies thrive. Many world religions embrace triple deities or concepts of deity, including the Hindu Trimurti of Brahma, Vishnu, and Siva, (Creator, Preserver, and Changer), the Three Jewels of Buddhism, the Three Pure Ones of Taoism, and the Triple Goddess of Wicca. For these reasons and more, Pythagoras called the number 3 the noblest of all digits.

Classical mythology explores the trios of Graces, that are Fates, Furies, and Muses. The Graces were charm, beauty, and creativity. The Fates were Clotho, who spun the thread of life, Lachesis, who chose one's lot in life and measured how long it was to be, and Atropos, who at death cut the thread of life with her shears. The Furies were the Greek goddesses of vengeance. The Muses were the inspiration for literature, science, and the arts. Poseidon carried a trident, a three-pronged spear representing, among other things, birth, life, and death, mind, body, and spirit, and past, present, and future. The Greek Gorgons were Stheno, Euryale and Medusa, who had hair made of living, venomous snakes, as well as a horrifying face that turned to stone those who beheld it. The three judges of Hades were Minos, Æacus, and Rhadamanthus. Pluto's dog Cerberus had 3 heads. During the siege of Troy by the Greeks, Hector's body was dragged around the city three times.

In ancient Ireland, among the household officials of the High King of Erin were three royal jugglers, three jesters, three head charioteers, three equerries, three swineherds, three janitors, and three drink-bearers. The emblem of the Emerald Isle, the Shamrock, has a three-lobed leaf. Harder to explain are The Three Stooges: Moe, Larry, and Curly, and The Pep Boys: Manny, Moe, and Jack.

It is said that it is our nature to fall into sin, which is human, to lie in sin, which is diabolical, and to rise out of it again, which is angelical. Harmony contains 3 symphonies, the Diapason, the Diapente, and the Diatessaron. In civil life, the usher of a court 3 times repeats the warning Oyez, Oyez, Oyez, which means "hear" or "listen." In religious ceremonies, the expression of sacred covenants may be repeated three times. We eat three meals a day. Dinner often consists of an appetizer, an entrée, and dessert. Theatre often consists of a prelude, a main act, and a postlude. The three-act play is familiar to all. Writers often use the device of a prologue and epilogue to frame the main body of the work. The bounds of education are limited by the 3 Rs. The third time is the charm, and three is company, but four is a crowd. There is nothing particularly sacred about the number 4, however. Consider the dreadful Four Horsemen of the Apocalypse: War, Famine, Pestilence, and Death.

Many superstitions utilizing the number 3 have been a part of Jewish life through the ages. One is to spit three times for good luck in reaction to something that is either especially worthwhile or particularly evil. Solomon's Temple was divided into three important areas: the Holy of Holies, the Holy Place, and the outer courtyard. In Jewish tradition, there will be three temples, Solomon's Temple (the first temple), the Temple of Zerubbabel (the second temple), and a third temple, to be built on Mount Zion at some future date. When Catholics are greatly excited, they sometimes cry out: "Jesus, Mary, and Joseph!" Shakespeare's "Macbeth" prominently features three witches.

In our own Latter-day Saint religious tradition, we express some of our most cherished concepts with three words. For example, justice and mercy, articles of faith, Abraham, Isaac (and) Jacob, The Holy Bible, Garden of Gethsemane, The Old Testament, The New Testament, Doctrine and Covenants, Book of Mormon, The Holy Trinity, Our Heavenly Father, Jesus The Christ, The Holy Ghost, prophet, priest (and) king, baptism by water, baptism by fire, take the

Sacrament, bear your testimony, choose the right, serve a mission, return with honor, Latter-day Saints, brothers and sisters, child of God, our ward family, share the gospel, perfect the Saints, redeem the dead, keep the commandments, follow thou Me, love your neighbors, families are forever, time and eternity, family home evening, stay the course, Word of Wisdom, Law of Tithing, Law of Sacrifice, Law of Consecration, Law of Chastity, the temple endowment, The First Presidency, The Telestial Kingdom, The Terrestrial Kingdom, The Celestial Kingdom, The Three Witnesses, and The Eight Witnesses. In our religious educational programs, we have Duty to God, Young Women Values, early morning Seminary, Institute of Religion, and Seminaries and Institutes. Our religious tradition also includes three degrees of glory, and three levels of glory within the Celestial Kingdom. The Fulness of The Godhead is expressed in the number three. (Colossians 2:9). We are all familiar with the three-fold admonition to get ready, get set, and go, and with President Spencer W. Kimball's encouragement to "Do it. Do it right. Do it right now."

Three times is the blessing given in Numbers 6:23-24: "The Lord bless thee and keep thee; The Lord make His face shine upon thee; and be gracious unto thee; The Lord lift up His countenance upon thee, and give thee peace." King Solomon's Seal (the Star of David) is expressed by interlaced triangles. The Divine Feminine (popularized in the movie: "The Da Vinci Code") is represented by a downward facing triangle. There are three primary colors, (red, green, and blue) from which all other colors may be created.

The scriptures identify these three things as essential: water, spirit, and blood. "By the water ye keep the commandment; by the Spirit ye are justified, and by the blood ye are sanctified. (Moses 6:60). In baptismal fonts, twelve oxen support the font itself, with three looking to each of the cardinal points of the compass. In the mouths of three witnesses, and in the testimony of three witnesses, was The Book of Mormon prophesied to be established. (Ether 5:4). In the sacramental prayer, we promise to do three things: Take upon ourselves the name of Christ, always remember Him, and keep His commandments. (See D&C 20:77).

The waters of the River Jordan were thrice divided. (Exodus 24, Joshua 4, & 2 Kings 2:8). During His 40-day fast in the wilderness, the Savior was three times tempted by the adversary. (Luke 4:1-13). His subsequent ministry lasted three years. During that time, He raised three persons, that we know about, from the dead. (Luke 7:15, 8:55, & John 11:44). At His crucifixion, Pilate had the inscription "Jesus of Nazareth the King of the Jews" put on the cross in three languages: Hebrew, Latin, and Greek. (John 19:19-20). At the crucifixion, there was great destruction in the Land of Zarahemla for the space of three hours. (3 Nephi 8:19). Following the destruction, darkness covered the land for three days. (Helaman 14:27). The voice of the Risen Savior was heard three times by the Nephites in Bountiful before they understood His words. (See 3 Nephi 11:5-6). Suffering, sacrifice, and resurrection figure prominently in our liturgy.

The angels who usher the faithful through the veil into the presence of God announce their intention to do so with three distinct knocks, and heavenly messengers on God's errand often seek the attention of mortals with three inquiries or exhortations. (Genesis 18:21, Daniel 3:24, Isaiah 6:3). Likewise does the Savior. (See Matthew 26:44, & Mark 14:41). In the Garden of Gethsemane, thrice did Jesus come to Peter, James, and John only to find them asleep each time. He was crucified at the third hour, Peter denied him three times before the cock crowed, and He rose from the dead on the third day. The third time Jesus showed Himself to His disciples following his crucifixion, He asked Peter three times if he loved Him. Three times the same answer was given: "Feed my sheep." (John 21:17). Three years elapsed after the First Vision before the visit to Joseph Smith by the Angel Moroni. Then, three times in a single night did the Angel Moroni appear to the boy prophet in his bedchamber.

Perhaps the most significant questions we can ask ourselves are these three: "Where did I come from? Why am I here?" and "Where am I going?" These inquiries relate to the Plan of Salvation. The number three also pops up repeatedly when we consider church government. There were Three Witnesses, there are three members of The Quorum of The

First Presidency, in Temple presidencies, and in the composition of Area Authorities, Stake Presidencies, Bishoprics, Aaronic Priesthood Quorum Presidencies, Auxiliary Presidencies, not to mention The Godhead itself. Even acronyms frequently employed by church members come in groups of three: These include L.D.S., C.E.S., C.T.R., E.F.Y., P.P.I., P.E.C., B.Y.C., F.H.E., M.T.C., C.C.H., and B.Y.U.

Pythagoras may have been right, that reality can be expressed mathematically, and that the number 3 is at the foundation of the Divine Proportion. However, there are no built-in scholastic prerequisites relating to our accessibility to the principles of the Plan of Salvation. Those without formal education are welcome to participate, as are those with advanced degrees from the most prestigious institutions of higher learning, like M.I.T. (Hmmm. There is the number three again!) It is the poor in spirit, those with broken hearts and contrite spirits, who seem to have an advantage, though, when it comes to fully embracing and implementing the principles of the Plan.

Nor does the Plan impose any age restrictions. Three-year-olds, thirty-year-olds, and ninety-year-olds may all sing with equal fervency: "I Am a Child of God." The Plan is non-discriminatory, as well. It was designed for the world's heaviest person, who weighed in at 1,400 pounds, for the world's tallest person, at 8 feet 11 inches, for the world's shortest adult, at just 21.5 inches, the world's wealthiest person, who boasts hundreds of billions of dollars in assets, as well as the world's smartest person whose I.Q. breaches 200, as well as for the other 8 billion of us who fall somewhere within these extremes. As a matter of fact, God invites all of us to "partake of his (Plan); and he denieth none that come unto him, black and white, bond and free, male and female; and he remembereth the heathen; and all are alike unto God, both Jew and Gentile." (2 Nephi 26:33).

There is no enrollment expiration date built into the Plan of Salvation. While an unrefrigerated creampuff will spoil in 2 hours, a banana will turn black in a few days, potatoes will grow "eyes" in a few months, and although wheat may stop germinating only after decades of storage, the Plan's vitality remains in effect forever. Its boundaries encompass the theories of evolution, relativity, quantum mechanics, the Big Bang, string theory, and every other theory that may have been or ever will be conceived by our finite minds to bring order out of chaos. Its operating parameters include the three laws of thermodynamics that define the fundamental physical quantities of temperature, energy, and entropy. The Plan trumps every postulate, supposition, or theoretical construct devised by man in an attempt to explain why the sun rises and sets, what keeps the planets in motion, and how the order of the cosmos was created and is maintained. Because it circumscribes every physical law governing the temporal universe, it is able to embrace every spiritual law governing the eternities.

God gave Abraham a glimpse of all "the works which his hands had made...which were many; and they multiplied before (his) eyes, and (he) could not see the end thereof," so comprehensive was the scope of the Plan. (Abraham 3:11-12). In 2015, NASA reported the discovery of a single quasar (WISE J224607.57-052635.0), sitting at the edge of the visible universe, that shines with the light of 300 trillion stars. This discovery reminds us of the line from the Anglican hymn: "All things bright and beautiful. The Lord God made them all." (Cecil Francis Alexander).

As it turns out, the benefits that spring from the "Plan of Salvation" will never cease to exist. New discoveries will continue to be made, at an accelerating rate, as we expand the boundaries of our knowledge. When we turn our cheeks to be bathed in warm sunlight, we will feel the gentle caresses of the hand of our Father in Heaven. It was He Who organized the forces of nature, (the strong force, the weak force, electromagnetism, and gravity), that have held our universe together for 13.7 billion years. It was He, Who anticipated the cosmic microwave background radiation that is left over from the Big Bang, and caused it to uniformly radiate at 2.73 degrees Kelvin, which happens to be just enough to warm our blood. His Plan of Salvation shines with an ethereal luster that supersedes anything in the cosmos.

The Plan has been humming along at a constant and unchanging level of energy since He implemented it following the Council in Heaven before the world was. When its elements were first explained to us, we jumped to our feet and "shouted for joy." (Job 38:7). We can almost hear the faint echo of the exclamations: "Hosanna, to God and the Lamb!" (D&C 109:79). When Jacob taught it to his brethren, he too was moved to exclaim: "How great the Plan of our God!" (2 Nephi 9:13).

The Plan of Salvation considers every conceivable exigency that could confront us. It has no finite depth or breadth, is temporally boundless, and has no restricting spatial conditions. To comprehend its universal applicability, we must make fundamental postulations about time that stretch our minds, expand our presumptions, and nudge us out of our complacency. As Steven Hawking said: "One can think of ordinary, real, time as a horizontal line. On the left, one has the past, and on the right, the future. (This is the linear aspect of time with which we are all familiar. The arrow of time moves in one comfortable direction only, and that is forward). But there's another kind of time that moves in a vertical direction (in the sense that we are moved out of our three spatial dimensions, at right-angles to them, if you will). (See my essay: "Higher Dimensional Realities"). This is called imaginary time, because it is not the kind of time we normally experience. But in a sense, it is just as palpable as what we call real time." It even makes more sense than real time, when you stop to think about it, because it helps us to better understand the matrix within which the Plan finds expression; or, in pragmatic terms, the space-time continuum that for more than a hundred years has provided a new physical definition of existence that was needed to help to explain Einstein's theories of relativity.

The new reality of space and time existing in four interrelated dimensions (3 physical dimensions and one temporal dimension) is a continuum in the sense that there are no missing points in space or in moments in time, and both can be subdivided without limits in size or duration. Additionally, space-time does not evolve; it simply exists. Once again, the Plan of Salvation trumps the accumulated wisdom of science by embracing these concepts, and more. When the veil is parted and you have been privileged to see God's realty more clearly, (what we might now call "imaginary time"), if you could "hie to Kolob in the twinkling of an eye, and then continue onward with that same speed to fly, do you think that you could ever, through all eternity, find out the generation where Gods began to be, or see the grand beginning, where space did not extend, or view the last creation, where Gods and matter end? Methinks the Spirit whispers, 'No man has found pure space,' nor seen the outside curtains, where nothing has a place. The works of God continue, and worlds and lives abound; improvement and progression have one eternal round. There is no end to matter; there is no end to space; there is no end to spirit; there is no end to race. There is no end to virtue; there is no end to might. There is no end to wisdom; there is no end to light. There is no end to union; there is no end to youth. There is no end to priesthood; there is no end to truth. There is no end to glory; there is no end to love; there is no end to being; there is no death above. There is no end to love; there is no end to being; there is no death above." (William W. Phelps, "If You Could Hie to Kolob,").

While there may be metaphorical interpretations relating to Kolob, no one can dispute that William W. Phelps was a keen observer and visionary who understood his place in the cosmos. He was one who related it to the elements of the Plan of Salvation. Hie to Kolob is yet another triad that grabs our attention.

In this vein, Steven Hawking continued: "One could say that the boundary condition of the universe (read: "of the Plan") is that it has no boundary. (Joseph Smith simply said that Kolob is the star that is nearest to the throne of God. See Abraham 3:2-3). Yet, the universe is completely self-contained and is not affected by anything outside itself. It has neither been created nor will it be destroyed. It just is. (Here, Hawking gets tantalizingly close to the mark). This might suggest that so-called imaginary time is the real time, and that what we call real time is just a figment of our imaginations. In real time, the universe has a beginning and an end at singularities that form a boundary to space-time and at which the laws of science break down. But in imaginary time, there are no singularities or boundaries. So maybe what we call imaginary time is really more basic, and what we call real is just an idea that we invent to help us describe what we think the universe is like."

Perhaps God has fabricated real time to deal with the veil that has been drawn across our minds, preventing us from seeing the bigger picture that would compromise our opportunity to fully participate in the Plan during a brief period of mortality that is not our natural condition. Perhaps, when the veil is parted and we are more visionary, imaginary time will flood over us in a surge that envelops us in a new reality, as it carries us to new heights of awareness and new appreciation of the magnitude of The Plan. Were we to paraphrase both Hawking and Phelps, we might then realize that "there is no end to matter; there is no end to space; there is no end to spirit, and there is no end to race. The boundary condition of the Plan of Salvation would be that it has no boundary."

Even though we can only "imagine" what that "time" might be like, we can take comfort in the Lord' counsel: "My thoughts are not your thoughts, neither are your ways my ways. …For as the heavens are higher than the earth, so are my ways higher than your ways, and my thoughts than your thoughts." (Isaiah 55:8-9). Maybe our physical universe had a beginning in real time, at the Big Bang, the point of singularity when all things were circumscribed in one great whole. But maybe, in a stroke of creative genius, The Plan has considered and utilizes "imaginary time" that exists at right angles to real time, in a vertical dimension, as it were. In this larger context, the universe would have no beginning and no end. This fits in neatly with our understanding of the Plan of Salvation.

Daniel was told: "God hath numbered thy kingdom, and finished it." (Daniel 5:26). The grand design of our Father in Heaven is evidence that He plans His work and works His Plan. It validates our testimony that proper prior planning prevents poor performance. As we have seen, He has quietly woven a golden tapestry on a cosmic loom, and has ennobled His efforts with the frequent insertion of the number 3 into His master design to subtly remind us to make course corrections and re-focus our efforts in the right direction.

(The) Plan of Salvation: 15 Names

"O how great
the plan of our God!"
(2 Nephi 9:13).

In the New Testament, there are tantalizingly few verses that speak of the Plan of Salvation. In Titus 1:2, Paul spoke of the promise of "eternal life, which God, that cannot lie, promised before the world began." (Titus 1:2). Peter wrote that Jesus Christ was "foreordained before the foundation of the world," to be the Redeemer. (1 Peter 1:20). In his letter to the Hebrews, he wrote that the Savior "became the author of eternal salvation" (Hebrews 5:9).

Abraham wrote of the creative process, and of the Gods' reasoning in creating the earth: "And we will prove them herewith, to see if they will do all things whatsoever the Lord their God shall command them; And they who keep their first estate shall be added upon; and they who keep not their first estate shall not have glory in the same kingdom with those who keep their first estate; and they who keep their second estate shall have glory added upon their heads for ever and ever." (Abraham 3:25-26). Moses spoke of "the Plan of Salvation unto all men. (Moses 6:62).

But it is in The Book of Mormon that we really get a feel for the Plan. In several verses, (1 Nephi 13:26, 29, 32, 35, 35, 40, 1 Nephi 14:23, 1 Nephi 19:3), Nephi explained that in the Last Days, the Gentiles would "stumble exceedingly, because of the most plain and precious parts of the gospel of the Lamb" which had been distorted within or deleted from the scriptures. (1 Nephi 13:34).

But there would be a light provided at the end of the tunnel, for those whose minds had been "blinded by the subtle craftiness of men." (D&C 123:12). Through His prophet, the Lord promised: "I will proceed to do a marvellous work among this people, even a marvellous work and a wonder: for the wisdom of their wise men shall perish, and the understanding of their prudent men shall be hid." (Isaiah 29:14).

The Merciful Plan of the Great Creator (2 Nephi 9:6).

"Mercy claimeth the penitent, and mercy cometh because of the atonement; and the atonement bringeth to pass the resurrection of the dead; and the resurrection of the dead bringeth back men into the presence of God. For behold, justice exerciseth all his demands, and also mercy claimeth all which is her own; and thus, none but the truly penitent are saved." (Alma 42:23-24). Our conscience is a celestial spark that God has put into each of us. It is part of the Merciful Plan of the Great Creator Whose purpose is the saving of our souls.

The Plan of our God (2 Nephi 9:13).

The "great and eternal purposes" of the Plan of our God, "were prepared from the foundation of the world." (Alma 42:26). John Taylor taught: "To the Son is given the power of the resurrection, the power of the redemption, the power of salvation, the power to enact laws for the carrying out and accomplishment of the design. Hence, life and immortality are brought to light, the gospel is introduced, and He becomes the Author of eternal life and exaltation." ("Mediation and Atonement," p. 171-172).

The Great and Eternal Plan of Deliverance from Death (2 Nephi 11:5).

One of the foundation teachings of the gospel is that we came into this world to die. "And now behold, I say unto you that if it had been possible for Adam to have partaken of the fruit of the tree of life at that time, there would have been no death, and the word would have been void, making God a liar, for he said: If thou eat thou shalt surely die." (Alma 12:23). It was clearly understood before we came here that our experience would be part of the Great and Eternal Plan of Deliverance from Death. When Adam was sent into the Garden of Eden, it was with the understanding that he would violate or transgress a law in order to bring to pass mortality for the human family.

The Plan of Salvation (Alma 24:14).

The Plan of Salvation is the Plan of Redemption, the Plan of Mercy, and the Plan of Happiness, because it makes possible the resurrection of otherwise imperfect mortals to an eternal life of glory. "Now, if it had not been for the plan of redemption, which was laid from the foundation of the world, there could have been no resurrection of the dead; but there was a plan of redemption laid, which shall bring to pass the resurrection of the dead." (Alma 12:25).

The Plan of Redemption (Alma 29:2).

"According to justice, the plan of redemption could not be brought about" and "mercy could not take effect except it should destroy the work of justice." (Alma 42:13). The beauty of the Plan of Redemption, then, is that it meets the demands of justice through the infinite mercy of a loving Heavenly Father. The Plan allows God to be both just and merciful at the same time.

The Great Plan of the Eternal God (Alma 34:9).

None of us can hope to find meaning in our lives if we treat the integral elements of the Plan superficially or carelessly. A conscious appreciation of its value must be earned. If we take it for granted or if we abandon its core principles, its power to bless our lives may slip away and be lost forever. While the Great Plan of the Eternal God guarantees free will, it also gives us wide latitude to use our agency inappropriately to make poor choices. It provides us with currency sufficient for our needs, but also allows us to substitute for legal tender wads of counterfeit cash with which late payments may be made with interest tacked on for bad behavior. If we attempt to subvert the Plan in futile efforts to obtain and retain blessings we do not deserve, our destabilizing efforts will reward us with a pyrrhic victory at best.

The Great and Eternal Plan of Redemption (Alma 34:16).

Nephi clearly taught that "it is by grace that we are saved, after all we can do." (2 Nephi 25:23). Latter-day Saints, however, tend to emphasize works to the point that it may seem to others that the grace of God takes a back seat to their own efforts to earn salvation. In spite of their focus on accountability, agency, industry, and labor, as they are exhorted to greater dedication, diligence, and duty, the truth is that nothing we can do will ever qualify us to enjoy eternal life. It is only because of the Great and Eternal Plan of Redemption that we are saved. Paul and Luke echoed Nephi, writing that it is "by grace ye are saved, through faith, and that not of yourselves. It is the gift of God." (Ephesians 2:8). "We believe that through the grace of the Lord Jesus Christ we shall be saved." (Acts 15:11). It is "the grace of God that bringeth salvation." (Titus 2:11).

The Great Plan of Redemption (Alma 34:31).

The Great Plan of Redemption required that "an atonement should be made; therefore, God Himself atoneth for the sins of the world, to bring about the plan of mercy, to appease the demands of justice, that God might be a perfect, just God, and a merciful God also." (Alma 42:15). The Atonement allowed God to satisfy justice and still mercifully reclaim us from physical and spiritual death. The Savior thus became the Master of the situation. In His sacrifice, the debt would be paid, the redemption made, the covenant fulfilled, justice satisfied, the will of God done, and all power, including the keys of resurrection, now given to the Son.

The Plan of Restoration (Alma 41:2).

The Book of Mormon clearly teaches that the purpose of the Fall was to give us the opportunity to come to the earth in order to prepare for a resurrection. "And we see that death comes upon mankind, yea, the death which has been spoken of by Amulek, which is the temporal death; nevertheless there was a space granted unto man in which he might repent; therefore this life became a probationary state; a time to prepare to meet God; a time to prepare for that endless state which has been spoken of by us, which is after the resurrection of the dead." (Alma 12:24). The Atonement is the keystone of the Plan of Restoration, that allows us to be raised in the resurrection clothed in exactly the kinds of bodies for which we have prepared ourselves.

The Great Plan of Salvation (Alma 42:5).

Without its light, we are doomed to suffer in the shadows where we experience only illusions and caricatures of reality. The discrepancy between our marginalized behavior and the ideals of the Great Plan of Salvation will become so great that our short-lived pleasure in worldly ways will surely evaporate as the morning dew in the full light of day. Sooner or later, when this disparity has become so great that it reaches "critical mass," the requisite readjustment will tear down the façade of corruption and hypocrisy to allow the cultivation of a more nurturing lifestyle made possible by obedience to the principles of the Plan.

The Great Plan of Happiness (Alma 42:8).

Alma taught that in the absence of repentance for our sins, and without the benefit of saving principles of the Plan, we must ultimately be in a wretched state, living forever in our sins. "And now behold, if it were possible that our first parents could have gone forth and partaken of the tree of life they would have been forever miserable, having no preparatory state; and thus, the plan of redemption would have been frustrated, and the word of God would have been void, taking none effect." (Alma 12:26). Without redemption from sin, if Adam and Eve were to have partaken of the fruit of the tree of life, without first having received a remission of their sins through the Atonement of Christ, it would not be possible for them to sustain a celestial existence, inasmuch as in their fallen condition they would have been incapable of obedience to celestial principles. Thus, the Great Plan of Happiness would have been forever frustrated.

The Plan of Mercy (Alma 42:15).

One of the foundation teachings of the gospel is that we came into this world to die. "And now behold, I say unto you that if it had been possible for Adam to have partaken of the fruit of the tree of life at that time, there would have been no death, and the word would have been void, making God a liar, for he said: If thou eat thou shalt surely die." (Alma 12:23). It was clearly understood before we came here that our experience would end in the deaths of our mortal bodies as part of the Plan of Mercy. When Adam was sent into the Garden of Eden, it was with the understanding that he would violate or transgress a law in order to bring to pass mortality for the human family.

The Plan of Happiness (Alma 42:16).

The cherubim guaranteed that the Plan of Happiness would not be frustrated. "For behold, if Adam had put forth his hand immediately, and partaken of the tree of life, he would have lived forever, according to the word of God, having no space for repentance." (Alma 42:5). This would have posed an immediate problem that begged a solution. Because of the transgression in the Garden, justice demanded that "man became lost forever, yea, they became fallen man. And now, ye see by this that our first parents were cut off both temporally and spiritually from the presence of the Lord." (Alma 42:6-7). So it was, that "they became subject to follow after their own will." The crowning principle of agency was to be honored, even if it meant that justice must be served. Therefore, "it was appointed unto man to die" (Alma 42:6), rather than to reclaim him "from this temporal death, for that would destroy the great plan of happiness." (Alma 42:8).

The Great Plan of Mercy (Alma 42:31).

The Great Plan of Mercy gives us the opportunity to live our lives, push the envelope, and dare to take risks. When we fail to measure up to its laws, Jesus Christ intervenes in our behalf. When we Recognize our mistakes, when we experience Remorse for having made them, when we attempt to make Restitution if our behavior has wronged others, when we learn from the mistake and Reform our ways, and Resolve to Refrain from repeating it, we will be free to continue the path of progress, with a complete Resolution of what would have otherwise been an incapacitating shortcoming.

Positive Mental Attitude

"Half this game is 90% mental."
(Yogi Berra).

"Look forward with one eye,
having one faith and one baptism,
having (your) hearts knit together in
unity and in love one towards another."
(Mosiah 18:21).

Pre-play before you replay. Follow an established plan. "Ask for the old paths, where is the good way, and walk therein, and ye shall find rest for your souls." (Jeremiah 6:16).

Learn to quickly recognize and deal with negative thoughts. As Isaiah said: "Seek ye the Lord while he may be found, call ye upon him while he is near." (Isaiah 55:6). Avoid negative self- talk because it becomes a self-fulfilling prophecy. "Where there is no vision, the people perish." (Proverbs 29:18). Believe the Lord when He says: "Even as you desire of me so it shall be done unto you." (D&C 6:8, 11:8). Avoid participating in pity-parties. Remember the admonition: "How beautiful upon the mountains are the feet of those that (publish) peace." (Mosiah 15:16). When we promote the cause of Zion, we proclaim the promise of peace of mind in a world gone mad.

"If I regarded my life from the point of view of the pessimist," wrote Helen Keller, "I should be undone. I should seek in vain for the light that does not visit my eyes and the music that does not ring in my ears. I should beg night and day and never be satisfied. I should sit apart in awful solitude, a prey to fear and despair. But since I consider it a duty to myself and to others to be happy, I escape a misery worse than any physical deprivation." ("Optimism").

Find yourself a sacred grove. We all need time to "get away" to maintain our sanity. The Psalmist's excellent advice was: "Be still and know that I am God." (Psalms 46:10). By physically or emotionally retreating to our "happy place," we are following the counsel to "stand ... in holy places, and be not moved." (D&C 87:8).

Listen to good, wholesome, uplifting music. The purpose of music is to inspire, to motivate, to invite the Spirit, to comfort, to strengthen, and to calm our unruly spirits. The intrinsic harmony of music is inseparably related to inner peace and contentment.

Be an eternal optimist, as was Joseph Smith, who encouraged the Saints: "Courage, brethren; and on, on to the victory! Let your hearts rejoice, and be exceedingly glad." (D&C 128:22). We know that reverses are a part of life, but our optimism carries us past these minor inconveniences and impediments to our progress. "To every thing there is a season, and a time to every purpose under the heaven." (Ecclesiastes 3:1).

Count your blessings. In everything give thanks, for God has made promises to us "with an immutable covenant that they shall be fulfilled; and all things wherewith (we) have been afflicted shall work together for our good." (D&C 98:3). Recognize the blessings in all the things that touch your life. Remember that the Savior is our "light in the wilderness" and "His arm of mercy is extended towards (us) in the light of the day." (1 Nephi 17:13 & Jacob 6:5). Be like the one who said: "I have a hobby! I have the world's largest seashell collection. I keep it scattered on beaches all over the planet." The fact is, you never know what the next tide is going to bring in.

Find a trusted priesthood leader and get a blessing. Moroni was speaking to us, when he wrote: "I am mindful of you always in my prayers, continually praying unto God the Father in the name of his Holy Child, Jesus, that he, through his infinite goodness and grace, will keep you through the endurance of faith on his name to the end." (Moroni 8:3). Solomon was in the thoughts and prayers of "Zadok the priest (who) took an horn of oil out of the tabernacle, (and he) anointed Solomon. And they blew the trumpet; and all the people said, God save king Solomon." (1 Kings 1:39).

Re-read your patriarchal blessing and view its promises as a catalyst to release the powers of Heaven in your behalf. The spirit of God expressed in the blessing is the spirit of hope and not the spirit of gloom. As you ponder your blessing, the Spirit will invite you to read between the lines to take encouragement and to be inspired.

Understand that the only way to truly comprehend the Atonement is to feel it through suffering. As Paul wrote: "For unto you it is given in the behalf of Christ, not only to believe on him, but also to suffer for his sake." (1 Philippians 1:29).

Pray more earnestly. James' wise counsel was to: "Confess your faults one to another, and pray one for another, that ye may be healed. The effectual fervent prayer of a righteous man availeth much." (James 5:16).

Read the scriptures to gain an eternal perspective. Jacob revealed his formula for success: "We search the prophets," he wrote, "and we have many revelations and the spirit of prophecy; and having all these witnesses we obtain a hope, and our faith becometh unshaken." (Jacob 4:6).

Remember that The Book of Mormon is true. About half its verses state a life-preserving truth: "It came to pass." It did not come to stay! Life unfolds before our eyes, often in surprisingly delightful ways.

Honestly evaluate your life to see if the stain of unresolved sin is creating negative energy. Remember what Alma taught his son: "If there were "no space for repentance … the word of God would have been void, and the great plan of salvation would have been frustrated." (Alma 42:5). Actively relying on the power of the Atonement is a strong generator of positive mental energy.

Deal with, learn from, and let go of the past. The future lies ahead, not behind! You cant go back and start a new beginning, but you can start today and make a new ending. (Anonymous). The apostle Paul's formula for ridding ourselves of the past was "forgetting those things which are behind, and reaching forth unto those things which are before." (Philippians 3:13-14).

"Finish each day and be done with it. You have done what you could. Although some blunders and absurdities no doubt crept in, you must forget them as soon as you can. Tomorrow is a new day. You shall begin it well and serenely and with too high a spirit to be encumbered with your old nonsense." (Ralph Waldo Emerson).

Know yourself well enough to recognize when you are starting to feed on negative energy. It may require spending some practice time with yourself. Never forget that when you are on an emotional roller coaster, it is driven, in part, "in consequence of evils and designs which do and will exist in the hearts of conspiring men in the last days." (D&C 89:4). To be forewarned is to be forearmed.

When we find ourselves losing our self-confidence and positive mental attitude, we must remember to walk "in obedience to the commandments." Then we "shall receive health in (our) navel and marrow to (our) bones; And shall find wisdom and great treasures of knowledge, even hidden treasures; And shall run and not be weary, and shall walk and not faint." Unto such are given "a promise, that the destroying angel shall pass by them, as the children of Israel, and not slay them. Amen." (D&C 89:18-21).

Tackle one problem at a time. Don't try to fix everything all at once. The next life is required to achieve perfection. For now, we learn "precept upon precept; line upon line; here a little, and there a little." (Isaiah 28:10). Doing so, we are given "consolation by holding forth that which is to come, confirming our hope!" (D&C 128:21). Joseph Smith was comforted with the promise that his trials would give him experience and should be for his good. (D&C 122:7). Even Jesus, who led a sinless life, "still grew up with his brethren, and waxed strong, and waited upon the Lord for the time of his ministry to come." (J.S.T. Matthew 3:24).

We may not see daily progress and in the short term there may be reverses. But over the long haul, we will steadily move to higher plateaus. We have a Plan to pull ourselves up. In times of difficulty, we remember the observation of the Apostle James: "We count them happy which endure." (James 5:11). We also acknowledge any and all progress, and that "miracles (are) worked by small means." (Alma 37:41).

Talk courage and perseverance, and not gloom and doom. We acknowledge "opposition in all things. If not so," Lehi explained to his son, "righteousness could not be brought to pass, neither wickedness, neither holiness nor misery, neither good nor bad." (2 Nephi 2:11). As Job said, we should "forget (our) misery, and remember it as waters that pass away." (Job 11:16). In other words, it's water under the bridge.

Use physical exercise to neutralize and dissipate depression-causing toxins. No wonder the Lord counseled: "Cease to be idle; cease to be unclean; cease to find fault one with another; cease to sleep longer than is needful; retire to thy bed early, that ye may not be weary; arise early, that your bodies and your minds may be invigorated" with a healthy shot of endorphins. (D&C 88:124).

Hang on. Outlast and counteract negative influences by doing everything you can to be positive and uplifted. Unless we "endure to the end, in following the example of the Son of the living God, (we) cannot be saved" from self-defeating behaviors that eat away at our foundation. (2 Nephi 31:16). But we take consolation in "the patience of Job." (James 5:11).

Follow the advice of the prophets. "Mine heart within me is broken because of the prophets," wrote Jeremiah. "All my bones shake; I am like a drunken man, and like a man whom wine hath overcome, because of the Lord, and because of the words of his holiness." (Jeremiah 23:9). In these circumstances, his frame was reduced to quivering jelly. Jacob explained how the process can lead to renewal, and to a solid footing within the fortress of faith. "We search the prophets," he revealed, "and we have many revelations and the spirit of prophecy; and having all these witnesses we obtain a hope, and our faith becometh unshaken." (Jacob 4:6).

Get help from priesthood leaders (including husbands, fathers, sons, and brothers). Speaking of his relationship to his brethren, Nephi wrote: "And I know that the Lord God will consecrate my prayers for the gain of my people. And the words which I have written in weakness will be made strong unto them; for it persuadeth them to do good; it maketh known unto them of their fathers; and it speaketh of Jesus, and persuadeth them to believe in him, and to endure to the end, which is life eternal." (2 Nephi 33:4)

Renew your baptismal covenants by participating in the ordinance of the Sacrament. The key to your deliverance is come, said the Savior: "If thou wilt hearken to my voice, which saith unto thee: Arise and be baptized, and wash away your sins, calling on my name, and you shall receive my Spirit, and a blessing so great as you never have known." (D&C 39:10).

In order to keep ourselves "unspotted from the world," we have been commanded to "go to the house of prayer and offer up (our) sacraments." (D&C 59:9). Painting with a broad brushstroke, keeping ourselves unspotted may mean maintaining a positive self-image with an unshakeable conviction that we are sons and daughters of God with promises to keep and miles to go before we sleep.

Follow the example of Father Abraham. Remember the Covenant. Remember his account from the Pearl of Great Price: "Finding there was greater happiness and peace and rest for me, I sought for the blessings of the fathers, and the right whereunto I should be ordained to administer the same; having been myself a follower of righteousness, desiring also to be one who possessed great knowledge, and to be a greater follower of righteousness, and to possess a greater knowledge, and to be a father of many nations, a prince of peace, and desiring to receive instructions, and to keep the commandments of God, I became a rightful heir, a High Priest, holding the right belonging to the fathers." (Abraham 1:2).

Turn your focus outward in service. Get outside yourself and serve others. Benjamin's words to the people of Zarahemla may be among the most oft' quoted passages in The Book of Mormon: "When ye are in the service of your fellow beings ye are only in the service of your God." (Mosiah 2:17). In this verse, the question of how to serve God is unambiguously answered. As we minister to our fellow men, we come to realize that there is "a time to get, and a time to lose; a time to keep, and a time to cast away." (Ecclesiastes 3:6). We recognize the profound wisdom in the Savior's statement that "whosoever will save his life shall lose it: but whosoever will lose his life for my sake, the same shall save it." (Luke 9:24). Perhaps we will be prompted to write a letter to a depressed friend to help ease his burden. Sometimes the answers to our own problems are revealed within the counsel we give to others.

"Once I knew the depth where no hope was, and darkness lay on the face of all things. Then love came and set my soul free. Once I knew only darkness and stillness. Now I know hope and joy. Once I fretted and beat myself against the wall that shut me in. Now I rejoice in the consciousness that I can think, act, and attain heaven. My life was without past or future; death, the pessimist would say, "a consummation devoutly to be wished." But a little word from the fingers of another fell into my hand that clutched at emptiness, and my heart leaped to the rapture of living. Night fled before the day of thought, and love and joy and hope came up in a passion of obedience to knowledge. Can anyone who escaped such captivity, who has felt the thrill and glory of freedom, be a pessimist?" (Helen Keller, "Optimism").

The Prophet Joseph Smith said: "Happiness is the object and design of our existence, and will be the end thereof if we follow the path that leads to it." ("Teachings," p. 255-256). We walk the walk, and talk the talk. We read ourselves full, think ourselves straight, pray ourselves hot, and let ourselves go.

Power: The Ultimate Test of Character

"Wo be unto
him that hearkeneth
unto the precepts of men, and
denieth the power of God, and
the gift of the Holy Ghost!"
(2 Nephi 28:26).

There are but a very few beings in the world who understand rightly the nature of God (and) if men do not understand the character of God they do not comprehend themselves." (Joseph Smith, "Teachings" p. 343). Those who come to know the Savior develop the burning desire to model their behavior after Him. They begin to realize that He alone holds the power to effect lasting change, and that in Him "there should come every good thing." (Moroni 7:22). That is why He invites us to be born again through faith on His name. As Marion G. Romney taught: "No person whose soul is illuminated by the burning Spirit of God can in this world of sin and darkness remain passive." (C.R., 10/1941). Thus did Parley P. Pratt declare: "I have received the holy anointing, and I can never rest until the last enemy is conquered, death destroyed, and truth reigns triumphant." (C.R., 4/1853).

When we are focused on the Savior, the clarity of our vision gives us the ability to see our weaknesses more clearly so that we might overcome them. Stumbling blocks become stepping stones, and our experiences teach us that "all things which are good cometh of Christ." (Moroni 7:24). But whenever our priorities are out of order, we lose the power to bring about positive change. The Lord has re-defined His gospel in the Dispensation of the Fulness of Times, so that our perspective might be crystal clear, enabling us to comprehend and build upon principles of perfection that are in His revealed words, taught by His authorized servants, emulated by His example, and validated by the Spirit. Without His protective influence and guidance, we are vulnerable to the lethal storms initiated by the destroyer that are sweeping the face of the earth. If we mistakenly trivialize celestial sureties, we become susceptible to telestial tempests and their suffocating winds that would suck the very life-sustaining marrow from our bones.

"Men should be anxiously engaged in a good cause, and do many things of their own free will, and bring to pass much righteousness; for the power is in them, wherein they are agents unto themselves." (D&C 58:28-29). This power stems from holiness, in contrast to the elusive and transient power that is driven by greed, avarice, lust, and the desire for dominion. It is not too difficult to identify Satan's fingerprints smeared all over the plans, pronouncements, proclamations, and parties that promote petty, provincial, paltry, and personal policies that pander to his program.

Because the word of God is superior to the trifling efforts of the adversary, those who lack spiritual strength often resort to violence in a vain attempt to strengthen their position and shore up their crumbling argument. But power and violence are mutually exclusive; where one is present the other is absent. Those who are least prepared for positions of trust and responsibility seem to be most inclined to abuse authority, which is a poor substitute for leadership and is antithetical to real power, especially when violence is engaged in its supposed exercise.

Those who manipulate the masses through counterfeit means are easily contrasted with those endowed with power in the priesthood that legitimately "administer(s) the gospel and hold(s) the key of the mysteries of the kingdom, even the key of the knowledge of God. Therefore, in the ordinances thereof, the power of godliness is manifest." (D&C 84:19-20). It is in the temple sanctuary from worldly influences that sacred covenants are ratified, divine investiture of authority takes place, and the endowment of spiritual and priesthood power is initialized. (See D&C 124:39).

As all save the elect God brush off the message of the Restoration, in its own twisted fashion Spiritual Babylon strangely craves the theological titillation of priesthood power. But it is not a change in the inner vessel that is desired. It is a wicked generation that seeks a sign. An adulterous society that is 'past feeling' needs greater and greater stimulation of the physical senses, mistakenly substituting that brief rush of endorphins for the sustaining influence of the Spirit.

Undisciplined minds are easily swayed by the siren song so seductively suggested by Satan, and unprincipled character crumbles in the face of telestial temptations that are so tantalizing and yet so traumatizing. The more our society focuses on the idols of the day, the less prevalent is the legitimate rule of priesthood authority. This substitution of the sacred by the profane is an abomination in the sight of God. Idol worship can be the epitome of taking His name in vain.

However, the power of the devil may be overwhelmed, his influence surmounted, his enticements resisted, and his doctrine refuted. His company is not so comely, contagious, or coveted, that we cannot live without it. In spite of his insufferable determination, he cannot forcibly wrest from us our moral agency to determine our own fate. As The Book of Mormon revealed, so it could be said of Latter-day Saints who fail to honor their sacred covenants: They "did not sin ignorantly, for they knew the will of God concerning them, for it had been taught unto them; therefore, they did willfully rebel against God." (3 Nephi 6:18).

"A favorite theme of Brigham Young was that the dominion God gives to man is designed to test him and enable him to show to himself, his fellows, and all the heavens just how he would act if entrusted with God's power." (Hugh Nibley, "Subduing the Earth," p. 89-90). We learn in The Book of Helaman that because Nephi had been unwavering, he was made "mighty in word and in deed, in faith and in works." (Helaman 10:5). He was "clothed with power and authority," because he could be trusted to do exactly as God would do in similar circumstances. (See D&C 138:30).

Joseph Smith clearly taught that the exercise of priesthood power is based solely upon the principles of righteousness. He wrote to the Saints, explaining that if, in the capacity of the priesthood, we "undertake to cover our sins, or to gratify our pride, our vain ambition, or to exercise control or dominion or compulsion upon the souls of the children of men, in any degree of unrighteousness," the power and authority of the priesthood is taken from us. (D&C 121:34-37).

As we exercise of agency, the power of God moves us along the path of eternal progression in the direction of our potential. "You are, and always will be, independent in that stage of development to which your voluntary decisions and divine powers have led," taught Truman Madsen. "There are limits along the way to what you can be and do. But you are not a billiard ball. No power in the universe can coerce your complete assent or dissent. This thesis on capacity translates Bergson's metaphor into breath-taking fact: 'The universe is a machine for the making of gods.'" ("Eternal Man," p. 18).

When it dawns on us that our power derives from God, we come to the startling realization that we are completely helpless to alter the progress, or affect the outcome, of any activity in which God is an active participant. It was when Moses finally recognized his utter dependence upon God that he exclaimed: "Now, for this cause, I know that man is nothing, which thing I never had supposed." (Moses 1:10). He understood, perhaps for the first time, that his dependence upon his Creator was total, complete, and all encompassing, that his debt to God was fathomless, that its magnitude was incomprehensible, the accounting beyond amortization, and that it could never be reconciled by anything less than the Atonement. God's impenetrable wisdom put Moses in an attitude of total reliance upon the power of God for his salvation and exaltation. And so it is with all of us.

Nothing we do can ever satisfy our debt to God. In that sense, King Benjamin asked his people: "Can ye say aught of yourselves? I answer you, Nay. Ye cannot say that ye are even as much as the dust of the earth; yet ye were created of the dust of the earth; but behold, it belongeth to him who created you." (Mosiah 2:25). It is for this reason that Brigham Young was moved to declare: "There is no man who ever made a sacrifice on this earth for the kingdom of heaven except the Savior. I would not give the ashes of a rye straw for that man who feels that he is making a sacrifice for God. We are doing this for our own happiness, welfare, and exaltation, and for nobody else's. What we do, we do for the salvation of the inhabitants of the earth, not for the salvation of the heavens, the angels, or God." (J.D., 16:114).

In a sublime act of compassion and condescension, God transfers His power to us with no thought or purpose other than to bless us as completely as possible. The only limiting factor is the extent to which we will allow God to grant us grace. It is in this context that we work out our salvation with fear and trembling before the Lord. (See Philippians 2:12). It is this transfer of power that makes mortality such an exciting learning laboratory of rich experiences. Perhaps this is why Nephi called the Plan of Salvation "The Great and Eternal Plan of Deliverance from Death" (2 Nephi 11:5), and why Alma called it "The Great Plan of Happiness." (Alma 42:8).

Since everything we are or ever hope to become is dependent upon His grace, one of the greatest acts we can perform is to show our gratitude to God. Gratitude is deeper than thanks. Thankfulness is the beginning of gratitude and may consist merely of words, but gratitude is shown in action. Because it is independent of circumstances, penetrates the deepest undercurrents of life, and is founded upon God, gratitude can serve us as well, as it unleashes the reservoirs of spiritual power waiting dormant within us.

Ultimately, "it is not the work of God that is frustrated, but the work of men." (D&C 3:3). This is because our work is illegitimate and must ultimately fail if it has no rightful claim upon the sustaining power by which righteous acts are accomplished. Joseph Fielding Smith, Jr. declared: "No power on earth or hell can overthrow or defeat that which God has decreed. Every plan of the Adversary will fail; for the Lord knows the secret thoughts of men, and sees the future with a vision clear and perfect, even as though it were in the past." ("Church History and Modern Revelation, 1:26). His omniscience and omnipotence are inseparable and irreducible. In the ultimate sense, knowledge is power. As the Lord God said to his Only Begotten while Adam was yet in the Garden: "The man is become as one of us to know good and evil." (Moses 4:28).

Courageous men and women can stand the refining heat of celestial fire. It is their destiny to become an army of God, and when the force is assembled, the enemies of righteousness will be delivered into its hands. The prophet Joseph Smith had unshakable confidence in this power, and was moved to declare: "No unhallowed hand can stop the work from progressing. Persecutions may rage, mobs may combine, armies may assemble, calumny may defame, but the truth of God will go forth boldly, nobly, and independent, until it has penetrated every continent, visited every clime, swept every country, and sounded in every ear; till the purposes of God shall be accomplished, and the Great Jehovah shall say 'The work is done.'" (H.C., 4:540).

"Did I not speak
peace to your mind concerning the
matter?" the Lord asked Oliver Cowdery.
"What greater witness can you have than
from God?" (D&C 6:22). He had learned
what so many of us have experienced
as we have prayed about The Book
of Mormon, that the Spirit is
quiet, unobtrusive, and
peaceful, and that
God works in
mysterious
ways.

Pragmatism in The Book of Mormon

Although it could certainly be argued that The Book of Mormon is not a pragmatic text, (but is a religious text), there are within its pages many examples of pragmatism. They include the following verses: 1 Nephi 8:17, 1 Nephi 15:3, 1 Nephi 19:8, 2 Nephi 33:12, Jacob 5:27, Enos 1:13, Words of Mormon 1:2, Mosiah 8:12, Mosiah 28:1-2, Alma 17:23, Alma 20:18, Alma 24:13, Alma 26:26, Alma 29:9, Alma 33:21, Helaman 11:4, 3 Nephi 3:13, 4 Nephi 1:6, and Mormon 9:6.

Pragmatism views language as a tool for prediction, problem solving, and action, rather than for describing, representing, or mirroring reality. Pragmatists contend that most philosophical topics, such as the nature of knowledge, language, concepts, meaning, belief, and science, are all best viewed in terms of their practical uses and successes. A person who is pragmatic is concerned more with matters of fact, result, and consequence, rather than with what could or should be. They evaluate beliefs in terms of the success of their practical application. Their emphasis is on actionable knowledge, a recognition of the relationships between experience, knowing, and acting, and inquiry as an experiential process. Although it could certainly be argued that The Book of Mormon is not a pragmatic text, (but is a religious text), there are within its pages examples of pragmatism. They include the following verses: 1 Nephi 8:17, 1 Nephi 15:3, 1 Nephi 19:8, 2 Nephi 33:12, Jacob 5:27, Enos 1:13, Words of Mormon 1:2, Mosiah 8:12, Mosiah 28:1-2, Alma 17:23, Alma 20:18, Alma 24:13, Alma 26:26, Alma 29:9, Alma 33:21, Helaman 11:4, 3 Nephi 3:13, 4 Nephi 1:6, and Mormon 9:6.

Although it could certainly be argued that The Book of Mormon is not a pragmatic text, (but rather a religious text), there are within its pages examples of pragmatism.

Premortal Life

"And this is the manner after which they were ordained – being called and prepared from the foundation of the world according to the foreknowledge of God, on account of their exceeding faith and good works; in the first place being left to choose good or evil."
(Alma 13:3).

I had never thought of the possibility that we lived before we were born, until I took the missionary lessons. I was unaware of William Wordsworth's poem that reads: "Our birth is but a sleep and a forgetting. The Soul that rises with us, our life's Star, hath had elsewhere its setting, and cometh from afar. Not in entire forgetfulness, and not in utter nakedness, but trailing clouds of glory do we come from God, Who is our Home." ("Ode on Intimations from Early Childhood, from Recollections of Early Childhood"). Had I been familiar with these lines, I am sure they would have touched tender chords.

I had read the King James Version of the Bible, but had overlooked the verses that provide hints about our pre-earth life. Among them are the following: "Before I formed thee in the belly I knew thee; and before thou camest forth out of the womb I sanctified thee, and I ordained thee a prophet unto the nations." (Jeremiah 1:5). "Ye are the children of the Lord your God." (Deuteronomy 14:1). We "are the sons of the living God." (Hosea 1:10). "All of you are children of the most High." (Psalms 82:6). He is "the Father of all." (Ephesians 4:6). "In him we live, and move, and have our being (for) we are the offspring of God." (Acts 17:28-29). I did not yet know that, when I die, "shall the dust return to the earth as it was: and the spirit shall return unto God who gave it." (Ecclesiastes 12:7).

If I had deeply pondered these things, I might have received answers to the questions I had not yet thought to ask. Emerson wrote: "The man who has seen the rising moon break out of the clouds at midnight has been present like an archangel at the creation of light and of the world." On another occasion, he declared: "If the stars should appear but one night in a thousand years, how would men believe and adore, and preserve for many generations the remembrance of the city of God which had been shown." Abraham (and Moses) were given key doctrinal information that would have astonished even Emerson, because they answer the fundamental questions of existence, such as pre-mortal life, agency, creation, and foreordination.

As he stood before the Burning Bush on Sinai, Moses became the first person in recorded history to ask: "Who am I?"

(Exodus 3:11). In the Book of Moses, which was received as revelation by Joseph Smith when he was translating the Bible, and which is probably one of the plain and precious parts of the bible that is missing from our K.J.V. of Exodus, we learn how Moses discovered who he was.

He was defined by his relationship with God. (See Moses 1:1-2). In fact, his identity was intertwined with that of God. "And God spake unto Moses, saying: Behold, I am the Lord God Almighty, and Endless is my name; for I am without beginning of days or end of years; and is not this endless? And behold, thou art my son." (Moses 1:3-4).

Today, we describe ourselves in the same way. The missionaries teach investigators, and we teach our children who they are, using the same parameters. Think of the words of the Primary hymn: "I am a Child of God." (Lyrics by Naomi W. Randall), Because of the restoration of priesthood authority, our character is largely defined by our covenant relationship with God. This begins with the Baptismal Covenant and only ends, really, with our Calling and Election.

We know that God is moral, because he has put us under covenant to obey the law of chastity. We know that He has charity, because he commands us to love Him and each other. We better understand His discipline as we conform our lives to the Law of Obedience. We know that He must have been a righteous steward, because He has provided us with the Law of Consecration. We learn how much He must love His less fortunate children, because he has given us the opportunity to obey the Law of the Fast. Our observance of the Word of Wisdom reminds us of His perfected, resurrected body. Our desire to seek knowledge recalls His omniscience. We carry a prayer of thanksgiving in our hearts for the laws that are anchored to the principles of the Plan of Salvation, and realize that if it were not possible to become as God is, covenants would be unnecessary. Covenants ground our almost unimaginable destiny to reality. They are the cables in air that anchor eternity to our temporal world.

We know that we are begotten spirit children of Heavenly parents, and that we lived in a pre-earth existence with them before we began our sojourn in this second estate known as mortality. In moments of deep reflection, we "think of stepping on shore, and finding it heaven! We visualize taking hold of a hand, and finding it God's hand. We envision breathing a new air, and finding it celestial air. We imagine feeling invigorated, and finding it immortality. We dream of passing from storm and tempest to an unbroken calm, and of waking up, and finding it home." (Anonymous).

We imagine what it will be like coming home from our mortal mission. "It will seem like the time passed too quickly. We will think of the people we met, the people we helped, and of how our experiences helped us to grow spiritually. We will recall that we were like children, so immature, when we left home such a short time ago. We will find mother waiting to embrace us, standing just a bit behind father, who is bursting with pride. We will see tears of happiness falling from mother's cheeks. Father will be the first to strike hands with us, and then warmly embrace us. Our feelings will resonate with familiarity, and we will feel the Spirit as we never have before. We will know this is where we belong, and it will be a real homecoming as we return with honor to Heavenly Father and Mother." (Anonymous).

God taught these fundamental truths to Abraham, who was pondering, as so many of us have, the majesty of God's handiwork. "Thus I, Abraham, talked with the Lord, face to face, as one man talketh with another; and he told me of the works which his hands had made; And he said unto me: My son, my son (and his hand was stretched out), behold I will show you all these. And he put his hand upon mine eyes, and I saw those things which his hands had made, which were many; and they multiplied before mine eyes, and I could not see the end thereof." (Abraham 3:11-12).

As He had earlier done with Moses, the Lord defined Abraham based on His relationship with him. Then God revealed to Abraham "the intelligences that were organized before the world was; and among all these there were many of the noble and great ones; And God saw these souls that they were good, and he stood in the midst of them, and he said: These I will make my rulers; for he stood among those that were spirits, and he saw that they were good; and he said unto me: Abraham, thou art one of them; thou wast chosen before thou wast born." (Abraham 3:22-23).

Joseph F. Smith saw in vision those who "were also among the noble and great ones who were chosen in the beginning to be rulers in the church of God." (D&C 138:55). He taught that these were chosen during a Council that was held in Heaven. We know we were also present at this council, because Job rhetorically asked: "Where wast thou when I laid the foundations of the earth? … When the morning stars sang together, and all the sons of God shouted for joy." (Job 38:4 & 7).

"It is extremely important to get straight what happened in that premortal council," taught Neal A. Maxwell. "It was not an unstructured meeting, nor was it a discussion between plans, nor a brain-storming session, as to how to formulate the plan for salvation and carry it out. Our Father's plan was known, and the actual question put was whom the Father should send to carry it out." ("Deposition of a Disciple," p. 11).

Satan did not offer a viable alternative plan. His suggestion was an unworkable, counterfeit. That he was a Liar from the beginning, and drew so many away from Heavenly Fathers Plan, underscores the effectiveness of his strategy to engage in "ideological warfare." But just who (and how many) were cast out of heaven as a result of rebellion remains unclear. "For behold, the devil was before Adam, for he rebelled against me, saying, Give me thine honor, which is my power; and also (not a third, but) a third part of the hosts of heaven turned he away from me because of their agency. And they were thrust down, and thus came the devil and his angels." (D&C 29:36-37). "He had drawn away many after him." (Moses 4:6). "Many followed after him." (Abraham 3:28). The Father's Plan suggests that the mighty doctrine of foreordination underlies this pure knowledge offered unto Abraham.

On the other side of the coin, Lucifer became the author of propaganda. With bias, he promoted what was really a political cause, that he might further his agenda and form a consensus among his brothers and sisters, that was in opposition to His Father's Plan. His counterfeit alternative produced an emotional, rather than a rational, response among those who listened to him. Rebellion, or war in heaven, inevitably followed.

God, Who always sees the bigger picture, explained how the divine gift of agency interacts with foreordination to give our lives purpose and meaning. Immediately after describing Abraham's seeds of greatness, He declared: "We will go down, for there is space there, and we will take of these materials, and we will make an earth whereon these may dwell; And we will prove them herewith, to see if they will do all things whatsoever the Lord their God shall command them; And they who keep their first estate shall be added upon; and they who keep not their first estate shall not have glory in the same kingdom with those who keep their first estate; and they who keep their second estate shall have glory added upon their heads for ever and ever." (Abraham 3:24-26).

This revelation makes clear that our divine right to exercise our agency in an atmosphere of opposition was intertwined with our creation, that we might freely choose God and his commandments. We are foreordained, because of the Plan, to have glory added upon our heads forever, on the condition of our faithfulness to God as we assist Him in His great work. We can better understand the blessings and foreordinations specific to our lives if we turn to the personal scriptures from the Lord that are known as our patriarchal blessings.

Foreordination is like any other blessing. It is a conditional bestowal of gifts that is subject to our faithfulness. "Prophecies foreshadow events without determining their outcomes, because of a divine foreseeing of that outcome. So, foreordination is a conditional bestowal of a role, responsibility, or a blessing that, likewise, foresees but does not fix the outcome." (Neal Maxwell, "B.Y.U Devotional," 10/10/1978).

"Our Heavenly Father has a full knowledge of the nature and disposition of each of His children, a knowledge gained by long observation and experience in the past eternity of our primeval childhood. By reason of that surpassing knowledge, God reads the future of men individually and of men collectively as communities and nations. He knows what each will do under given conditions, and sees the end from the beginning. He foresees the future and as a state which naturally and surely will be; not as one which must be because He has arbitrarily willed that it should be." (James E. Talmage, "The Great Apostasy," p. 20).

Harold B. Lee taught: "Now a further word about this matter of foreordination. The Prophet Joseph Smith taught that "every man who has a calling to minister to the inhabitants of the world was ordained to that very purpose in the grand council of heaven before this world was." ("Teachings," p. 365). So, likewise, declared the Apostle Paul, "for whom he did foreknow ... them he also called." (Romans 2:29-30). But do not misunderstand that such a calling and such foreordination pre-determine what you must do. A prophet on this western continent has spoken plainly on this subject: "Being called and prepared from the foundation of the world, according to the foreknowledge of God on account of their exceeding faith and good works; in the first place being left to choose good or evil." (Alma 13:3). This last passage makes the other preceding passages more understandable. God may have called and chosen men in the spirit world or in their first estate to do a certain work, but whether they will accept that calling here and magnify it by faithful service and good works while in mortality is a matter in which it is their right and privilege to exercise their agency to choose good or evil." ("Decisions for Successful Living," p. 168-169).

Moses asked: "Tell me, I pray thee, Why are these things so?" (Moses 1:30). In response, the Lord gave the most simple, yet powerful, reply: "This is my work and my glory, to bring to pass the immortality and eternal life of man." (Moses 1:39). Creation was instituted that we might have a greater opportunity to exercise our agency, that we might participate with God in his marvelous work of bringing to pass our immortality and eternal life.

The more we contribute to this work, the greater will be our happiness and joy, and the more fully will we fulfil our own foreordained destiny. Let us ever be faithful in this great cause. Knowledge of our pre-mortal existence sanctifies our lives, dignifies our individual effort, rewards our timid achievements, and validates our faltering progress toward our goals. One of our greatest personal challenges is to live our lives in sufficient humility to recognize, and then to magnify, our foreordained callings.

Preparation

"This life is the time for
men to prepare to meet God; yea,
behold the day of this life is the day
for men to perform their labors."
(Alma 34:32).

We need "clean hands, a pure heart, and a willing mind, to touch heaven." (Thomas S. Monson). We need to "go and do the things which the Lord hath commanded, for (we) know that the Lord giveth no commandments unto the children of men, save he shall prepare a way for them that they may accomplish the thing which he commandeth them." (1 Nephi 3:7).

President Monson said to the brethren of the church: "May we be filled with gratitude for the right of choice, accept the responsibility of choice, and ever be conscious of the results of choice. As bearers of the priesthood, all of us qualify for the guiding influence of our Heavenly Father as we choose carefully and correctly. We are engaged in the work of the Lord Jesus Christ. We, like those of olden times, have answered His call. We are on His errand. We shall succeed in the solemn charge: "Be ye clean, that bear the vessels of the Lord." (C.R., 4/2010).

It is wonderful when The First Presidency and Quorum of the Twelve give apostolic blessings. I still remember the dedicatory prayer at the Pacific Palisades, California, chapel, delivered by Elder Robert D. Hales in the late 1970s. I specifically recall him blessing our new chapel, that it would be protected from the fires that periodically ravaged the Santa Monica Mountains, in which it was nestled. That protection was required just a few years later, when a raging wildfire, fanned by the flames of a Santana Wind, burned the hillsides surrounding the chapel, but spared the building itself. I also remember Boyd K. Packer's April 2010 General Conference address, and how he closed his address by saying: "I invoke the blessings of the Lord upon you who are struggling against this terrible plague (of immorality), to find the healing that is available to us in the priesthood of the Lord."

I once read that Elder Holland "left an apostolic blessing on those attending a stake conference, in Bahrain. He challenged the brethren to live up to their priesthood offices and become true disciples of Christ, counseled the sisters to be proud they are women in the kingdom of God, and the young people to be safe, happy, and loved. He blessed the children, the sick, the ill and the grieving, saying his greatest desire was to bear the same witness and extend the same blessings that the Savior would, if He were present." (Reported in the "Church News," 3/7/2009).

In his April 2010 Conference Address, President Monson said: "One of my most vivid memories is attending priesthood meeting as a newly ordained deacon and singing the opening hymn "Come, All Ye Sons of God." Tonight,

I echo the spirit of that special hymn and say to you, 'Come, all ye sons of God who have received the priesthood.' The message of that hymn is to spread the gospel, listen to the Shepherd, repent, and be baptized, get the Spirit's zeal, and pray."

President Monson continued: "Twenty years ago I attended a sacrament meeting where the children responded to the theme "I Belong to The Church of Jesus Christ of Latter-day Saints." One of my grandsons, who was 11 years old at that time, had spoken of the First Vision as he presented his part on the program. Afterward, as he came to his parents and grandparents, I said to him, "Tommy, I think you are almost ready to be a missionary." He replied, "Not yet. I still have a lot to learn."

We all still have a lot to learn, and hopefully, we have the gift of time on our side. If we do, perhaps we should think about what we would like to learn, say, in the next twelve months. How would we like to be different then, from what we are now? How could President Monson's counsel help us to make positive changes in our lives? How could we prepare to receive his apostolic blessing?

We can begin by making conscious efforts to avoid temptation. "God … will not suffer you to be tempted above that ye are able; but will with the temptation also make a way to escape, that ye may be able to bear it." (1 Corinthians 10:13). This puts the responsibility for yielding to temptation squarely where it belongs, on our own heads.

We can cultivate good friendships. Gordon B. Hinckley famously said that every convert needs three things: "a friend in the church, an assignment, and to be nourished by the good word of God." We all need these things.

We can treat everyone with kindness and dignity. We can do as Thumper counseled, in the Disney film "Bambi." "If you can't say nuttin' nice, don't say nuttin' at all." We can strive to be the kinds of people our dogs think we are.

We can be honest. George Washington famously wrote: "I hope I shall always possess firmness and virtue enough to maintain what I consider the most enviable of all titles, the character of an 'Honest Man." A young man who sought employment, in competition with a number of other equally qualified applicants, echoed Washington's wish. "If I hire you," asked the owner of the company, "can I count on you to be honest?" "You can count on me to be honest whether you hire me or not!" responded the young man. Do you think he got the job?

We can use uplifting language. Mark Twain said that we should so live that we would be willing to sell our parrot to the town gossip. We can avoid murmuring and idle conversation. In fact, "there is so much good in the worst of us, and so much bad in the best of us, that it hardly behooves any of us to talk about the rest of us." (Anonymous).

We can seek after "anything virtuous, lovely, or of good report or praiseworthy." (12th Article of Faith). This includes avoiding the use of illicit hard drugs, the abuse of prescription medication, and the use of coffee, tea, alcohol, and tobacco products that destroy our physical, mental, and spiritual well-being. Then we shall be as those who "wait upon the Lord (who) shall renew their strength, (and) mount up with wings as eagles. (Then) they shall run, and not be weary, and they shall walk, and not faint." (Isaiah 40:31).

As we strive to abide by the principles of The Word of Wisdom, we think of Heraclitus, a philosopher of the Golden Age of Greece, who left this sage observation that is applicable in every time, but especially in our own: "When health is absent, then wisdom cannot reveal itself, culture cannot become manifest, strength cannot fight, wealth becomes useless, and intelligence cannot be applied."

We can listen to wholesome music that invites us to draw closer to our Heavenly Father. Its purpose is to inspire, to motivate, to comfort, to strengthen, and to calm our souls. Music and worship are inseparably interrelated. Because music is part of a unified whole, the instruments utilized, the way they are played, the volume and tempo, the lyrics if a vocal, the accompaniment, the attire and attitude of musicians, and the atmosphere in which the music is presented significantly influence the message conveyed and its impact on the listener. When we have been privileged to touch the face of God, it has often been facilitated by the medium of music. Even before the foundations of the earth were laid, there was music in the celestial air, when "the morning stars sang together, and all the sons of God shouted for joy." (Job 38:7).

We can be sure that we maintain absolute fidelity in marriage, and think clean thoughts. "This much I can tell you," declared Mosiah, "that if ye do not watch yourselves, and your thoughts, and your words, and your deeds, and observe the commandments of God, and continue in the faith…ye must perish." (Mosiah 4:30). As President Monson said: "May each of you be able to echo in truth the line from Tennyson spoken by Sir Galahad: "My strength is as the strength of ten, because my heart is pure."

We can remember that prayer is our passport to spiritual power, and is an excellent way to seek the companionship of the Holy Ghost. We want to collect as many of His visa stamps as possible. These validate that we have been keeping the commandments of God and repenting when necessary. President Monson closed the October 2010 General Conference with these words: "May God bless you, my brothers and sisters. May heaven's blessings be with you. May your homes be filled with love and courtesy and with the Spirit of the Lord. May you constantly nourish your testimonies of the gospel, that they will be a protection to you against the buffetings of Satan. Conference is now over. As we return to our homes, may we do so safely. May the spirit we have felt here abide with us as we go about those things that occupy us each day. May we show increased kindness toward one another. May we ever be found doing the work of the Lord. I love you. I pray for you."

Meet Joe Black was a film that was loosely based on the 1934 motion picture "Death Takes a Holiday." At its conclusion, the protagonist, who is about to die, asks Death: "Should I be afraid?" When Death answers him and says: "Not a man like you," we know that, in the face of the inevitable, everything is going to be all right. May we so live that when we reach out and are embraced by heaven, we are similarly blessed.

"Our birth is but a sleep and a forgetting. The Soul that rises with us, our life's Star, hath had elsewhere its setting, and cometh from afar. Not in entire forgetfulness, and not in utter nakedness, but trailing clouds of glory do we come from God, Who is our Home." (William Wordsworth, "Ode on Intimations from Early Childhood, from Recollections of Early Childhood").

Pride

"Because of pride, and
because of false teachers, and false
doctrine, their churches have become
corrupted, and their churches are
lifted up; because of pride,
they are puffed up."
(2 Nephi 28:12).

This essay is as much about humility as it is about pride, because for every character trait that is synonymous with pride, its counterpart defines humility. For example, pride looks over to man and argues who is right, while humility looks up to God and cares about what is right. Pride asks only: "What do I want out of life?" while humility quietly implores: 'What would God have me do?' Pride is motivated by self-will, while humility is inspired by God's will. Pride is driven by the fear of man, while humility is nurtured by the love of God. The applause of the world rings in the ears of pride, while the accolades of heaven warm the hearts of the humble.

The Book of Mormon repeatedly speaks of pride, which could have just as easily been called "Nephite Disease." Remembering that the past is prologue, we read Moroni's warning: "Behold, the pride of this nation, or the people of the Nephites, (that) hath proven their destruction." (Moroni 8:27). To the Latter-day Saints, the Lord cautioned: "Beware of pride, lest ye become as the Nephites of old." (D&C 38:39). In the beginning, before the world was made, it was pride that was at the root of the rebellion of Lucifer, who not only competed with his Father's Plan, but also desired to dethrone Him by seeking honor for himself. The Savior, on the other hand, was moved by humility. As His Father declared: "Behold, my Beloved Son, which was my Beloved and Chosen from the beginning, (Who) said unto me - Father, thy will be done, and the glory be thine forever." (Moses 4:2).

The prideful are self-centered, conceited, boastful, arrogant, and haughty, as opposed to the modesty, self-effacement, and deference of the humble, but the central feature of pride is enmity toward God and our fellowmen. There is no room for charity in the hearts of the proud. Hatred, hostility, and blind opposition are the raw manifestations of pride by which Satan wishes to reign over us, and with which he feeds his lust for power, while the sociability, approachability, and accommodation of the humble starve his strategy for domination.

The proud feel more comfortable with their own perception of truth than they do with God's omniscience. They pit their own abilities against His priesthood power, their own paltry accomplishments against His mighty works, and their stubborn will against His gentle counsel, never recognizing that it is from Him that all blessings flow. Those who refuse to accept His influence and authority have hard-hearts, stiff-necks, and are unashamedly rebellious.

They lack the pliability and malleability of the humble. The proud are unrepentant because they are smitten with themselves, while the humble are smitten by the Spirit with remorse as they realize they are less than the dust of the earth. The proud are easily offended, and are sign seekers, and because they are past feeling, they require greater and greater levels of stimulation to receive the same level of temporal or theological gratification. The humble are long suffering and faithful, and when things seem that they could not be worse, they are at their best, because they are particularly sensitive to the influence of the Holy Ghost.

The proud secretly wish that God would agree with them more frequently. They are uninterested in changing their opinions or in aligning themselves with His direction. They believe that they don't get what they deserve. Instead, they consume themselves in a senseless scramble of self-serving negotiation. Their objective is to receive more than their fair share. But too often, their lives become a series of compromises, with no end in sight. They blindly make every man their adversary by pitting their intellect, opinion, works, wealth, and talents against all others. The humble, on the other hand, foster an atmosphere of cooperation and conciliation, and they pool their resources with those with whom they work in order to achieve mutually agreeable solutions to their problems.

The proud believe that it's not about having enough of the world's goods for their needs, but rather it's about accumulating more than their neighbors have. It's not about keeping up with the Joneses. It's about stepping on and climbing over the Joneses as they scramble up what they mistakenly think is the ladder of success. It's not about cooperation, but competition. As C. S. Lewis observed: "Pride gets no pleasure out of having something, only out of having more of it than the next man. It is the comparison that makes you proud, the pleasure of being above the rest." ("Mere Christianity," pp. 109-110). Pride feeds on competition, and once that is gone, it hasn't got a leg to stand on.

The fear of what others may think of them blinds the proud to their potential, and to what God sees in them. Pride was the engine that drove the Jews to demand the crucifixion of the Savior. It was pride that compelled Saul to see David as his enemy, and to seek his life. An appeal to the pride of King Noah sent Abinadi to the flames. Because of pride, Herod's hands were stained with the blood of John the Baptist.

The proud argue, fight, exercise unrighteous dominion, and abuse their position. The humble speak softly, seek peaceful solutions, invite the Spirit to guide them in their interpersonal relationships, and honor the priesthood of God as the engine that drives their righteous behavior. The proud set the stage for secret combinations that are built up with one purpose in mind: To get gain and the glory of the world. The humble work openly. They know that "nothing is secret, that shall not be made manifest; neither any thing hid, that shall not be known and come abroad." (Luke 8:17). Their lives are open books, for all to read, and to profit thereby.

The proud correctly believe that life is about opposition, but they have chosen poorly, by entering the fray on the wrong side of the line between right and wrong. "They have sown the wind, and they shall reap the whirlwind." (Hosea 8:7). They are in a constant state of competition for the approval of others, and love "the praise of men more than the praise of God." (John 12:42-43). Their sin lies in their motivation, as well as in their execution. The proud are not concerned about whether their wages meet their needs, and do not believe in equal pay for equal labor. They only want to be sure that they receive more than their co-workers do. The humble, on the other hand, are only vaguely aware of the promise that "he that exalteth himself shall be abased, and he that abaseth himself shall be exalted," because it is inherent to their nature to be their brother's keeper. (D&C 101:42, see Genesis 4:9).

When we are caught up in the snare of pride, we can lose both our physical and spiritual independence because we deliver our freedom to the bondage of the judgment of those who do not really matter, do not really care about us or our welfare, and who, ironically, may not even wield significant influence over either our successes or our failures. When we succumb to pride, we lose our perspective and can no longer make sound judgments, because the Holy Ghost, Who has no desire to compete with the noise and commotion of the world, withdraws to a safe distance to wait out the storm. When the proud allow the wiles of the adversary to overwhelm the revelations of God, they are quick to let go of the Rod of Iron, and even to rail against the truth.

The haughty recognize pride as a poison in others, but they rarely treat, or even acknowledge, their own infection. Their feverish appetite for telestial fast-food is a self-defeating addiction, and they ignore the dietary counsel of the One Who could teach them how to adopt a healthier lifestyle. They may point to the pride of the rich and the learned, but they fail to recognize the beam in their own eye, and they never look in the mirror, other than to admire themselves. Were they to do so, they might recognize the telltale signs of arrogance and egotism, such as murmuring, which is the subdued and continually repeated expression of indistinct or inarticulate complaints or grumbling. Like an earthquake, the murmuring of the smug can build into harmonic waves with the power to undermine the foundations of relationships and institutions. Because the conceited and the proud expect results without responsibility, their murmuring is a cowardly act. While it is often conducted anonymously or behind the cloak of secrecy, its effects are felt publicly. The pride of those who murmur compels them to expect tangible returns without having made legitimate initial individual investments.

The proud are prone to gossip, which is a kindred spirit of murmuring, but is more focused on mindless chatter and speaking without real purpose. It is just as damaging, however, because it feeds voraciously on rumor, hearsay, second-hand information, innuendo, and vanity. Left unchecked, it may build into a self-perpetuating wave leading to a cascade of unfortunate consequences. In its many forms, gossip has one common characteristic. The words once so loosely spoken cannot be gathered up later on. Gossip is like a pile of feathers left on the doorstep of those with whom one engages in idle conversation. As it drifts to the four winds, it cannot be recalled. Words so carelessly scattered about in gossip suggest that the mouth has been brought on-line before the brain.

The proud are faultfinders, who throw dirt, but lose ground in the process. With revulsion, we have all witnessed flies passing over healthy parts of the body to feed only at open sores. At the dedication of the Kirtland Temple, Joseph Smith referred to those predatory individuals who sought to tear down the Latter-day work through fault finding. "We ask thee," he prayed, "to confound, and astonish, and to bring to shame and confusion, all those who have spread lying reports abroad, over the world, against thy servants, if they will not repent." (D&C 109:29).

Too often, the proud forget that when they point their finger at someone, there are three other fingers pointing right back at them. On the other hand, when the humble seek to discover the best in others, they somehow bring out the finest in themselves. How refreshing, when their appraisals reflect a nobler estimate of others and celebrate their potential. Even if but little good is known, the humble still speak in glowing terms of that which they do know to be true. If the humble are the first to discover a fault in others, they are the last to make it known to the world. They practice restraint, and are always ready to give courage and hope, and to speak kind words that come from the heart to awaken the soul to cheerfulness, "'til heart meets with heart and rejoices in friendship that ever is true." ("Let Us Oft Speak Kind Words," Joseph L. Townsend).

In their twisted thinking, the proud believe that they are somehow demeaned by those who have earned their authority and respect. They do not feel that they need guidance or direction from priesthood leaders, and do not easily receive counsel or take correction. Their disobedience is the manifestation of a power struggle against those who legitimately rule over them, who may be parents, priesthood leaders, teachers, or even God. The proud do not easily admit their mistakes, and are not easily taught. They fanatically cling to their beliefs, because they redouble their efforts even as they lose sight of their objectives. They feel uncomfortable with the thought of changing their minds, because to do so would imply they had been wrong.

Their behavior contrasts with that of the humble, who in their assessments and judgments are prone to praise loudly and blame softly. The humble understand that when straightening a bent nail, a pat on the back is better than a bump on the head. Before being critical of others, the humble remember that they may have had fewer advantages. The humble have learned to seek out supportive and sustaining experiences in the peaceful and pastoral countryside of clarity of the spirit, and they encourage others to remove themselves from the madding crowd, to clear their heads, to listen more attentively and see more clearly, to breathe more deeply, to inhale the fresh air of truth, and to be caressed by its gentle breeze, if they have not beforehand been refreshed by such influences and invigorated by such whisperings.

The proud often have only a weak foundation of doctrinal understanding of the gospel, and risk falling into transgression in consequence of their shallow comprehension of its principles. As they pick apart the scriptures or the words of those who preach, they distort the doctrines into meaningless fragments without any coherent connection. As Alma declared to the inhabitants of Ammonihah: "Behold, the scriptures are before you; if ye will wrest them it shall be to your own destruction." (Alma 13:20).

The appearance of pride is multi-faceted, but the Spirit provides face-recognition software to help identify its shape-shifting manifestations. What may have begun as a selfish tendency can morph into self-absorbed and self-seeking character flaws such as self-conceit, self-pity, self-fulfillment, and self-gratification. The humble rely upon intrinsic and self-reinforcing countermeasures such as altruism, self-denial, self-discipline, self-restraint, and self-sacrifice. The proud are easily offended and hold grudges, believing that others have wronged them and do not deserve their forgiveness, which they perversely withhold to keep others in their debt and to justify their injured feelings. In their defensiveness, they rationalize their weaknesses, frailties, and failures, rather than seeking the peace that comes with repentance and forgiveness by God. Their self-esteem hinges upon their approval by the world. They only feel validated if others suffer disapprobation. Pride is particularly ugly because it says: "If you succeed, I am a failure," and "If I have value, that makes you worthless."

The antidote to pride is humility, meekness, and submissiveness. As Rudyard Kipling put it: "The tumult and the shouting dies; the captains and the kings depart. Still stands, thine ancient sacrifice, an humble and a contrite heart. Lord God of Hosts, be with us yet, lest we forget, lest we forget." ("Recessional").

We can choose to humble ourselves by accepting counsel and chastisement, by forgiving those who have offended us, by rendering selfless service, and by our good example that teaches others. We can unconsciously choose to humble by adopting a lifestyle that complements and honors God, and that acknowledges His "glory, honor, power, majesty, might, dominion, truth, justice, judgment, mercy, and an infinity of fulness, from everlasting to everlasting." (D&C 109:77).

The antidote to pride, the principle that has been woven into this essay, is frustratingly simple. The quiet example of the Savior is illustration enough. Humility will conquer our pride and cleanse our inner vessel as we yield to the enticings of the Holy Spirit, put off the natural man, and become saints through the atonement of Christ.

(The) Priests of Baal in Our Lives

"Priestcrafts are that men preach and set themselves up for a light unto the world, that they may get gain and praise of the world; but the seek not the welfare of Zion."
(2 Nephi 26:29).

"Born in poverty but nurtured in faith, José García prepared for a mission call. I was present the day his recommendation was received. There appeared the statement: 'Brother García will serve at great sacrifice to his family, for he is the means of much of the family support. He has but one possession, a treasured stamp collection, which he is willing to sell, if necessary, to help finance his mission.' President Spencer W. Kimball listened attentively as this statement was read to him, and then he responded: 'Have him sell his stamp collection. Such sacrifice will be to him a blessing.'

Then, with a twinkle in his eye and a smile on his face, this loving prophet said, 'Each month at church headquarters we receive thousands of letters from all parts of the world. See that we save these stamps and provide them to José at the conclusion of his mission. He will have, without cost, the finest stamp collection of any young man in Mexico.'" (Thomas S. Monson).

When we put the things of God first in our lives, the rewards we receive are far greater than anything we may have had to sacrifice along the way. But we sometimes don't receive these blessings right away. More often than not, we need to be patient.

Jeroboam, who led the kingdom of Israel into idolatry, was followed by a succession of idolatrous kings. Of those rulers, Ahab was the worst. He "did more to provoke the Lord God of Israel to anger than all the kings of Israel that were before him." (1 Kings 16:33). He married Jezebel, adopted her practice of Baal worship, and encouraged his people to join him in the worship of false gods.

In consequence of their idolatry, the prophet Elijah was sent to deliver words of warning to Ahab and his kingdom. Because of the wickedness of Ahab and his people, Elijah declared, "There shall not be dew nor rain these years, but according to my word." (1 Kings 17:1).

In The Book of Mormon, Nephi, the son of Helaman, was given the same power: "Blessed art thou, Nephi, for those things which thou hast done; for I have beheld how thou hast with unwearyingness declared the word, which I have given unto thee, unto this people. And thou hast not feared them, and hast not sought thine own life, but hast sought my will, and to keep my commandments. And now, because thou hast done this with such unwearyingness, behold, I will bless thee forever; and I will make thee mighty in word and in deed, in faith and in works; yea, even that all things shall be done unto thee according to thy word, for thou shalt not ask that which is contrary to my will." (Helaman 10:4-5).

After Elijah declared that no rain would fall in the kingdom, the Lord commanded him to flee from the presence of Ahab. "And the word of the Lord came unto him, saying, Get thee hence, and turn thee eastward, and hide thyself by the brook Cherith, that is before Jordan. And it shall be, that thou shalt drink of the brook; and I have commanded the ravens to feed thee there. So he went and did according unto the word of the Lord." (1 Kings 17:2-5).

President Gordon B. Hinckley, as a latter-day counterpart to the Prophet Elijah, said: "I draw strength from a simple statement made concerning the Prophet Elijah: 'So he went and did according unto the word of the Lord.' (1 Kings 17:5). There was no arguing. There was no excusing. There was no equivocating. Elijah simply 'went and did according unto the word of the Lord.' And he was saved from the terrible calamities that befell those who instead scoffed and argued and questioned."

After the brook in the wilderness dried up, the Lord sent Elijah to the Widow of Zarephath. "And it came to pass after a while, that the brook dried up, because there had been no rain in the land. And the word of the Lord came unto him, saying, Arise, get thee to Zarephath…and dwell there: behold, I have commanded a widow woman there to sustain thee. So, he arose and went to Zarephath. And when he came to the gate of the city, behold, the widow woman was there gathering of sticks: and he called to her, and said, Fetch me, I pray thee, a little water in a vessel, that I may drink. And as she was going to fetch it, he called to her, and said, Bring me, I pray thee, a morsel of bread in thine hand.

And she said, As the Lord thy God liveth, I have not a cake, but an handful of meal in a barrel, and a little oil in a cruse: and, behold, I am gathering two sticks, that I may go in and dress it for me and my son, that we may eat it, and die. And Elijah said unto her, Fear not; go and do as thou hast said: but make me thereof a little cake first, and bring it unto me, and after make for thee and for thy son. For thus saith the Lord God of Israel, the barrel of meal shall not waste, neither shall the cruse of oil fail, until the day that the Lord sendeth rain upon the earth. And she went and did according to the saying of Elijah: and she, and he, and her house, did eat many days. And the barrel of meal wasted not, neither did the cruse of oil fail, according to the word of the Lord, which he spake by Elijah." (1 Kings 17:7-16).

The Lord often helps those in need through the service of other people. Jeffrey Holland said: "I know we can each do something, however small that act may seem to be. We can pay an honest tithe and give our fast and freewill offerings … and we can watch for other ways to help. To worthy causes and needy people, we can give time if we don't have money, and we can give love when our time runs out. We can share the loaves we have and trust God that the cruse of oil will not fail."

Elder Holland said that the widow's response when Elijah asked her for food was an "expression of faith, as great, under these circumstances, as any I know in the scriptures. Perhaps uncertain what the cost of her faith would be, she first took her small loaf to Elijah, obviously trusting that if there were not enough bread left over, at least she and her son would have died in an act of pure charity."

Ezra Taft Benson counseled: "When we put God first, all other things fall into their proper place or drop out of our lives. Our love of the Lord will govern the claims for our affection, the demands on our time, the interests we pursue, and the order of our priorities. May God bless us to put Him first and, as a result, reap peace in this life and eternal life with a fulness of joy in the life to come."

When the widow's son later became sick and died, Elijah "carried him up into a loft, where he abode, and laid him upon his own bed. And he cried unto the Lord, and said, O Lord my God, I pray thee, let this child's soul come into him again. And the Lord heard the voice of Elijah; and the soul of the child came into him again, and he revived." (1 Kings 17:17-22).

The priesthood power of Elijah did not go unnoticed in the land. Before long, he found it necessary to contend with all of the priests of Baal, who were the lackeys of Ahab and Jezebel: "Now therefore send, and gather to me all Israel unto mount Carmel, and the prophets of Baal four hundred and fifty, and the prophets of the groves four hundred, which eat at Jezebel's table. So, Ahab sent unto all the children of Israel, and gathered the prophets together unto mount Carmel." (1 Kings 18:19-20).

When the people gathered to hear Elijah speak, he asked them, "How long halt ye between two opinions?" (1 Kings 18:21). To halt between two opinions is to serve two masters. But no-one can do this, "for either he will hate the one, and love the other; or else he will hold to the one, and despise the other. Ye cannot serve God and mammon." (Matthew 6:24). A house divided against itself cannot stand.

We sometimes halt between two opinions in our struggle to be obedient. There is a constant battle between maintaining church dress standards and adopting the standards of the world, keeping the Sabbath or enjoying the weekend, honoring the Word of Wisdom or pushing the envelope in the cafés of convenience that are scattered all along the broad boulevards of Idumea, memorizing the Thirteenth Article of Faith or practicing it, following the counsel of the brethren or analyzing it to find some weakness within it, or some way around it, so that we can justify our behavior and feel better about our disobedience.

Sometimes, we must contend with "the Priests of Baal" lurking in our own lives. "The stirring words of various prophets urge us to choose, to decide, and not to halt. Elijah's message has tremendous relevancy today, for all must finally choose between the gods of this world and the God of eternity." (Neal A. Maxwell).

Following Elijah's spiritually exhausting confrontation with the priests of Baal, (1 Kings 18) he was comforted by the Holy Ghost and was instructed to continue in God's work. (1 Kings 19). He became discouraged, just as we sometimes do in our daily struggles. "There are 1,200 kids in my high school, and I'm the only member." "None of my teammates support my standards." "I've tried giving out copies of The Book of Mormon, but all I seem to get is rejection." "Everyone else got to date at 14, but I have to wait 'til I'm 16." "While everyone else is out enjoying the weekend, I'm be on a service project on Saturday, and in church on Sunday."

Elijah said: "The children of Israel have forsaken thy covenant, thrown down thine altars, and slain thy prophets with the sword; and I, even I only, am left; and they seek my life, to take it away." (1 Kings 19:10). Despite the people's response to God's spectacular display of power, Elijah still felt that he was the only Israelite left who worshiped the true God.

The Lord responded to Elijah by declaring: "Yet I have left me seven thousand in Israel, all the knees which have not bowed unto Baal, and every mouth which hath not kissed him." (1 Kings 19:18). In the midst of the community of unbelievers (and apostate members of the church) there were thousands who were still faithful to their covenants (or who, as the elect of God, would respond enthusiastically to overtures from members of the church). Today, there are many who just don't know where to find the truth. If we are sensitive to the whisperings of the Spirit, the Lord will direct us to them.

The Lord communicated with Elijah in the same way He often counsels us. (See 1 Kings 19). Gordon B. Hinckley said: "I think the best way I could describe the (communication) process is to liken it to the experience of Elijah as set forth in the book of First Kings. Elijah spoke to the Lord, and there was a wind, a great wind, and the Lord was not in the wind. And there was an earthquake, and the Lord was not in the earthquake. And there was a fire, and the Lord was not in the fire. And after the fire, a still, small voice, which I describe as the whisperings of the Spirit." (C.R., 10/1996).

Ezra Taft Benson, asked that we take time to listen to the promptings of the Spirit. "Answers to prayer," he said, "come most often by a still voice and are discerned by our deepest, innermost feelings. I tell you that you can know the will of God concerning yourselves if you will take the time to pray and to listen." The lesson of Elijah contending with the priests of Ball teaches us that we will be comforted and guided as we put God first and heed the whisperings of the Holy Ghost.

(The) Prime Directive

*'Ye have not come thus far
save it were by the word of Christ
with unshaken faith in him, relying
wholly upon the merits of him who is might
to save. Wherefore, ye must press forward with a
steadfastness in Christ, having a perfect brightness
of hope, and a love of God and of all men. Wherefore,
if you shall press forward, feasting upon the word
of Christ, and endure to the end, behold, thus
saith the Father: Ye shall have eternal life.
(2 Nephi 31:19-20).*

In the fictional universe of Star Trek, the Prime Directive, Starfleet's General Order #1, is the most prominent guiding principle of the United Federation of Planets. The Prime Directive dictates that there can be no interference with the internal development of pre-warp civilizations, consistent with the historical real world concept of Westphalian sovereignty.

The rationale behind the Prime Directive is that civilizations with advanced technologies should not alter, modify, revise, amend, adjust, improve, develop, expand, or change in any way the natural development of emerging societies, wherever they may be found, even if the aid is well-intentioned or kept secret. To do so might radically influence the natural evolution of such a civilization. This could be detrimental to the society or the celestial neighbors within the sphere of its expanding power, or it could beneficial, but the effect would most certainly not be neutral. In any case, the culture's natural progression, and that of those with whom it might come in contact, would be artificially influenced in ways that would be difficult to anticipate and impossible to control. No matter the outcome, there would be no going back.

The Prime Directive works well for Starships boldly going where no one has gone before, but it runs counter to the nurturing philosophy of our Heavenly Father. His stated mission is to care for His children to such an extent that they will flourish under His guidance until they reach the point in their progression that they receive everything He is and has. No matter in what condition they may currently live, at some point, He will provide the means for them to be reborn by generation and not by maturation, and receive immortality and eternal life. His version of The Prime Directive has been radically altered, and goes something like this: "Come now, and let us reason together." (Isaiah 1:18).

For all practical purposes, Heavenly Father is the President of The United Federation of Planets, and He enjoys life tenure. He has at His disposal skills, knowledge, expertise, know-how, tools, and technologies that are beyond our comprehension. Were they to be given to us all at once, they would probably do us more harm than good. It would be of no benefit to us to receive a cascade of information that would simply overwhelm us and overload our ability to process and utilize information. So, instead, He gives us "line upon line, precept upon precept; here a little, and there a little; giving us consolation by holding forth that which is to come, confirming our hope!" (D&C 128:21).

Sir Isaac Newton recognized his woeful inadequacies, writing late in his life: "I do not know what I may appear to the world, but to myself I seem to have been only like a boy playing on the seashore, and diverting myself now and then in finding a smoother pebble, or a prettier shell than ordinary, while the great ocean of truth lay all undiscovered before me." ("The Ascent of Man," p. 236).

He understood that the mind of man is generally locked on telestial targets, and that when we even attempt so-called higher-level thinking we risk becoming "as sounding brass, or a tinkling cymbal." (1 Corinthians 13:1). "For my thoughts are not your thoughts," chided the Lord.. "Neither are your ways my ways ... For as the heavens are higher than the earth, so are my ways higher than your ways, and my thoughts than your thoughts." (Isaiah 55:8-9). Newton realized that "the best of life is always further on. Its real lure is hidden from our eyes somewhere behind the hills of time." (Sir William Murdock). Good things come to those who are willing to wait.

Divine tutorial training is a process. As we receive guidance, we "hear truth spoken with clarity and freshness; uncolored and untranslated, it speaks from within ourselves in a language original but inarticulate, heard only with the soul." (Hugh B. Brown). The Holy Ghost educates us about eternal truths; it teaches us things that we can learn in no other way. "Hearken unto me," urged King Benjamin, "and open your ears that ye may hear, and your hearts that ye may understand; and your minds that the mysteries of God may be unfolded to your view." (Mosiah 2:9). When we allow the Holy Ghost to influence our lives, we are cast off into a stream of revelation and carried along in the quickening currents of direct experience with God. The philosophy of The Prime Directive is repudiated by the very mechanics of The Plan of Salvation.

And that is just how God wants it. In effect, He says, "Stop thinking about The Prime Directive." Forget the crooner who sings: "And now, the end is near, and so I face the final curtain. My friend, I'll say it clear; I'll state my case, of which I'm certain. I've lived a life that's full. I've traveled each and every highway; and more, much more than this, I did it my way." ("My Way," lyrics by Paul Anka). What a pathetic waste, to be so arrogant, haughty, egotistical, and proud to have summarily declined the helping hand of God.

The "lives of great men all remind us we can make our lives sublime, and, departing, leave behind us footprints on the sands of time." (Henry Wadsworth Longfellow). Sometimes there are two sets of footprints, and during times of particular difficulty, there may be only one set. Of course, it is during those trying times that the Savior carried us on his shoulders. We are comforted that He will lead us out of the bondage of ignorance "by power, and with a stretched-out arm." (D&C 103:17). The very fact that He is "mighty to save" suggests that we must allow Him to become involved in our lives so He may rescue us. (2 Nephi 31:19).

For many millions of people, "religion consists of a humble admiration of the illimitable superior spirit who reveals himself in the slight details we are able to perceive with our frail and feeble minds." (Albert Einstein). Einstein also said: "I am satisfied with a glimpse of the marvelous structure of the existing world, together with the striving to comprehend a portion of the Reason that manifests itself in nature. ("The World as I See It").

The scientist's Unknowable Reason notwithstanding, it is the poets' heartstrings that are often moved by the rustling robes of the Spirit. As Eliza R. Snow wrote: "Oft times a secret something whispered, 'You're a stranger here,' and I felt that I had wandered from a more exalted sphere." ("O My Father").

She intuitively knew that God intervenes in our lives, whether we specifically recognize His influence or not. Ralph Waldo Emerson declared: "The man who has seen the rising moon break out of the clouds at midnight has been present like an archangel at the creation of light and of the world." Truly, when God said, "Let there be light," it was a simple statement of fact as much as a command. It was an invitation to embrace His Light, to celebrate it, and to revel in it. As are most of His entreaties, the formula is simple. Truly, "earth is crammed with heaven, and every bush with fire of God. But only those who see take off their shoes. The rest stand around picking blackberries." (Elizabeth Barrett Browning, "Aurora Leigh," Book Seven, 1856).

We are intertwined with God in a palpable connection. He takes notice of sparrows falling from trees but also of supernovas exploding in distant galaxies. He does not play dice with His creations. He does not leave things to chance. As a loving Parent, He is an active participant in the growth and development of His children. He always attends Parent/Teacher conferences. He never misses the extracurricular activities of His children. He has a season pass to every game we play. He is forever in the bleachers, in the middle of the cheering section. He is in the "wave" when it passes through the stands. He sits up late in the evening, with the porch light on, waiting for us to come back home to safety. He has our phone number on speed dial and regularly uses voice mail. He is at the top of our "friends-and-family" list. If the character "Q," from Star Trek, the Next Generation, had a benevolent side, it would be characteristic of Heavenly Father's nature.

Even if we try to ignore Him, we cannot make Him go away. "This is My Prime Directive," He has told us, "to bring to pass the immortality and eternal life of man." (Moses 1:39). To accomplish that purpose, He explained, "I will go before your face. I will be on your right hand and on your left, and my Spirit shall be in your hearts, and mine angels round about you, to bear you up." (D&C 84:88). "For he hath said, I will never leave thee, nor forsake thee." (Hebrews 13:5).

When we are caught up in the snare of pride, we can lose both our physical and spiritual independence because we deliver our freedom to the bondage of the judgment of those who do not really matter, do not really care about us or our welfare, and who, ironically, may not even wield significant influence over either our successes or our failures. When we succumb to pride, we lose our perspective and can no longer make sound judgments, because the Holy Ghost, Who has no inclination to compete with the noisy commotion the world, withdraws to a safe distance to wait out the storm. When the proud allow the wiles of the adversary to overwhelm the revelations of God, they are quick to let go of the Rod of Iron, and even to rail against the truth.

Professors

"Pride ... began to enter ... into
the hearts of the people who professed
to belong to the church of God."
(Helaman 3:33).

The Lord is mindful of His covenant relationship with the members of His church, and so He requires extraordinary performance of those "who profess (His) name." (D&C 50:4). Professors represent themselves as independent witnesses. Memorable professors back up their words with deeds, and give vitality, or life to desire. Good intentions, after all, are only dreams. As Harold B. Lee observed: "Vision without work is dreamery. Work without vision is drudgery. But work with vision is destiny!"

Professors are persevering and stay focused on the tasks at hand. They begin with the end in mind and settle for more, and not for less. They are purposeful, determined, disciplined, focused, and are not easily distracted or persuaded. Their foundation is on bedrock. They have depth and breadth, and have made regular deposits to their spiritual bank accounts, from which they may take timely, strategic, and significant withdrawals.

Professors are guided by the Spirit, and teach by example. They are leaders, and not just managers. They help others to clarify their own feelings, and their teachings are founded on principles rather than values. Professors are not easily swayed by conventional wisdom or politically correct ideology and are uninfluenced by situational ethics or expediency. If the testimony of Jesus is the spirit of prophecy, then every professor of the name of Christ, every member of His church who carries the burden of a testimony of His divinity, is a facilitator who helps to bring others of Heavenly Father's children into the light. Thus, professors are light bearers who carry the torch of truth as a beacon to guide others who are having difficulty finding their own way. The best among them wear the heavy robes of responsibility of God's true priesthood or operate under its influence and by its direction.

Professors "are faithful and endure, whether in life or in death, for they shall inherit eternal life." (D&C 50:5). They endure to the end and lay claim to the promise of the Lord, Who said He would disperse the powers of darkness from before them, and cause the heavens to shake for their good. (D&C 21:6). The doors to the spirit prison of the unjust shrink in significance, and, as the Lord has promised, the confidence of professors will wax strong in the presence of God; and the doctrine of the priesthood will distill upon their souls as the dews from heaven. The Holy Ghost will be their constant companion, and their scepter will be an unchanging scepter of righteousness and truth; and their dominion will be an everlasting dominion, and without compulsory means it will flow unto them forever. (See D&C 121:45-46, & D&C 76:13, 23, & 73, 138:8 & 28, Isaiah 61:1, 1 Peter 3:19, & Moses 7:57).

The real tragedy in life is not that we set our sights too high, and then fail to achieve our goals. Rather, it is that those who have not participated in the curriculum of the gospel aim too low, easily reaching their objectives but having little to show for their consistently timid efforts.

Professors do not accept mediocrity in their lives; instead, their behavior is in harmony with the nature of God, Who dwells in perfection in the Celestial Kingdom. What He has, He could easily give to us, if He chose to do so. But we would likely squander the inheritance, failing to recognize its value. Instead, God has provided a mortal experience for us, and complimented it with moral testing, so that we can learn to be what He is. These are the conditions under which His grace may be granted, and this is the only way we may claim the reward that is intricately interwoven within the elements of the Plan.

Professors "hunger and thirst after righteousness," and are "filled with the Holy Ghost." (3 Nephi 12:6). Nephi encouraged professors, saying: "If ye shall press forward" with complete dedication, "feasting upon the word of Christ" or receiving physical and spiritual strength and nourishment, "and endure to the end" with continuing responsibility and accountability, "behold, thus saith the Father: Ye shall have eternal life," which is the greatest of God's gifts. (2 Nephi 31:20).

For professors, endurance is positive and pleasant. Their faith motivates them to be spiritually fit, for the exalting principles of the gospel bestow upon them gifts that to be earned require effort. Consequently, they are sometimes admonished: "Behold, you have not understood; you have supposed that I would give it unto you, when you took no thought save it was to ask me. But, behold, I say unto you, that you must study it out in your mind." (D&C 9:7-8). One noted professor named Lorenzo Snow declared: "It is impossible to advance in the principles of truth, to increase in heavenly knowledge, except we exercise our reasoning faculties and exert ourselves." (J.D., 18:371). Agency is not free, but is purchased at a substantial price. "For all who will have a blessing at my hands," explained the Lord, "shall abide the law which was appointed for that blessing, and the conditions thereof, as were instituted from before the foundation of the world" when the Plan was ratified by its future participants. (D&C 132:5). The Lord said that professors should press forward, not with the crowd who jostles for position in the circus of telestial trivialities, but rather with the Saints who seek "wisdom; and ... the mysteries of God" that are those truths that can only be known by revelation from the Holy Ghost. (D&C 11:7).

"But wo unto them that (in contrast to professors) are deceivers and hypocrites." (D&C 50:6). The word "hypocrite" is from the Greek, where it describes the mask used by actors. A hypocrite, then, is someone who professes to be one thing, when actually it is a charade; he is an entirely different person behind his mask. Satan exults in hypocrisy and is a master of the techniques whereby we are methodically moved by subtraction from brilliant, dazzling white, through every shade of grey, to a fathomless black that is the absence of every good thought, word, deed, or worthy principle. His flattery and subtle suggestions that he does not exist leads us to judge ourselves to be deserving of peace and plenty without having earned the reward. (2 Nephi 30:22). We seek to subvert the curriculum as if it were possible to hack into the system that records our grades and give ourselves undeserved high marks. Meanwhile, as C.S. Lewis wrote: "Little people, like you and me, if our prayers are sometimes granted beyond all hope and probability, had better not draw hasty conclusions to our own advantage. If we were stronger, we might be less tenderly treated. If we were braver, we might be sent, with far less help, to defend far more desperate posts in the great battle." ("The World's Last Night," p. 10-11).

"Wherefore, let every (professor) beware lest he do that which is not in truth and righteousness before me." (D&C 50:9). "That ye may not be deceived," Joseph was counseled, "seek ye earnestly the best gifts, always remembering for what they are given." (D&C 46:8). God will continue the ministry, and work miracles among the children of men, as "long as time shall last, or the earth shall stand, or there shall be one (professor) upon the face thereof to be saved." (Words of Mormon 1:36).

Proper Prior Preparation

"Salvation cometh to none such
except it be through repentance and faith on
the Lord Jesus Christ. And the Lord God hath sent
his holy prophets among all the children of men, to
declare these things to every kindred, nation, and
tongue, that thereby whosoever should believe the
Christ should come, the same might receive
remission of their sins, and rejoice
with exceedingly great joy."
(Mosiah 3:12-13).

LaVell Edwards taught that the measure of successful athletes is that they "have the will to prepare" rather than "the will to win." So too, our lives are times of personal preparation and joint preparation with our loved ones. In life, as in sports, those who will wear the laurel crown of the victor will be those who have prepared well.

Historical examples illustrate the point. Perhaps it was difficult for young David to see why lions and bears so frequently attacked his flocks, but when the time came for him to select five smooth stones for his sling, as he stood alone against Goliath in the Valley of Elah, he was prepared.

Prior to his election to the Presidency of the United States, Abraham Lincoln was guided through many years of difficulty and disappointment by this magnificent principle: "I will prepare myself," he wrote, "and some day my chance will come."

In the Book of Alma, we learn how Ammon paid the price to spiritually prepare himself. His opportunity to deliver the message of the gospel to the Lamanites came soon enough. God set the stage and provided a golden teaching moment. When ruffians came to scatter the flocks of King Lamoni, Ammon's heart swelled with the confidence that God would manifest his power. He eagerly anticipated the same opportunity that caused his companions to "weep exceedingly." (Alma 17:28). In our day we all face our own 'Lamanites by the waters of Sebus.' As always, proper prior preparation will prevent poor performance in the hour of need.

A successful evangelical minister offered this recipe for success: "Read yourself full, think yourself straight, pray yourself hot, and let yourself go!" (J. Douglas Gibb). The first three admonitions involve preparation and set the stage for purposeful action, when we can really "let ourselves go."

The Prime Directive works well
for those on Starships boldly going
where no one has gone before, but it runs
counter to the nurturing philosophy of our Father
in Heaven. His stated mission is to care for us to such
an extent that we will flourish under His guidance until
we reach a point in our progression that we receive everything
He is and has. No matter in what condition we may currently
find ourselves, at some point, God will provide the means for us to
be reborn and to receive immortality and eternal life. His version of
The Prime Directive, that is found in The Book of Mormon, has been
radically altered. We cry unto Him for our support, and we counsel
with Him in all that we do. When we lie down at night, He watches
over us in our sleep, and in the morning when we rise up, our
hearts are full of thanks, and throughout the day, He
gives us uninterrupted guidance and direction.
(See Alma 37:36-37).

(The) Prophet Joseph Smith

"Yea, Joseph truly said: Thus
saith the Lord unto me: A choice seer
will I raise up out of the fruit of thy loins.
Ad unto him dwill I give commandment that
he shall do a work ... which shall be of great worth
unto them, even to the bringing of them to the knowledge
of the covenants which I have made with thy fathers. And
his name shall be called after me; and it shall be after
the name of his father. And he shall be like unto me;
for the thing, which the Lord shall bring forth
by his hand, by the power of the Lord shall
bring my people unto salvation."
(2 Nephi 3:7 & 15).

Asked, how he could govern so many people, the Prophet Joseph replied: "I teach them correct principles, and they govern themselves." (Quoted by John Taylor and others, 5/18/1862 - Salt Lake Tabernacle, see J.D., 10:57). He was a staunch believer in our inherent ability to obey correct principles in an atmosphere of intellectual freedom without temporal restraints. On one occasion, he said: "It is one of the first principles of my life, and one that I have cultivated from my childhood, having been taught it by my father, to allow everyone the liberty of conscience. I am the greatest advocate of the Constitution of the United States there is on the earth. In my feelings, I am always ready to die for the protection of the weak and oppressed in their just rights." (H.C., 6:56-57).

He viewed life from an unusual perspective, having received divine tutorial training from his youth. As a prophet, seer, and revelator, he declared: "Could we read and comprehend all that has been written from the days of Adam on the relation of man to God and angels in a future state, we should know very little about it. Reading the experience of others, or the revelation given to them, can never give us a comprehensive view of our condition and true relation to God. Knowledge of these things can only be obtained by experience through the ordinances of God set forth for that purpose. Could you gaze into heaven five minutes, you would know more than you would by reading all that has ever been written on the subject." (H.C., 6:50).

Many people believe, as did Joseph F. Smith, that "the greatest event that has ever occurred in the world since the resurrection of the Son of God from the tomb and his ascension on high, was the coming of the Father and of the Son to that boy Joseph Smith, to prepare the way for the laying of the foundation of His kingdom, never more to cease nor be overturned. Having accepted this truth, I find it easy to accept every other truth that he enunciated and declared during his mission of fourteen years in the world. He saw; he heard; he did as he was commanded to do." ("Deseret Evening News," 7/14/1917, p. 9).

His presence dominates the history of The Church of Jesus Christ of Latter-day Saints. "From his birth to his martyr's death at the age of 38, (we feel) his power and influence. He emerges the prophet, seer, organizer, lawgiver, promoter, architect, and teacher. His religious concept includes fashioning the kingdom of God upon the earth, changing the lives of men, and preparing everyone who will listen for Christ's advent, along with the building of the New Jerusalem and the great temple in Missouri where the Lord will make his appearance and usher in the millennial reign of peace." (Ivan Barrett, "Joseph Smith & The Restoration," p. 2).

He had a knack for reducing even weighty doctrine down to its lowest common denominator in a way that simplified eternal principles. He struck familiar chords with people from all walks of life, making everyone in his company feel at ease. He taught by precept and by example. He would have been comfortable with princes, as he certainly was at ease with paupers. He could roll up his sleeves and toil from dawn to dusk with the working man. One of his greatest contributions was "his knowledge of what is to come after death. He did much to clarify men's understanding of heaven and to make it seem worth working for." ("My Religion & Me," Sunday School Course Manual). He crafted in words a formula that has been the Holy Grail of philosophers everywhere: "Happiness is the object and design of our existence, and will be the end thereof, if we pursue the path that leads to it, and this path is virtue, uprightness, faithfulness, holiness, and keeping all the commandments of God." ("Teachings," p. 255).

He could knock conventional wisdom on its ear with an innocent and yet profoundly penetrating indictment. "We shall at last have to come to this conclusion," he said, that "whatever we may think of revelation, without it we can neither know nor understand anything of God, or the devil." ("Millennial Star," 19:275). He spoke as one having authority, and was fluent not only in English but also in the language of the Spirit, testifying: "I thank God that I have got this old book (as he held up the Bible); but I thank him even more for the gift of the Holy Ghost. I have got the oldest book in the world, but I also have the oldest book in my heart, even the gift of the Holy Ghost." ("Teachings," p. 349).

Ultimately, all will come to a knowledge of his mission, and many will develop a testimony of the work he began. After all, he "holds the keys of this last dispensation, and no man or woman in this dispensation will ever enter into the celestial kingdom of God without the consent of Joseph Smith." (Brigham Young, J.D., 7:289-290).

Many champions of truth have followed in the footsteps of the Prophet. Having gone word by- word and line-by-line through his writings, "and having read everything he could find on his life, B.H. Roberts found Joseph Smith to be possessed of a deeper and richer comprehension of Christ than anyone he had read in the Christian tradition since the apostles. Through all Roberts' buffetings and his intellectual probings, honing his own mind with the major figures in the history of Western thought, this conviction never diminished. And as his extensive knowledge of the alternatives increased, his conviction deepened: Joseph Smith told the truth. He was a prism of the Lord Jesus Christ." (Truman Madsen, "Defender of The Faith," p.93). "Roberts was once asked an intricate question on the life and teaching of the Prophet. As he answered, the elders saw their beginning curiosity expanded to vast proportions. They nodded in grateful admiration. All of a sudden, he looked up and raised his hands and said: "Brother. Joseph, I have fought for you, I have defended you, I have loved you!" and made one of the most spiritual and emotional outbursts. I have never heard a stronger testimony of the Prophet." ("Defender of The Faith," p. 388).

He could muster courage in even the most difficult circumstances. His close associate Parley P. Pratt described his reaction to vile guards at Liberty Jail who had been boasting of their depredations against the Mormons: "Silence, ye fiends of the infernal pit!" Joseph cried. "In the name of Jesus Christ, I rebuke you, and command you to be still. I will not live another minute and hear such language. Cease such talk, or you or I die this instant!"

He ceased to speak. He stood erect in terrible majesty. Chained, and without a weapon; calm, unruffled and dignified as an angel, he looked upon the quailing guards, whose weapons were lowered or dropped to the ground, whose knees smote together, and who, shrinking into a corner, or crouching at his feet, begged his pardon, and remained quiet 'til a change of the guards.

I have seen the ministers of justice, clothed in magisterial robes, and criminals arraigned before them, while life was suspended on a breath, in the courts of England; I have witnessed a Congress in solemn session to give laws to nations; I have tried to conceive of kings, of royal courts, of thrones and crowns; and of emperors assembled to decide the fate of kingdoms; but dignity and majesty have I seen but once, as it stood in chains, at midnight, in a dungeon in an obscure village in Missouri." ("Autobiography of Parley P. Pratt," Classics in Mormon Literature Series, p. 179-80).

In 1823, Moroni counseled Joseph Smith: "Wherever the sound (of the marvelous work) shall go, it shall cause the ears of men to tingle, and wherever it shall be proclaimed, the pure in heart shall rejoice, while those who draw near to God with their mouths, and honor him with their lips, while their hearts are far from him, will seek its overthrow, and the destruction of those by whose hands it is carried. Therefore, marvel not if your name is made a derision and had as a by-word among such, if you are the instrument in bringing it, by the gift of God, to the knowledge of the people." (Oliver Cowdery, "The Messenger and Advocate," "The Gathering of Latter-day Israel, p. 79-80).

When we study his life, we are drawn inevitably to the conclusion that, when he receives his exaltation in the Celestial Kingdom of God, "Joseph Smith will be seated on the right hand of Christ." (Bruce R. McConkie, C.R., 10, 1949).

In the best sense of the word,
professors of religion are persevering
and stay focused on the tasks at hand. They
begin with the end in mind and settle for more,
and not for less. They are purposeful, determined,
disciplined, focused, and are not easily distracted
or persuaded. Their foundation is on bedrock. They
have depth and breadth, and have made regular
deposits to their spiritual bank accounts,
from which they may take timely,
strategic, and significant
withdrawals.

Prophet, Seer, and Revelator

"And Ammon said that a seer is a revelator and a prophet also; and a gift which is greater can no man have."
(Mosiah 8:16).

Prophet, seer, and revelator is an ecclesiastical title used in The Church of Jesus Christ of Latter-day Saints (LDS Church) that is currently applied to the members of the First Presidency and the Quorum of the Twelve Apostles. In the past, it has also been applied to the Presiding Patriarch of the church and the Assistant President of the Church.

The phrase "prophet, seer, and revelator" is derived from a number of revelations received by church founder Joseph Smith, Jr. The first revelation received by Smith after the organization of the church on 4 6, 1830 declared that "there shall be a record kept among you; and in it thou (Smith) shalt be called a seer, a translator, a prophet, an apostle of Jesus Christ, an elder of the church through the will of God the Father, and the grace of your Lord Jesus Christ"

In 1835, Smith further clarified the role of the presidents of the church. "The duty of the President of the office of the High Priesthood is to preside over the whole church, and ... to be a seer, a revelator, a translator, and a prophet." In 1841, Smith recorded a revelation that again restated these roles: "I give unto you my servant Joseph to be a presiding elder over all my church, to be a translator, a revelator, a seer, and prophet."

In 1836, approximately one year after Smith organized the church's Quorum of the Twelve Apostles, he instructed that the members of the First Presidency and the Apostles should also be accepted by the church as prophets, seers, and revelators: "I (Smith) made a short address, and called upon the several quorums, and all the congregation of Saints, to acknowledge the Presidency as Prophets and Seers and uphold them by their prayers ... I then called upon the quorums and congregation of Saints, to acknowledge the Twelve, who were present, as Prophets, Seers, Revelators, and special witnesses to all the nations of the earth holding the keys of the kingdom, to unlock it, or cause it to be done among them, and uphold them by their prayers."

Later revelations of Smith further confirmed that those other than the president of the church may hold these titles. For example, in 1841, a revelation described the role of Smith's brother Hyrum Smith as Assistant President of the Church. "And from this time forth I appoint unto him that he may be a prophet, and a seer, and a revelator unto my church, as well as my servant Joseph."

At the biannual general conference of the LDS Church, the name of the President of the Church is presented to the membership of the church as "prophet, seer, and revelator and President of The Church of Jesus Christ of Latter-day Saints." The membership of the church is invited to vote to "sustain" the president in these roles by the raising of the hand. The signaling of any opposing votes is also called for. Additionally, the counselors in the First Presidency and the members of the Quorum of the Twelve Apostles are sustained by the membership as "prophets, seers, and revelators." Until October 1979, the Presiding Patriarch the church was also sustained as a "prophet, seer, and revelator." Apostles that are not members of the Quorum of the Twelve or the First Presidency are not sustained as prophets, seers, and revelators.

The procedure of "sustaining" the prophets, seers, and revelators is repeated in local congregations of the church several times per year at stake, district, ward, or branch conferences. These procedures are mandated by the theology of the LDS Church, which dictates that the church shall be governed by the common consent of the membership. Prophet was first mention in Genesis 20:7. Prophets were first called seers in 1 Samuel 9:9.

The words prophet, seer, and revelator have separate and distinct meanings in the language of the Latter-day Saint movement. Apostle John A. Widtsoe described the meanings of the terms and the differences between them: "What Is the Meaning of The Title 'Prophet, Seer, And Revelator'?

"The three separate titles in the general title have much the same meaning in popular usage, yet there are differences sufficiently important to justify their use. "A prophet is a teacher. That is the essential meaning of the word. He teaches the body of truth, the gospel, revealed by the Lord to man; and under inspiration explains it to the understanding of the people. He is an expounder of truth. Moreover, he shows that the way to human happiness is through obedience to God's law. He calls to repentance those who wander away from the truth. He becomes a warrior for the consummation of the Lord's purposes with respect to the human family. The purpose of his life is to uphold the Lord's plan of salvation. All this he does by close communion with the Lord, until he is 'full of power by the spirit of the Lord.' (Micah 3:8; see also D&C 20:26, 34:10, & 43:16).

"The teacher must learn before he can teach. Therefore, in ancient and modern times there have been schools of the prophets, in which the mysteries of the kingdom have been taught to men who would go out to teach the gospel and to fight the battles of the Lord. These 'prophets' need not be called to an office; they go out as teachers of truth, always and everywhere.

"A prophet also receives revelations from the Lord. These may be explanations of truths already received, or new truths not formerly possessed by man. Such revelations are always confined to the official position held. The lower will not receive revelations for the higher office.

"In the course of time the word 'prophet' has come to mean, perhaps chiefly, a man who receives revelations, and directions from the Lord. The principal business of a prophet has mistakenly been thought to foretell coming events, to utter prophecies, which is only one of the several prophetic functions.

"In the sense that a prophet is a man who receives revelations from the Lord, the titles 'seer and revelator' merely amplify the larger and inclusive meaning of the title 'prophet.' Clearly, however, there is much wisdom in the specific statement of the functions of the prophet as seer and revelator, as is done in the conferences of the church.

"A seer is one who sees with spiritual eyes. He perceives the meaning of that which seems obscure to others; therefore, he is an interpreter and clarifier of eternal truth. He foresees the future from the past and the present. This he does by the power of the Lord operating through him directly, or indirectly with the aid of divine instruments such as the Urim and Thummim. In short, he is one who sees, who walk in the Lord's light with open eyes. (Mosiah 8:15-17).

"A revelator makes known, with the Lord's help, something before unknown. It may be new or forgotten truth, or a new or forgotten application of known truth to man's need. Always, the revelator deals with truth, certain truth (D&C 100:11) and always it comes with the divine stamp of approval. Revelation may be received in various ways, but it always presupposes that the revelator has so lived and conducted himself as to be in tune or harmony with the divine spirit of revelation, the spirit of truth, and therefore capable of receiving divine messages.

"In summary: A prophet is a teacher of known truth; a seer is a perceiver of hidden truth, a revelator is a bearer of new truth. In the widest sense, the one most commonly used, the title, prophet, includes the other titles and makes the prophet a teacher, perceiver, and bearer of truth."

Asked, how he could govern so many people, the Prophet Joseph said: "I teach them correct principles, and they govern themselves." He was a staunch believer in our inherent ability to obey correct principles within an atmosphere of intellectual freedom that is free of temporal restraints. On one occasion, he declared: "It is one of the first principles of my life, and one that I have cultivated from my childhood, having been taught it by my father, to allow everyone the liberty of conscience."

(The) Q Continuum

"The light
of the body is the
eye; if, therefore, thine
eye be single, thy whole
body shall be full of light."
(3 Nephi 13:22).

In the Star Trek Universe, the Q Continuum is a hyper-dimensional plane of existence inhabited by a race known as the Q. The Q have powers similar to those possessed by the seers of whom Ammon spoke, who "know of things which are past, and also of things which are to come, and by them shall all things be revealed, or, rather, shall secret things be made manifest, and hidden things shall come to light, and things which are not known shall be made known by them, and also things shall be made known by them which otherwise could not be known." (Mosiah 8:17).

We do not possess the powers of the Q; in fact, in one episode Q tells Grand Nagus Zek: "I worship stupidity, and you're my new god." With our poor lenses cannot discern what they see, but when our eye is single to faith, our bodies "shall be full of light." (3 Nephi 13:22). Joseph Smith confirmed the reality of that promise when he said of the revelatory process with which he was becoming increasingly familiar: "My whole body was full of light, and I could see even out at the ends of my fingers and toes." (N.B. Lundwall, "The Vision," p. 11). This may be why the angel Moroni hovered in the air during his visits to Joseph Smith in his chamber and why his hands and his feet were naked, for he could "see" with every part of his body. Every child of God potentially possesses this gift of the Q that only waits to be revealed. "If your eye be single to my glory," the Lord promised, "your whole bodies shall be filled with light, and there shall be no darkness in you; and that body which is filled with light comprehendeth all things." (D&C 88:67).

Orson Pratt was familiar with neither the Q nor their Continuum, but he did appreciate the ramifications of the truth that celestial beings have the ability to perceive with all parts of their bodies. "The spirit," he said, "is inherently capable of experiencing the sensations of light. I think we could then see in different directions at once. Instead of looking in one particular direction, we could then look all around us at the same instant." (J.D., 2:238-248).

The Q are on a higher plane of existence and thus is not subject to the same laws of physics as is normal space. Their influence may be analogous to that of the Lord, of Whom the Psalmist wrote: "Fire goeth before (Him), and burneth up his enemies round about. His lightnings enlightened the world: the earth saw, and trembled. The hills melted like wax at the presence of the Lord of the whole earth." (Psalms 97:3-5). As Mormon observed: "The dust of the earth moveth hither and thither, to the dividing asunder, at the command of our great and everlasting God. Yea, behold at his voice do the hills and the mountains tremble and quake. And by the power of his voice, they are broken up, and become smooth, yea, even like unto a valley. Yea, by the power of his voice doth the whole earth shake; Yea, by the power of his voice, do the foundations rock, even to the very center. Yea, and if he say unto the earth - Move - it is moved. Yea, if he say unto the earth - Thou shalt go back, that it lengthen out the day for many hours - it is done." (Helaman 12:8-14). Thus is manifest the awful power of His Presence. It may not be so much that God commands the earth to tremble, but rather that it is the proximal influence of His nature itself that causes the foundation of our world to rock to its very core.

The Q can manipulate time, space, matter, and energy. They are the products of our imagination, and we know that in the beginning, it was "the Gods (and not the Q, who) organized and formed the heavens and the earth" by defining the boundaries of both the temporal universe and the eternal world. (Abraham 4:1). By the power of faith, They set the conditions "by which the worlds were framed, (and) all things in heaven, on the earth, or under the earth. (These) exist by reason of faith as it existed in (the mind of the Gods). Had it not been for this principle of faith, the worlds would never have been framed, neither would man have been formed of the dust. It is this principle by which Jehovah works, and through which He exercises power over all temporal as well as eternal things." (Joseph Smith, "Lectures on Faith," #1).

Perhaps the writers of TNG inherited their creative "Q" from the Prophet himself. The Q are omnipotent, omniscient, and for all practical purposes omnipresent. W.W. Phelps presaged the Q when he wrote: "If you could hie to Kolob in the twinkling of an eye, and then continue onward with that same speed to fly, do you think that you could ever through all eternity find out the generation where Gods began to be? Or see the grand beginning where space did not extend? Or view the last creation where Gods and matter end? Methinks the Spirit whispers, 'No man has found pure space nor seen the outside curtains where nothing has a place.' The works of God continue and worlds and lives abound. Improvement and progression have one eternal round. There is no end to matter; there is no end to space; there is no end to spirit; there is no end to race. There is no end to virtue; there is no end to might; there is no end to wisdom; there is no end to light. There is no end to union; there is no end to youth; there is no end to priesthood; there is no end to truth. There is no end to glory; there is no end to love; there is no end to being; there is no death above." ("If You Could Hie to Kolob").

The Q are invulnerable and immortal. Perhaps the Q are as God, Who was described by John the Revelator as One Whose "head and his hairs were white like wool, as white as snow; and his eyes were as a flame of fire; and his feet like unto fine brass, as if they burned in a furnace; and his voice as the sound of many waters." (Revelation 1:14-15). Joseph Smith said that under the feet of God "was a paved work of pure gold, in color like amber ... His countenance shone above the brightness of the sun; and his voice was as the sound of the rushing of great waters." (D&C 110:2-3).

The Q have the ability to perceive events in the past, present, and future. So too does the Lord our "God, even Jesus Christ, the Great I Am, Alpha and Omega, the beginning and the end, the same which looked upon the wide expanse of eternity, and all the seraphic hosts of heaven, before the world was made; the same which knoweth all things, for all things are present before (His) eyes; (I am) the same which spake and the world was made, and all things came" by Me. (D&C 38:1-3).

Both physics and the Q Continuum (not to mention theology) would suggest that there are no privileged frames of reference. The galaxies are imbedded in time and attached to space, but the fabric of the universe is constantly expanding. If we ask where and when the creation took place, the answer is everywhere and forever. The universe is warped temporally and spatially and expands like a balloon and may explain why the Lord said to Moses: "As one earth shall pass away, and the heavens thereof even so shall another come, and there is no end to my works." (Moses 1:38). "For by him were all things created that are in heaven, and that are in earth, visible and invisible, whether they be thrones, or dominions, or principalities, or powers: all things were created by him." (Colossians 1:16).

The Q can manipulate the fabric of existence, weaving it into fantastically intricate patterns. Carl Sagan suggested an idea that may have been familiar to inhabitants of the Q Continuum, but which to the human mind is "strange, haunting, evocative, and one of the most exquisite conjectures in science or religion. It is entirely undemonstrated, and it may never be proven. But it stirs the blood. There is, we are told, an infinite hierarchy of universes, so that an elementary particle, such as an electron, in our universe, would, if penetrated, reveal itself to be an entire closed universe. Within it, organized into the local equivalent of galaxies and smaller structures, are an immense number of other, much tinier elementary particles, which are themselves universes at the next level, and so on forever, an infinite downward regression, universes within universes, endlessly. And upward as well. Our familiar universe of galaxies and stars, planets, and people, would be a single elementary particle in the next universe up, the first step of another infinite progress. This is the only religious idea I know that surpasses the endless number of infinitely old cycling universes in Hindu cosmology. What would those other universes be like? To enter them, we would somehow have to penetrate a fourth physical dimension. Poised at the edge of forever, we would jump off" into life's ultimate incredible journey. ("Cosmos," p. 262-267).

Perhaps the title sequence of Star Trek Enterprise episodes should be amended to declare: "Time and Space and even Existence are the final frontiers. These are the voyages of the Starship Enterprise. Its continuing mission: To explore strange new worlds, to seek out new life and new civilizations, to boldly go where no one has gone before."

The Q Continuum is unconstrained by linear time and the three familiar dimensions of space. When Enterprise crewmembers are plucked from the ship by Q, we are reminded how in similar fashion, John was taken from his temporal and spatial surroundings into the presence of God. He was brought into the "depths of eternity" in the "hereafter," somehow at the same time both "here" and "after," which although vague is about as specific as one can get when referring to a higher dimension that may be analogous to the Q Continuum. Thus, John described what he both saw and heard as "lightnings and thunderings and voices" from the unseen world. (Revelation 4:5). To Joseph Smith, the voice of the Great Jehovah struck a similar chord "as the sound of the rushing of great waters." (D&C 110:3).

For the Q, the arrow of time moves in two directions. Our stable temporal frame of reference allows us to live within a timeline that overlays the tapestry of our familiar three-dimensional space. It reassures us that the sun will come up tomorrow, and that there will be 24 hours in each day. Without the veil insulating us from God's unrestrained, unencumbered, unreserved, and uninhibited temporal reality, life would be too confusing for most people. This is corroborated by the chaotic consequences of the manipulation of time by the Q. In several episodes of TNG, Enterprise crewmembers are bewildered by sensory overload that follows the mischievous manipulation of time by the Q.

In the real world, when the veil that encloses us evaporates, time will be no more, and as we ease into eternity, we will become increasingly comfortable with the transformation to the native and natural environment of our former home. (D&C 84:100). "Thus it is that we are never really at home in time," wrote Neal A. Maxwell. "Alternately, we find ourselves impatiently wishing to hasten its passage or to hold back the dawn. We can do neither, of course. Whereas the bird is at home in the air, we are clearly not at home in time because we belong to eternity. As much as any one thing, time whispers to us that we are strangers here. If it were natural to us, why is it that we have so many clocks, and wear wristwatches? "Without the veil," he concluded, "we would lose the precious insulation so necessary for our mortal probation and maturation. Our brief mortal walk in a darkening world would lose its meaning, for one would scarcely carry the flashlight of faith at noonday and in the presence of the Light of the world." ("B.Y.U. Speeches of The Year," 1979).

The Q can move about in time and space by the power of their will. Brigham Young said: "I long for the time that a point of the finger, or motion of the hand, will express every idea without utterance." When men, like the Q, are "full of the light of eternity, then the eye is not the only medium through which he sees, nor the brain the only means by which he understands. When the whole body is full of the Holy Ghost, he can see behind him with as much ease, without turning his head, as he can see before him. If you have not had that experience, you ought to have. It is not the optic nerve alone that gives the knowledge of surrounding objects to the mind. I shall yet see the time that I can converse with this people, and not speak to them. We are at present low, weak, and groveling in the dark, but we are planted here in weakness for the purpose of exaltation." (J.D. 1:70-71).

The Q can "look down upon" our affairs from a perspective that is to us both foreign and indescribable. Brigham Young taught that when we die we go into the spiritual world, "Do the spirits go beyond the boundaries of this organized earth?" He asked. "No, they do not. They can see us, but we cannot see them, unless our eyes are opened." ("The Contributor," 10:9, quoted in N.B. Lundwall, "The Vision," p. 55-56, See "Discourses of Brigham Young," p. 376). This only makes sense if beings from the unseen world exist in a parallel spatial dimension, which may be for them like our being in a room with a one-way mirror. They, like the Q, can witness the every-day world on a whim, but to those of us trapped in the here-and-now, trying to see what lies in the other "direction" beyond the mirror's reflective surface is fruitless. Many Star Trek episodes suggest that because we are bound by the laws and conditions of our temporal and spatial reality, all we can hope to gain by venturing onto the unstable curricula of theoretical physics is a confirmation of the validity of that which we already know, which is really only our reflection in the mirror of experience.

The Q can move from one point in the universe to another by overriding the normal constraints of the laws of physics. At the speed of light, it would take at least 10 or 15 billion years for a Q to traverse the known universe. So, in the real world, physically plodding along at light speed from one point to another seems unlikely because those of us who have gotten the Lord's attention know that His intercession can be instantaneous. Samuel was once moved to exclaim: "In my distress I called upon the Lord, and cried to my God: and he did (immediately) hear my voice out of his temple, and my cry did enter into his ears. Then the earth shook and trembled; the foundations of heaven moved and shook," as God instantly responded to His disciple's entreaty in a powerful manifestation from His higher dimensional reality. (2 Samuel 22:7-8). So it is when the faithful pray to Heavenly Father. As James declared: "The effectual fervent prayer of a righteous man availeth much." (James 5:16). God hears us even as we cry out to Him, and He has the power to immediately respond to our needs, wherever and whenever He or they may be. Existing in another dimension that is analogous to the Q Continuum might give God the ability to hear all of our petitions simultaneously, without the inherent limitations of three-dimensional time and space, time warp notwithstanding. The omnipresent example of the Q gives God more plausible credibility.

Additional insight into God's dominion may come from accounts of the creation of the earth. Brigham Young used very unusual language when referring to the earth as it was at the time of the Fall and when it will receive its paradisiacal glory. He said: "When the earth was framed and brought into existence and man was placed upon it, it was near the throne of our Father in Heaven. And when man fell … the earth fell into space, and took up its abode in this planetary system, and the sun became our light. This is the glory the earth came from, and when it is glorified, it will return again unto the presence of the Father, and it will dwell there." (J.D., 17:143). This description of falling into space and then leaving space to return to the presence of the Father suggests adjacent spatial dimensions that are also inferred by the characteristics of the Continuum. The Q mimic the prophecy of Micah: "The Lord cometh forth out of his place, and will come down, and tread upon the high places of the earth." (Micah 1:3). At the very least, the various scenarios and plot twists in TNG episodes involving the Q make more sense when viewed against the backdrop of religious experience.

The Q jealously guard their powers. Heavenly Father is more expansive than the Q, and promises to use His influence to sanctify the immortal world and transform it so that it "will be made like unto crystal and will be a Urim and Thummim to the inhabitants who dwell thereon, whereby all things pertaining to an inferior kingdom, or all kingdoms of a lower order, will be made manifest to those who dwell on it." (D&C 130:9). Nevertheless, with a bit of whimsy, Q does confide to Captain Picard that he is "the closest thing in this universe that I have to a friend." ("Deja Q").

The Q are not confined by the narrow limitations of corruptible flesh. What will our faculties be when our spirits are free of the incarceration within our mortal bodies? Orson Pratt spoke of the ability to consider many different ideas at the same time, instead of focusing our attention and following only one course of reasoning. "Suppose He should give us a sixth sense, a seventh, an eighth, a ninth, or a fiftieth?" he asked. "All these different senses would convey to us new ideas, as much so as the senses of tasting, smelling, or seeing communicate different ideas from that of hearing. Do we suppose our five senses converse with all the elements of nature? No."

The Q nourish the mind-expanding idea that "knowledge will rush in from all quarters; it will come in like the light which flows from the sun, penetrating every part, informing the Spirit, and giving understanding concerning ten thousand things at the same time; and the mind will be capable of receiving and retaining all. Not one object at a time, but a vast multitude of objects will rush before our vision, and will be present before us, filling us in a moment with the knowledge of worlds more numerous than the sands of the seashore. Will we be able to bear it? Yes, our minds will be strengthened in proportion to the amount of information imparted. It is this tabernacle in its present condition that prevents us from a more enlarged understanding. When we burst beyond the confines of our mortal clay, he continued, "we shall look not in one direction, but in every direction. This will be calculated to give us new ideas concerning the creations of God, (and) information and knowledge we never can know as long as we dwell in this mortal tabernacle. We shall have other sources of gaining knowledge besides these inlets called senses. We will be endowed, after we leave this tabernacle, with powers and faculties which we now have no knowledge of, by which we may learn what is round about us." ("The Increased Powers of Faculties of Mind in a Future State," Excerpted from "Temples of the Most High," p. 299-312, also J.D., 2:238-248).

The Q do not grow old. When we move into eternity, or into the Q Continuum, time will lose all significance, and "See you later," will cease to be in our vocabulary. Time, that we too frequently viewed as a predator that stalked us all our lives, may then be fondly remembered as a companion that accompanied us on our journey through mortality, reminding us to cherish every moment. We will find that mortality itself was only one of innumerable layers of reality, and that our perspective was faulty as long as we believed it to be unique. We may be shocked to learn for the first time that it was not our natural dimension. We will come to understand why it was that we were never entirely comfortable in our mortal circumstances, that we were "strangers and pilgrims on the earth." (Hebrews 11:13). This will, in turn, explain our innate thrust always toward the future and beyond the horizon.

We will even find that growing "old" was strictly and uniquely a quality of mortality and a brilliant mechanism designed by Heavenly Father that afforded us an opportunity to gauge the approach of our reunion with Him in a higher-dimensional world. We will discover that because we lived in only one dimly lighted corner of reality, it was difficult for us to really appreciate our potential and the power of our position, that we would one day "flourish in immortal youth, unhurt amidst the war of elements, the wreck of matter, and the crash of worlds." (Joseph Addison, "Cato," Act 5, Scene 1). From our very narrow perspective, frozen in time as it were, death seemed so distant, and its consequences so remote. Too often, we grew complacent in our indifference to the subtle message reflected in the passage of time, and failed to understand its eternal consequences.

The Q are consummate multi-taskers. Hugh Nibley reasoned: "As to taking a calm and deliberate look at more than one thing at a time, that is a gift denied us at present. I cannot imagine what such a view of the world would be like, but it would be more real and correct than the one we have now. Once we can see the possibilities that lie in being able to see more than one thing at a time, the universe takes on new dimensions and God (never mind the Q) takes over." ("Zeal Without Knowledge," "Nibley on The Timely and Timeless," p. 263-264). We shall then be as the Brother of

Jared, who, when overshadowed by the Spirit, could look upon past, present, and future generations at once. "They all came before him, and there was not a soul that he did not behold." (Mormon 8:35).

"The heavens they are many," explained the Lord, "and they cannot be numbered unto man; but they are numbed unto me, for they are mine." (Moses 1:36). Plainly, we are dealing with two orders of minds, that of mortals, and that of God and the Q Continuum. "For my thoughts are not your thoughts, neither are your ways my ways, saith the Lord. For as the heavens are higher than the earth, so are ... my thoughts than your thoughts." (Isaiah 55:8-9). The Q roam the wide expanse of the universe, much as Federation starships do, for whom space is the Final Frontier. One particularly bold explorer, perhaps an ancestor of Jean Luc Picard, declared that he intended to go not only "farther than any man has been before me, but as far as I think it is possible for a man to go." ("Captain James Cook: Explorer, Navigator, and Pioneer," BBC). The Q might brazenly recite an even more audacious couplet: "As Q is God once was, as God is Q may become."

The time will come when we shall enter into the spatial reality of God's Rest, when we have gained a perfect knowledge of the divinity of the work, and by our actions no longer suffer from fear, doubt, apprehension of danger, the religious turmoil of the world, or from the vagaries of men. These are the self-limiting conditions that blind us to a larger view of life. His Rest is born of a settled conviction of the truth in our minds, and an assurance that obedience to celestial principles will bring His reality within our reach. His invitation to follow Him is prefaced by the action verb "to come." If we do come to Him, just where and how far will that journey carry us?

After we have kept our second estate, and have had glory added upon our heads, what shall we be like? What does it mean to be clothed with immortality and eternal life? Will we then more closely resemble in image and likeness our Father in Heaven? Are we now gods and goddesses in embryo? Is our genetic code divine? Is it our destiny to mature to the stature of our Heavenly Parents? The evolutionary progress of the Q envisioned by the writers of TNG would suggest an affirmative answer. In the final episode of Star Trek: The Next Generation, Captain Picard joins the crew's regular poker game, expressing regret that he had not done so before. The stakes are outlined, and he says: "The sky's the limit," suggesting the Final Frontier has borders yet to be probed, opportunities to be had, and adventures to be experienced.

Perhaps the interest of the Q in humanity was first kindled by the exploits of Captain James T. Kirk, captain of the Enterprise (NCC-1701). Captain Kirk's middle name was Tiberius. Tiberius Julius Caesar Augustus was born 2,275 years before Kirk, and was one of ancient Rome's greatest generals and tacticians. Thus, Tiberius would have been an appropriate name for the youngest graduate of Starfleet Academy to be given his own command. It may have been his bold daring that caught the attention of Q. They may have thought, as did Hamlet: What a piece of work is a man, how noble in reason, how infinite in faculties, in form and moving how express and admirable, in action how like an angel, in apprehension how like a god! The beauty of the world, the paragon of animals." (Shakespeare, "Hamlet," Act 2, Scene 2). However, this description would come back to bite Q, in the episode entitled "Hide and Q." As long as their powers remain intact, the Q have little apparent need for redemption. In the episode entitled "Deja Q," after he has lost his powers, Q is told by Captain Picard: "For all your protestations of friendship, your real reason for being here is protection." Q responds: "You're very smart, Jean-Luc. But I know human beings. They're all sopping over with compassion and forgiveness. They can't wait to absolve almost any offense. It's an inherent weakness in the breed." To which Picard says: "On the contrary, it is a strength."

The Q show a unique interest in the development of humanity. As Q told Captain Picard: "The hall is rented, the orchestra engaged. It's now time to see if you can dance." ("Q Who"). But the Lord goes a step further, promising to give His children at least a portion of His own powers, but only after they have prepared themselves, submitted to instruction, and better understood their responsibilities. He suggests patience, "that they themselves may be prepared, and that my people may be taught more perfectly, and have experience, and know more perfectly concerning their duty, and the things which I require at their hands. And this cannot be brought to pass until mine elders are endowed with power from on high." (D&C 105:9-11).

The Q believe that humanity is compelled to explore the very nature of existence itself. In the episode "All Good Things," Q mentions that Jean Luc Picard was destined to consider possibilities that he had never before imagined, implying that there are states that are natural to the Q but foreign to mortal experience. The Q became the catalyst for motivation that stirred the Enterprise crew as a fire in the bones. Christopher Columbus recounted the similar impetus for his voyage of discovery by simply saying: "The Holy Spirit gave me fire for the deed." Our hearts burn within us when God gives us "knowledge by His Holy Spirit, yea, by the unspeakable gift of the Holy Ghost." (D&C 121:26 & 28). Thus did Jeremiah describe his feelings: "His word was in mine heart as a burning fire shut up in my bones, and I was weary with forbearing, and I could not stay." (Jeremiah 20:9). The Spirit worked on Belshazzar's troubled conscience to the extent that his "countenance was changed, and his thoughts troubled him, so that the joints of his loins were loosed, and his knees smote one against another." (Daniel 5:6). Joseph Smith was moved to declare of his revelatory experiences: "The still small voice ... whispereth through and pierceth all things, and often times it maketh my bones to quake while it maketh manifest."(D&C 85:6).

As the process unfolds and our maturity disciplines our unsteady steps, we recognize the wisdom in the observation of Hans Christian Anderson, who said: "Our lives are fairy tales waiting to be written by the finger of God." A number of the chapters in our stories have already been set to paper, and we don't know how many remain to be written. But we do know this: We cannot start over and make a new beginning, but we can begin now and make a new ending. We believe God when He says: "If your eye be single to my glory, your whole bodies shall be filled with light, and there shall be no darkness in you; and that body which is filled with light comprehendeth all things." (D&C 88:67). For "that which is of God is light; and he that receiveth light, and continueth in God, receiveth more light; and that light groweth brighter and brighter until the perfect day." (D&C 50:24). In marvelous ways, as we gain spiritual maturity, "by doing our duty, faith increases until it becomes perfect knowledge." (Heber J. Grant, C.R., 4/1934).

As the seasons of our lives unfold, we learn that "Life is a sheet of paper white, where each of us may write a line or two, and then comes night. Greatly begin! If thou hast time for but a line, make that sublime. Not failure, but low aim, is crime." (James Russell Lowell).

In one episode of Star Trek, Q is stripped of his powers and becomes human. ("Deja Q"). He is "the king who would be man," lamenting: "I have no powers! Q, the ordinary! Q, the miserable, Q, the desperate!" The difference between the Q and our Alpha progenitors is that Adam and Eve had a longitudinal view and perspective on life that was denied the Q, who seem to have been myopic in their vision, their omniscience notwithstanding. Our first parents cherished the opportunity to become mortal. "Blessed be the name of God," Adam declared, "for because of my transgression my eyes are opened, and in this life I shall have joy, and again in the flesh I shall see God. And Eve, his wife, heard all these things and was glad, saying: Were it not for our transgression we never should have had seed, and never should have known good and evil, and the joy of our redemption, and the eternal life which God giveth unto all the obedient." (Moses 5:10-11). Due to an apparent genetic anomaly during their evolution, the Q seem to be incapable of experiencing the adrenalin rush that comes when mortals yield themselves to the power of the Atonement and become new creatures in Christ.

Q confided to Captain Picard: "Truthfully, Jean-Luc, I've been entirely preoccupied by a most frightening experience of my own. A couple of hours ago, I realized that my body was no longer functioning properly. I felt weak. I could no longer stand. The life was oozing out of me. I lost consciousness." The captain replied: "You fell asleep." Q exclaimed:

"Oh, how terrifying. How can you stand it day after day?" To which the captain said: "You'll get used to it." "What other dangers await me? Q protested. I'm not prepared for this. I need guidance."

When his powers are later restored, he exclaims: "I'm forgiven! My brothers and sisters of the Continuum have taken me back. I'm immortal again! Omnipotent again!" Q does not realize that mortality is a brief but welcome interlude in the grand scheme of things, and that all that is necessary may be accomplished before the book is closed on this chapter in our lives and we move on to perfection. They cannot understand that death is as much a part of life as is birth, and Adam's transgression was integral to the execution of the Plan, inasmuch as it gave us the opportunity to be born into this world, to live, and to die. Living in eternity before our births, we were able to preview the big picture and so we shouted for joy. (Job 38:7). When it was finally our time to come to earth, others smiled at our birth, while we cried. When it is our time to leave, our loved ones will cry at our departure, while we will smile. Only then will death be seen for what it really is, "a mere comma, and not an exclamation point." (Neal A. Maxwell, "Ensign," 5/1983). It is "not extinguishing the light, but rather putting out the lamp because the dawn has come." (Ramindraneth Tagore).

The Q generally observe the principle of free will (but only if it suits their fancy). Among the shortcomings of the Continuum is the fact that it has not embraced the concept of opposition and does not realize that progress is dependent upon the opportunity to choose in an atmosphere without external constraints. The stagnation within the Continuum that is suggested by the plot lines of several episodes reflects its ignorance of this eternal principle. However, Q did warn Captain Picard: "You judge yourselves against the pitiful adversaries you've encountered so far - the Romulans and the Klingons. They're nothing compared to what's waiting. Picard, you are about to move into areas of the galaxy containing wonders more incredible than you can possibly imagine, and terrors to freeze your soul." He continued: "It's not safe out here! It's wondrous, with treasures to satiate desires both subtle and gross. But it's not for the timid." ("Q Who?").

The Q anticipate with prescience the actions of the crew. As Q told Captain Picard (noted above): "Con permiso, Capitan. The hall is rented, the orchestra engaged. It's now time to see if you can dance." ("Q Who"). The Lord's interest in our performance is remarkable, for He already "knoweth the thoughts of man." (Psalms 94:11). But the difference between His interest and the curiosity of the Q is that the latter look at mortality as the whole of existence, and pain, sorrow, failure, and short life as misfortunes. The vantage point of the Q Continuum may be expansive, but it lacks the capacity to develop the moral element of responsibility we call faith that is provided by the mortal expression of God's perspective that is within the Plan of Salvation.

The Q are always lingering in the background, watching with interest the activities of the Enterprise crew, even though they characterized Twenty-Fourth Century Earth as a "dreary place" and "mind-numbingly dull." For our part, we intuitively wish we "could remember the days before our birth, and if we knew the Father before we came to earth. In quiet moments when we're all alone, we close our eyes and try to see our Heavenly home. Although we can't remember and cannot clearly see, we listen to the spirit and so we must believe. But still we wonder, and we hope to find the answer to the question that is on our minds. Where is Heaven? Is it very far? We would like to know if it's beyond the brightest star." (Janice Kapp Perry).

The Q allow Starship personnel to experience both the positive and negative consequences relating to their exploration of the universe. As Q told Jean Luc Picard after a particularly traumatic encounter with the Borg: "If you can't take a little bloody nose, maybe you ought to go back home and crawl under your bed. It's not safe out here. ("Q Who"). Joseph Smith similarly exhorted the Saints: "Brethren, shall we not go on in so great a cause? Go forward and not backward. Courage, brethren; and on, on to the victory." (D&C 128:22).

The Q recognize the fact that "the galaxy can be a dangerous place when you're on your own." ("Q-Less"). Although they have the power to change circumstances, God has the power to transform lives. They would shoot the arrow blindly, and then move the target so we would think we had scored a bullseye. He would teach us to aim with precision to hit the bullseye 100% of the time. They would say "You miss 100% of the shot you don't take." He would encourage us to practice as often as possible, and learn to make 100% of the shots we do take.

Unconsciously, the Q may reflect the feelings of God that He is too frequently unappreciated. In "Tapestry," Q says: "I gave you something most mortals never experience – a second chance at life. And now all you do is complain." At least superficially, they are alike. When we cultivate gratitude, wonderful things happen. Good eclipses evil. Love overpowers jealousy, hate, and prejudice. Light drives away darkness. Knowledge banishes ignorance. Humility overwhelms pride. Courtesy checks rudeness. Appreciation overcomes thanklessness. Abundance overshadows poverty. Well-being replaces weakness. Simplicity supplants perplexity. Harmony displaces discord. Faith controls fear. Hope casts out despair. Charity subdues selfishness. Joy deposes unhappiness, sadness, dejection, and misery. Confidence is substituted for timidity. Certainty dethrones bewilderment. Assurance dislodges discouragement and even despair. "Those who live in thanksgiving daily have a way of opening their eyes to the wonders and beauties of this world as though seeing them for the first time. Those who live in thanksgiving daily are usually among the happiest people on earth." (Joseph Wirthlin, "B.Y.U. Devotional," 10/31/2000).

The Q Continuum validates Lehi's aphorism that "there must needs be opposition in all things. (2 Nephi 9:24). Q exclaims: "Of course there's no suffering! They're all happy! Happy people! Look at them!" To which Q3 responds: "They don't dare feel sad. If only they could! It would be progress." ("Deathwish"). "If pain and sorrow and total punishment immediately followed the doing of evil, no soul would repeat a misdeed. If joy and peace and rewards were instantaneously given the doer of good, there could be no evil. All would do good and not because of the rightness of doing good. There would be no test of strength, no development of character, no growth of powers, no free agency only Satanic controls. Should all prayers be immediately answered according to our selfish desires and our limited understanding, then there would be little or no suffering, sorrow, disappointment or even death, and if these were not there would also be an absence of joy, success, resurrection, eternal life, and Godhood." (Spencer W. Kimball, "B.Y.U. Devotional," 12/6/1955).

The unity within the Q Continuum is only a shadow of that found within the Godhead. Strength, safety, sanctuary, solidarity, stability, security, and steadiness are qualities of the Continuum. But it is still only a shadow of the unity of the faithful who are as one, able to "stand independent above all other creatures beneath the celestial world." (D&C 78:14). The Saints recognize that they may enjoy "the unity of the Spirit in the bond of peace." (Ephesians 4:3) Unity in conviction and of purpose is one of the characteristics of the Lord's true church, which is "of one accord, (and) of one mind." (Philippians 2:2). It is a miracle that within its organizations, all things are "done by common consent ... by much prayer and faith." (D&C 26:2). Church members echo Paul, who declared to the Romans: "We, being many, are one body in Christ." (Romans 12:5). No wonder that the Lord told His disciples that it would be possible for them to "be one," and then warned, "and if ye are not one ye are not mine." (D&C 38:27). The Continuum stands in stark contrast to the endless possibilities of mortality's learning laboratory. Q3 observed: "When I was a respected philosopher, I argued that the purity of the Continuum was a great thing, the road, the endless possibilities; only they're not so endless after all. At the beginning of the 'New Age,' there was the exhilaration of discovery, the animated discussions of new things learned. But after a time, all had been learned. All had been shared. Listen to their dialogues now. They haven't spoken for millennia. There's nothing left to say!" He continued: "Your mission is to explore. Imagine you'd explored everything, that there's nothing left. Would you want to live forever? For us, the disease is immortality." ("Deathwish"). Q3 described the living hell of an immortal vacuum in the absence of morality. The intellectual prowess of those inhabiting his Continuum would be equivalent to the dull, monotonous, and mind-numbing hum of a super-computer that for all its binary capabilities and permutations is incapable of experiencing the qualities of morality and feeling.

The evolution of the Q to a plateau of omniscience and omnipotence has selectively eliminated the very things that would have guaranteed eternal happiness. In the episode entitled "The Q and The Grey," Q mused to Captain Janeway: "I've been single for billions of years. It was fun at first, gallivanting all over the galaxy, using my omnipotence to impress women of every species. The fact is, it's left me empty. I want someone to love me for myself. I guess what I'm saying is, I want a relationship. I just thought if you and I had a child, it would give me the kind of stability and security that I've been missing."

The Continuum would have done well to consider the Plan that encompasses God's ordained core curriculum leading to family exaltation. The Plan diagrams safe passage through the minefields of mortality, documents potential perils and pitfalls, charts the recommended route to refuge, measures our progress on the pathway to perfection, and maps out success strategies for abundant living. Its elements are similar to the World Wide Web that requires only computer literacy, an I.P address with a network, and relevant hardware and software. It has the potential to order our chaotic world, to bless us with clarity rather than confusion, to teach fluency in the language of the spirit, and to educate those who are functionally illiterate to be mesmerized by the power of the Word. In simple binary terms, the Plan is our access code and our password leading to happiness. It is far superior to the heartless curriculum of the Continuum, that would have done well to heed the counsel of Jacob: Because the Q "are learned they think they are wise, and they hearken not unto the counsel of God, for they set it aside, supposing they know of themselves, wherefore, their wisdom is foolishness and it profteth them not. (2 Nephi 9:28).

The "gift" of immortality enjoyed by the Q, is eerily reminiscent of the counterfeit plan of the adversary. As Jacob taught: "Death hath passed upon all men, to fulfil the merciful plan of the great Creator," Whose omniscience, it would seem, is greater than that of the Q. (2 Nephi 9:6). Q wished: "If only I could let you see what my life is like. You're all mortals! Oh, how I envy you! The thing I want more than any other is to die!" ("Deathwish"). For all their talk, the Q seem unable to grasp the comforting concept that "death is not extinguishing the light; it is putting out the lamp because the dawn has come." (Rabindraneth Tagore). The Q are functionally illiterate when it comes to the grammar of the gospel. They may be "immortal," but at a terrible cost. They have forgotten that the three most important days of their lives are the day they were born, the day they find out why, and the day they die. They have become inured to the "resonance with realities on the other side of the veil" alluded to by Neal Maxwell. ("B.Y.U. Devotional," 11/1979).

Sometimes, the Q exert their powers on behalf of the crew, and in one specific episode, Q actually bestowed his powers upon Commander William Riker. ("Hide and Q"). Nevertheless, God is more benevolent than the Q, and the Latter-day work testifies to the truth of His declaration: "I have conferred upon you the keys and power of the priesthood, wherein I restore all things, and make known unto you all things." (D&C 132:45).

The existence of the Q Continuum is evidence that the Plan of Salvation is necessary for an evolving species like homo sapiens. Q says: "When I look at a gas nebula, all I see is a cloud of dust, but seeing the universe through your eyes allowed me to experience wonder." ("Q-Less").

We have been given a glimpse of the powers of God, who "hath given a law unto all things, by which they move in their times and their seasons; And their courses are fixed, even the courses of the heavens and the earth, which comprehend the earth and all the planets. And they give light to each other in their times and in their seasons, in their minutes, in their hours, in their days, in their weeks, in their months, in their years—all these are one year with God, but not with man. The earth rolls upon her wings, and the sun giveth his light by day, and the moon giveth her light by night, and the stars also give their light, as they roll upon their wings in their glory, in the midst of the power of

God. Unto what shall I liken these kingdoms, that ye may understand? Behold, all these are kingdoms, and any man who hath seen any or the least of these hath seen God moving in his majesty and power. (D&C 88:42-47).

When the Q choose to remain hidden from view, they leave the crew of the Enterprise with tantalizing clues relating to their presence. In contrast, God sends love letters to His children with His return address prominently displayed on the envelopes, so they are instantly identifiable, eagerly engaged, and carefully considered. "Earth is crammed with heaven, and every common bush with fire of God. But only those who see take off their shoes. The rest stand around picking blackberries." (Elizabeth Barrett Browning, "Aurora Leigh," Book Seven, 1856).

R.W. Emerson was particularly sensitive to these love letters. On one occasion, he wrote, "Those who have seen the rising moon break out of the clouds at midnight, have been present like archangels at the creation of light, and of the world." On another, he observed: "If the stars should appear but one night in a thousand years, how would we believe and adore, and preserve for many generations, the remembrance of the city of God which had been shown." ("Nature," Chapter 1).

From the quiet perspective of his home in Concord, Massachusetts, he mused: "I see the spectacle of morning from the hilltop over against my house, from daybreak to sunrise, with emotions which an angel might share. The long, slender bars of cloud float like fishes in a sea of crimson light. From the earth, as a shore, I look out into that silent sea. I seem to partake its rapid transformations; the active enchantment reaches my dust, and I dilate and conspire with the morning wind. How does nature deify us with a few and cheap elements! Give me health and a day, and I will make the pomp of emperors ridiculous."

Perhaps the evolutionary development of the Q was only achieved at a terrible cost, with the sacred secularized, profound truths homogenized into easily digestible forms, ennobling principles sacrificed, and expediency replacing undeviating commitment to moral standards of behavior. With sensitivity and insight William Wordsworth penned these lines: The Q Continuum "lies about us in our infancy! Shades of the prison house begin to close upon the growing boy. But he beholds the light, and whence it flows; he sees it in his joy. The youth, who daily farther from the east must travel, still is nature's priest, and by the vision splendid, is on his way attended. At length," the Q "perceives it die away, and fade into the light of common day." ("Ode: Intimations of Immortality").

The Q cannot know the exhilaration that mortals feel after having made the effort to squeeze through the strait and narrow gate, when their way opens up into broad boulevards lined with fig trees laden with fruit, flooded by sunlight, caressed by soothing breezes, and paved with cobblestones that glint of gold. Only then will there be no billboards to clamor for our attention, no neon lights to distract us, and no cacophony of voices assaulting us from every direction to suppress the serenity of a gospel-centered life. Instead, we will burst free of the most glaring limitations of the Q and be as the aviator who exulted, "Oh, I have slipped the surly bonds of earth and danced the skies on laughter-silvered wings. Sunward I've climbed, and joined the tumbling mirth of sun-split clouds, and done a hundred things you have not dreamed of; Wheeled and soared and swung high in the sunlit silence. Hovering there, I've chased the shouting wind along, and flung my eager craft through footless halls of air. Up, up the long, delirious, burning blue I've topped the windswept heights with easy grace, where never lark, or even eagle flew. And, while with silent, lifting mind I've trod the high untrespassed sanctity of space, I put out my hand, and touched the face of God." (John G. Magee, Jr., "High Flight").

For all their powers, the Q cannot appreciate the value of our innate desire to reach for the stars. "Humans are such commonplace little creatures," said Q. "They roam the galaxy searching for something they know not what." ("Deja Q"). The Q cannot appreciate that our emotions are nurtured by our Father in Heaven Who has given something of Himself that our lives might be inlaid with His as we learn to pattern ourselves after His example. His priesthood "administereth the gospel and holdeth the key of the mysteries of the kingdom, even the key of the knowledge of God. Therefore, in the ordinances thereof, the power of godliness is manifest. And without the ordinance thereof, and the authority of the priesthood, the power of godliness is not manifest unto men in the flesh. For without this no man can see the face of God, even the Father, and live." (D&C 84:19-22).

The interaction of the Q with humans subtly, ingeniously, and perhaps unconsciously reinforces the fact that gospel principles carry within themselves their own witness. They need no external warrant. Thus, Joseph Smith declared: "I teach people correct principles and let them govern themselves." (Cited by John Taylor, "Millennial Star," 13:22, p. 339). As impish as Q is with Jean Luc Picard, his pranks always leave the captain better for having had the experience.

The evolutionary development of the Q is similar to that experienced by mortals living within the dynamic matrix of the Plan of Salvation. Even the Continuum would grudgingly admit that our heritage "is richer than ever before. It is richer than that of Pericles, for it includes the Greek flowering that followed him; richer than Leonardo's, for it includes him and the Italian Renaissance; richer than Voltaire's, for it embraces all the French Enlightenment and its ecumenical dissemination. If progress is real, it is because we are born on a higher level of that pedestal which the accumulation of knowledge and art raises as the ground and support of our being. The heritage rises, and man rises in proportion as he receives it. Consider education as the transmission of our mental, moral, technical, and aesthetic heritage as fully as possible to as many as possible, for the enlargement of our understanding, control, embellishment, and enjoyment of life." (Will Durant, "The Lessons of History," p. 100-102). When we examine the Q, it is apparent that they have evolved in a similar fashion, but somewhere along the way lost their innocence.

At first blush, the existence of the Q would seem to obviate the need for God. With congenital short-sightedness, the Continuum would agree with Steven Hawking, who said: "The quantum theory of gravity has opened up a new possibility, in which there is no boundary to space-time and no need to specify behavior at the boundary. There are no singularities at which the laws of science break down and no edge of space-time at which one has to appeal to God or some new law to set new boundary conditions for space-time. One could say: 'The boundary condition of the universe is that it has no boundary.' The universe is completely self-contained and not affected by anything outside itself. It is neither created nor destroyed. It just IS." (Steven Hawking, "A Brief History of Time: From the Big Bang to Black Holes," p. 136).

On closer inspection, however, the existence of the Q Continuum demands the existence of God. Their very presence betrays our need for the irreducible qualities of faith, light, and truth that establish a baseline for our acquisition of knowledge that inevitably leads to testimony. Every time the Q manifest themselves, they broadcast the news that God is alive and well and is not living in hiding under an assumed name in Argentina as some have supposed. He continues to enjoy tremendous popularity. His book is still on the best-seller list. In fact, it has enjoyed such success that He has authored additional volumes, and it is rumored that He is even now in negotiation for new book deals. How foolish are the Q are when they get a whiff of fame or fancy themselves as celebrities, while all the time, the character and reputation of God remains unblemished and untarnished. He, alone, deserves theatrical encores, and it is He who, in the end, will receive standing (or kneeling) ovations from His children.

You just don't get it, do you?" said Q to Captain Picard. "The trial never ends. We wanted to see if you had the ability to expand your mind and your horizons, and for one brief moment, you did. For one fraction of a second, you were open to options you had never considered. That is the exploration that awaits you. Not mapping stars and studying nebulae, but charting the unknown possibilities of existence." ("All Good Things"). Just so, our Heavenly Father has promised to reveal "all mysteries, yea, all the hidden mysteries of my kingdom from days of old, and for ages to come, will I make known unto them the good pleasure of my will concerning all things pertaining to my kingdom." (D&C 76:7).

The Q would probably be bemused to find that their omnipotence is evidence of the reality of God. When the Savior said: "I am come (into the world) that they might have life, and that they might have it more abundantly," He was speaking of the entire alphabet, including the letter Q. (John 10:10). He was speaking of Atonement, baptism, celestial glory, deification, exaltation, faith unto salvation, grace, and so on, all the way to Zion (including qualifications for the priesthood). His Atonement and Resurrection were not in vain if we are all anxiously engaged, hungering and thirsting after righteousness, boldly declaring the word, and with fear and trembling working out our salvation before the Lord. His Springtime sacrifice will make a difference to us only if we are carried away by personal visions of our individual potential, if we smite the destroyer with the power of the word, live life enthusiastically with divine fire, are filled with the Spirit, and if we ultimately are caught up unto eternal life to continue our mission to explore strange new worlds, to seek out new life and new civilizations, and to boldly go where no-one has gone before.

A prophet is a teacher of known truth, a seer is a perceiver of hidden truth, and a revelator is a bearer of new truth. In the broadest application of the titles, a prophet is also a seer and a revelator, making him at once a teacher, a perceiver, and a bearer of truth. (See Mosiah 8:13).

Quorum Sensing

"This is the doctrine of Christ, and
the only and true doctrine of the Father,
and of the Son, and of the Holy Ghost,
which is one God, without end."
(2 Nephi 31:21).

The phenomenon of "quorum sensing" has been described in both behavioral and natural sciences as a type of decision-making process used by decentralized groups to coordinate behavior. It functions as long as individuals within the group have a means of assessing the numbers of those they interact with and as long as they are able to initiate a standard response once a threshold number of other individuals is detected. Even bacteria use quorum sensing to coordinate their gene expression according to the local density of their population. Similarly, insects may use quorum sensing to make collective decisions about where to nest. Think of colonies of ants, swarms of bees, and clouds of locusts, not to mention flocks of birds, schools of fish, and herds of gazelles, impala, and wildebeest that all move in concert with each other.

Quorum sensing seems to function within human populations, as well. When successful businessmen work together, quorum sensing may be at work. The collective creative genius of Apple Computers' Steve Jobs and Steve Wyzniak, or Microsoft's Bill Gates and Paul Allen comes to mind. Warren Buffett had Benjamin Graham as a friend, confidant, and lasting influence. John Huntsman may have been referring to quorum sensing when he revealed the secret of his success: "What I've learned to do," he said, "is put people who are smarter than me around me." Even the great Sir Isaac Newton acknowledged: "If I have been able to see further than others, it is because I have stood on the shoulders of giants." Albert Einstein presaged quorum sensing when he mused: "Of all the communities available to us, there is not one I would want to devote myself to except for the society of the true searchers, which has very few living members at any one time."

The church intuitively participates in quorum sensing. Its priesthood is organized into bodies called quorums, from the First Presidency, to the Twelve, the Seventy, Stake Presidencies, High Councils, Bishoprics, High Priests, Elders, Priests, Teachers, and Deacons. There is even a quorum of the Godhead. Nephi characterized the Father, Son, and Holy Ghost as "one God" utilizing a title that is reminiscent of the sense of "quorum," or the minimum number of members of a deliberative assembly necessary to conduct its business. (2 Nephi 31:21). The Priesthood auxiliary organizations are organized into presidencies that are the basic equivalents of quorums.

The Presidency of the Church or The First Presidency is a quorum consisting of at least one apostle (the President of the Church) and two or more high priests who may or may not be apostles, who serve as counselors and are called presidents. The Presidency presides over the entire church, while the President is authorized to exercise all priesthood keys to the benefit of the church. His quorum "sense" as a shepherd over the flock encompasses members and nonmembers alike.

The Quorum of the Twelve Apostles is a group of men ordained to the office of apostle, that have been called as special witnesses of Jesus Christ. There may be twelve or more members of this quorum. This quorum is equal in authority and power to the First Presidency. The priesthood keys held by members of this quorum are only used under the direction of the First Presidency. Because their quorum sense is "general" in its scope and influence, the members of this quorum are referred to as General Authorities.

The Presiding Bishopric is a quorum consisting of three men who are called to preside over the Aaronic priesthood and who report to the First Presidency and Quorum of The Twelve. This quorum consists of the Presiding Bishop and two counselors, who hold all of the keys of the Aaronic Priesthood. These "keys" represent the quorum sense to direct the temporal affairs and finances of the church. In our day, these men are always high priests who have been ordained bishops.

The Quorums of the Seventy are special witnesses who are equal in authority to the Twelve. Each Quorum consists of up to seventy individuals who have been ordained Seventies. Each is presided over by seven presidents who hold the keys of authority and responsibility to direct the affairs of the quorum. There is no limit to the number of quorums of the Seventy that may be organized, but currently only the First and Second Quorums of The Seventy are authorities whose quorum sense is general in its scope and influence. (D&C 107:93). The Third through Eighth Quorums of The Seventy are not General Authorities, but are Area Authorities.

A High Priests Quorum is organized in each stake and is presided over by the local Stake Presidency that holds the keys of the Melchizedek Priesthood to unlock the power to exercise a quorum sense of concern for members of the stake. Melchizedek Priesthood members who have been ordained to the office of High Priest and live within the stake are automatically and by nature members of this quorum. Its meetings are generally held twice a year, but ward High Priest Group meetings are held weekly in order to reinforce the sense of quorum or of belonging. A Group Leader in each ward is responsible to the quorum president to nurture this sense of quorum within his sphere of accountability.

Stake Patriarchs and Bishops belong to their stake High Priest Quorum. The only high priests who do not belong to stake high priest quorums are those who belong instead to the Quorum of The First Presidency, Quorum of The Twelve, or First through Ninth Quorums of the Seventy. An Elders Quorum is organized in each ward and is presided over by a president who exercises priesthood keys under the direction and authority of the local Stake Presidency, and under the direction of the bishop, who is the presiding High Priest in the ward. Its quorum sense is more narrowly defined than that of the stake High Priest Quorum and consists of a maximum of ninety-six Elders.

A Melchizedek Priesthood Group is formed when there are not enough High Priests to justify a High Priest group within a ward or branch (usually less than 20). In these cases, a High Priest is called to oversee the direction of both the High Priests and Elders and is set apart as the Melchizedek Priesthood Group Leader under the direction of the Stake President. Even in those situations where church membership is few in numbers, priesthood programs nurture emotional and spiritual attachments that lead to a sense of quorum.

A Priests Quorum consists of up to forty-eight members at least sixteen years of age who have been ordained to the office of Priest. As a preparatory priesthood, quorum members are relatively few in number, making it easier to identify with the group and nurture the sense of quorum. If there are more than forty-eight Priests in the ward, then additional quorums are organized. They are presided over by the ward Bishop who as the president of the quorum(s) has the responsibility to develop the bonds of brotherhood within the Aaronic Priesthood in the ward. The bishop typically calls two assistants to oversee the day-to-day affairs of the quorum(s).

A Teachers Quorum consists of up to twenty-four members at least fourteen years of age, ordained to the office of Teacher. These quorums are organized at the ward level under the direction of the Aaronic Priesthood president who is the bishop. The Teachers Quorum President holds keys to direct the affairs of the quorum.

A Deacons Quorum consists of up to twelve members at least twelve years of age, ordained to the office of Deacon. Quorums of the Aaronic Priesthood start out small, and get progressively larger as identification with the group strengthens. These quorums are organized at the ward level and act under the direction of the ward Bishop who is the Aaronic Priesthood president.

The Deacons Quorum President holds priesthood keys to direct the affairs of the quorum. An Aaronic Priesthood Group is formed in a ward or branch where there are not enough Aaronic priesthood holders to form individual quorums (usually less than 10 total). In these cases, a senior Aaronic priesthood holder (a Priest if available, then a Teacher if available) is called to "assist" the bishop to develop a sense of quorum within the Aaronic priesthood in the ward. This individual may be called as "Aaronic Priesthood group leader," "Aaronic Priesthood class president," or as an assistant to the bishop.

A Stake Presidency consists of a Stake President and two counselors who are high priests charged with the responsibility to govern ecclesiastical organizations called stakes. The inherent sense of quorum is found in a much less centralized pattern within stakes.

A Stake High Council is an administrative quorum consisting of twelve men who assist in the nurturing of the sense of quorum within stakes. Each of its members is ordained to the office of high priest and also belongs to the High Priests Quorum in the stake as well as to individual High Priest Groups in wards within the stake. This nurtures a sense of interdependency within the different quorums of related church units.

A Bishopric is a quorum consisting of a Bishop and two counselors, who are high priests charged with the responsibility to govern church congregations called wards. The bishop is also set apart as the quorum president of the Priests Quorum, and therefore the bishopric is the presidency of that quorum. Auxiliary presidencies of groups such as the Relief Society, Primary, Sunday School and Young Men's and Young Women's organizations do not form quorums, as they are auxiliary to the priesthood.

The affairs of each of these quorums is closely aligned with the behavior characterized by quorum sensing, for both nurture a sense of community that focuses on members' perceptions, understandings, attitudes, and feelings, in relation to those of others. Members of quorums in the church generally consider themselves to be part of a greater whole, and view their quorum experience to be a major factor in self-definition.

Quorums forge links that are strengthened by perceptions of similarity to others, foster acknowledged interdependence, and generate a willingness to maintain interdependence by giving to or doing for others what is expected of themselves, and solidify feelings that larger structures are unwavering and dependable. The sense of community within quorums includes the feeling of belonging, the sense of shared commitments, the assurance that each member is important to others in the group, and the shared faith that their individual and collective needs will be met through mutually shared exertion. There are both territorial and relationship components that contribute to the sense of community within the quorums of the church. Most quorums have discernable geographical demarcations, while a few operate in far-reaching disparate locations. Those that are territorially defined cannot by themselves comprehensively describe the community, since the relationship dimension exerts a significant influence that has no physical boundaries. Their material and immaterial sum really is greater than their parts.

Membership in communities or quorums that are defined by the priesthood government of the church has a number of tangible and intangible benefits, including the psychological comfort afforded by well-defined boundaries, emotional safety, a sense of belonging and identification, personal investment, and recognition through a common symbol system. The dynamic interrelationship between quorums and the benefits of the sense of community may be illustrated by the following examples:

1). Someone puts an announcement in a ward bulletin about the formation of a basketball team. Interested ward members attend the organizational meeting to define their individual talents (integration and fulfillment of needs). The team is delineated by place of residence (ward boundaries) and spends time together in practice. They play a game and win, (thereby experiencing a successfully shared event). Members of the team exert energy on its behalf, (thereby making personal investments in the group). As they continue to win, announcements are made in priesthood meeting opening exercises, (thus bestowing honor and status on team members). The suggestion is made that they all wear matching shirts and shoes, (thereby unconsciously establishing common symbols).

2). The bishop encourages a young man who has just celebrated his twelfth birthday to prepare for a mission, and for the next seven years, he matures in the expanding responsibilities of the Aaronic Priesthood quorums of the ward (integration and fulfillment of needs). He is bound by his place of residence and spends time with other quorum members (well-defined boundaries). His quorum helps him to resist negative peer pressures at school and in his community (emotional safety). He learns to define himself by his quorum (sense of belonging and identification). He spends time carrying out the responsibilities of the priesthood, including serving as a home teacher (personal investment). Eventually, he is interviewed by the bishop, who recommends him to the Stake President to receive the Melchizedek Priesthood and receive his endowment in the temple, preparatory to his departure for the Missionary Training Center and full-time service as a representative of the Lord (a common symbol system).

3). The Stake President encourages young adults to marry in the temple, and the church provides opportunities for integration and fulfillment of needs, including Institute and Stake and Regional Young Adult activities. Temple preparation seminars reinforce behavioral boundaries that are consistent with temple attendance. Upon completion of the seminar, priesthood and Relief Society leaders invite participants to go to the temple as a group, where they might enjoy a successfully shared event. Heavenly Father is the penultimate behavioral psychologist. We should take His counsel and avoid trying to second-guess Him. "Be still, and know that I am God," we are gently reminded. (Psalms 46:10). We should remember Sir Isaac Newton, who reflected: "I was like a boy playing on the seashore, and diverting myself now and then finding a smoother pebble or a prettier shell than ordinary, whilst the great ocean of truth lay all undiscovered before me." We all need to develop to a greater extent our quorum sense that will help us to release in ways scarcely understood the glimmering facets of the life of the Spirit.

Receiving Revelation

(D&C 8)

"The words which are sealed he shall not deliver neither shall he deliver the book. For the book shall be sealed by the power of God, and the revelation which was sealed shall be kept in the book until the due time of the Lord, that they may come forth; for behold, they reveal all things from the foundation of the world until the end thereof. And the day cometh that the words of the book which were sealed shall be read upon the house tops; and they shall be read by the power of Christ; and all things shall be revealed unto the children of men which ever have been among the children of men, and which ever will be even unto the end of the earth." (2 Nephi 27:10-11).

To receive revelation, we must "ask in faith, with an honest heart, believing that (we) shall receive." (V. 1). Perhaps the most dramatic spiritual manifestation of revelation was that of Joseph Smith in The Sacred Grove. He had read the words of James: "If any of you lack wisdom, let him ask God, that giveth to all men liberally, and upbraideth not; and it shall be given him. But let him ask in faith, nothing wavering." (James 1:5-6). He soon learned that wisdom leading to salvation comes from God by revelation.

Joseph learned, as have countless others, that revelation comes to those who prepare themselves. As Chauncey Riddle wrote: "I felt I had received some revelation before. However, I saw that random revelation was not sufficient. To be a rock, a bastion of surety, revelation must be something on which one can count and receive on every occasion of real need. I began to seek it actively. I prayed, fasted, and I lived the gospel as best I knew. I was faithful in my church duties. I tried to live up to every scruple that my conscience enjoined upon me. And dependable revelation did come. Intermittently, haltingly at first, then steadily, over some years it finally came to be a mighty stream of experience. I came to know that at any time of day or night, in any circumstance, for any real need, I could get help. That help came in the form of feelings of encouragement when things seemed hopeless. It came in ideas to unravel puzzles that blocked my accomplishment. It came in priesthood blessings that were fully realized. It came in whisperings of prophecy that were fulfilled. It came in support and even anticipation of what the General Authorities of the church would say and do in general conference. It came in the gifts of the Spirit, as the wonders of eternity were opened to the eyes of my understanding. That stream of spiritual experience is today for me a river of living water that nourishes my soul in every situation. It is the most important factor of my life. If it were taken away, all that I have and am would be dust and ashes. It is the basis of my love, life, understanding, hope, and progress. My only regret is that though this river is so wonderful, I have not been able to take full advantage of it as yet. My life does not yet conform to all that I know. But now I do know; I do not just believe." ("Sunstone," 5/1988, p. 8).

The revelation known as D&C Section 8 came because Oliver Cowdery wanted to know about "the engravings of old records, which are ancient." (V. 1). When Mormon described the events surrounding the ministry of Jesus among the Nephites, he wrote that those in the Last Days would receive The Book of Mormon "to try their faith, and if it shall so be that they shall believe these things then shall the greater things be made manifest unto them. And if it so be that they will not believe these things then shall the greater things be withheld from them, unto their condemnation." (3 Nephi 26:9-10). Consequently, in 1829, Oliver found himself on "scripture probation," to see if he would accept and utilize that with which he had already been entrusted. Oliver was put on notice that the Lord's people were to be a people who possessed scripture, who actively read scripture, who were scripturally literate, and who were scripturally obedient, as well.

The Lord revealed to Oliver: "I will tell you in your mind and in your heart, by the Holy Ghost, which shall come upon you, and which shall dwell in your heart." (V. 3). "This is the spirit of revelation." (V. 4). Revelation "is light; and he that receiveth light, and continueth in God, receiveth more light; and that light groweth brighter and brighter until the perfect day." (D&C 50:24). Those who receive light find that "strait is the gate, and narrow is the way, which leadeth unto life, and few there be that find it." (3 Nephi 14:14). The danger is that when our hearts are set upon temporal things, our spirituality is weakened until interactive communication with our Father in Heaven is no longer a part of our daily lives. We ought instead to "lay aside the things of this world, and seek for the things of a better." (D&C 25:10). But how can we do that? How can we find the truth? Where can we turn for guidance and direction? Who on the earth is authorized to speak in the name of God to help us? Have the heavens closed? Are they silent? Are we to be left alone, to wander to and fro, like flotsam on the sea of life? Does God answer our prayers? Has revelation ceased? The Savior's instruction in Third Nephi confirms that the answer to these questions is found in revelation, and "if any man preach any other gospel unto you than that ye have received, let him be accursed." (Galatians 1:9, See D&C 50:13-20).

The Savior warned against "false prophets, who come to you in sheep's clothing, but inwardly they are ravening wolves." (V. 15, See Matthew 7:15, & Alma 31:30). Some enemies have used this scripture to attack the church, claiming that it speaks directly of its prophet. This is quite a claim, coming as it does from a people "who never had faith enough to call down one scrap of revelation from heaven, and for all they have now are indebted to the faith of another people who lived hundreds and thousands of years before them. Does it remain for them to say how much God has spoken and how much he has not spoken?" (Joseph Smith, H.C. 2:17-18).

Granting that their claim could be reasonable, where then are the true prophets suggested by Christ's warning? They must exist, for "Adam's revelation did not instruct Noah to build his ark; nor did Noah's revelation tell Lot to forsake Sodom; nor did either of these speak of the Exodus. These all had revelations for themselves, and so had Isaiah, Jeremiah, Peter, Paul, John, and Joseph Smith." (John Taylor, "The Gospel Kingdom," p. 34).

God exists in the present tense and is the Great I Am. In the Doctrine & Covenants, the Lord testified that Joseph Smith was given "power from on high, by the means which were before prepared, to translate The Book of Mormon; which contains a record of a fallen people, and the fulness of the gospel of Jesus Christ to the Gentiles and to the Jews also; which was given by inspiration and is confirmed to others by the ministering of angels, and is declared unto the world by them - Proving to the world that the holy scriptures are true, and that God does inspire men and call them to his holy work in this age and generation, as well as in generations of old; Thereby showing that he is the same God yesterday, today, and forever." (D&C 20:8-12).

Something wonderful surrounds our testimonies of the living Prophet, Seer, and Revelator of The Church of Jesus Christ of Latter-day Saints. Many years ago, John Greenleaf Whittier said: "Of these modern prophets, I discovered, as I think, the great secret of their success in making converts. They speak to a common feeling; they minister to a universal want. They speak a language of hope and promise to the weak, weary hearts, tossed and troubled, who have wandered from sect to sect, seeking in vain for the primal manifestations of the divine power." ("A Mormon Conventicle," p. 461).

Whittier recognized the grand key: "By their fruits ye shall know them." (V. 20). Do these prophets, or teachers who speak in the name of the Lord, bless the lives of their people? Is their doctrine edifying and uplifting? Do they encourage a religion that promotes chastity, morality, and fidelity to family values? Do they hold dear the sanctity of life and the rights of the unborn? Do they believe that free will is an eternal principle with a moral foundation that is vital to the successful completion of our mortal probation? Do they believe in obeying, honoring, and sustaining the law of the land? Do they believe in being honest, true, chaste, benevolent, virtuous, and in doing good to all? Do they believe all things, hope all things, have they endured many things and hope to be able to endure all things? If there is anything virtuous, lovely, or of good report or praiseworthy, do they seek after these things? (See Philippians 4:8, & the Thirteenth Article of Faith). To have these qualities was to be Oliver's gift. (V. 4 & 5).

He was given the power to receive revelation from God through the medium of the Holy Ghost. But this was not all. The Lord told him: "You have another gift, which is the gift of Aaron." (V. 6). This alluded to his opportunity to be a spokesman and scribe for the Prophet Joseph Smith. This was a sacred calling, for the Lord said: "There is no other power, save the power of God, that can cause this gift of Aaron to be with you. No power shall be able to take it away out of your hands, he was promised, "for it is the work of God." (V. 7-8). "No power on earth or hell (can) overthrow or defeat that which God (has) decreed. Every plan of the Adversary (will) fail, for the Lord knows the secret thoughts of men, and sees the future with a vision clear and perfect, even as though it were in the past." (Joseph Fielding Smith, Jr., "Church History and Modern Revelation," 1:26).

"Therefore, whatsoever you shall ask me to tell you by that means, that will I grant unto you, and you shall have knowledge concerning it." (V. 9). Oliver was poised on the cusp of a profound understanding of the doctrine of Christ that is a blessing reserved for the faithful. Nephi had mourned "because of the unbelief, and the wickedness, and the ignorance, and the stiffneckedness of men; for they will not search knowledge, nor understand great knowledge, when it is given unto them in plainness." (2 Nephi 32:7). His concern was real, for his focus was on the future at the time of the Restoration when many would lack the desire to change, and would be swept to and fro in a sea of moral relativism and experiential mediocrity. Within the gospel framework, however, their lives would be dynamic and changing, for as their knowledge would increase, their responsibility and commitment to obedience would increase as well. As their testimonies of Christ would swell, faith would intensify their desire to repent. Oliver was learning that if he brought his life in harmony with gospel principles, he would be in a constant state of improvement leading to perfection. Becoming Christ-like would become his ultimate, incredible journey. It would be the road less traveled, but the rewards would make completing the trip worth the effort.

"Remember that without faith you can do nothing;" he was cautioned, "therefore ask in faith. Trifle not with these things; do not ask for that which you ought not." (V. 10). For if you "ask anything that is not expedient for you, it shall turn unto your condemnation." (D&C 88:65). As Mormon had written: "I judge that ye have faith in Christ because of your meekness; for if ye have not faith in him then ye are not fit to be numbered among the people of his church." (Moroni 7:39). He was likewise old Tevya, who had told his daughters: "In Anatevka, God knows who you are, and what you may become." (Joseph Stein, "Fiddler on The Roof").

One who had the opportunity to be present when Joseph Smith prayed said of the experience: "There was no ostentation, no raising of the voice as by enthusiasm, but a plain conversational tone, as a man would address a present friend. It appeared to me as though, in case the veil were taken away, I could see the Lord standing facing His humblest of all servants. It was the crowning of all the prayers I ever heard." (Hyrum & Helen Mae Andrus, "They Knew the Prophet," p. 52).

In our petitions, the Lord has asked that we "use not vain repetitions." (3 Nephi 13:7). Alma taught: When your "prayer is vain, (it) availeth you nothing, and ye are as hypocrites who do deny the faith." (Alma 34:28, see Mosiah 4:16-27). Because thoughtless repetition in prayers bespeak faithlessness, they are ineffectual. If we are full of faith, however, we will ask only for those blessings that we ought to have, for Heavenly Father "knoweth what things ye have need of, before ye ask him." (3 Nephi 13:8, See Matthew 6:8). Moreover, Christ has said: "If ye are purified and cleansed from all sin, ye shall ask whatsoever you will in the name of Jesus, and it shall be done. But know this, it shall be given you what you shall ask." (D&C 50:29-30).

"Ask," Oliver was counseled, "that you may translate and receive knowledge from all those ancient records which have been hid up, that are sacred; and according to your faith shall it be done unto you." (V. 11). Joseph Smith's Book of Mormon translation, with Oliver Cowdery acting as scribe, was afterward completed in just six weeks, between April 7, 1829, and the first week of June 1829. The translation was unlike that of any other text, because it was accomplished "through the mercy (and) power of God." (D&C 1:29). This is as specific an explanation as is found regarding just how Joseph Smith accomplished the task. It is appropriate that he let the record speak for itself, because when we understand that it is an inspired translation, we are drawn to The Book of Mormon itself, and without distraction can put to the test the challenge left by Moroni: "And when ye shall receive these things, I would exhort you that ye would ask God, the eternal Father, in the name of Christ, if these things are not true; and if ye shall ask with a sincere heart, with real intent, having faith in Christ, he will manifest the truth of it unto you, by the power of the Holy Ghost." (Moroni 10:4).

Jesus Christ Himself testified of the divine authenticity of the completed work. "He translated the book, even that part which I have commanded him, and as your Lord and your God liveth it is true." (D&C 17:6, See D&C 19:26). As if to confirm that His influence was instrumental in the work of translation, the Lord reminded Oliver Cowdery that it was He that had earlier spoken to him. (V. 12). "Did I not speak peace to your mind concerning the matter?" the Lord asked. "What greater witness can you have than from God?" (D&C 6:22). Oliver had learned that the Spirit is quiet, unobtrusive, and peaceful, and that God works in mysterious ways.

Recognizing The Church of Christ

"How be it my church
save it be called in my name?
For if a church be called in Moses'
name then it be Moses' church; or if it
be called in the name of a man then it be
the church of a man; but if it be called in
my name then it is my church; if it so
be that they are built upon my
gospel." (3 Nephi 27:8).

Today, just where I live (in Spokane, Washington) there are a lot of churches. Among them are the following fifty: Jehovah's Witnesses, The Church of The Resurrection, The Cornerstone Pentecostal Church, Jesus is The Answer, The Living Truth Tabernacle, Amazing Grace Fellowship, The Assembly of God, The Crosswind Church, The Glad Tidings Church, The Trinity Lighthouse, The Baptist Church, The Living Water Community Church, The Shiloh Hills Fellowship, Christ Our Hope Bible Church, The Church of The Nazarene, The Catholic Church, The Christian Life Church, The Calvary Chapel, The Presbyterian Church, The Methodist Church, The Holy Temple Church of God in Christ, The Slavic Christian Church, The Refreshing Soaring Church of God in Christ, The Unity Church of Truth, The Life River Fellowship, The Cornerstone Pentecostal Church, The Northview Bible Church, The Lutheran Church, The New Beginnings Church, The Pentecostal Evangelical Church, The River of Life Open Bible Church, The Spokane Dream Center Women's Discipleship, The Unity Church of Truth, The New Hope Christian Reformed Church, The First Church of Christ Scientist, The Church of Christ, The Jesus Lord Church of the Living God International, The Church of Jesus Christ of Latter-day Saints, The Heritage Congregational Church, The First Covenant Church, The All Nations Christian Center, The Christ our Hope Bible Church, The Christ the Savior Orthodox Church, The First Church of The Open Bible, The Shalom Church, The Fellowship of The Messiah, A Fresh Start Ministries, and The Unitarian Universalist Church.

You would think that Christians of all faiths would ask the questions: "Does my church have, at the very least, these seven features?" (1). "Does my church believe that God speaks to its leaders who have the authority to act in His name?" (See Amos 3:7). (2). "Does the organization of my church bear a resemblance to the church during the ministry of Christ and His Apostles?" (Ephesians 2:19-20). (3). "Does my church believe, as Peter taught on the Day of Pentecost, that the first principles and ordinances of the gospel are faith in the Lord Jesus Christ, repentance for sins, baptism by immersion for the remission of sins, and receiving the gift of the Holy Ghost by the laying on of hands by those who hold the authority of the holy priesthood?" (See Acts 2:37-38). (4). "Does my church believe, as did Paul, that God is no respecter of persons, whether living or dead, and that the dead have the same opportunities as the living to accept the ordinances of the gospel and to make covenants with Him?" (1 Peter 4:6). (5). "Does my church believe, as did Paul, in the gifts of the Spirit?" (1 Corinthians 112:4-10). (6). "Does my church believe in the biblical prophecies relating to an apostasy?" (Acts 20:28-30). (7). "Does my church believe not only in the Reformation and the Protestant movement, but also in the necessity of the Restoration foretold by Paul and others?" (2 Thessalonians 2:1-3).

Perhaps the reason that people don't ask these questions is because they are only aware of Act Two of the Three Act Play (The Plan of Salvation: Where did we come from? Why are we here? Where are we going?). Somehow, the religious educational system upon which they rely, that is supposed to teach these foundation truths, has been broken. They behave as though they skipped kindergarten and don't recognize the need for college-level courses. They are as the honorable men and women among the sects, parties, and denominations, "who are blinded by the subtle craftiness of men (who) lie in wait to deceive, and (who are) are only kept from the truth because they know not where to find it." (D&C 76:75 & 123:12).

It is Satan who is responsible for darkening the minds of many who dwell upon an earth that has been corrupted, and is scarcely fit for sacred use. Isaiah suggested that it has been defiled and is polluted, "under the inhabitants thereof; because they have transgressed the laws, changed the ordinance, (and) broken the everlasting covenant." (Isaiah 24:5). It is hard to understand how a church could function today without even one of the seven features of revelation, authority, organization, first principles, work for the dead, and spiritual gifts, and the illumination of restoration following a long night of apostasy.

Our Sixth Article of Faith states: "We believe in the same organization that existed in the primitive church, namely, apostles, prophets, pastors, teachers, evangelists, and so forth." For some reason, this fundamental structure is not obvious to Christians of other faiths, who simply don't see things as we do. And yet, the Pope himself has stated the obvious: "Even the humblest human beings," he observed, "are naturally philosophic, asking themselves such questions as "Who am I? Where do I come from, and where am I going?" Religious revelation provides answers to these questions, the pope acknowledged." ("Time Magazine," 10/26/1998).

Paul believed in a "God, who at sundry times and in divers manners spake in time past unto the fathers by the prophets, (and who) hath in these last days spoken unto us by his Son." (Hebrews 1:1-2). "Whom say ye that I am?" the Savior asked. "And Simon Peter answered and said, Thou art the Christ, the Son of the living God. And Jesus answered and said unto him, Blessed art thou, Simon Bar-jona, for flesh and blood hath not revealed it unto thee, but my Father which is in heaven. And I say also unto thee, That thou art Peter, and upon this rock" of revelation "I will build my church." (Matthew 16:15-18). We believe in the Father, and in the Son, and in the Holy Ghost. The Savior taught: The Holy Ghost is a Revelator, "whom the Father will send in my name. He shall teach you all things, and bring all things to your remembrance, whatsoever I have said unto you." (John 14:26).

The concept of authority builds upon this established revelation, and is given to ecclesiastical leaders. Martin Luther lamented the homogenization of the exercise of supposed authority that traces back to indiscriminate revelation: "A shoemaker, a smith, a farmer, each has his manual occupation and work; and yet, at the same time, all are eligible to act as priests." Walt Whitman said: "There will soon be no more priests. They may wait awhile, perhaps a generation or two, dropping off by degrees. A superior breed shall take their place. A new order shall arise, and they shall be the priests of man, and every man shall be his own priest." Whitman, however, did not understand what had inspired Luther to resist the profane and apostate authority of Catholicism, that institutional revelation comes only to those whose lives merit the bestowal of divine authority, for as Paul correctly understood it, "no man taketh this honour unto himself, but he that is called of God, as was Aaron." (Hebrews 5:4).

"For the Son of man is as a man taking a far journey, who left his house, and gave authority to his servants, and to every man his work, and commanded the porter to watch." (Mark 13:34). "Ye have not chosen me," Jesus explained, "but I have chosen you, and ordained you." (John 15:16). Following His ministry, the Apostles "ordained them elders in every church." (Acts 14:23). Their authority was intertwined with a formal church organization that was quickened by the functional foundation of revelation and authority. Jesus Christ established a church that was a carefully crafted construct compared by Paul to a structure that was "built upon the foundation of the apostles and prophets, Jesus Christ himself being the chief corner stone." (Ephesians 2:20). Accordingly, "he gave some, apostles; and some, prophets, and some, evangelists; and some, pastors and teachers; For the perfecting of the saints, for the work of the ministry, for the edifying of the body of Christ: Till we all come in the unity of the faith, and of the knowledge of the Son of God, unto a perfect man, unto the measure of the stature of the fulness of Christ." (Ephesians 4:11-13).

Jesus foresaw the need for other priesthood leaders to assist the Apostles in the work of the ministry. He sent officers called Seventies in pairs to preach the gospel. (See Luke 10:1). Others who held callings in the church included evangelists (patriarchs), pastors (presiding leaders), high priests, elders, bishops, priests, teachers, and deacons. These positions were established to instruct and inspire church members, perform missionary work, and perform saving ordinances, or, in other words, to perfect the Saints, preach the gospel, and cement family relationships both in time and in eternity. Those who labored in these callings helped the members come to a "unity of the faith, and of the knowledge of the Son of God." (See Ephesians 4:13).

Authority empowered the leaders of the church to administer the first principles and ordinances of salvation. Those who held the priesthood in former times taught the two basic principles of faith and repentance, and then, the two basic ordinances of baptism and the receipt of the Holy Ghost. As the Savior taught: "Except a man be born of water and of the Spirit, he cannot enter into the kingdom of God." (John 3:5).

A dramatic application of this principle of authority that had been taught by the Savior occurred on the Day of Pentecost, when over three thousand people "were pricked in their heart, and said unto Peter and to the rest of the apostles, Men and brethren, what shall we do? Then Peter said unto them, Repent, and be baptized every one of you in the name of Jesus Christ for the remission of sins, and ye shall receive the gift of the Holy Ghost." (Acts 2:37-38). "And they continued steadfastly in the apostles' doctrine and fellowship, and in breaking of bread, and in prayers." (Acts 2:42). The ordinances of salvation propelled them along on the pathway of progression leading to exaltation in the kingdom of God.

These ordinances were for the living as well as for the dead. The scriptures plainly teach that Christ preached to the dead, between His Own death and resurrection. "For Christ also hath once suffered for sins, the just for the unjust, that he might bring us to God, being put to death in the flesh, but quickened by the Spirit: By which also he went and preached unto the spirits in prison. Which sometime were disobedient, when once the longsuffering of God waited in the days of Noah, while the ark was a preparing, wherein few, that is, eight souls were saved by water." (1 Peter 3:18-20).

He performed these labors because the requirements to enter heaven are the same for all. They are equivalent for the living and for the dead, because God is no respecter of persons. (See Acts 10:34). As Peter further explained: "For this cause was the gospel preached also to them that are dead, that they might be judged according to men in the flesh, but live according to God in the spirit." (1 Peter 4:6). "Else what shall they do which are baptized for the dead," asked Paul, "if the dead rise not at all? Why are they then baptized for the dead?" (1 Corinthians 15:29).

While we tarry on earth, ordinances expose the Saints to a multitude of spiritual gifts that allow them to walk in the light of the gospel. Paul told the Corinthians: "Now there are diversities of gifts." (1 Corinthians 12:4). These gifts enabled the image of God to be engraven upon their countenances. "Who shall ascend into the hill of the Lord," asked the Psalmist, "or who shall stand in his holy place" to partake of the Divine Nature? "He that hath clean hands and a pure heart; who" is a partaker of spiritual gifts, and "hath not lifted up his soul unto vanity, nor sworn deceitfully." (Psalms 24:4-5).

Unfortunately, the seven features that distinguish the church of Christ have been neutralized by apostasy from the truth, that has resulted in a darkening of the minds of men. When the Saints in former times closed their hearts to spiritual promptings, darkness superseded the light. The loss of spiritual gifts resulted in apostasy. Paul prophesied to the Thessalonian Saints: "Be not soon shaken in mind, or be troubled, neither by spirit, nor by word, nor by letter as from us, as that the day of Christ is at hand. Let no man deceive you by any means: for that day shall not come, except there come a falling away first." (2 Thessalonians 2:2-3). "For behold," an angel taught Nephi, the apostasy has "taken away from the gospel of the Lamb many parts which are plain and most precious; and also many covenants of the Lord have they taken away." (1 Nephi 13:26).

Even if they are not Catholic, and their evangelical roots trace back to the Protestant Reformation, conscientious Christians may not realize that there has been a Great Apostasy. (See Amos 8:11-12). Perhaps Latter-day Saints need to learn how to explain that reality in different words that might be more easily understood. When Christians of all faiths acknowledge the reality of the Apostasy, it will be easier for them to accept the Restoration. When that is the case, it will be easier to establish a dialogue relating to the features of the primitive church (the church in former times), such as revelation, authority, church organization, first principles, work for the dead, spiritual gifts, apostasy, and restoration, that should be identifying markers of the Lord's restored church in the latter days, that was foretold by the Apostles so long ago. (See Acts 3:21 & D&C 27:6).

A restoration has been eagerly anticipated by visionaries seeking to redress the wrongs resulting from the corruption of the basic principles relating to the covenants we make with God. "I have sought nothing beyond reforming the church in conformity with the Holy Scriptures," declared Martin Luther. "I simply say that Christianity has ceased to exist among those who should have preserved it." ("Luther and His Times," p. 509). Roger Williams is reported to have declared: "There is no regularly constituted church on earth, nor any person authorized to administer any church ordinance; nor can there be until new apostles are sent by the Great Head of the church for Whose coming am seeking." (See: "TimesandSeasons.org "For whose coming I am seeking," 6/15/2012).

After the Reformers paved the way, it was only natural that a Restoration would burst upon the scene. John saw in vision the angel Moroni, who would, in the Last Days, "fly in the midst of heaven, having the everlasting gospel to preach unto them that dwell on the earth, and to every nation, and kindred, and tongue, and people." (Revelation 14:6). How wonderful it would be to put the icing on the cake with a visit by the Resurrected Lord Himself. As Luke had prophesied: "He shall send Jesus Christ, which before was preached unto you: whom the heavens must receive until the times of restitution of all things, which God hath spoken by the mouth of all his holy prophets since the world began." (Acts 3:20-21).

Revelation, authority, organization, first principles, work for the dead, and spiritual gifts are illustrations of principles in which "the power of godliness is manifest. And without" the driving force of these principles, "the power of godliness is not manifest unto men in the flesh," and there can be no Restoration. "For without this no man can see the face of God, even the Father, and live." (D&C 84:20-22). The manifestation of energy that animates the latter-day church speaks for itself, and is a seamless continuation of the vitality that quickened the church in former times.

Resource Material

1. Concerning the name of His church, the Lord told the Nephites: "If it be called in my name then it is my church." (3 Nephi 27:8). The essential qualifying prerequisite of the church was, as the Savior said, that it be "built upon my gospel." (3 Nephi 27:8).

Interestingly, of all the churches in the world when the Lord restored His Church in this dispensation, there was not a single one that bore His name. It must have been very satisfying for Him to declare to Joseph Smith: "For thus shall my church be called in the last days, even the Church of Jesus Christ of Latter-day Saints." (D&C 115:4). Before this revelation, the Lord's church was variously called The Church of Christ, The Church of Jesus Christ, The Church of God, and The Church of The Latter-day Saints. Even today, it is sometimes inaccurately called The Mormon Church, or The L.D.S. Church. But in 1830, this revelation from the Lord resolved the issue once and for all.

Today, "there is no valid reason why the Latter-day Saints should speak of themselves as 'Mormons,' or of the church as 'The Mormon Church.' We emphasize that we belong to The Church of Jesus Christ of Latter-day Saints, the name the Lord has given by which we are to be known and called." (Joseph Fielding Smith, Jr., "Answers to Gospel Questions," 4:174-175).

2. "The word 'saint' is a translation of a Greek word also rendered 'holy,' the fundamental idea being that of consecration or separation for a sacred purpose; but the word came to mean 'free from blemish,' whether physical or moral. In the New Testament, the saints are all those who by baptism have entered into the Christian covenant." ("Bible Dictionary," p. 768).

Hence, Paul addressed "all that be in Rome, beloved of God, called to be saints." (Romans 1:7). He saluted "the church of God which is at Corinth, to them that are sanctified in Christ Jesus, called to be saints." (1 Corinthians 1:2). He introduced himself and his missionary companion Timothy as "the servants of Jesus Christ, to all the saints in Christ Jesus which are at Philippi." (Philippians 1:1).

Book of Mormon prophets also characterized the members of the church as 'saints.'. "Behold, the righteous," Nephi declared, "the saints of the Holy One of Israel." Then he described them as those "who have believed in the Holy One of Israel, (and) who have endured the crosses of the world." (2 Nephi 9:18).

Benjamin taught: "The natural man is an enemy to God, and has been from the fall of Adam, and will be, forever and ever, unless he yields to the enticings of the Holy Spirit, and putteth off the natural man, and becometh a saint through the atonement of Christ the Lord." He characterized the Saints as children, "submissive, meek, humble, patient, full of love, willing to submit to all things which the Lord seeth fit to inflict upon him, even as a child doth submit to his father." (Mosiah 3:19).

Moroni explained that "the remission of sins bringeth meekness, and lowliness of heart; and because of meekness and lowliness of hearth cometh the visitation of the Holy Ghost, which Comforter filleth with hope and perfect love, which love endureth by diligence unto prayer, until the end shall come, when all the saints shall dwell with God." (Moroni 8:26).

Our journey to Christ via The Book of Mormon reminds us of the description by Job relating to his receipt of heavenly instruction: "For God speaketh once, yea, twice, yet man perceiveth it not. In a dream, in a vision of the night, when deep sleep falleth upon men, in slumberings upon the bed; then he openeth the ears of men, and sealeth their instruction." (Job 33:14-16).

Removing the Barnacles of Life

"I will give away all my sins
to know thee, and that I may be raised
from the dead, and be saved at the last day."
(Alma 22:18).

Portland, Oregon lies on the Columbia River, over 75 miles from the Pacific Ocean. Yet ocean-going ships regularly cross the treacherous Columbia Bar at the mouth of the river, to steam upstream to deliver and take on cargo at Portland's bustling wharves. There are easier ports of call, but a trip to Portland every now and then is worthwhile for at least one special reason.

The barnacles that attach to the hulls can proliferate and create significant drag as the ship makes its way through the water. This creates inefficiency that translates into increased fuel costs that can become prohibitively expensive. Additionally, if the barnacles work their way onto the rudder mechanism, they can seriously compromise the ability of the captain to move the ship forward toward its intended destination.

But those barnacles thrive only in salt water. Fresh water kills them, and when they die, they lose their grip on the ship's hull and fall off in the water. Thus, the accumulation from months or years of contamination can be eliminated in just a few days as the ship moves through fresh river water, leaving it "as good as new."

In a similar fashion, we can rid ourselves of "the barnacles of life" that would otherwise compromise our life's mission or purpose. This can be done by completely immersing ourselves in cleansing water that leave us afresh and anew, and with the feeling afterward that can be almost indescribable.

There is a way
to rid ourselves of the barnacles
of life that may compromise our initial
forays into The Book of Mormon. This can
be done as we completely immerse ourselves
in the stream, in the cleansing waters of
baptism that leave us afresh and anew,
with feelings afterward that are
almost indescribable.

Restoration – The Early Days

We need prophets who are of the caliber of Moses,
Isaiah, Jeremiah, and Joseph Smith to drive the law of the
Lord into our inward parts, to help us internalize its principles, to
experience sanctification, and to be cleansed by repentance from the
effects of sin. (See Jeremiah 31:33). We need prophets to facilitate
our spiritual renewal, so that we may stand prepared to enter the
presence of the Lord. We must submit to the will of the Lord,
yield our hearts to Him, and be obedient to all of the
teachings of His prophet. "Therefore, if ye do
these things blessed are ye, for ye shall
be lifted up at the last day."
(3 Nephi 27:22).

December 23, 1805 - Joseph Smith is born in Sharon, Vermont.

April 1815 - Mount Tambora, in Indonesia, explodes, ejecting so much sulphur dioxide, ash, and dust into the atmosphere that, the following Spring, it caused "the year without a summer" around the world. Temperatures in New England persisted in the 40s throughout July and August, and there were killing frosts. The Smiths lost their farm in Norwich, Vermont, settled their accounts, and moved to the western New York frontier in search of new opportunities. They settled in a town called Palmyra, over 300 miles away, in fertile, wheat-growing country.

Early Spring, 1820 - At the age of 14, Joseph experiences the First Vision in the nearby Sacred Grove.

When he walked out of the grove of trees that beautiful spring morning in 1820, he would never be the same again. He knew the Father and the Son lived, and he would testify of this truth throughout his life. It was three years, however, after he experienced his vision of God before Joseph received further instructions concerning the important work to which he had been called.

During this period, Joseph passed through his mid-teens, a time when sympathetic teachers and a congenial community could have strengthened him. But his testimony instead aroused hostility. Even trusted friends turned against him; however, Joseph continually had the unconditional support of his family.

He acknowledged that during this period he "frequently fell into many foolish errors, and displayed the weakness of youth" (Joseph Smith History 1:28). His native cheery temperament was one reason he gave for sometimes associating with jovial company and being guilty of levity, which he considered inconsistent with the character of one called of God. (See JSH 1:28). He was not, however, guilty of any "great or malignant sins." (See JSH 1:28). During this time, he labored with his father on the family farm, working in the fields, clearing trees, or tapping sugar maples. Occasionally, he had an odd job, such as digging a building foundation or working in the corn fields for Martin Harris. This three-year interval gave young Joseph the time to grow, mature, gain experience, and receive further nurturing.

The First Appearance of Moroni: September 21-22, 1823 – This is the first of at least 22 documented appearances of Moroni to Joseph Smith. (See H. Donl Peterson, "Moroni - Joseph Smith's Tutor", "Ensign", 1/1992, p. 22-29).

In 1822, Joseph had begun helping his older brother Alvin build a new frame house for the family. By September of 1823, it was two stories high but without a roof, and so, the family continued to live in their small log cabin just down the road.

It was in this log cabin, late in the evening of Sunday, September 21, 1823, that seventeen-year-old Joseph retired for the night. Concerned about his standing before the Lord, he earnestly prayed for forgiveness of his sins. Suddenly, his room began to fill with light, until a heavenly messenger stood by his bedside in partial fulfillment of the great prophecy of John the Apostle. (See Revelation 14:6-7).

In his history, Joseph later described this resurrected being: "He had on a loose robe of most exquisite whiteness. It was a whiteness beyond anything earthly I had ever seen; nor do I believe that any earthly thing could be made to appear so exceedingly white and brilliant. His hands were naked, and his arms also, a little above the wrist; so, also, were his feet naked, as were his legs, a little above the ankles. His head and neck were also bare. I could discover that he had no other clothing on but this robe, as it was open, so that I could see into his bosom.

Not only was his robe exceedingly white, but his whole person was glorious beyond description, and his countenance truly like lightning. The room was exceedingly light, but not so very bright as immediately around his person. When I first looked upon him, I was afraid; but the fear soon left me." (JSH 1:31-32).

The messenger introduced himself as Moroni, a prophet who had lived on the American continent. As holder of the keys of the "stick of Ephraim" (see D&C 27:5) the purpose of Moroni's visit was to reveal the existence of a record written on metal plates which had lain hidden in the ground for fourteen centuries. It was "an account of the former inhabitants of this continent. ... He also said that the fulness of the everlasting gospel was contained in it, as delivered by the Savior to the ancient inhabitants." (JSH 1:34).

Joseph recounted: "While he was conversing with me about the plates, the vision was opened to my mind that I could see the place where the plates were deposited, and that so clearly and distinctly that I knew the place again when I visited it."

"This messenger (Moroni) proclaimed himself to be an angel of God, sent to bring the joyful tidings that the covenant which God made with ancient Israel was at hand to be fulfilled, that the preparatory work for the second coming of the Messiah was speedily to commence; that the time was at hand for the gospel in all its fullness to be preached in power, unto all nations, that a people might be prepared for the millennial reign. I was informed that I was chosen to be an instrument in the hands of God to bring about some of His purposes in this glorious dispensation" ("History of the Church", 4:536-37).

Joseph was to translate the record and publish it, and because of this, his name would be known for good and evil among all people. (See JSH 1:33). Moroni cited several passages from the Bible quoting prophets such as Malachi, Isaiah, Joel, and Peter concerning the preparations to be made in the last days for the millennial reign of Christ. Thus commenced the gospel tutorship of Joseph Smith by Moroni, in September 1823, three years after his First Vision in what came to be known as the Sacred Grove, near his home.

"After this communication, I saw the light in the room begin to gather immediately around the person of him who had been speaking to me, and it continued to do so until the room was again left dark, except just around him; when, instantly I saw, as it were, a conduit open right up into heaven, and he ascended till he entirely disappeared, and the room was left as it had been before this heavenly light had made its appearance."

So important was Moroni's message and the need to impress it on the mind of the young boy that Moroni returned twice more that night, and once the following morning, to repeat the same instructions, adding additional information each time. On the first occasion, Joseph saw in vision the location of the plates. (See JSH 1:42). They were buried in a hillside about three miles from his home. During the second visit, Joseph was told of judgments which were coming upon the earth. (See JSH 1:45). Near the conclusion of the third visit, Moroni warned Joseph that Satan would try to wrest the plates from his possession, for their temporal value. The angel directed seventeen-year-old Joseph that there was to be one purpose only for obtaining the plates, and that was to glorify God. Only one motive should influence him, and that was to build up God's kingdom. (See JSH 1:46). Joseph's interviews with Moroni occupied most of the night, for at the end of the third visit he heard a rooster crow. Indeed, a new day of spiritual light was about to dawn. Isaiah had spoken of this day as a time when a "marvellous work and a wonder" would come forth. (Isaiah 29:14).

One is reminded of the description by Job, relating to his receipt of heavenly instruction. "For God speaketh once, yea twice, yet man perceiveth it not. In a dream, in a vision of the night, when deep sleep falleth upon men, in slumberings upon the bed; Then he openeth the ears of men, and sealeth their instruction." (Job 33:14-16).

Continued Instruction From the Angel Moroni. Moroni instructs Joseph about restoring the gospel of Jesus Christ and teaches him from scripture. John Taylor explained: "Joseph Smith was set apart by the Almighty according to the councils of the Gods in the eternal worlds, to introduce the principles of life among the people … The principles which he had, placed him in communication with … Abraham, Isaac, Jacob, Noah, Adam, Seth, Enoch, Jesus and the Father, and the apostles that lived on this continent as well as those who lived on the Asiatic continent … Why? Because he had to introduce a dispensation which was called the dispensation of the fulness of times, and it was known as such by the ancient servants of God" ("Deseret News", 6/9/1880, p. 280).

Joseph also learned about the ancient inhabitants of the Americas, "who they were, and from whence they came; a brief sketch of their origin, progress, civilization, laws, governments, of their righteousness and iniquity, and the blessings of God being finally withdrawn from them as a people" (History of the Church, 4:537).

Joseph Smith's first sees the Plates (but is not allowed to handle them). – His first visit to Cumorah. After Moroni departed, Joseph related, "I … went to the place where the messenger had told me the plates were deposited; and owing to the distinctness of the vision which I had had concerning it, I knew the place the instant that I arrived there." (JSH 1:50). Near the top of the hill Joseph found a large stone, "thick and rounding in the middle on the upper side, and thinner towards the edges." (JSH 1:51). It was the lid of a stone box. We can only imagine his excitement as he opened the box. There were the plates, the Urim and Thummim, and the breastplate, just as Moroni had explained.

"The box in which they lay was formed by laying stones together in some kind of cement. In the bottom of the box were laid two stones crossways of the box, and on these stones lay the plates and the other things with them." (JSH 1:52).

As Joseph had approached the Hill Cumorah, he had thoughts about his family's poverty, and the possibility that the plates or the popularity of the translation would produce enough wealth to "raise him above a level with the common earthly fortunes of his fellow men, and relieve his family from want." (Related by Oliver Cowdery, in "Messenger and Advocate", October 1835, p. 198).

As he harbored these thoughts, he reached down to handle the plates, but received a shock and was thus prevented from taking them out of the box. Twice more he tried, and was thrown back. In frustration, he cried out, "Why can I not obtain this book?" Moroni appeared, and told him it was because he had not kept the commandments, but had yielded to the temptations of Satan to obtain the plates for riches instead of having his eye single to the glory of God as he had been commanded. ("History of Joseph Smith", p. 81).

Repentant, Joseph humbly sought the Lord in prayer and was filled with the Spirit. A vision was opened to him, and the "glory of the Lord shone round about and rested upon him. ... He beheld the prince of darkness, (and) the heavenly messenger (Moroni) said, 'All this is shown, the good and the evil, the holy and impure, the glory of God and the power of darkness, that you may know hereafter the two powers and never be influenced or overcome by that wicked one ... You now see why you could not obtain this record; that the commandment was strict, and that if ever these sacred things are obtained, (it) must be by prayer and faithfulness in obeying the Lord. They are not deposited here for the sake of accumulating gain and wealth for the glory of this world: they were sealed by the prayer of faith, and because of the knowledge which they contain, they are of no worth among the children of men, only for their knowledge." (See H.C., 4:537; George Q. Cannon, in "Journal of Discourses", 13:47; John Taylor, in "Journal of Discourses", 17:374 & 21:94).

Moroni concluded by warning Joseph that he would not be allowed to obtain the plates "until he had learned to keep the commandments of God - not only till he was willing, but able to do it. "The ensuing evening, when the family were all together, Joseph made known to them all that he had communicated to his father in the field, and also of his finding the record, as well as what passed between him and the angel while he was at the place where the plates were deposited." ("History of Joseph Smith", p. 83).

Every September for four years, from 1823 to 1827, Joseph returns to the Hill Cumorah to view the plates, and to be taught by Moroni. Joseph was 17 when he first saw the plates, but he wasn't allowed to remove them from the hill until 4 more years had passed. The monumental work of bringing forth The Book of Mormon had been foretold by ancient prophets. (See Isaiah 29, Ezekiel 37:15-20, & Moses 7:62). A work of this magnitude required careful preparation, necessitating four more years of tutoring. During that time, Joseph met annually with Moroni at the Hill Cumorah to receive instructions in preparation for receiving the plates. Other Nephite prophets who had a vital interest in the coming forth of The Book of Mormon also played a significant role in Joseph's preparation. Nephi, Alma, the twelve disciples chosen by the Savior in America, and Mormon all instructed Joseph. (See "History of Joseph Smith", p. 87).His religious education was intense during this period. (See Buddy Youngreen, "Reflections of Emma, Joseph Smith's Wife", p. 4).

Interim Events. Between Moroni's first appearance, and when Joseph received the plates, several significant events occurred in his life. In November of 1823, tragedy struck the Smith home, when Alvin, Joseph's oldest brother, became ill. On his deathbed, he counseled Joseph: "I want you to be a good boy, and do everything that lies in your power to obtain the record. Be faithful in receiving instruction, and in keeping every commandment that is given you." (H.C., 3:29). Years later, Joseph learned by revelation that Alvin was an heir to the Celestial Kingdom. (See D&C 137:1-6).

October 1825 - Joseph works for Josiah Stowell, and meets Emma Hale. Following Alvin's death, Joseph and his brothers hired out as day-laborers, performing whatever work was available. Treasure hunting, or "money-digging" as it was then called, was a craze in the western United States at this time. Josiah Stowell, a farmer, lumber mill owner, and deacon in the Presbyterian church, came to ask Joseph to assist him in the search for a legendary lost silver mine that was thought to have been opened by Spaniards in northern Pennsylvania. Stowell had heard that Joseph was able to discern invisible things and desired his assistance in the project. The impressionable boy was reluctant, but Stowell persisted, and since Joseph's family was in need, he and his father, together with other neighbors, agreed to help. It was a decision that would have a significant impact on Joseph's life, and on the future of the church.

In preparation for the venture, Joseph and his associates boarded with Isaac Hale in Harmony township, in Pennsylvania, not far from the supposed mine site. While boarding with the Hales, Joseph and Isaac's daughter Emma were attracted to each other, although she was Joseph's senior by a year and a half. The budding romance, however, was frowned upon by Emma's father, who disliked money digging and disdained Joseph's lack of education. His cultured daughter was a schoolteacher, and he thought she could do better. Meanwhile, the search for the silver mine proved to be unproductive. After nearly a month's work, Joseph was able to persuade Josiah Stowell that his efforts were in vain, and the pursuit of the mine in Harmony was abandoned.

Emma Hale was the seventh of nine children, and "a tall, attractive young woman with comely features. Dark-complexioned, with brown eyes and black hair, she possessed a singular, regal beauty of form and of character." ("History of Joseph Smith", pp. 100-101).

Ever since this episode in Joseph's young life, his detractors have used what they have described as "money digging" to question his motives, and to disparage the church he later organized. However, the circumstances are best understood in the context of their time and place. In New England and western New York, such activities were not frowned upon the way they would be many decades later. In his History, Joseph candidly acknowledged his participation in the venture, but characterized it as "insignificant." (See "History of Joseph Smith", p. 108).

While working in the borderlands of New York and Pennsylvania, Joseph made another contact that became important to him and to the early church in New York. Joseph Knight, Sr., a friend of Josiah Stowell, was a humble farmer and miller who lived in Colesville, Broome County, New York. Joseph Smith also worked for him for a time, and in the process developed close friendships with him and his sons, Joseph, Jr., and Newel. They accepted the testimony of the young Prophet, as he recounted his sacred experiences to them.

January 18, 1827 - Joseph marries Emma Hale. Between working for Josiah Stowell, Joseph Knight, Sr., and visiting his own family in Manchester, Joseph continued to court Emma Hale. Because of her father's strong opposition to the marriage, Joseph and Emma eloped. They were married by a justice of the peace in South Bainbridge, New York, on January 18, 1827. Immediately afterward, Joseph moved his new bride to the family home in Manchester, where he spent the succeeding summer farming with his father. Emma was well received by Joseph's family, and a close relationship developed between Emma and Joseph's mother, Lucy Mack Smith.

On September 22, 1827, the Prophet finally receives the plates from the angel Moroni. Little is known of Joseph's visits with Moroni between 1824 and 1827, but sometime before the fall of 1827, Joseph returned home one evening, later than usual. His family was concerned, but he told them he had been delayed because he had just received a severe chastisement from Moroni. He said that as he passed by the Hill Cumorah, "The angel met me, and said that I had not been engaged enough in the work of the Lord; that the time had come for the record to be brought forth; and that I must be up and doing and set myself about the things which God had commanded me to do." (See "History of

Joseph Smith", p. 114; "Joseph Smith 1832 History", "Joseph Smith Letterbook," cited in Dean C. Jessee, "The Personal Writings of Joseph Smith" P. 7-8).

Much had transpired during Joseph's four years of preparation. He passed through his teens largely uninfluenced by the precepts of men. He enjoyed the emotional support of his family, and he took on the responsibilities associated with marriage. Angels prepared him to translate a divinely inspired record and taught him the necessity of self-discipline, repentance, patience, and obedience. He was undoubtedly anxious to begin translating The Book of Mormon.

September 22, 1827 - Joseph is entrusted by Moroni with the records. The work of translation of the plates begins. During the process, his scribes include Martin Harris, Oliver Cowdery, Emma Smith, and John Whitmer.

Before sunrise on September 22, 1827, Joseph and his wife hitched Joseph Knight's horse to Josiah Stowell's spring wagon and drove three miles to the Hill Cumorah. Leaving Emma at its base, Joseph climbed the hill for another interview with Moroni. Moroni gave him the plates, the Urim and Thummim, and the breastplate. He also gave Joseph a specific warning and promise concerning his responsibilities. Joseph now had possession of these sacred objects, and if he were careless or negligent and lost them, he would be cut off. On the other hand, if he used all his efforts to preserve them until Moroni returned for them, he was assured that they would be protected. (See JSH 1:59).

For the first time in over fourteen hundred years, the records were entrusted to a mortal. In what might seem to some to be a surprising move, Joseph carefully hid the plates in a hollow log near his home. The Prophet's friends were not the only ones who eagerly anticipated his receipt of the plates. Others in the neighborhood had heard that Joseph was going to bring home valuable metal plates. Some of them may have also been involved in searching for the silver mine, and now felt that they should have a share in any treasure that had been found.

Joseph soon learned why Moroni had strictly charged him to protect the plates. "Every stratagem that could be invented" was used to get them from him. (See J.S.H. 1:60). For example, Willard Chase, a neighboring farmer, along with other treasure seekers, sent for a sorcerer to come and find the place where the plates had been hidden. When the Smiths learned of the plot, they sent Emma to get Joseph, who was working in Macedon a few miles west of Palmyra. He returned immediately and retrieved the plates. Wrapping them in a linen frock, he started through the woods, thinking that route might be safer than the well-traveled road. But just as he jumped over a log, he was struck from behind with a gun. Joseph, however, was able to knock his assailant down and flee. Half a mile later, he was again assaulted, but managed to escape once more, and before he arrived home, he was accosted a third time. His mother said that when he reached home he was "altogether speechless from fright and the fatigue of running." (See Stanley B. Kimball, "I Cannot Read a Sealed Book," "Improvement Era", 2/1957).

Efforts to steal the plates only intensified, but Moroni's promise of protection was also fulfilled. Joseph often moved the plates from their hiding places just minutes before the treasure seekers arrived. Once, he hid them under the hearthstone of the fireplace of his home, and later he hid them under the wooden floor of the cooper shop on the Smith farm, before moving them to the loft.

The Prophecy of Isaiah is fulfilled. During this period, Joseph's life was in danger, so he decided to take Emma back to Harmony, where he hoped to begin the translation of the record in peace. Before they left, Martin Harris, a citizen of Palmyra who would later play a role in the Restoration, stepped forward and offered to help. He was a prosperous farmer who had met the Smiths when they had first settled in Palmyra, and over the years, he had hired various family members to work for him. Now, he provided money so Joseph and Emma could liquidate their debts, and he also gave them fifty dollars to finance their trip to Harmony. With the plates hidden in a barrel of beans in the back of the wagon, they left town in December of 1827, headed for Harmony. Prior arrangements had been made to board temporarily with Emma's parents.

Except for Joseph Smith, no man played a more varied role in the coming forth of The Book of Mormon than Martin Harris. He served as a scribe, became a witness of the coming forth of The Book of Mormon, financially assisted in its publication, and testified of the truthfulness of the book throughout his life.

Following a brief stay with the Hales, the couple purchased a house from Emma's eldest brother, Jesse. It was a small two-story home on a thirteen-acre farm bordering the Susquehanna River. For the first time in weeks, Joseph was able to work in relative peace. Between December 1827 and February 1828, he copied many of the characters from the plates and translated some of them by using the Urim and Thummim. In the early stages of the work, Joseph spent considerable time and effort becoming familiar with the language of the plates and learning how to translate.

According to previous arrangements, Martin Harris visited Joseph in Harmony sometime in February of 1828, it having been revealed to him that the Lord had a work for him to do. In 1827, several personal manifestations had convinced Harris that Joseph Smith was a prophet, and that he should assist him in publishing The Book of Mormon. Therefore, he went to Harmony to obtain a copy of some of the characters from the plates to show several noted linguists of the time, thereby unintentionally fulfilling the prophecy of Isaiah 29:11-12, to help convince an unbelieving world. (See H.C., 1:20). This ancient prophecy of Isaiah continues to mystify Bible scholars, but Martin Harris and Joseph Smith linked it to The Book of Mormon. This has been verified by an expanded version of Isaiah's prophecy that appears in 2 Nephi Chapter 27.

February 1828 - Martin Harris visits Charles Anthon in New York City. Martin visited Professor Charles Anthon, affiliated with Columbia College in New York City, who was among the leading classical scholars of his day. At the time of Harris's visit, Anthon was adjunct professor of Greek and Latin. He spoke French, German, Greek, and Latin, and was familiar with the latest discoveries pertaining to the Egyptian language, including the early work of Champollion. (See "History of Joseph Smith", p. 116-17, & 122).

According to Harris, Professor Anthon examined the characters and their translation and willingly gave him a certificate stating that the writings were authentic. Anthon further told Harris that the characters resembled Egyptian, Chaldean, Assyrian, and Arabic, and expressed his opinion that the translation was correct. Martin put the certificate in his pocket and was about to leave when Anthon called him back, and asked how Joseph Smith had found the plates in the hill. Martin explained that an angel of God had revealed the location to Joseph, whereupon Anthon asked for the certificate, which Martin gave to him. "He took it and tore it to pieces, saying, that there was no such thing as ministering of angels, and that if I (Martin) would bring the plates to him, he would translate them. I informed him that part of the plates were sealed, and that I was forbidden to bring them. He replied, 'I cannot read a sealed book.'" ("History of Joseph Smith", pp. 128-29).

Martin Harris's experience with Anthon was significant for several reasons. First, it demonstrated a scholarly interest in the characters, and that there were academicians who were willing to give them serious consideration, as long as an angel was not part of the story. Secondly, it was, in the view of Harris and Joseph, the direct fulfillment of prophecy that related to The Book of Mormon. Thirdly, it demonstrated that translating the record would require the assistance of God; intellect alone would be insufficient. (See Isaiah 29:11-12 & 2 Nephi 27:15-20). Finally, it solidified Harris's own faith. He returned home, confident that he now had evidence to convince his neighbors of Joseph Smith's work. He was now ready to wholeheartedly commit himself and his worldly treasure to the publication of The Book of Mormon.

February – June 1828 - The first 116 pages of the record are translated from the Large Plates of Nephi, which was Mormon's translation of the Book of Lehi, but the manuscript copy is lost. Consequently, Joseph loses the gift of translation, and the plates and the Urim and Thummim are taken from him.

Martin's wife, Lucy, had been suspicious of Joseph Smith. She had questioned him about the plates and had demanded to see them. He had told her she could not, "for he was not permitted to exhibit them to any one except those whom the Lord should appoint to testify of them."

Lucy was angry that her husband had been spending so much time away from her, and she wondered if the Smiths might be trying to defraud him. She insisted on going to Harmony again, to meet with Joseph. This time, she announced that she was not going to leave until she saw the plates. She ransacked the entire house looking for them, but did not find them. From that day on, she claimed that her husband had been duped by "a grand imposter." After two weeks, Martin took her home. Despite her attempts to dissuade him, he returned to Harmony. In Martin's absence, Lucy continued her vocal criticism in Palmyra. (See "History of Joseph Smith", p. 135).

In Harmony, Joseph and Martin labored together on the translation until June 14, 1828. By that time, the translation filled 116 roughly legal-size pages, and Martin asked if he could take this manuscript home to show his wife and friends. He hoped this would convince Lucy that the work was legitimate, and that it would put an end to her opposition. Through the Urim and Thummim, Joseph inquired of the Lord regarding what he should do. The answer was no, do not release the 116 pages to the care of Martin Harris. Not satisfied, Harris persisted until Joseph once again asked the Lord. Still, the answer was no. Martin's pleadings and solicitations continued unabatedly. Joseph wanted to satisfy his benefactor; he was young and inexperienced, and he relied upon the age and maturity of Harris. Moreover, Harris was the only one Joseph knew who was willing to both work as scribe and finance the publication of the book. These considerations moved him to ask one more time. Finally, the Lord granted a conditional permission. Harris agreed in writing to show the manuscript to only four or five people, including his wife; his brother, his father, his mother, and Lucy's sister. Harris then left for Palmyra with the only copy of the manuscript.

Shortly after his departure, Emma Smith bore a son who died the day he was born. Emma nearly died herself, and for two weeks, Joseph was constantly at her bedside. When she improved, his attention turned to the manuscript. By this time, Harris had been gone for three weeks, and they had heard nothing from him. Harris had not been totally irresponsible during this time. He had spent time with his wife, taken care of business in Palmyra, and served on a jury.

Emma encouraged Joseph to take a stage to Palmyra, to check on the matter. After walking the last twenty miles during the night, Joseph finally arrived at his parents' home in Manchester. He immediately sent for Harris, who usually came quickly, so breakfast was prepared for him and the Smiths. Several hours passed before Harris finally plodded up the walk with head hung down. He climbed on the fence and sat there with his hat down over his eyes. Finally, he came in and sat down at the breakfast table, but he could not eat. Lucy Mack Smith, Joseph's mother, recorded: "He took up his knife and fork as if he were going to use them, but immediately dropped them. Hyrum, observing this, said 'Martin, why do you not eat; are you sick?' Upon which Harris pressed his hands upon his temples, and cried out in a tone of deep anguish, 'Oh, I have lost my soul! I have lost my soul!'

"Joseph who had not expressed his fears till now, sprang from the table, exclaiming, 'Martin, have you lost that manuscript? Have you broken your oath, and brought down condemnation upon my head as well as your own?' "'Yes; it is gone,' replied Harris, 'and I know not where.'"
Joseph exclaimed, "'All is lost! all is lost! What shall I do? I have sinned. it is I who tempted the wrath of God. I should

have been satisfied with the first answer which I received from the Lord; for he told me that it was not safe to let the writing go out of my possession.' He wept and groaned, and walked the floor continually.

"At length he told Harris to go back and search again. "'No", said Harris, 'it is all in vain; for I have ripped open beds and pillows looking for the manuscript; and I know it is not there.' "'Then must I,' said Joseph, 'return with such a tale as this? I dare not do it. And how shall I appear before the Lord? Of what rebuke am I not worthy from the angel of the Most High?' ... "The next morning, he set out for home. We parted with heavy hearts, for it now appeared that all which we had so fondly anticipated, and which had been the source of so much secret gratification, had in a moment fled, and fled forever." ("History of the Church", 5:423).

September 1828 - Joseph regains possession of the plates and the Urim and Thummim. The gift of translation is restored, and the translation of the plates recommences.

Upon returning to Harmony without the 116 pages of manuscript, Joseph immediately began to pray for the Lord to forgive him for acting contrary to his will. Moroni appeared to Joseph and required him to return the plates and the Urim and Thummim, but promised that he could receive them back if he were humble and penitent. Some time later, he received a revelation which chastised him for negligence and for "setting at naught the counsels of God" but it also comforted him that he was still chosen to perform the work of translation if he repented. (See D&C 3:4-10). Joseph did repent, and again received the plates and the Urim and Thummim, along with a promise that the Lord would send a scribe to assist him in the translation. There was a special message: "The angel seemed pleased with me ... and he told me that the Lord loved me, for my faithfulness and humility." ("H.C., 2:170.)

With his divine gift restored, Joseph learned by revelation that wicked men intended to entrap him. They had altered the words of the manuscript, and if he translated the same material again and published it, they would say he was unable to do it the same way twice, and therefore, the work must not be inspired. (See D&C 10). God, however, had anticipated this scenario. The lost document was the Book of Lehi taken from Mormon's abridgment of the Large Plates of Nephi. But Mormon had been inspired to attach the Small Plates of Nephi to his record for "a wise purpose," which at the time he did not understand. (See Words of Mormon 1:3-7). These small plates contained an account similar to that in the Book of Lehi. Joseph was instructed not to retranslate, but to continue on and at the appropriate time to include the material from the Small Plates of Nephi. These records were the account of Nephi which the Lord said was "more particular concerning the things which, in my wisdom, I would bring to the knowledge of the people." (D&C 10:40).

The Prophet's Preparation. The five and one-half years between September 1823 and April 1829 had been important in Joseph Smith's preparation for translating The Book of Mormon and leading the church in the dispensation of the fulness of times. In 1829, he was now twenty-three years old. He was tall and strong; he worked on the farm, in the fields, and at odd jobs. Although he had had little formal schooling, Joseph had a hungry and curious mind. He liked to discover things for himself and to seek his answers from the scriptures. (See JSH 1:11-12). This thirst for knowledge, especially spiritual knowledge, never left him.

Twenty years later, in June of 1843, Joseph told the Saints: "I am a rough stone. The sound of the hammer and chisel were never heard on me until the Lord took me in hand. I desire the learning and wisdom of heaven alone." (H.C., 5:423). Courage, optimism, and faith were hallmarks of his personality. He had shown great courage at an early age, when he had endured a painful leg operation. He later faced moblike neighbors who were trying to get the plates from him. Despite his poverty and lack of education, he was optimistic about himself and life. Rebuked by the Lord and corrected by Moroni, he was always submissive, repentant, and energetic. He despaired when the 116 pages had been lost, but from that experience he learned obedience, and was later able to say, "I made this my rule: When the Lord commands, do it." (History of the Church, 2:170). He also learned valuable lessons about controlling his motives and purposes and was, therefore, able to keep his "eye single to the glory of God" (D&C 4:5) and channel his energies and thoughts toward building the kingdom.

By this time, Joseph Smith had gained considerable experience with various means of revelation. He had communed with God and his Son and with angelic messengers. He had seen visions, felt the promptings of the Spirit, and become skilled using the Urim and Thummim. But, we should not conclude that revelation came easy to him, for another lesson he learned during this time was the price in faith, diligence, persistence, worthiness, and obedience he had to pay to receive communication from God.

April 7, 1829 - Oliver Cowdery begins his service as scribe to Joseph Smith. He continued to serve until the translation of The Book of Mormon is completed, in June 1829.

May 15, 1829 - While Joseph translates passages of The Book of Mormon about the necessity of baptism, he and Oliver Cowdery ask the Lord who has authority to baptize in His name. They knelt in a secluded spot near Joseph's home in Harmony, Pennsylvania, when "the voice of the Redeemer spake peace to us," Oliver later wrote, and a heavenly messenger, John the Baptist, "came down clothed with glory." He conferred upon the two men the Aaronic Priesthood, which holds the priesthood keys "of the gospel of repentance, and of baptism by immersion for the remission of sins." Subsequent to their ordination, and on that same day, Joseph baptized Oliver, and Oliver baptized Joseph.

June 1, 1829 - Joseph and Oliver move to Fayette, to continue the work of translation.

June 1829 (?) - The Melchizedek Priesthood is restored, and Joseph Smith and Oliver Cowdery are ordained under the hands of Peter, James, and John, although there remains a question about the actual month and year of their ordination (See BYU Studies, 35:4, "Priesthood Restoration Documents" Brian Q. Cannon).

It is impossible to precisely date this heavenly manifestation from existing sources. The only firsthand account from Joseph that provides details about the circumstances of the vision is an 1842 letter (now canonized as Doctrine and Covenants 128) in which he testified he heard "the voice of Peter, James, and John in the wilderness between Harmony, Susquehanna County, and Colesville, Broome County; on the Susquehanna river, declaring themselves as possessing the keys of the kingdom."

In a blessing that Joseph Smith gave to Oliver Cowdery, recorded in October 1835, he spoke of Oliver's receiving "the holy priesthood under the hands of they who had been held in reserve for a long season, even those who received it under the hand of the Messiah." ("Blessing to Oliver Cowdery, 10/2/1835," in Patriarchal Blessing Book 1, 12, josephsmithpapers.org).

How long did it take to translate The Book of Mormon? The work of translation proceeded haltingly through 1828. Joseph's wife, Emma, and others served as scribes until the spring of 1829, when Oliver Cowdery took over, recording the bulk of the 275,000-word text from Joseph's dictation, concluding near the end of June 1829, during a period of about 60 to 90 days.

What was the language of the ancient plates? According to Moroni, the record was written in "reformed Egyptian." He further explained that if the "plates had been sufficiently large we should have written in Hebrew; but the Hebrew hath been altered by us also; and if we could have written in Hebrew, behold, ye would have had no imperfection in our record. But the Lord knoweth the things which we have written, and also that none other people knoweth our language … therefore he hath prepared means for the interpretation thereof" (Mormon 9:32-34).

June 1829 - The sacred records are shown to the Three Witnesses, (Oliver Cowdery, David Whitmer, and Martin Harris) who declare that an angel of God appeared to them and showed them The Book of Mormon plates and that they heard the voice of the Lord declare that Joseph Smith's translation had been accomplished "by the gift and power of God." This takes place in June 1829, near the home of Peter Whitmer Sr. in Fayette, New York.

June 28, 1829 - The sacred records are shown to the Eight Witnesses. Subsequently, on June 28, 1829, near the Whitmer farm, the Three Witnesses have their own experience. Thereafter, the Smith and Whitmer families travel to the Joseph Smith, Sr. home in Palmyra, New York. On July 2, 1829, near the Smith home, the Eight Witnesses say that they had seen and handled the plates.

March 26, 1830 - The Book of Mormon is published under the direction of printer Egbert B. Grandin, and goes on sale in Palmyra, New York. The printing cost is $.60 per copy, but many are given away. Joseph is 24 years of age. The typesetting, printing, and calf-leather binding of 5,000 copies, consisting of nearly 3 million total pages, had begun in August 1829, at a cost of $3,000, paid for through the sale of part of Martin Harris's farm. It is estimated that around 700 copies of that first edition have survived to the present day. Their value has increased significantly.

April 6, 1830 - The Church of Jesus Christ of Latter-day Saints is formally organized, in Fayette, New York. Initially, and in accordance with the laws of New York State, there are 6 members. Although about thirty people are present, only those six – Joseph Smith, Jr., Oliver Cowdery, Hyrum Smith, Peter Whitmer, Jr., Samuel H. Smith, and David Whitmer - become the first legal members of the church.

April 6, 1830 - The first elders of the church are ordained. Joseph and Oliver ordain each other. During the first few years after the church is organized, Joseph Smith and other early members of the church do not use the terms 'Aaronic Priesthood' or 'Melchizedek Priesthood' to describe the authority they had received. Their understanding of priesthood only develops over time and with the aid of continuing revelation.

April 6, 1830 - The Sacrament is first administered for the first time in the church, on the day it is organized, on Tuesday, April 6, 1830, when the thirty men and women referenced above gather "to partake of bread and wine in the remembrance of the Lord Jesus" (D&C 20:75).

April 3, 1836 – Priesthood keys are restored in the Kirtland Temple, with the keys of authority being given to Joseph Smith and Oliver Cowdery. First comes Moses to restore the keys of the gathering of Israel. Then comes an Elias from Abraham's day to restore the sealing power of the priesthood. Then comes Elijah, with the keys by which all gospel ordinances are sealed. When the sealing power of the priesthood is restored, it is on the second day of the Passover Feast, when many Jews throughout the world symbolically open their doors to invite the prophet in to their homes and their lives.

Testimony of Emma Smith, Wife of the Prophet Joseph Smith. "Joseph Smith could neither write nor dictate a coherent and well-worded letter; let alone dictate a book like The Book of Mormon. And, though I was an active participant in the scenes that transpired, and was present during the translation of the plates, and had cognizance of things as they transpired, it is marvelous to me, 'a marvel and a wonder,' as much so as to any one else" ("Last Testimony of Sister Emma," "Saints' Herald", 10/1/1879, p. 290).

June 27, 1844 – After leading the church for just over 14 years, Joseph Smith is martyred at Carthage Jail, Illinois. He was 38 years old.

If we ever hope to successfully free ourselves from the quicksands of self-pity and escape the inequalities of life, we must personalize the lessons of the Atonement. We must change our nature and become new creatures in Christ. We must practice in front of a mirror, if necessary, and recite the following over and over again until we get it right: "Father, forgive them, for they know not what they do." We must become more Amish.

Revelation

We are cast off into a
stream of revelation and carried
along in the quickening currents
of direct experience with God.

"And we also had many
revelations, and the spirit of much
prophecy; wherefore, we knew of Christ
and his kingdom, which should come."
(Jacob 1:6, see Jacob 4:6).

Before the Restoration, during the theophany in the Sacred Grove, Joseph Smith was told that he must join none of the sects of Christendom, "for they were all wrong; and the Personage who addressed (him) said that all their creeds were an abomination in his sight; that those professors were all corrupt; that 'they draw near to me with their lips, but their hearts are far from me, they teach for doctrines the commandments of men, having a form of godliness, but they deny the power thereof.'" (J.S.H. 1:19). In reality, the abomination of their creeds was that their actions were all form and no substance, the sizzle without the steak. Insult was added to injury when hypocrisy became a part of humanized, spiritually impotent dogma, when people did not really believe, but were only professors of religion. Too often they revealed their true character, when "every man (was) lifted up in the imagination of the thoughts of his heart, being only evil continually." (Moses 8:22).

Religion in Joseph Smith's day had become magical, when the power by which churches operated was transferred from God to those who professed to be His earthly representatives, but who were only competing for market share. Priesthood had acquired the status of an office that mechanically bestowed power and grace, without regard for the spiritual or moral qualifications of its possessor. The Bible itself had become a magical book in the eyes of many, conveying power and knowledge without the aid of revelation. Moroni saw that there would be many in the Last Days who had "transfigured the holy word of God," or who had changed the appearance and substance of the scriptures. (Mormon 8:33).

When we recognize priesthood authority, ordinances, and covenants, Christ becomes "the way, the truth, and the life," while those who will not hear the voice of the Lord, neither the voice of his servants, neither give heed to the words of the prophets and apostles, shall be cut off from among the people. For they have strayed from mine ordinances," said the Lord, "and have broken mine everlasting covenant." (John 14:6 & D&C 1:14-15). Joseph Smith once declared that his generation was "as corrupt as the generation of the Jews that crucified Christ." (H.C., 5:68). If this accurately described behavior in the early years of the nineteenth century, it would be an absolute condemnation of those now living in the barren desert wastes of spiritual Babylon.

Today, our world is in a self-destruct mode that seeks "not the Lord to establish his righteousness, but every man (desperately) walketh in his own way, and after the image of his own god, whose image is in the likeness of the world, and whose substance is that of an idol, which waxeth old and shall perish in Babylon, even Babylon the great, which shall fall." (D&C 1:16). The devil rules in the earth by the manipulation of those who worship such idols. In contrast to his profane authority, John Taylor taught: "Priesthood is the legitimate rule of God and is the only legitimate power that has a right to rule upon the earth, and when the will of God is done on the earth, as it is done in heaven, no other power will bear rule." (J.D., 5:187).

Those who fight against Zion are wicked and adulterous in the sense that they have fornicated with the devil by being unfaithful to gospel principles. Individuals and institutions are promiscuous and corrupt when idols are the focus of their worship. Those who are not with God are against Him. As Ezekiel wrote, those who allow themselves to be led into spiritual bondage, become "as the heathen, as the families of the countries, to serve (idols of) wood and stone." (Ezekiel 20:32).

In our day, Babylon has become firmly entrenched in the world and is "the great whore that sitteth upon many waters, with whom the kings of the earth have committed fornication." (Revelation 17:1-2). To some extent, all of the profane governments of the earth are institutionally corrupt and have prostituted themselves.

One of the terrible consequences of the fascination of the world with Babylon is its spiritual insensitivity. Isaiah foresaw the Last Days, when he wrote: "Stay yourselves, and wonder; cry ye out, and cry: they are drunken, but not with wine; they stagger, but not with strong drink. For the Lord hath poured out upon you the spirit of deep sleep, and hath closed your eyes: the prophets, and your rulers, and seers hath he covered." (Isaiah 29:9-11).

Those who are steeped in iniquity are spiritually unprepared to receive revelation from God. The Lord told His prophet Daniel: "Shut up the words, and seal the book, even unto the time of the end." (Daniel 12:4). When John saw God the Father on His holy throne in heaven, he noticed "a book written within and on the backside, sealed with seven seals. And (he) saw a strong angel proclaiming with a loud voice, Who is worthy to open the book, and to loose the seals thereof? And no man in heaven, nor in earth, neither under the earth, was able to open the book, neither to look thereon. And (he) wept much, because no man was found worthy to open and to read the book, neither to look thereon." (Revelation 5:1-4).

The Apocalypse of John is incomplete, but the Lord has promised that if we are faithful, we "shall receive the fulness of the record of John." (D&C 93:18). An angel confirmed to Nephi that many things have been written that are "sealed up to come forth in their purity, according to the truth which is in the Lamb, in the own due time of the Lord, unto the house of Israel." (1 Nephi 14:26). Joseph Smith was forbidden to translate a portion of the plates delivered by Moroni. Nephi explained: "For the book shall be sealed by the power of God, and the revelation which was sealed shall be kept in the book until the own due time of the Lord, that they may come forth; for behold, they reveal all things from the foundation of the world unto the end thereof." (2 Nephi 27:10).

When the church has proven itself worthy and capable of accepting it, God will reveal the contents of these sealed scriptures. "And the day cometh that the words of the book which were sealed shall be read upon the house tops; and they shall be read by the power of Christ; and all things shall be revealed unto the children of men which ever have been among the children of men, and which ever will be even unto the end of the earth." (2 Nephi 27:11).

After the Lord selects those who are humble and worthy, "the weak things of the word," He tutors and mentors them by revealing His will to them. (D&C 1:19). In consequence of the great power exerted by Satan in the Last Days, and "knowing the calamity which should come upon the inhabitants of the earth," the Lord chose Joseph Smith to be

His prophet, seer, and revelator, and "spake unto him from heaven, and gave him commandments." (D&C 1:17). As Spencer W. Kimball once stated, "Christianity did not go from Rome to Galilee. It was the other way around. In our day, the routing is from Palmyra to Paris, not the reverse." ("Ensign," 5/1976).

It is the Lord's hope that "every man might speak in the name of God the Lord, even the Savior of the world." (D&C 1:20). Certainly, this is one of the most powerful evidences of both the Apostasy and the Restoration, that the authority to invoke the name of God rests with His priesthood servants who are scattered across the face of the earth.

Because of the ministry of Joseph Smith and others, faith has increased so that the covenant promises God made with Abraham may be realized. It is becoming possible for the fulness of the gospel to be "proclaimed by the weak and the simple unto the ends of the world, and before kings and rulers." (D&C 1:23). In the early days of the latter-day work, it was the Lord's way to use unlettered and untutored servants, and so grammatical errors in the revelations were to be expected. Changes made in some of the revelations actually confirm that Joseph Smith received revelation. Knowing the mind and will of God, he edited them before they were published, so that the wording of each would accurately reflect the thoughts, impressions, and inspiration the Lord had given him.

In fact, we have both clarification and confirmation from Deity: "Behold, I am God and have spoken it; these commandments are of me, and were given unto my servants in their weakness, after the manner of their language, that they might come to understanding. And inasmuch as they erred, it might be made known; And inasmuch as they sought wisdom they might be instructed; And inasmuch as they sinned they might be chastened, that they might repent; And inasmuch as they were humble they might be made strong, and blessed from on high, and receive knowledge from time to time." (D&C 1:24-28).

The Lord Himself testified of the divine mission of Joseph Smith and of the truthfulness of The Book of Mormon in language reminiscent of ancient Hebrew oaths. "And he has translated the book, even that part which I have commanded him, and as your Lord and your God liveth it is true." (D&C 17:6). As Paul wrote: "Because he could swear by no greater, he sware by himself." (Hebrews 6:13). Joseph Smith was given the "power to lay the foundation of this church, and to bring it forth out of obscurity and out of darkness, the only true and living church upon the face of the whole earth, with which I, the Lord, am well pleased." (D&C 1:30).

The realities of the apostasy and the subsequent restoration of priesthood authority are well documented in the scriptures and in the history of the church. No other church has the authority required to bind and ratify the covenants we make with God or to break the iron grip of Satan, who would drag our souls down to hell in an instant if he were given the opportunity to do so. No other church has the authority to receive revelation to direct God's work, or the full and unabridged support of "the only living and true God." (D&C 20:19).

"Of the other churches, we do not say they are wrong, so much as we say they are incomplete." (Boyd K. Packer, C.R., 10/64). All the branches of the House of Israel, as well as the Gentiles who were grafted in, had become corrupted by the time the gospel was restored to the earth in 1830. As the prophet Zenos taught: "Notwithstanding all the care with which we have taken of my vineyard, the trees thereof have become corrupted, that they bring forth no good fruit." (Jacob 5:46). A hallmark of The Church of Jesus Christ of Latter-day Saints is that its members believe in both personal and institutional continuing revelation. However, "looking for the spectacular, we often miss the constant flow of revealed communication that comes." (Spencer W. Kimball, Munich Germany Area Conference, 1973, p. 77). Because this is true of society as well as of Saints, the Lord's authorized servants who have been commissioned to preach the saving principles of the gospel frequently have a difficult time finding an audience. In contrast to the messages of Madison Avenue that are pleasing to those with itching ears and carnal natures, theirs strike more sensitive and selective chords.

For too many, "our age is retrospective," Ralph Waldo Emerson sadly observed, "building only on the "sepulchres of the fathers. It writes biographies, histories, and criticism. The foregoing generations beheld God and nature face to face; we, through their eyes. Why should not we also enjoy an original relation to the universe? Why should not we have a poetry and philosophy of insight and not (only) of tradition, and a religion by revelation to us, and not (just) the history of theirs?" (Introduction, "Nature").

The church has the answer to these questions. The Restoration confirms that it is possible to tap into the fountain of life-giving waters. "These currents and many more are part of the flowing fountain of the church. If we do not drink, if we die of thirst while only inches from the fountain, the fault comes down to us. For the free, full, flowing, living water is there." (Truman Madsen, "Christ & The Inner Life," p. 31).

Chauncey Riddle wrote of his own intensely personal journey to a state of peace that surpasseth understanding: "I felt I had received some revelation before," he said, "However, I saw that random revelation was not sufficient. To be a rock, a bastion of surety, revelation must be something on which one can count and receive on every occasion of real need. I began to seek it actively. I prayed, I fasted; I lived the gospel as best I knew. I was faithful in my church duties. I tried to live up to every scruple that my conscience enjoined upon me. And dependable revelation did come. Intermittently, haltingly at first, then steadily, over some years it finally came to be a mighty stream of experience. I came to know that at any time of day or night, in any circumstance, for any real need, I could get help. That help came in the form of feelings of encouragement when things seemed hopeless. It came in ideas to unravel puzzles that blocked my accomplishment. It came in priesthood blessings that were fully realized. It came in whisperings of prophecy that were fulfilled. It came in support and even anticipation of what the General Authorities of the church would say and do in General Conference. It came in the gifts of the Spirit, as the wonders of eternity were opened to the eyes of my understanding. That stream of spiritual experience is today for me a river of living water that nourishes my soul in every situation. It is the most important factor of my life. If it were taken away, all that I have and am would be dust and ashes. It is the basis of my love, life, understanding, hope, and progress. My only regret is that though this river is so wonderful, I have not been able to take full advantage of it as yet. My life does not yet conform to all that I know. But now I do know; I do not just believe." ("Sunstone," 5/1988, p. 8).

We know, as members of The Church of Jesus Christ of Latter-day Saints, that God will continue to reveal many great and important things pertaining to the kingdom. We believe that he sends us tenderly crafted letters of love and encouragement, hoping that they will be opened and read with care. We also believe that these lines of communication may be nurtured to become avenues of freely flowing correspondence between heaven and earth.

"The builder who first bridged Niagara's gorge, before he swung his cable, shore to shore, sent out across the gulf his venturing kite, bearing a slender cord for unseen hands to grasp upon the further cliff and draw a greater cord, and then a greater yet, 'til at last across the chasm swung The Cable and then the mighty bridge in air. So may we send our little timid thoughts across the void, out to God's reaching hands; send our love and faith to thread the deep, thought after thought until the little cord has greatened to a chain no chance can break, and we are anchored to the infinite!" (Edwin Markham).

Reverence

"Their meetings were conducted
by the church after the manner of the
workings of the Spirit, and by the power
of the Holy Ghost; for as the power of
the Holy Ghost led them whether to
preach, or to exhort, or to pray,
or to supplicate, or to sing,
even so it was done."
(Moroni 6:9).

David O. McKay said: "People come to church for light and knowledge, and when they do they have a right to find it." (C.R., 10/1950. He went on to say that "the greatest manifestation of spirituality (during the worship service) is reverence; indeed, reverence is spirituality." ("Instructor" 10/1966, p. 371).

Reverence is first a state of being and then a condition of action. "Be still, and know that I am God," said the Lord. (D&C 101:16). After that quiet confirmation, comes the admonition to "see that ye serve him with all your heart, might, mind and strength." (D&C 4:2). God simply asks that we focus upon Him all our affections, will power, reasoning faculties, and physical efforts as we worship. The Lord explained that the Spirit teaches us "that (we) may understand and know how to worship, and know what (we) worship, that (we) may come unto the Father in (His) name, and in due time receive of his fulness." (D&C 93:19). Indeed, the hour has come, "and now is, when ... true worshippers shall worship the Father in spirit and in truth." (John 4:23). For "this is life eternal," the Savior explained, "that they might know thee the only true God, and Jesus Christ, whom thou hast sent." (John 17:3).

"Reverence," wrote John Ruskin, "is the noblest state in which a man can live in the world. Reverence is one of the signs of strength, while irreverence one of the surest indications of weakness. No man will rise high who jeers at sacred things. The fine loyalties of life must be reverenced or they will be foresworn in the day of trial." (Quoted by David O. McKay, C.R., 10/1950). Some things should be held in such high esteem that they could never legitimately fall under the scrutiny of a critical eye, never be subjected to judgment, and never be compromised in conversation by association with the profane. The standard of our relationship with Heavenly Father, Jesus Christ, and the Holy Ghost is so high that, if we cross the line and demean any member of the Godhead, our guilt is immediately and incontrovertibly established, and without repentance the consequences of our irreverence are irrevocably sealed. Charles Jefferson wrote: "Men in many circles are clever, interesting, brilliant, but they lack one of the three dimensions of life. They have no reach upward. Their conversation sparkles, but it is frivolous and often flippant. Their talk is witty, but is often at the expense of high and sacred things." ("The Character of Jesus," p. 313-314). In his youth, even Joseph

Smith was, by his own admission, guilty of levity, and sometimes associated with jovial company. His conduct was "not consistent with that character which ought to be maintained by one who was called of God." (J.S.H. 1:27). Modern sophists and others fall into the same trap, when "intellectual embroidery is preferred to the whole clothing of the gospel, the frills to the fabric." (Neal A. Maxwell, Salt Lake Institute of Religion, 1/2/1974).

Latter-day Saints believe that reverence is an integral part of an eternal relationship with God. Much is expected of those to whom much has been given, and so those who enjoy the guidance of the Holy Ghost have a special responsibility to develop noble traits of character. "An irreverent man is not a believing man. He may profess belief in Christ, but as the king in Hamlet, his words will fly up, but his thoughts remain below." (David O. McKay, C.R., 10/1951). Reverence cannot tolerate hypocrisy. When all the trappings and pretenses have been shorn away, when outward observances and phylacteries have been stripped from the ritual of our worship, when the façade and hypocrisy of our supposed devotion have been dismantled, when only our true feelings remain, it will be the reverent who will be found to be blameless and without guile. But there is hope, even for the worst of us. The wounds that are so easily inflicted by worldly influences, the raw and ugly sores of pseudo-sophistication, and the cankers of the cares of the world, can be promptly and effectively healed with the Balm of Gilead. Reverence will prevail over even the most virulent assaults that Babylon can muster. Reverence is meek, but it is not passive. It actively fosters both creativity and purposeful action. It disciplines our minds, strengthens our bodies, and enlarges the capacities of our hearts, making room for the Spirit to find expression. While it is not always articulated, it can be the greatest facilitator of the most profound communication, centering our efforts and our attention on the things that truly make a difference, and prompting us to ask ourselves how we can make everything with which we relate more beautiful and harmonious with their surroundings. Everything we do in the church, every priesthood action, every ordinance, every covenant, every prayer, and every act of compassionate service, every sacrifice, has greater meaning and purpose because of the reverence that is consciously and unconsciously integrated into our actions.

"Reverence embraces regard, deference, honor, and esteem. Without some degree of it, therefore, there would be no courtesy, no gentility, no consideration of others' feelings, or of others' rights. It is the fundamental virtue in religion. If there were more reverence in human hearts, there would be less room for sin and sorrow, and increased capacity for joy and gladness. Reverence for God and sacred things is the chief characteristic of a great soul." (David O. McKay, C.R., 10/1956).

We can see why, in a world with less reverence, there is more selfishness. When reverence wanes, spiritual power is sapped, and strife and contention move in to fill the void. With less reverence, human sophistry is substituted for the counsel of Almighty God. With less reverence, it is easier to rationalize behavior that is inconsistent with gospel principles. With less reverence, "freedom weeps, wrong rules the land, and justice sleeps." (Josiah Gilbert Holland).

"Learn the power and lesson of self-mastery," urged David O. McKay. "The principle of self-control lies at the basis of reverence." (C.R., 10/1950). There is a perpetual battle raging in our hearts. It is a battle pitting reverence against telestial tendencies that twist our focus inward, toward ourselves and away from our Creator. These two ways always "lie open before us, one leading to an ever lower and lower plane, where are heard the cries of despair and the curses of the poor, where manhood shrivels and possessions wear down the possessor; and the other leading to the highlands of the morning where are heard the glad shouts of humanity, and where honest (and reverent) effort is rewarded with immortality." (John P. Altgeld). In our technologically sophisticated society, it is all too easy "to fill space, as if what we have, what we are, is not enough. Being affluent, we strangle ourselves with what we can buy, things whose opacity obstructs our ability to see what is really there." (Gretel Erlich, "Under Wyoming's Skies," The Atlantic Magazine). Materialism is like a cancer that chokes out the capacity of our hearts for reverence. Focusing on the work of the Kingdom helps us to maintain our perspective and strengthen our reverence for God's work. Indeed, the earth, sun, moon, and stars "roll upon their wings in their glory ... and any man who hath seen any or the least of these hath seen God moving in his majesty and power." (D&C 88:45-46).

Because Latter-day Saints tend to be sociable, they are periodically reminded of the importance of reverence in meetings. Those who come to worship God in His sanctuary have a right to b carried by the Spirit into a mystical union with the Infinite. Gordon B. Hinckley stated; "We encourage the cultivation of friends with happy conversations among our people. However, these should take place in the foyer, and when we enter the chapel we should understand that we are in sacred precincts. All who come into the Lord's house should have a feeling they are walking and standing on holy ground." ("Ensign," 5/1987). We should reverence that sacred house, as did Moses on Sinai, when the mount "was altogether on a smoke, because the Lord descended upon it in fire." (Exodus 19:18).

God gave our hearts the capacity for reverence because He knew that it would bring us into complete harmony with His nature. Reverence can be the catalyst that propels us upward to discover the personal levels of experience of the Savior, for when the scriptures speak of "knowing Him," they must be referring to a special sense of the word. It is not enough that we know about Him, by reading the Gospels, or by listening to others speak of Him. We must know Him through the bonds of common experience and common feeling. After all, religion is more involved with recovery than discovery. Our destiny is not union, but reunion with divine realities. Religious recognition is a relearning of that which we have already understood. The only way we can "approach" the Savior either figuratively or literally is reverently.

Melvin J. Ballard related an experience that might be shared by all who have learned the power of reverence. He said: "I found myself one evening in the dreams of the night in the sacred building, the temple. After a season of prayer and rejoicing, I was informed that I should have the privilege of entering into one of those rooms, to meet a glorious Personage, and, as I entered the door, I saw, seated on a raised platform, the most glorious Being my eyes have ever beheld or that I ever conceived existed in all the eternal worlds. As I approached to be introduced, he arose and stepped towards me with extended arms, and he smiled as he softly spoke my name. If I shall live to be a million years old, I shall never forget that smile. He took me in his arms and kissed me, pressed me to his bosom and blessed me, until the marrow of my bones seemed to melt. When he had finished, I fell at his feet, and as I bathed them with my tears and kisses, I saw the prints of the nails in the feet of the Redeemer of the world. The feeling that I had in the presence of Him who hath all things in his hands, to have his love, his affection and his blessing was such that if I ever can receive that of which I had but a foretaste, I would give all I am, all that I ever hope to be, to feel what I then felt." ("Sermons and Missionary Experiences of Melvin Joseph Ballard," p. 156).

Serious investigators come to The Book of Mormon expecting to receive light and knowledge. The greatest manifestation of spirituality during that holy quest is reverence; indeed, reverence is spirituality.

(The) Sabbath

"The people of Nephi
had waxed strong in the land.
They observed to keep the law of
Moses, and the sabbath day
holy unto the Lord."
(Jarom 1:5).

First it was called the Holy Sabbath, then the Sabbath, then Sunday. Now, it is called the Weekend. Nevertheless, holy days must never be confused with holidays. "Wherefore the Sabbath was given unto man for a day of rest; and also, that man should glorify God." (J.S.T. Mark 2:26-27). The Lord has given us the Sabbath to help us to have the Spirit more fully in our lives.

The word "Sabbath" comes from the Hebrew, meaning "day of rest." "And on the seventh day God … rested … from all his work which he had made. And God blessed the seventh day, and sanctified it: because that in it he had rested from all his work." (Genesis 2:2-3).

Later, God made the seventh day of the week a holy day for Israel, and incorporated into the Decalogue the commandment: "Remember the Sabbath day, to keep it holy. Six days shalt thou labor, and do all thy work: But the seventh day is the Sabbath of the Lord thy God: in it thou shalt not do any work." (Exodus 20:8-10).

The Nephites also "observed to keep the Law of Moses and the Sabbath day holy unto the Lord." (Jarom 1:5). Following the ministry of Christ among the Nephites, after members of the church "had been received unto baptism, and were wrought upon and cleansed by the power of the Holy Ghost, they were numbered among the people of the church of Christ; and their names were taken, that they might be remembered and nourished by the good word of God, to keep them in the right way, to keep them continually watchful unto prayer, relying alone upon the merits of Christ who was the author and the finisher of their faith. And the church did meet together oft, to fast and to pray, and to speak one with another concerning the welfare of their souls. And they did meet together oft to partake of bread and wine, in remembrance of the Lord Jesus." (Moroni 6:4-6).

To commemorate the Resurrection, the first day of the week was made the Sabbath in the Lord's church: "And upon the first day of the week, when the disciples came together to break bread, Paul preached unto them." (Acts 20:7).

The Lord has reaffirmed the observance of the Sabbath in the Last Days. In a revelation given through Joseph Smith, in Zion, Jackson County, Missouri, August 7, 1831, He told the Saints: "And that thou mayest more fully keep thyself unspotted from the world, thou shalt go to the house of prayer and offer up thy sacraments upon my holy day. For verily this is a day appointed unto you to rest from your labors, and to pay thy devotions unto the Most High. And on this day thou shalt do none other thing, only let thy food be prepared with singleness of heart." (D&C 59:9-11 & 13).

Blessings are always associated with obedience to specific eternal laws, and observance of the Law of the Sabbath is no exception. "There is a law, irrevocably decreed in heaven before the foundations of this world, upon which all blessings are predicted. And when we obtain any blessing from God, it is by obedience to that law upon which it is predicated." (D&C 130:20-21). The blessings associated with the Sabbath day are described in the Doctrine and Covenants: "And inasmuch as ye (keep the Sabbath day holy) with thanksgiving, with cheerful hearts and countenances ... the fulness of the earth is yours ... even peace in this world, and eternal life in the world to come." (D&C 59:15-15 & 23).

How do we determine what it means to keep the Sabbath day holy? Because individual circumstances differ, it is best to follow general principles rather than specific rules for every conceivable situation. We should follow scriptural guidelines, listen to the promptings of the Spirit, and ask questions such as: "Are my actions holy, or of service to God? Are my actions doing good? Do they keep me unspotted from the world? In my actions, am I honoring the Lord?"

Specifically, He has promised, "If thou turn away ... from doing thy pleasure on my holy day, and (instead) call the Sabbath a delight, the holy of the Lord, honourable; and shalt honour him, not doing thine own ways, nor finding thine own pleasure, nor speaking thine own words, then shalt thou delight thyself in the Lord, and I will cause thee to ride upon the high places of the earth, and feed thee with the heritage of Jacob thy father." (Isaiah 58:13-14).

Those who honor the Sabbath follow Isaiah's counsel: "Everyone that thirsteth, come ye to the waters, and he that hath no money; come ye, buy, and eat; yea, come, buy wine and milk without money and without price. Wherefore do ye spend money for that which is not bread? And your labour for that which satisfieth not? Hearken diligently unto me, and eat ye that which is good, and let your soul delight itself in fatness. Incline your ear, and come unto me; hear, and your soul shall live, and I will make an everlasting covenant with you." (Isaiah 55:1-3). The Lord's formula is not complicated. If we draw near to Him, He will make binding promises with us.

"A Favorite theme of Brigham Young was that the dominion God gives us is designed to test him and enable us to show to ourselves, our fellows, and all the heavens just how we would act if entrusted with God's power." (Hugh Nibley, "Subduing the Earth," p. 89-90). Our agency allows us to do with the Sabbath as we please. But we are not left without guidance. We are not as ships without rudders, for the commandment has been reiterated: "Blessed is the man that doeth this, and the son of man that layeth hold on it; that keepeth the Sabbath from polluting it." (Isaiah 56:2).

Alternatively, there is a curse associated with polluting the Sabbath. "Ye shall keep the Sabbath therefore; for it is holy unto you; everyone that defileth it shall surely be put to death; for whosoever doeth any work therein, that soul shall be cut off from among his people. Six days may work be done; but in the seventh is the Sabbath of rest, holy to the Lord: whosoever doeth any work in the Sabbath day, he shall surely be put to death." (Exodus 31:14-15).

Today, we no longer put to death those who violate the Law of the Sabbath, yet we die spiritually when we deliberately alienate ourselves from God's influence, because our actions put a halt to our eternal progression. "Broad is the gate, and wide they way that leadeth to the deaths; and many there are that go in thereat, because they receive me not, neither do they abide in my law." (D&C 132:25). God has prepared the Sabbath as a "work release program" for us, to see how we will behave if we are left on our own, after having received instruction regarding what we ought to do.

"That which the Spirit testifies unto you even so I would that ye should do in all holiness of heart, walking uprightly before me, considering the end of your salvation, doing all things with prayer and thanksgiving, that ye may not be seduced by evil spirits or doctrines of devils, or the commandments of men." (D&C 46:7). "This life (after all, is) a probationary state, a time to prepare to meet God." (Alma 12:24). It is a time of testing, for the Lord has said: "I will prove you in all things, whether you will abide in my covenant." (D&C 98:14).

On the Sabbath Day: "We should perform no labor that would keep us from giving our full attention to spiritual matters." (Gospel Principles Lesson Manual). Our focus sanctifies the Sabbath. "Reverence (for the Sabbath day) embraces regard, deference, honor, and esteem. Without some degree of it, therefore, there would be no courtesy, no gentility, no consideration of others' feelings, or of others' rights. It is the fundamental virtue in religion. If there were more reverence in human hearts, there would be less room for sin and sorrow, and increased capacity for joy and gladness. Reverence for God and sacred things is the chief characteristic of a great soul." (David O. McKay, C.R., 10/1956).

It is our responsibility to make the Sabbath Day the most special day of the week, when we can renew ourselves through the ordinances of the priesthood, partake of the spirit in our meetings, and mutually edify and strengthen each other in our exhortations. But "we must not be caught in the bind of building a church and killing the articles of its faith, or permitting form to triumph over spirit. The church and kingdom of God is built by the ardor and conviction of its members. We must be alert to the expansion of its assets at the cost of lost conviction. When buildings or institutions grow bigger and bigger, let us be fearful lest the Spirit will thin out." (Alvin R. Dyer, "A Foundation for Education).

Rather than enslaving us in good habits, Heavenly Father repeatedly gives us opportunities to recommit ourselves to covenants of obedience to true and eternal principles, as we receive the Sacrament every Sunday. This is one of the most important reasons why the Sabbath day, church membership, and faithful attendance at our meetings is vital to our spiritual well being. In so doing, we expand our awareness, rededicate ourselves, magnify our efforts, and realize our potential. By developing the qualities and attributes of our Heavenly Father, we "keep our second estate," and we are rewarded with the opportunity to have glory added upon our heads forever.

President Gordon B. Hinckley said, "The Sabbath is such a precious thing. The Lord wrote concerning the sanctity of the Sabbath when His finger touched the tablets of stone on Sinai: 'Keep the Sabbath day holy.' And that commandment has been reiterated in modern times as set forth in the fifty-ninth section of the Doctrine and Covenants. Let us (therefore) be a Sabbath keeping people. Now I do not want to be prudish. I do not want you to lock your children in the house and read the Bible all afternoon to them. Be wise. Be careful. Make that day a day when you can sit down with your families and talk about sacred and good things." ("Teachings of Gordon B. Hinckley," p. 559-560). In so doing, the Sabbath will become a day of renewal and a day of fortification against the affronts to spirituality that constantly assault us. It will be a day to look forward to with joyful anticipation, for, as the Savior promised, "Come unto me, all ye that labour and are heavy laden, and I will give you rest." (Matthew 11:28).

When we read
The Book of Mormon,
we are cast off into streams of
revelation and carried along in
the quickening currents
of direct experience
with God.

(The) Sacrament

"The manner of
their elders and priests
administering the flesh and
blood of Christ unto the church;
and they administered it according
to the commandments of Christ;
wherefore we know the manner
to be true; and the elder or
priest did minister it."
(Moroni 4:1).

If you have ever witnessed an automobile accident, you may have seen everything related to it unfold in slow motion. At the same time, it's like your brain sped up, allowing you to process information more comprehensively, so that you could see every element in fine detail. I have had such an experience, and it reminded me of the account of Moses, who "cast his eyes and beheld the earth, yea, even all of it; and there was not a particle of it which he did not behold, discerning it by the Spirit of God." (Moses 1:27). Although neuroscientists cannot tell us why, in extreme situations we sometimes have this ability, in the case of Moses, he was able to see in fine detail because he was full of the Spirit of God.

When we consider the Sacrament, it is helpful to step back and view it in slow motion, if you will. We are able to do so, particularly because of the influence of the Spirit that is woven into the tapestry of the ordinance. As we listen to the prayer, we are struck by how deliberately the powers of heaven are invoked in our behalf. "O God, the Eternal Father." Immediately after beseeching God, there is often a "pregnant pause" suggesting that birth is imminent. Something wonderful is about to happen, and we're waiting with bated breath to find out what it is.

The Sacramental Prayer is part of a priesthood ordinance, and is not an ordinary prayer of thanksgiving in the traditional sense. After addressing God, the prayer gets right down to the business at hand: "We ask thee in the name of thy Son Jesus Christ …" Now this really grabs our attention. It positions us as supplicants squarely in the center of the petition, catapults us into a highly emotional state, and gets the tightly wound chords of our spiritual sensitivities vibrating with intensive anticipation. We've just invoked the name of the Son of God!

There follow several entreaties, each charged with a rising tide of energy, and we close the prayer with one final plea: "That they may always have His spirit to be with them." The power and promise of this final appeal call to mind practical benefits that we've all experienced. Fundamentally, the Spirit influences us to ratchet down the hectic pace of our lives. The Lord knows how busy we are. He also knows what it feels like to be neglected, to be ignored, and to be in competition with telestial trivialities. In fact, He may have been thinking of the Sacrament when He urged David: "Be still, and know that I am God." (Psalms 46:10).

The Spirit clears our minds, and impels us to see things unambiguously. Once, in preparation for the holidays, I was hanging strings of lights on the outside of my house. Unraveling them as I took them out of the boxes in which they had been stuffed the previous winter, I realized I was faced with a hopelessly tangled mess. We can compare that Gordian Knot of tangle wires and bulbs with the cacophony of the "Christmas Lights of Confusion" that are so prevalent in the world today.

So, what can we do "to have His Spirit to be with us," to be able to see, and hear, and feel, with unmitigated transparency? First of all, let's consider the Pandora's Box of social media, that once opened, can be used for good or for evil. For better or for worse, it has become part of our experience, if it is not already part of our lives. If you haven't already done so, read or watch David Bednar's address at the 2014 BYU Education Week Devotional, that explores this subject. (Available at LDS.Org, in its Media Library).

Elder Bednar warned of the dangers related to the improper use of technology. "Too much time can be wasted, too many relationships can be harmed or destroyed, and precious patterns of righteousness can be disrupted," he said. "We should not allow even good applications of social media to overrule the better and best uses of our time, energy, and resources." If we want to have His Spirit to be with us, instead of texting, surfing the net, twittering, or feeding our dependency on Facetime, Pinterest, or Instagram, we might consider spending our time in other, arguably more worthwhile, activities.

If we want to have His Spirit to be with us, we might want to turn off our cell phones and put away our tablets, especially during Sacrament meeting. Instead of answering e-mail, we might quietly use our time seeking answers to prayer. Instead of focusing our attention on the cares of the world, and sampling the flavor of the day, we could instead savor the moment and relish our relationship with our Father in Heaven. Instead of burning the candle at both ends, or trying to run faster than we have strength, we could step back, take a deep breath, and realize that when we have given our best, our best is good enough. If we want the Spirit to be with us, we will re-group, re-assess, re-prioritize our time, re-focus on matters of substance, and get to work, while ignoring petty pursuits. We will cultivate the feeling I had when I witnessed that automobile accident. We will learn to speed up our brains, even as we quietly perceive things in slow motion. In a world that is filled with smoke and mirrors and artful deception that can only lead to conceptual cul-de-sacs, doctrinal dead-ends, and religious round-abouts, we will more clearly see what is real because we have moved to a more spiritually advantageous point of view.

The Sacrament has the power to do this because it immobilizes time, which reminds me of a line from the motion picture "Frozen." "For the first time in forever, nothing's in my way!" So too, nothing gets in the way of the Sacrament. There is no pomp and circumstance, no splendid celebration with ceremony and fuss, and no histrionics to detract from the simplicity of the ordinance. No outside interferences compete for our attention, and there are no distractions to obstruct our direct conduit to God's listening ear. For the first time in forever, nothing's in our way!

Administered at the beginning of a week that is sure to have its ups and downs, the Sacrament is an independent constant with a powerful and influential capacity. It is a bastion of stability in the midst of turmoil, and it never gets old. There is no update 10.4.1 to worry about. There is enough Random Access Memory within the Sacrament to bind us to unchanging principles, and the code of its working vocabulary calls us to action in a clear and unmistakable voice. The language of the Sacrament is the gospel standard, whether it is expressed in English or any of the other 188 languages spoken in the Lord's church. (Source: LDS Newsroom – November 21, 2014).

Its irreducible elements define a lowest common denominator that breaks down the Plan of Salvation into easily digestible bite-sized principles. At the same time, the Sacrament positions the solemnities of eternity right in the cross hairs. We can take our understanding as far as our capacity allows us to go, because the Sacrament is individually tailored to suit our circumstances, and yet it is collectively understood and is universally applicable. Insofar as the Sacrament is concerned, God "doeth nothing save it be plain unto (us); and he inviteth (us) all to come unto him and partake of his goodness; and he denieth none that come unto him … and all are alike unto God." (2 Nephi 26:33).

Many years ago, Melvin J. Ballard counseled: "The road to the Sacrament table is the path of safety for the Latter-day Saints." (Improvement Era, 10/1919). We live in a different world today, almost a century after Elder Ballard made that remark. One thing that hasn't changed, however, is that we still place a high priority on our personal security. It has been said that there are only two or three places where one can find maximum security: in a prison cell, in a hospital's intensive care unit, or possibly in a Doomsday Prepper's Panic Room.

We don't want or need that kind of security because we have Elder Ballard's "path of safety" that leads us to the emblems of Christ. It makes you wonder: Why would anyone willfully neglect to follow the clearly marked "path of safety?" Who would say to themselves: "I think I'll just blow off Sacrament Meeting this week." It just doesn't make sense to do so.

Our testimonies grease the wheels and allow us to move us along on the Path of Safety. It's no coincidence that our hearts swell during its administration, and that immediately thereafter, on Fast Sunday, it's customary to pour out their contents in testimony of the truths of the gospel. In sharp contrast to the world's orientation toward confrontation and its insatiable appetite for conflict, the spirit of the ordinance bears a witness of peace. Its inarticulate stirrings are evidence of personal revelation, as we remember the powerful promise of the ordinance: "…that His spirit might be with (us)."

Joseph Smith said we "may profit by noticing the first intimation of the spirit of revelation; for instance, when you feel pure intelligence flowing into you, it may give you sudden strokes of ideas … By learning the Spirit of God and understanding it, you may grow into the principle of revelation." The Sacrament, then, is the perfect schoolmaster to bring us to Christ. (See Galatians 3:24).

When you stop to think about it, everything about the church is revelatory. We've all had these experiences. Hugh B. Brown spoke for all of us, when he said: "Sometimes during solitude, I hear truth spoken with clarity and freshness; uncolored and untranslated it speaks from within myself in a language original but inarticulate, heard only with the soul, and I realize I brought it with me, was never taught it nor can I efficiently teach it to another." But as President Kimball observed: "Expecting the spectacular, (we) may not be fully alerted to the constant flow of revealed communication." (C.R., 4/1977). The Sacrament, that lowest common denominator that puts us all on an equal footing, gives each of us an opportunity to recognize these universal feelings and to act on them.

I've now taken the Sacrament close to 2,500 times. I'm not expecting the spectacular, and yet I recognize the repetitive nature of the ordinance as theatrical encore on a cosmic level. Like a beautiful sunset, or a rainbow after a summer shower, or a baby's birth, or the sound of a loved one's voice, or passing through the veil of the temple, it doesn't get old, it stirs my most intimate sensitivities, and it continues to amaze me.

The Sacrament raises our testimony temperature and gets our juices flowing. It gives us a healthy "whack" right in our status quo, where we need it the most. It makes us feel complete, whole, at peace, and it binds up our wounds. We feel forgiveness through the Atonement, and have a burning desire to re- commit ourselves to be disciples of Christ.

We understand what Joseph Smith meant, when he exclaimed: "I can taste the principles of eternal life, and so can you. They are given to me by the revelations of Jesus Christ." (H.C. 6:304-5, 312, & 317). We understand what it means when we hear the promise in the Sacrament prayer, that we may have His Spirit to be with us.

In the church, we often hear a member of the Bishopric say: "We will now prepare for the Sacrament…by singing a hymn." We are encouraged to sing with devotion, worshipfully, reverently, fervently, with conviction, solemnly, thoughtfully, and with dignity. But at the very least, our preparation really begins in the hours immediately following our last Sacrament meeting. In this sense, also, the Sacrament is "frozen in time."

Of course, our preparation is tied to the Atonement of Jesus Christ, a process that began during our pre-earth existence. It's one of the reasons we "sang together and … shouted for joy." (Job 38:7). That spontaneous outburst of emotion was in response to the explanation that during mortality we would be able to partake of the Sacrament, to renew not only our covenant of baptism, but also, perhaps, the covenants we undoubtedly had made with our Father during that great council.

Groundwork for the ordinance of the Sacrament was laid during the mortal ministry of the Savior, with clarity first established in the upper room at Jerusalem. Luke recorded how the Savior taught His disciples to administer the Sacrament of the Last Supper. (See Luke 22). Later events in the Garden of Gethsemane give further context to the Sacrament, with unmistakable definition provided on the cross, and incontrovertible finality shaped by an empty tomb. For added emphasis, Latter-day Saints have the additional witness of Book of Mormon scriptures that deal with the Savior's instruction to priesthood brethren during His post-mortal ministry among the Nephites. (See 3 Nephi 18:7).

These Book of Mormon scriptures also testify that the Sacrament is frozen in time. As pre-occupied as the prophet Moroni must have been after Cumorah, he was still able to write a few more things on the plates of Mormon. Included in those precious engravings was specific instruction dealing with the ordinance of the Sacrament. (See Moroni 4). Moroni knew that the Sacrament would be "the path of safety" for his descendants, and even for his brethren the Lamanites. (See Moroni 1:4).

As Joseph Smith organized the Latter-day church, he received a revelation known as The Lord's Preface to The Doctrine & Covenants. In it, he recorded a warning that was reminiscent of Isaiah, and meant for the world: "Prepare ye for that which is to come (for) they have strayed from mine ordinances, and have broken mine everlasting covenant." (D&C 1:12-13, see Isaiah 24:5). Through Joseph, the Lord would see to it that the ordinance of the Sacrament would be properly restored.

He prioritized the ordinance of the Sacrament when He revealed to His prophet specific instructions regarding its administration. (See D&C Section 20, recorded in its entirety soon after the church was organized on April 6, 1830). This revelation provides instruction not only on how the Sacramental Prayers should be offered, but also gives us insight into the necessity of our own preparation prior to participation in the ordinance. "The duty of the members after they are received by baptism - The elders or priests are to have a sufficient time to expound all things concerning the church of Christ to their understanding, previous to their partaking of the sacrament." (D&C 20:68).

To take advantage of the real power of the Sacrament, it is necessary to develop a solid foundation of doctrinal understanding through new member discussions, and then to participate in repetitive instruction in Gospel Essentials and Gospel Doctrine classes, and in Primary, Sunday School, Priesthood and Relief Society meetings. Continuing religious education is the constant companion of the priesthood-administered ordinances of the gospel.

D&C 20 continues: "And the members shall manifest before the church, and also before the elders, by a godly walk and conversation, that they are worthy of it, that there may be works and faith agreeable to the holy scriptures - walking in holiness before the Lord." (D&C 20:69). This is where works meet faith, where the rubber hits the road - walking in holiness before the Lord. As Martin Luther observed: "Good works do not make a good man, but a good man does good works. And what makes a man good? Faith in God, and Christ."

Then, in this same revelation, we have the Sacramental Prayer itself. Without the recurring, repetitive infusion of power through the Sacrament, living a Christ-centered life is possible and can be wonderful, but it is not ideal. Trying to negotiate the minefields of mortality on our own, without the protective priesthood ordinance of the Sacrament, we will fall short and cannot measure up. The Lord condemned the world specifically because it had "changed the ordinance, and (had consequently) broken the everlasting covenant." (D&C 1:13). Without the Sacrament, neither Latter-day Saints nor the world can hope to enjoy the protection of a covenant relationship with the Good Shepherd.

On September 30, 2014, I celebrated a milestone in my life: 25,000 days on earth. I hope if I have done anything with the indescribable gift of a long life, I have been able to teach my children and grandchildren about the importance of the Sacrament. My daughter Tara shared with me the following: "When I have a moment to breathe, be calm, and then watch my boys pass the Sacrament to the congregation, my spirit has a moment to be still. To some, that quiet moment might not seem like a very long time, but in my busy life it seems like a lifetime!" The Sacrament, once again, is frozen in time.

My son-in-law Nate told me: "A couple of Sundays ago, as I sat down with my family on our favorite row and prepared my bag as a road block in an attempt to keep the kids from escaping, I said a quick prayer that maybe today I could be a little more in tune during the Sacrament; that maybe I could direct my thoughts more toward the Savior and His Atonement. Almost immediately after that silent prayer, a young man tapped me on the shoulder and asked me if I would participate in the administration of the ordinance and help pass the Sacrament. It was a very humbling experience that I will record as an answer to a prayer for an increased desire to focus on the Sacrament and the Savior."

My daughter Elizabeth said: "The bishop challenged our ward to avoid distractions for our children during the Sacrament. So, I made a book with pictures of Jesus and His life, and I have my 5 & 9 year-old boys look through it before the Sacrament. They have learned to listen and to feel the Spirit, and although it has taken them some time, they are now more accustomed to focusing on the words of the prayers."

One of my heroes is William Tyndale, who has been called "the mostly unrecognized translator of the most influential book in the world." He was an English priest, who died a martyr, on October 5, 1536, 480 years ago. He is one, like Joseph Smith, whose influence defies measurement. He has helped countless millions make the transition to a higher spiritual plane. He was the first to translate the Bible and publish it in English, the language of the people. He did this in 1526, only 72 years after Gutenberg turned the world upside down with his publication, utilizing his invention of the printing press, of a Latin Bible, in 1454.

In order to accomplish the task, Tyndale studied the New Testament in its original Hebrew and Greek. He was a true polyglot: fluent in Greek, Latin, French, German, Italian, and Spanish in addition to his native English. The result of his scholarship was so spectacular that, in the following century, the theologians revising the Bible relied heavily on his interpretations when creating the King James Version. 83% of the New Testament in the K.J.V. can be attributed to Tyndale. With feeling, passion, and excitement, he bequeathed to us its poetical language. These same emotions wash over us as we listen to the recitation of the Sacrament Prayer.

Tyndale crafted familiar phrases that flow like honey from our lips: "Let there be light." "In the beginning, God created the heaven and the earth." "In the beginning was the Word and the Word was with God and the Word was God." "Our Father, which art in heaven, hallowed be thy name." "The spirit is willing, but the flesh is weak." "Blessed are they that mourn, for they shall be comforted." And even "It came to pass," that familiar phrase found 1,407 times in The Book of Mormon, and 672 times in the K.J.V.

Tyndale wrote about "the tongues of men and of angels, "sounding brass and tinkling cymbals," "the salt of the earth," "the signs of the times," and "Atonement. He is responsible for these expressions, as well: "Blessed are the peacemakers," "Seek and ye shall find," "Ask and it shall be given you, "The Lord bless thee and keep thee. The Lord make his face to shine upon thee and be merciful unto thee. The Lord lift up his countenance upon thee, and give thee peace. "

It would be nice if Tyndale were responsible for the word "Sacrament," but alas, he is not – it derives from the ecclesiastical Latin sacrāmentum, from sacrō ("hallow, or consecrate"), and from sacer ("sacred, or holy").

One day, a priest visiting his parish openly attacked Tyndale's beliefs. He replied: "If God spare my life, before very long I shall cause a plough boy to know the scriptures better than you do!" In fulfillment of that prophetic statement, as of November 2014, the Bible has been translated into 531 languages, and 2,883 languages have at least some portions of the Bible. (Source: Wikipedia).

The next time we partake of the Sacrament, we might ask ourselves: "Who are the modern-day plough boys, of whom Tyndale referred?" Surely, they are our 16-year-old Priests, our 14-year-old Teachers, and our 12-year-old Deacons, who know the scriptures better than many theologians. Tyndale prophetic vision has come true.

Thanks to the restoration of the gospel, each of us, proverbial "ploughboys" and commoners in the Church, can understand the scriptures as well as any. The Restoration has calibrated our heartstrings to vibrate in harmony with celestial melodies, as when we listen to the Sacramental Prayers. In the musicality of these prayers, we can "taste" the principles of eternal life.

To quote two more of William Tyndale's contributions to our liturgy, and these may be my favorites: By the "still small voice" we can know the truth of all things. And second: "In him we live, and move, and have our being."

Thank God for all those who have sacrificed so much that we might enjoy the Sacrament, and for all that it means to us. Within its administration lies the key to our perfection. According to Brigham Young, "The sin that will cleave to all the posterity of Adam and Eve is, that they have not done as well as they knew how." (J.D., 2:130). The road to the Sacrament table is our path of safety. May we resolve, from this hour, to better understand and to keep the covenant of the Sacrament, by doing as well as we know how.

Sacramental Waters

"The manner of administering the wine – Behold, they took the cup, and said: O God, the Eternal Father we ask thee, in the name of thy Son, Jesus Christ, to bless and sanctify this wine to the souls of all those who drink of it, that they may do it in remembrance of the blood of thy Son, which was shed for them; that they may witness unto thee, O God, the Eternal Father, that they do always remember him, that they may have His Spirit to be with them. Amen." (Moroni 5:1-2).

"In preparation for a religious service at which the sacrament of bread and wine was to be administered, Joseph set out to procure wine for the occasion. He was met by a heavenly messenger and received this revelation, a portion of which was written at this time, and the remainder in the September following." As a result of the instruction given by the angel at this time, "water is now used instead of wine in the sacramental services of the church." (Superscript to Doctrine & Covenants Section 27).

"It mattereth not what ye shall eat or what ye shall drink when ye partake of the sacrament," instructed the angel, speaking by divine investiture of authority, "if it so be that ye do it with an eye single to my glory - remembering unto the Father my body which was laid down for you," bringing the gift of immortality to all, "and my blood which was shed for the remission of your sins," thereby opening the portal to eternal life. (V. 2). This revelation stresses the simplicity of the ordinance of the Sacrament, emphasizing that it does not matter what we drink, as long as we do it in sincerity with an eye single to the glory of God. Wine is only symbolical of the redeeming blood of Christ. It does not become His blood through a mystical transformation, as many would believe. The Catholic doctrine of transubstantiation is false. The emblems of the Sacrament are designed to focus our attention where it belongs: on the Son of God and His sacrifice, and on the covenants we have made with Him at the waters of baptism.

This revelation was given some two and a half years before the revelation known as The Word of Wisdom was received. The church did not adopt the practice of using water in place of wine because of the Word of Wisdom, although the two are related. In each case, intervention by the Lord was prompted by the evil designs of conspiring men who would go to any length to destroy the order of the church.

It is the purpose of the ordinance of the Sacrament to recommit by priesthood ordinance to the covenant of baptism and to receive the Spirit of God that we might more surely hold fast to the iron rod. If the purpose of the Sacrament were to obtain a remission of sins, it would not be forbidden to those in greatest need. The reason that those who partake without proper preparation, that is to say, without repentance, drink damnation to their souls is that such an action blocks the channels through which spiritual power flows. It is the consequent halt in progress that is damning to the individual.

Conversely, this is why partaking of the Sacrament in worthiness infuses us with power. Heavenly Father blesses us that His promises might be freely fulfilled. Through Joseph Smith, He said: "Let thy bowels also be full of charity towards all men, and to the household of faith, and let virtue garnish thy thoughts unceasingly; then shall thy confidence wax strong in the presence of God; and the doctrine of the priesthood shall distill upon thy soul as the dews from heaven. The Holy Ghost shall be thy constant companion, and thy scepter an unchanging scepter of righteousness and truth; and thy dominion shall be an everlasting dominion, and without compulsory means it shall flow unto thee forever and ever." (D&C 121:45-46).

The covenants we make with God reflect His attributes. He is moral, so He gives us the Covenant of Chastity, and He has charity, so He commands us to love Him and each other. God is disciplined, so He gives us the Law of Obedience. Because He is a righteous steward, He gives us the Law of Consecration. Because He loves His less fortunate children, He gives us the Law of the Fast. Because His is a perfected, resurrected body, He gives us the Word of Wisdom. Because He is omniscient, He gives us the commandment to seek knowledge. In consequence of the Gift of His Son, He gives us the Law of Sacrifice. Because He rested from His labors on the seventh day, He gives us the Law of the Sabbath. Because He is Holy, He gives us the ordinance of the Sacrament.

Our perfect Father could give us everything He has, but what He is, we must earn for ourselves, as we struggle to overcome adversity and gain self-mastery. "Spirituality," David O. McKay said: "Is the consciousness of victory over self, and of communion with the infinite." (C.R., 10/1969). Our covenants help us to focus our efforts to become as He is. This is their purpose. If it were not possible to become as God is, they would be unnecessary. Thus, we partake of the emblems of the Sacrament because we want to be like our Father in Heaven.

"You shall not purchase wine neither strong drink of your enemies; wherefore, you shall partake of none except it is made new among you." (V. 3-4). In response to the wicked designs that existed in the hearts of his enemies, the Prophet Joseph Smith received this revelation regarding the use of wine in the Sacrament. He later wrote: "Early in the month of August (1830) Newel Knight and his wife paid us a visit at my place in Harmony, Pennsylvania; and as neither his wife nor mine had been as yet confirmed, it was proposed that we should confirm them, and partake together of the Sacrament, before he and his wife should leave us. In order to prepare for this, I set out to procure some wine for the occasion, but had gone only a short distance when I was met by a heavenly messenger, and received the following revelation:" (D&C 27).

What was the nature of the wine used in ancient times? There is little doubt that Jesus and His disciples drank fermented wine, and not "new wine" as so many Latter-day Saints would like to believe. There is nothing inherently wrong with drinking wine. The Word of Wisdom was only given "in consequence of the evils and designs which do and will exist in the hearts of conspiring men in the last days," who would subvert the drinking of spirits to suit their wicked purposes. (D&C 89:4). That this has occurred is readily attested by even a cursory review of the media, where the consumption of alcoholic beverages is glorified almost beyond imagination.

Satan

"Satan
did get great hold upon
the hearts of the people upon
all the face of the land."
(Helaman 16:23).

"Who Am I? I am a spirit child of God, which makes you my spirit brother or sister. I was present in the Council in Heaven. I offered to go to earth to redeem mankind. I want you to become as I am. I work hard to encourage you to follow me. Oh, yes. One more thing. I am your mortal enemy."

The more we know about our adversaries, the greater our tactical advantage in dealing with them. Fortunately, we have the scriptures to teach us about the greatest adversary of them all, and we can learn as much about Satan in The Pearl of Great Price as we can anywhere else. Much of this book was revealed to Joseph Smith when he was engaged in his translation of the Bible, so it clarifies themes that are only superficially addressed in the King James Translation. "And I, the Lord God, spake unto Moses, saying: That Satan, whom thou has commanded in the name of mine Only Begotten, is the same which was from the beginning, and he came before me, saying - Behold, here am I, send me, I will be thy son, and I will redeem all mankind, that one soul shall not be lost, and surely I will do it; wherefore give me thine honor." (Moses 4:1).

Lucifer was "a son of the morning," and was very influential in the pre-mortal world of spirits. His name literally means "Light Bearer," and so he was. In the Great Council he offered to redeem all mankind. But even then, he lacked the faith necessary to allow agency to rule. He concocted a plan that was, in fact, an inoperative counterfeit. It would not work because it would not permit its participants to exercise free will. This is why Satan is called "the father of lies," and "a liar from the beginning." (Moses 4:4, Ether 8:25, & D&C 93:25). He is also a "murderer from the beginning" in the sense that he was responsible for the spiritual death of the third part of the host of heaven. (John 8:44, & D&C 29:36). He promoted a bogus plan that, if embraced and ratified by a majority of God's spirit children, was calculated to elevate its author to a position of prestige and power. (See Moses 4:3).

"But, behold, my Beloved Son, which was my Beloved and Chosen from the beginning, said unto me - Father, thy will be done, and the glory be thine forever." (Moses 4:2). The Son of God was chosen and foreordained from the foundation of the world to be the Savior of mankind. (See 1 Peter 1:20). He was anointed to redeem mankind. (See D&C 138:42). He is the Messiah. (See Moses 7:53). He was the first born of the spirit children of our Heavenly Father, and the greatest of all. (Colossians 1:15). Some feel that he was greater than all the other spirit children of our Heavenly Father put together. (See Exodus 18:11). He understood the Plan of the Father, and by his actions had already demonstrated for his brethren and had put into proper perspective the principle of Sacrifice. (See Abraham 3:27). He knew that the Plan required the will of the Father, and was overjoyed that obedience would lead to the greater glory of the Father. (See Moses 4:2). His expression in the Council revealed his selfless nature.

There was ideological war in heaven, made possible by the eternal rule of agency. "Wherefore, because that Satan rebelled against me, and sought to destroy the agency of man, which I, the Lord God, had given him, and also, that I should give unto him mine own power; by the power of mine Only Begotten, I caused that he should be cast down." (Moses 4:3). The spirit children of our Father would be allowed to choose between His Plan and that of the adversary. However, the consequences of choosing unwisely would be eternally damaging.

Rebellion then and now, in its many forms, is among the most evil and pernicious of sins, because it leads to the destruction of the spirit. The rebellion of Lucifer was inspired, in part, by his lust for the power of God. He did not understand that Father's power is inseparable from His nature. Therefore, it was needful that Lucifer and those who sided with him be cast out of the presence of their Father, inasmuch as they could not abide by the principles that governed life in His Presence. It is Christ's way for us to act for ourselves. (2 Nephi 2:27). It is Satan's way for us to be acted upon. The 'perfect law of liberty' requires that we be free according to the flesh. (See James 1:25).

The choice is between liberty and eternal life, or captivity and spiritual death. But unless action is carried out within the context of the gospel and its laws, unbridled freedom will lead to tyranny. We are free to choose, but we cannot choose to escape the consequences of our poor choices. Satan's tactics and plan was a pipe dream that would have denied agency, requiring obedience based on compulsion. Even now, when force is applied or coercion obligates us under duress to conform to the will of others, though it may be legal, it tarnishes our actions and robs them of their intrinsic beauty and spontaneity. Coercion captures our attention, while free will captivates us. Satan sought to punish us because he thought his argument was strong, when in fact, he punished us because his argument was weak. But the fallout was that, living in a world of opposition, when we voluntarily give up our agency, we trade it for the grip of bad habits, and we are snared by Satan, bound by his strong chains, and feel the heavy cords around our necks that restrict our actions and drag us down to hell. It is very hard to break bad habits precisely because we have given up our agency in order to acquire them.

Heavenly Father does not operate this way. He always honors the eternal principle of agency. It is riskier this way, but it is the only sure way. Rather than enslaving us in good habits, He repeatedly gives us the opportunity to recommit ourselves to our covenants of obedience to true and eternal principles. This is one of the most important reasons why church membership, faithful attendance at meetings, and participation in the Sacrament service are all vital to our spiritual well being. "The Spirit is pure, and (is) under the special control and influence of the Lord, but the body is of the earth, and is subject to the power of the devil, and is under the mighty influence of that fallen nature that is of the earth. If the Spirit yields to the body, the devil then has power to overcome the body and spirit of that man, and he loses both." ("Discourses of Brigham Young," p. 69-70).

Unwittingly, Lucifer became a key player in the great gospel Plan of Salvation that invites us to live by obedience and by faith. He "became Satan, yea, even the devil, the father of all lies, to deceive and to blind men, and to lead them captive at his will, even as many as would not hearken unto (the Savior's) voice." (Moses 1:4). He is Perdition, which mean "utter ruin." (See Moses 5:24). His progression has stopped because he used his agency in the most inappropriate way. He rebelled against the light, while basking in its warmth. He blasphemed the name of God while yet in His very presence.

Even now, the war is far from over. The battlefields have changed, but Satan is still trying to lead people astray. Those who follow him become his captives. He wants us to believe that he does not exist, so that we will not take him seriously, so to know of his reality prepares us to recognize his tactics and resist them. Those who are susceptible to his propaganda, however, "he flattereth away, and telleth them there is no devil, for there is none - and thus he whispereth in their ears, until he grasps them with his awful chains, from whence there is no deliverance." (2 Nephi 28:22).

Satan has always raged "in the hearts of men, and stir(ed) them up to anger against that which is good." (2 Nephi 28:20). But sometimes he pacifies us, and lulls us into a false sense of worldly security, making us believe that we are gaining something when we are really losing. He does this very subtly, so as not to awaken our senses to the reality of what is happening. (2 Nephi 28:21). He is always at work to move us from brilliant, dazzling white, through every shade of gray, to a fathomless black that is, by subtraction, the very opposite of worthy thoughts, words, deeds, and principles. His flattery leads us to believe we are deserving of peace and plenty, when we have not paid the price to earn the reward. We would do well to remember, as C.S. Lewis wrote, that "little people, like you and me, if our prayers are sometimes granted beyond all hope and probability, had better not draw hasty conclusions to our own advantage. If we were stronger, we might be less tenderly treated. If we were braver, we might be sent, with far less help, to defend far more desperate posts in the great battle." ("The World's Last Night," p. 10-11). Satan failed to destroy our souls in the pre-earth existence, but he can still do so now by getting us to misuse our precious agency. "Wherefore, men are free according to the flesh; and all things are given them which are expedient…. They are free to choose liberty and eternal life, through the great Mediator of all men, or to choose captivity and death, according to the captivity and power of the devil; for he seeketh that all men might be miserable like unto himself." (2 Nephi 2:27).

"He knows all the tricks. He senses when we are susceptible to temptations, and moves in for the kill. He suggests evil by making drinking and smoking look enticing, by rationalizing cheating, lying, and shoplifting. He plays mind games with us to get us to use drugs, and he clothes gambling in fine twined linens. Immorality and swearing are woven into popular music, hit movies, and prime time TV. Hedonism is promoted as normal behavior, and "easy street" is a much sought-after home address.

He minimizes the seriousness of sin by repeatedly telling us "Everyone's doing it." "It doesn't hurt anyone else." "Just once won't hurt." "I can always repent later." "It can't be wrong if we love each other." "It's not a big deal." "It's only a movie rating." And how about this one, popularized by a television comedian: "The devil made me do it." (The Flip Wilson Show, 1970).

He makes sin appear inviting by emphasizing pleasure on TV, in the movies, and in magazines. He uses peer pressure to break down our resolve to do good, and recruits sports figures and movie stars whose lifestyles reflect the vulgar tastes of the world. He knows that we are least able to withstand his onslaughts when we are physically tired, mentally fatigued, operating on spiritual reserves, or when we are upset, irritable, distracted, discouraged, or preoccupied. His timetable could be a lifetime. He knows that if he starts with little things, and gradually builds up to serious transgressions, it is much easier for him to make inroads.

But he reveals his true colors when we resist him. "When he is challenged, Satan is angry, as he was with Moses. After that confrontation, he cried with a loud voice, trembled, and shook, and then departed from Moses, who remained resolute. There was nothing else for him to do. He has to leave when you say, 'Depart from me, Satan.' Every soul who has mortality is stronger than Satan, if that soul is determined." (Spencer W. Kimball, "Ensign," 3/1976).

Those who hold the priesthood or live within its influence are particularly well prepared to resist Satan. In fact, Joseph Fielding Smith, Jr. once declared: "I believe there has never been a moment of time since the creation but what there has been someone holding the priesthood on the earth to hold Satan in check." (Remarks at Ensign Stake Conference, 1/30/1966. Quoted by Harold B. Lee, "The Place of The Living Prophet, Seer and Revelator"). That is the essence of the matter. Priesthood weighs in on one side of the scale, and the counterfeit coin of Satan's spurious currency clatters down in a cacophony of confusion on the other side of the scale. Our destiny hangs in the balance, and ultimately, on every issue there are three votes cast. Heavenly Father casts His vote in favor of us, and Satan casts his against us. We cast the deciding vote, and all eternity depends on that single ballot. Our one vote really does count, and we will stand before God at the Last Day to render a personal accounting. The sooner we learn to govern our lives by priesthood principles the better, for we will we be on the path leading to God's kingdom. John Taylor taught: "Priesthood is the legitimate rule of God and is the only legitimate power that has a right to rule upon the earth, and when the will of God is done on the earth, as it is done in heaven, no other power will bear rule." (J.D. 5:187). Satan will have been vanquished, once and for all.

(The) Scope of Our Decisions

"Do ye remember, my brethren, that we
said unto our brethren in the land of Zarahemla,
we go up to the land of Nephi, to preach unto our brethren,
the Lamanites, and they laughed us to scorn? For they said
unto us: Do ye suppose that ye can convince the Lamanites of the
incorrectness of the traditions of their fathers as stiffnecked a
people as they are; whose hearts delight in the shedding
of blood; whose days have been spent in the grossest
iniquity; whose ways have been the ways of a
transgressor from the beginning?"
(Alma 26:23-24).

When I was baptized, on April 17, 1965, my brother, who, at the time, was a radioman in the U.S. Coast Guard, transmitted this message at 2,670 kilohertz: 'Phil is a Mormon!"

That message went out to the world, and beyond, in an ever-expanding electro-magnetic bubble, at the speed of light. In 8 minutes and 19 seconds, it had reached the sun, and traveling in the opposite direction, outward across the solar system, the message reached Neptune in just over 4 hours, and after 140 hours, it had reached the inner edge of the Ort Cloud, at the furthest reaches of our solar system.

In just 4.2 years, the message reached the star that is our nearest neighbor, Proxima Centauri. Within 10 years, it had passed by at least 12 stellar objects. As of today (April 17, 2024) it was sent over 59 years ago. Scientists have identified over a thousand stars within fifty light years of earth, and expect that about 4,000 planets orbit these stars. About 20 of these have been identified in "the habitable zone" but there could be as many as a thousand roughly earth-sized planets in the habitable zone.

I often think of the Beatles song, "Across the Universe," which NASA sent in the direction of Polaris, the North Star, on February 4, 2008. It was the fiftieth anniversary of the agency. If any extraterrestrials happen to be in the vicinity of Polaris, in 2439, they will get the message (Polaris is 431 light years from earth).

"Words are flowing out like endless rain (and) slither wildly as they slip away across the universe. Pools of sorrow (and) waves of joy are drifting through my opened mind, possessing and caressing me. Images of broken light, which dance before me like a million eyes ... call me on and on across the universe. Thoughts meander like a restless wind . They tumble blindly as they make their way across the universe. Sounds of laughter (and) shades of life are ringing through my opened ears, inciting and inviting me. Limitless undying love, which shines around me like a million suns … calls me on and on, across the universe."

We're surrounded by our own personal force fields, and our bodies contain electrical generators, which they use to send signals from head to toe. Virtually every process that is keeping us alive can be traced back to an electric field that some component of our body is creating. Not only is it possible that the human body creates EM fields — it is the only way we can possibly exist as a coherent entity. We are electric fields. They hold our atoms together, and are used to communicate with each other.

A one hundred forty-pound human being is made up of roughly ten trillion cells, and each one is composed of twenty billion protein molecules. Each protein molecule has, on average, fourteen thousand atoms. Each of those has around forty-nine matter particles, consisting of a nucleus, protons, and electrons, etc. Each of those average matter particles is composed of roughly one million photons, which are the basic units of electro-magnetic energy. Thus, the human body is one-billionth particle matter, composed of substance, and the rest is photons. Joseph Smith, as it turns out, was right on the mark. He trumped the best and brightest minds of the Twenty-First Century, when he wrote: "That which is of God is light; and he that receiveth light, and continueth in God, receiveth more light; and that light groweth brighter and brighter until the perfect day." (D&C 50:24). In 1831, 48 years before Einstein was born, Joseph Smith already knew by his own experience that, fundamentally, we are beings of light, and he used beautiful poetic symbolism to clothe his point. (See Joseph Smith History 1:17 & 30).

(The) Second Mile

*"God will consecrate my
prayers for the gain of my people.
And the words which I have written in
weakness will be made strong unto them
and persuade them to believe in him,
and to endure to the end."
(2 Nephi 33:4).*

"And behold, one came and said unto him, Good Master, what good thing shall I do, that I may have eternal life? And he said unto him … if thou wilt enter into life, keep the commandments. He saith unto him, Which?" Jesus then enumerated a number of commandments.

"The young man saith unto him, All these things have I kept from my youth. What lack I yet?" This young man had been a good and faithful member of the church. He had attended Primary and Sunday School, never missed a Seminary class, and had been ordained a Deacon at age twelve. He had been a faithful home teacher with his father, and had accepted opportunities to speak in church. He had done temple baptisms for the dead. He had attained the rank of Eagle Scout. He had received his endowment in the temple, had accepted the Law of the Gospel by covenant, and had faithfully served a two-year full-time mission for the church. In his obedience to the letter of the law, he had been perfect.

But the Savior knew his heart, and perceived that there was something missing from his life that was preventing him from achieving the gift of spiritual independence that would remove the veil of insensitivity to his destiny. What he lacked was not necessarily the same thing that was absent from the personal lives of his contemporaries. His challenges had been carefully tailored by a wise Father to meet his circumstances, that he might grow through opposition that had been specifically and pointedly fashioned to address his weaknesses. The Savior knew this young man's heart, and perceived that obedience to the Law of Consecration would be his greatest challenge.

And so, He "said unto him, If thou wilt be perfect, go and sell that thou hast, and give to the poor, and thou shalt have treasure in heaven: and come and follow me." The Savior knew this would have been an easy thing to do if the young man had been poor and destitute. "But when the young man heard that saying, he went away sorrowful: for he had great possessions." (Matthew 19:16-22).

This impressionable young man, like so many in the church, had not developed the seasoned maturity that comes with age. From the opposite end of the temporal spectrum near the end of his life, William Tyndale said that he would rather "be blessed with Christ, in a little tribulation, than to be cursed perpetually with the world for a little pleasure. Prosperity is a right curse," he wrote, "and a thing that God giveth to his enemies."

Mortality is, for each of us, a probationary state, a time in which we will be individually tried to see if we will put to the proof those things that we have been taught we must do if we are to inherit eternal life. In short, we are tested and tempted so that God can see if we are willing to "go the second mile." When I was younger, I ran 5 or 10 miles every morning, for an hour or two before sunrise. I ran through the Santa Monica Mountains, above Pacific Palisades, in Southern California. One day, as I neared the end of my run and began to trace my way back over the surface streets to my home, I stopped at an intersection, waiting for the traffic signal to change. I put my hands on my knees and allowed the perspiration to drip off the end of my nose. I thought about aborting my run, stopping right then and there, and letting my complaining muscles cool down as I returned home. However, through sweat-soaked eyes, I looked up, and saw as it were, a vision before me. Insistently flashing red with neon brightness, directly in front of me, were these words that urged me on: "Don't walk!"

That message, as if it had come from God Himself, urged me to go the second mile, and the experience has since prompted me to reflect upon this question: "What happens to us when we go the second mile?" I have come to the conclusion that as we learn to confront our trials and tribulations, by pushing just a little harder, we grow in the spirit. It is no coincidence that these two scriptures are linked together: "And whosoever shall compel thee to go a mile, go with him twain," and then: "Be ye therefore perfect, even as your Father which is in heaven is perfect." (Matthew 5:38-48).

I have been in the church long enough to have experienced the exhilaration of temporal, spiritual, emotional, and intellectual symmetry. But the world still tugs at me. Mortality is a probationary state, a time of testing, to see if we "will do all things whatsoever the Lord (our) God shall command (us)." (Abraham 3:25). We all have crosses to bear, and the ominous warning applies to every one of us: "Whosoever doth not bear his cross, and come after me, cannot be my disciple ... Whosoever he be of you that forsaketh not all that he hath, he cannot be my disciple." (Luke 14:27 & 33).

The question remains: What and who do I think the Savior was talking about when he said: "Whosoever shall compel thee to go a mile, go with him twain." (Matthew 5:41). When I joined the church, I was asked to go the first mile. I started to attend church on a weekly basis. I began to regularly repent. I established the habit pattern of consistently partaking of the Sacrament. I learned what it means to keep the Sabbath day holy, and I adjusted my habit patterns to do so to the best of my ability. I accepted a home teaching assignment together with its related responsibilities. I learned to express myself by employing modest speech that reflected the higher standard to which I aspired. I began to consistently pay my tithes and offerings. I worked to sustain my temple worthiness. I accepted and tried to magnify ward callings. I began to appreciate the temporal and spiritual benefits of obedience to the Word of Wisdom. I made regular deposits to my spiritual bank account by praying daily to my Heavenly Father, and learned how to make withdrawals in times of need. I made a conscious effort to internalize the Ten Commandments, and tried to be ever mindful of my baptismal covenants.

However, after a period of time I began to recognize that Heavenly Father had something more in mind for me, and I felt the urge to go the second mile. I had been attending church, but the second mile compelled me to take advantage of opportunities such as B.Y.U. Education Week, and other Conferences and Symposia, and to really internalize the scripture that encouraged me to seek "out of the best books words of wisdom," and to "seek learning even by study and also by faith." (D&C 109:7).

I had been repenting regularly, but His admonition to go the second mile put the Atonement in a new perspective. Against the backdrop of His marvelous light, my sins brought me real sorrow. I felt terrible about them. I felt profoundly filthy. I wanted to unload and abandon them. I became almost obsessive-compulsive about cleansing my soul. I was broken in heart, and had the spirit of contrition, and became zealous in my preparation to receive the Spirit, that I might be teachable. At a heightened level of preparation, I began to consistently ask, as did those on the Day of Pentecost: "What shall I do?" I listened for answers, and began to feel with greater intensity the promptings of the Spirit.

I had been receiving the Sacrament each Sunday, but the second mile urged me to consistently be receptive to new ways to have His spirit to be with me. I determined to prepare for the ordinance of the Sacrament hours and even days ahead of time, and to treat the service with newfound respect.

I felt that I had been keeping the Sabbath day holy, but the second mile encouraged me to visit the sick, and the elderly, and to look for opportunities to provide compassionate service and to perform other acts of quiet Christianity.

I had been doing my home teaching, but I began to realize that if I wanted to go the second mile, that responsibility would never be over, no matter the day of the month. I began to take an active interest in the on-going affairs of my families, and to be sensitive to their spiritual, emotional, intellectual, and temporal needs. With a second mile perspective, I began to see hidden truth in the scriptures that related to my responsibilities: "Verily I say unto you, Inasmuch as ye have done it unto one of the least of these my brethren, ye have done it unto me." (Matthew 25:40).

I had established habit patterns that supported my desire to express myself with soft and considerate words, but I took to heart the second mile admonition of Paul, who wrote: "Let no corrupt communication proceed out of your mouth, but that which is good to the use of edifying, that it may minister grace unto the hearers. (Ephesians 4:29).

I had been paying my tithing, but I began to regularly ponder the significance of the second mile covenant to obey the Law of Consecration.

I had maintained temple worthiness, and had received my own endowment, but I began to appreciate the second mile requirement to do my own family work, and to expand my temple service by participating in baptismal, initiatory and sealing ordinances, in addition to proxy endowments for the dead.

I had consistently accepted a number of ward callings, but realized that my second mile commitment would require me to go beyond an hour or two of service each week, and would compel me to consecrate my time and talents to the needs of those for whom I had a stewardship responsibility. I began to appreciate the observation of Job, who wrote: "For God speaketh once, yea twice, yet man perceiveth it not. In a dream, in a vision of the night, when deep sleep falleth upon men, in slumberings upon the bed; Then he openeth the ears of men, and sealeth their instruction." (Job 33:14-16).

I had learned to be undeviating in my obedience to the Word of Wisdom, but when I applied the second mile principle to this law of health, I began to see it in its greater context, as a conduit to enlightenment, and so I began to pay more strict attention to the spirit of the law, and to the delicate relationships between physical and spiritual stability, and between physical health and personal revelation.

I had established a habit pattern of praying daily to my Heavenly Father, but the second mile urged me to ask for His influence at the break of day, and to return and report at its end. The second mile reminded me of the Lord's commandment: "Go to the house of prayer and offer up thy sacraments upon my holy day; For verily this is a day appointed unto you to rest from your labors, and to pay thy devotions unto the Most High; Nevertheless thy vows shall be offered up in righteousness on all days and at all times." (D&C 59:9-11).

I had been obeying the Ten Commandments to the best of my ability, but the second mile asked me to live according to the principles defined by a higher spiritual law, to develop real compassion for others, and to shun the siren song coming from the great and spacious building.

I had been mindful of my baptismal covenants, but the second mile focused my thoughts on the command to be "willing to mourn with those that mourn; yea, and comfort those that stand in need of comfort, and to stand as witnesses of God at all times and in all things, and in all places that ye may be in, even until death." (Mosiah 18:9). I learned that the second mile would expose me to experience God's love, and to understand what Paul meant when he said: "By the grace of God I am what I am: and his grace which was bestowed upon me was not in vain; but I laboured more abundantly than they all: yet not I, but the grace of God which was with me." (1 Corinthians 15:10).

When they speak in General Conference, the General Authorities of the church often urge us to go the second mile. They talk about the first principles and ordinances of the gospel, because they are mindful that they may be instructing non-members and less-active members, but they realize that they are also speaking to members of the church who have already committed themselves to obedience. Their messages have multiple layers of meaning and application. They speak to the basic principles in such a way that non-members are encouraged to take the first steps toward commitment, while at the same time, seasoned members are encouraged to commit to go the second mile.

After Paul had traveled along the road to Damascus, he learned what it meant to go the second mile. He later ministered among the Corinthian Saints, whom he was pleased to discover had a working relationship with the laws of a gospel whose expression he characterized as being written upon "tables of stone." But he also took pains to explain their second mile commitment: "Ye are manifestly declared to be (living examples of) the epistle of Christ ministered by us, written not with ink, but with the Spirit of the living God; not in tables of stone, but in fleshy tables of the heart." (2 Corinthians 3:3).

Those who commit to the second mile are as the Nephites of old, who were encouraged by the sermon of King Benjamin. The scriptures record: And now, it came to pass that when king Benjamin had thus spoken to his people, he sent among them, desiring to know of his people if they believed the words which he had spoken unto them. And they all cried with one voice, saying: Yea, we believe all the words which thou hast spoken unto us; and also, we know of their surety and truth, because of the Spirit of the Lord Omnipotent, which has wrought a mighty change in us, or in our hearts, that we have no more disposition to do evil, but to do good continually. And we, ourselves, also, through the infinite goodness of God, and the manifestations of his Spirit, have great views of that which is to come; and were it expedient, we could prophesy of all things. And it is the faith which we have had on the things which our king has spoken unto us that has brought us to this great knowledge, whereby we do rejoice with such exceedingly great joy." (Mosiah 5:1-4).

Sooner or later, every member of the church is a second miler, who is manifestly encouraged to endure to the end in righteousness. During His mortal ministry, the Savior said: "He that shall endure unto the end, the same shall be saved." (Matthew 24:13). Going a little further, He explained to Joseph Smith: "If you keep my commandments (the first mile) and endure to the end (the second mile) you shall have eternal life, which gift is the greatest of all the gifts of God. (D&C 14:7).

Service

Mission Reflections
Sister Joanna Hudson

"I tell you these things that ye may learn wisdom; that ye may learn that when ye are in the service of your fellow beings ye are only in the service of your God." (Mosiah 2:17).

This is a world of constant extraction and absorption - a spiritual I.V. - a transfusion all rolled into one. I'm learning that the only way we can increase our strength is to give away that which we have received. I have realized that at the end of the days when I expend the least amount of energy serving others I am the most tired, and it is on the days when I serve my heart out that I feel so rejuvenated.

I have loved working with the people in Belgium. As I have served them, my desire to be better has been strengthened. Service is not the price we pay to get to the Celestial Kingdom. It is the very fabric of which the Celestial Kingdom is made.

More than ever before, on my mission I have looked to Christ as my example. Unselfishness marked His every action. Personal pleasures and comfort came last, if at all. He spent His ministry serving others. As great as was His suffering on the cross and in Gethsemane, I am touched by His example just hours before the appointed hour. As He explained to one disciple who wanted to join Him, "Foxes have holes, and birds of the air have nests; but the Son of man hath no where to lay his head." (Luke 9:58).

Prior to His mortal birth, during His mortal ministry, and in the eternities, the Savior has continued to give. His love for us is infinite. To feel that love is one of our greatest blessings. To feel that same quality of love for Him, to begin to have just a hint of that capacity, is yet another blessing. To feel that love for all of our brothers and sisters is the ultimate goal. Until we have the pure love of Christ, our love of the Savior is incomplete. We gain this love in small increments that are directly related to giving service to others.

The Savior is not looking forward to retirement and relaxation. He is, and will be throughout eternity, looking for new opportunities to serve. We see this philosophy in action, as He came to the earth to live in much less comfortable circumstances than those to which we are accustomed. During His ministry, He thought only of others. While here, He experienced all that we experience and more.

I love my mission because it allows me to join the Savior in His work to bring to pass our immortality and eternal life. I am grateful for it all; not only for the joy and the incredible happiness, but even for the heartache and frustration. Through it all, I have come to know my Savior. As we seek to become purified and sanctified as we move along the pathway that leads to exaltation, we must all pass through our own Gethsemane, the refiner's fire, so that our spirits will be malleable and ductile in the hands of the Lord. I know this holds true especially during a mission. We are asked to follow the road less traveled. Sometimes it hurts. But we look up to a God who loves us so much, whose outstretched hands are there to bring us into the warmth of His bosom, and turn us into instruments that can bless the lives of our fellow travelers.

Set Apart

"He changed their hearts; yea, he awakened them out of a deep sleep, and they awoke unto God. Behold, they were in the midst of darkness; nevertheless, their souls were illuminated by the light of the everlasting word."
(Alma 5:7).

When we are set apart to do a particular work in the church, the position becomes ours. It doesn't belong to anyone else, and no one else has a right to it. If we do not do our job, it will not be done. Therefore, positions in the church should be accepted with the intention to carry out our duties as though our lives depended on it, as indeed they do.

It is amazing what can happen when we set our mind to a task. The secret of success is to accept assignments without reservation and with strong hearts. When we become church members and we get the spirit into our bloodstream, things really begin to happen. Our burning zeal to serve God lifts us to greatness and gives us authority over all our weaknesses and over the defeats of life. But our efforts are strangely impotent when our hearts are not in the work. John Taylor said: "If you do not magnify your calling, God will hold you responsible for those whom you might have saved had you done your duty." ("Deseret News," 8/7/1878). Who among us can afford to be responsible for the loss of the eternal life of a human soul? If great joy is the reward for saving one soul, then how terrible must be the remorse of those whose timid efforts have allowed a child of God to be lost?

We who hold positions in the church should pledge our best efforts. Not only other lives, but our own depend on it, for those who were "not valiant in the testimony of Jesus" while in mortality cannot enter the Celestial Kingdom of God. (D&C 76:79).

We are the children of Divinity and have within us the seeds of greatness, for we have been endowed with celestial character traits. We call forth power through faithful efforts. We fight for eternal principles. We are "set apart" because ours is a work of eternal significance that is carried out in partnership with our Creator. We are "set apart" by our convictions, our enthusiasm, our righteousness, and our faith. Our constant prayer should be that after we have been "set apart" and His work has been given into our hands, everyone within the circle of our influence will be enriched.

Therefore," said the Lord, "Let every man stand in his own office, and labor in his own calling, that the system may be kept perfect." (D&C 84:109-110). As Joseph Fielding Smith declared: "The way to magnify these callings is to do the work designed to be performed by those who hold the particular office involved." (C.R., 10/1970).

The road to the Sacrament table is the path of safety. (See Moroni Chapters 4 & 5).

Sharing the Gospel

> The Sons of Mosiah had been teaching God's word "for the space of 14 years among the Lamanites, having had much success in bringing many to the knowledge of the truth; yea, by the power of their words many were brought before the altar of God, to call on his name and confess their sins before him.
> (Alma 17:4).

Our reluctance to share the gospel also has something to do with timidity, which is ironic, because the exhortation of Paul resonates within us. While a prisoner for the truth's sake in Rome, he declared: "I am not ashamed of the gospel of Christ: for it is the power of God unto salvation to everyone that believeth." (Romans 1:16). At one time or another, many of us have had similar missionary zeal. But we may have lost that fire in our belly. Parley P. Pratt never did. He exclaimed: "I have received the holy anointing, and I can never rest, till the last enemy is conquered, death destroyed, and truth reigns triumphant." (J.D., 1:15).

Perhaps we could re-acquire that fervor if we would adjust our attitudes a bit. Maybe we could be missionaries by simply teaching correct principles and by being more aware of the example we are setting. If we could be undeviatingly true to ourselves, we could be false to no man. (See Shakespeare, "Hamlet"). Perhaps missionary work is nothing more complicated than loving others as ourselves. (See Mark 12:31). After all, we do missionary work because God loves his children. If we just learn to love as He does, and if we live to learn, we'll love to live, and our charity will become infectious.

Perhaps we need to pay more attention to our own testimonies, and do a better job of nurturing them. On a daily basis, we might need to find a thermometer with which to take our own testimony temperature. Perhaps, if we put our hand to our forehead, we might detect its feverish pitch. As Alma asked: "Have ye spiritually been born of God? Have ye received his image in your countenances? Have ye experienced this mighty change in your hearts?" (Alma 5:14). "I say unto you, my brethren, if ye have experienced a change of heart, and if ye have felt to sing the song of redeeming love, I would ask, can ye feel so now?" (Alma 5:26).

We might need to step back, inhale deeply, take time, and prioritize our busy agendas. Missionaries typically tithe their time. What if we were to dedicate 10% of our waking hours to the service of the Lord? What if we were to serve more energetically, and pray with greater specificity. Ninety five percent of the members of the church do not pray for missionary opportunities. Five percent of the members of the church do. That five percent has ninety five percent of the missionary opportunities. Do you think the Lord is trying to tell us something?

We need to take the time to invite our neighbors to church activities or meetings, and to welcome them into our homes. We need to have real gospel conversations with them. Of course, we need to strive to obtain the Spirit, acquire humility, love the people, and work diligently. If we are waiting for spectacular results, we may need to ratchet down our expectations, and pay closer attention to the constant flow of revealed communication that comes from the Holy Ghost, that guides us into the warm embrace of daily spiritual experiences, and introduces our friends and neighbors to that same undiscovered country.

We need to act upon our spiritual promptings, for proper prior planning will prevent poor priesthood performance. As Spencer W. Kimball taught: "We have paused on some plateaus long enough. Let us resume our journey forward and upward, and quietly put an end to our reluctance to reach out to others, whether in our own families, wards, or neighborhoods. We have been diverted at times from fundamentals on which we must now focus, in order to move forward as a person or as a people." (C.R., 4/1979). Gordon B. Hinckley re-affirmed what an early church welfare pamphlet stated: "The church cannot hope to save a man on Sunday, if during the week it is a complacent witness to the destruction of his soul." Rather than only taking the glowing embers of a gospel-centered life out into the world, we need to bring others into the crackling fire of a church that illuminates the eternal burnings of the Kingdom of God.

Most of us have enjoyed the delicious texture and flavor of Swiss chocolate. If we hold up a poster of an assortment of Lindt chocolates and show it to our friends, they may or may not be inclined to try a piece for themselves. If we actually show them a real piece of chocolate, we might catch their interest, and they might begin to salivate with the stirrings of hopeful anticipation. But, in our enthusiasm, if we unwrap a piece before their eyes, and pop it into our own mouths, and then try to describe how wonderful it tastes, they might be disappointed and be underwhelmed by our gesture. They might even think it insincere or disingenuous. However, what if we were to take a piece of chocolate that had their name written upon it, and we unwrapped it with them, and on our open palms presented it to them, and then allowed them to savor it for themselves, encouraging them to roll it over and over on their tongues while it slowly and deliciously melted in their mouths? Better yet, what if we were to share in their gustatory delight, and enjoy a similar piece of chocolate with them? How much easier and more fluid would be our expressions relating to life with Swiss chocolate. If we further augmented their sensory delight with words of encouragement, their experience might expand to new proportions, and they would almost certainly forevermore enthusiastically endorse and desire, and perhaps even crave, Swiss chocolate. They might even be willing to pay a premium, just to relive the experience. From that day on, they might be hooked on Swiss chocolate.

Nearly everyone has a "sweet tooth," something that really hits their hot button and gets their juices flowing. For the two disciples on the Road to Emmaus, it was the Spirit. After their personal encounter with the resurrected Lord, one said to the other: "Did not our heart burn within us, while he talked with us by the way, and while he opened to us the scriptures?" (Luke 24:32). We do not know what happened to these travelers, but we can be sure that their lives were thereafter never the same. When we allow the Spirit to guide us with tailor-made messages to our friends and neighbors, sooner or later they will be moved upon to wash their flesh in water and put on holy garments. (See Leviticus 16:4).

Sharper Than a Two-Edged Sword
(D&C 33)

"O how great is the nothingness of the children of men; yea, even they are less than the dust of the earth. For behold, the dust of the earth moveth hither and thither, to the dividing asunder, at the command of our great and everlasting God. Yea, behold at his voice do the hills and the mountains tremble and quake. And by the power of his voice they are broken up, and become smooth, yea, even like unto a valley." (Helaman 12:7-10).

The word of the Lord is "quick" or living in a Biblical sense, "and powerful" or a source of life and energy, "sharper than a two-edged sword, to the dividing asunder of the joints and marrow, soul and spirit" or penetrating to our innermost parts. (V. 1). He is "a discerner of the thoughts and intents of the heart." (V. 1). At the Judgment Bar, "our words will condemn us, yea, all our works will condemn us and our thoughts will also condemn us." (Alma 12:14). "In the armory of thought we forge the weapons by which we destroy ourselves. We also fashion the tools with which we build for ourselves heavenly mansions of joy and strength and peace. Between these two extremes are all grades of character, and we are their maker and their master. We are the masters of thought, and the shapers of condition, environment, and destiny." (James Allen, "As a Man Thinketh").

King Benjamin had told his audience that there are many ways to commit sin. (Mosiah 4:29). There is a rule, however, that is the foundation for purposeful living, and the order of counsel is significant. When we have been taught the truth, and with a firm knowledge of that which is good, we must take care to watch our thoughts, words, and deeds. (Mosiah 4:30). When people are taught correct principles, they are left to govern their own behavior according to the light and knowledge they have received. (See D&C 58:26). Usually, the Lord gives us the overall objectives to be accomplished and some guidelines to follow, but He expects us to work out most of the details ourselves. These are developed through study and prayer with accompanied by the promptings of the Spirit.

If we stand condemned, "we would fain be glad if we could command the rocks and the mountains to fall upon us to hide us from his presence." (Alma 12:14). "In the last days an angel will sound his trump, and reveal the secret acts of men, and the thoughts and intents of their hearts." (D&C 88:109). When this happens, we will know that the Last Judgment has begun. Though we stand unrepentant at the Bar in the presence of God "in his glory, and in his power, and in his might, majesty, and dominion," we will still acknowledge His justice and mercy. (Alma 12:15). God, Who is the Author of Salvation and the Builder of the universe and all things therein, will be able to read the blueprint of our lives with unerring accuracy. In a sense, it would seem, we are after all is said and done, the architects of our own fate. Therefore, we should be vigilant to see that we are building temples, and not rickety shanties, for the eternal dwelling places of our souls. Life should be more than just an overnight stay in cheap, second-class hotel rooms.

"Ye are called to lift up your voices as with the sound of a trump." (V. 2). Trumpets were used anciently to call attention to danger or to announce the coming of royalty. "Blow ye the trumpet in Zion, and sound an alarm in my holy mountain: let all the inhabitants of the land tremble: for the day of the Lord cometh." (Joel 2:1-2). It will be a day of thick darkness and gloominess for the wicked, when even the sun, the moon, and the stars of heaven will obey the voice of the Master. "For the stars of heaven and the constellations thereof shall not give their light; the sun shall be darkened in his going forth, and the moon shall not cause her light to shine." (Isaiah 13:10). The purpose of the day of the Lord is to "destroy the sinners thereof out of (the land)." (Isaiah 13:9). They will be punished for iniquity, arrogance, pride, and haughtiness, because they have failed to repent.

In that day, a righteous man will be "more precious than fine gold." (Isaiah 13:12). This might be because they are few in number, or it could be because the true value of righteousness, when contrasted to the insignificance of telestial treasures will be apparent. Even the wealth of the Golden Wedge of Ophir will pale in comparison to one righteous man. (Isaiah 13:12).

The Lord called Ezra Thayre and Northrop Sweet to declare His gospel "to a crooked and perverse generation." (V. 2). Missionaries in all ages have been shocked by the distorted understanding of the spiritually illiterate. B.H. Roberts related an experience he had as a young Elder while serving in the Southern States Mission: "As Brother Palmer and I stepped into the church, we found the pastor engaged in prayer, and what was my surprise to hear him say: 'O Lord, help us to understand that we have enough of Thy word; that the canon of scripture is full. Help us to believe, O Lord, that the awful voice of prophecy will no more be heard; help us to believe that revelation has ceased, that Thou wilt no more speak to man.' Well, thought I, there is a wide difference between the ideas contained in that person's prayer and what we are going to preach!" ("Defender of The Faith," p. 108).

Set prayers can be riddled with expressions of false doctrine and the elements of apostasy. Some convey the sense that God is a Spirit. Others suggest a belief in pre-destination. For many, Sunday may be punctuated by institutional prayer. For others, weekday activities may be uninfluenced by belief in God, while whatever faith that is possessed lies dormant. When religious thoughts are confined to the Sabbath, they can be sterile and devoid of vitality, impotent and powerless expressions. With this in mind, James taught: "Faith without works is dead, being alone." (James 2:14). That so many can make prayer a stylistic ritual is astonishing to those who are accustomed to more intimate levels of conversations with God.

"For behold, the field is white already to harvest; and it is the eleventh hour, and the last time that I shall call laborers into my vineyard." (V. 3, See v. 7). This is the Parable of the Laborers in the Vineyard in the Dispensation of the Fulness of Times. Their continuing focus of attention on their less fortunate brethren will eventually bring the missionaries into complete harmony with the attributes of Heavenly Father. "And ye shall be even as I am, and I am even as the Father, and the Father and I are one," said the Savior to the Three Nephites. (3 Nephi 28:10). The Lord numbers His children by their willingness to accept covenants, and His missionary objective is really quite simple. Just find those who are the elect, and teach them by the Spirit. "And ye are called to bring to pass the gathering of mine elect," declared the Lord, "for mine elect hear my voice and harden not their hearts." (D&C 29:7).

The vineyard had become corrupted in "every whit … because of priestcrafts, all having corrupt minds." (V. 4). Doctrine is homogenized by "the loftiness of (the) vineyard," or the haughtiness and pride of the world. It occurs when the people disregard the word of the Lord, and "look beyond the mark" that is Jesus Christ. It happens when members of the church follow their own agenda and establish their own values on the shifting sands of expediency, rather than on the principles that are the bedrock of the doctrine of Christ. It is because even church members sometimes exercise unrighteous dominion, or take "strength unto themselves." (Jacob 5:48). It is then that we try to bring the world into the gospel, rather than take the gospel into the world. The Lord rhetorically asked: "What could I have done more for my vineyard?" (Jacob 5:49). This question is more personal when we realize that the Master is always in control and knows our individual and collective needs and weakness, and yet in His benevolence "His grace is sufficient for all men that (simply) humble themselves" before Him. (Ether 12:27).

Therefore, "out of the wilderness" of apostasy came the restoration of the gospel. (V. 5). In contrast to the wicked who groped about blindly, lurching to and from as flotsam and jetsam on the sea of life, the Lord described the events surrounding the Restoration as "the beginning of the rising up and the coming forth of my church out of the wilderness - clear as the moon, and fair as the sun, and terrible as an army with banners." (D&C 5:14, See Song of Solomon 6:10). The Savior indicated to the Nephites that in the day when the Latter-day Restoration would burst upon the world stage, it would be such a phenomenon "that kings shall shut their mouths." (3 Nephi 21:8). Its destiny is to become the greatest power the world has ever known. "For in that day," declared the Savior, "shall the Father (perform) a great and marvelous work among them." (3 Nephi 21:9).

To the church that was the fruits of the Restoration would be gathered "the elect ... even as many as will believe in me, and hearken unto my voice." (V. 6). It is the mission of The Church of Jesus Christ of Latter-day Saints to preach the gospel throughout the world because the blood of Israel is there, and they need the "roots" or the foundation covenants. We do not preach the gospel so that people can enjoy a better life. We do it so that they can be saved in the Celestial Kingdom of God.

"Open your mouths and they shall be filled" through the prompting of the Holy Ghost." (V. 8). The Lord asks only that we establish a spiritual rapport with Him by developing a relationship that is at first initiated, and then sustained, through intimate conversation. We do not draw near to God by constructing eloquent prayers or elaborate edifices in which to recite them by rote. The world's misconception of the nature of God is characterized by its secularization of the divine model, first represented by the ancient ziggurat of Babel, that the people constructed in the false hope that the top thereof would reach all the way to heaven. (See Genesis 11:4). But Heavenly Father's children cannot find Him that way. Cathedrals can be quiet stands of trees more easily than can piles of stones, glaring gargoyles, and stained-glass windows.

Those who practice priestcraft and engage in idolatry are more prone to focus their worship on their "elegant and spacious buildings and fine work of wood, and all manner of precious things." (Mosiah 11:8-11). One is reminded of the Emperor Justinian, who "began a new Santa Sophia. He summoned the most famous of living architects to plan and superintend the work. Abandoning the traditional Basilican form, they conceived a design whose center would be a spacious dome resting not on walls but on massive piers and buttressed by a half dome at either end. Ten thousand workmen were engaged, and 320,000 pounds of gold were spent on the enterprise. In five years and ten months the edifice was complete, and on December 26, 537 A.D., the Emperor led a solemn inaugural procession to the resplendent cathedral. Justinian walked alone to the pulpit, and lifting up his hands, cried out: "Oh Solomon! I have vanquished you!" (Will Durant, "The Lessons of History," 4:130).

Today, when we study the archaeological remains of ancient Meso-American cultures, we are probably seeing the remnants of apostate Lamanite civilizations, since it was they who worshipped gods of wood and of stone and focused their attention on temporal monuments to their profane deities. (See Ezekiel 20:32). Jeremiah might have asked of these apostates: "Shall a man make gods unto himself, and they are no gods?" (Jeremiah 16:20).

As Truman Madsen so keenly observed, the avenue through which we may approach our Father is intimate and heart-felt prayer, acting no hypocrisy. "At one level," he said, "we all indulge the daily clichés and more or less mean them: 'Forgive us,' or 'Help us to overcome our weaknesses.' At a deeper level, we voice actual present feelings, even when they are raw, ugly, miserable ones: 'Father, I feel awful,' or 'I am racked with anxiety.' But there is a deeper level, the inmost of which often defies words, even feeling words. This level may be likened to what the scriptures call 'groanings which cannot be uttered.' (Romans 8:26). Turned upward, they become the most powerful prayer-thrusts of all." ("Christ & The Inner Life," p. 17-18).

As we yearn for the wordless center in each of us, the Lord promised that we "shall become even as Nephi of old." (V. 8). He "was an extraordinary man. He was firm and as unflinching as a rock in standing up for the right. He was full of faith, and uncomplaining in the face of adversity, and yet was as humble and tender as a child. The Holy Ghost seems constantly to have attended him and instructed him. He is one of the very greatest spiritual characters of The Book of Mormon." (Sydney B. Sperry, "Book of Mormon Compendium," p. 253).

Nephi set a tremendous example for those who would follow him. He was self-effacing, and would have been embarrassed to have been held up as a role model. His Exemplar was Jesus Christ, and he would count his ministry a failure if it were unable to deepen our commitment to the Savior and strengthen our testimony of the principles of His gospel. The Tree of Life was very real to Nephi, and his constant prayer must have been to be sensitive to the whisperings of the Spirit to enable him to help as many as possible to be introduced to its delicious fruit. Those who pattern their lives after that of Nephi are they who follow the Lord, who cry: "Repent, repent, and prepare ye the way of the Lord, and make his paths straight; for the kingdom of heaven is at hand." (V. 10). They acknowledge His sovereignty and strive to make all necessary preparations for His earthly reception as King of kings and Lord of lords.

Faith and repentance lead us to the strait gate of baptism where we obtain a remission of sins, gain membership in the church, and enter on the way leading to personal sanctification through repentance and the gospel standard is undeviating, with no room for rationalization or compromise. There is no latitude in God's declaration, when He said: "For I the Lord cannot look upon sin with the least degree of allowance." (D&C 1:31).

"This seems a harsh scripture," wrote Stephen Robinson, "for it clearly states that God cannot tolerate sin in any degree. He can't wink at it, or ignore it, or turn and look the other way. He won't sweep it under the rug or say, 'Well, it's just a little sin. It'll be all right.' God's standard, the celestial standard, is absolute, and it allows no exceptions. There is no wiggle room. Many people seem to have the idea that the Judgment will somehow involve weighing or balancing, with their good deeds on one side of the scales and their bad deeds on the other. If their good deeds outweigh their bad, or if their hearts are basically good and outweigh their sins, then they can be admitted into the presence of God. This notion is false. God cannot allow moral or ethical imperfection in any degree whatsoever to dwell in his presence. He cannot tolerate sin 'with the least degree of allowance.' It is not a question of whether our good deeds outweigh our sins. If there is even one sin on our record, we are finished. The celestial standard is complete innocence, pure and simple, and nothing less will be tolerated in the kingdom of God." ("Believing Christ," p. 1-2).

"Yea, repent and be baptized, every one of you, for a remission of your sins; yea, be baptized even by water, and then cometh the baptism of fire and of the Holy Ghost … This is my gospel." (V. 11-12). All teaching should provide motivation to repent. "Behold," said the Lord, "this is my doctrine - whosoever repenteth and cometh unto me, the same is my church." (D&C 10:67). Moroni offered the same message: "Be wise in the days of your probation; strip yourselves of all uncleanness … ask with a firmness unshaken, that ye will yield to no temptation, but that ye will serve the true and living God." (Mormon 9:28).

The spirit of revelation teaches the principles of the gospel that are revealed in the scriptures. "And upon this rock" of revelation "I will build my church; yea, upon this rock ye are built, and if ye continue, the gates of hell shall not prevail against you." (V. 13). The key to our understanding of the mysteries of God is the spiritual illumination of our minds. Of secular Christianity, B.H. Roberts once wrote: "In their efforts to clarify (their consideration of Christ) they were often simply multiplying mirrors and studying angles without increasing the light. The New Dispensation brought a flood of light that did not simply replace the darkness, but illuminated elements and principles, and their relationships, that heretofore had been (only) dimly perceived." ("The Truth, The Way, The Life," p. 263).

Under most circumstances, though, the people to whom the glad message is offered "will not seek wisdom, neither do they desire that she should rule over them!" Under those circumstances, "how blind and impenetrable are the understandings of the children of men." (Mosiah 8:20). On the college portals in Moorish Granada (1300-1492) were inscribed these lines: "The world is supported by four things, the learning of the wise, the justice of the great, the prayers of the good, and the valor of the brave." (Mohammed). The casualties of every dispensation are those who try to let intellect do for intelligence, who suppose that they can judge both the truth and the morality of the word of the Lord and of His prophets. The Saints, however, gain knowledge and skill by both study and faith without confusing the two.

In addition, the Lord revealed that it would be necessary for every faithful Latter-day Saint to "remember the church articles and covenants to keep them." (V. 14). Doctrine and Covenants Section 20, a revelation on Church Organization and Government, and Section 22, that deals with the New and Everlasting Covenant, had been accepted and embraced by the membership of the church at its first conference, in June 1830.

Of the occasion of the organization of the church two months earlier, the Prophet Joseph Smith wrote: "After a happy time spent in witnessing and feeling for ourselves the powers and blessings of the Holy Ghost, through the grace of God bestowed upon us, we dismissed with the pleasing knowledge that we were now individually members of, and acknowledged of God, 'The Church of Jesus Christ.'" (H.C. 1:79). It must have been a very good feeling!

When studying the revelations dealing with church organization and government and the new and everlasting covenant, the members were to be guided by the Holy Ghost. Therefore, the Lord instructed: "Whoso having faith you shall confirm in my church, by the laying on of the hands, and I will bestow the gift of the Holy Ghost upon them." (V. 15). "The world does not have its guidance, but is blessed with the Light of Christ as a guide, which, if they are humble and seek the light, will lead them to the light." (Joseph Fielding Smith, Jr., "Answers to Gospel Questions," 4:89).

"And The Book of Mormon and the holy scriptures are given of me for your instruction; and the power of my Spirit quickeneth all things." (V. 16). These are the tools of conversion. The scriptures are the great equalizer, for the past is prologue, and holy writ can be likened to the circumstances of each individual who ponders its messages.

Marion G. Romney once admitted to the Saints: "I don't know much about the gospel other than what I've learned from the Standard Works. When I drink from a spring, I like to get the water where it comes out of the ground, not down the stream, after the cattle have waded in it. I appreciate other people's interpretation, but when it comes to the gospel, we ought to be acquainted with what the Lord says." (C.R., 4/1975).

Spencer W. Kimball said: "I ask us all to honestly evaluate our performance in scripture study. It is a common thing to have a few passages of scripture at our disposal, floating in our minds, as it were, and thus to have the illusion that we know a great deal about the gospel. In this sense, having a little knowledge can be a problem indeed. I am convinced that each of us must, at some time in our lives, discover the scriptures for ourselves, and not just discover them once, but rediscover them again and again." ("Ensign," 9/1976).

As President Kimball suggested, the Lord requires a constant state of spiritual readiness: "Be faithful, praying always, having your lamps trimmed and burning, and oil with you, that you may be ready at the coming of the Bridegroom." (V. 17). Those who pray to the Father continually are not likely to lose sight of their utter dependence on Him for both their temporal and spiritual welfare, nor will they forget from Whom both talents and blessings flow. They will have banked spiritual reserves sufficient for withdrawal in their time of need.

Prayer is only "in vain" when it is performed without effect or without the desired or intended result. To pray in vain is to pray without success. Using the name of the Lord during prayer may be blasphemous if it is used improperly without any intention of genuinely extending thanks, or hope of receiving desired blessings. Those who do so are imposters, invoking the name of Deity in a false, misleading, and counterfeit way. This is Satan's approach, in contrast to the righteous use of the name of God by those who bear His priesthood authority or act under its direction, are bound by His covenants, and act no hypocrisy.

From his confinement in Liberty Jail, Joseph Smith pleaded with the church to develop the behavioral characteristics of our Heavenly Father and Jesus Christ. "Let thy bowels also be full of charity towards all men, and to the household of faith," he wrote the Saints, "and let virtue garnish thy thoughts unceasingly; then shall thy confidence wax strong in the presence of God; and the doctrine of the priesthood shall distill upon thy soul as the dews from heaven. The Holy Ghost shall be thy constant companion, and thy scepter an unchanging scepter of righteousness and truth; and thy dominion shall be an everlasting dominion and without compulsory means it shall flow unto thee forever and ever." (D&C 121:45-46).

Nephi had similar concerns about his own brethren. He perceived that they were having difficulty with the doctrine of Christ, because they were not exercising faith sufficient to pray. He equated the acquisition of the knowledge and qualities necessary for salvation with our ability and willingness to pray. In his closing remarks to his people, he said: "If ye would hearken unto the Spirit which teacheth a man to pray, ye would know that ye must pray; for the evil spirit teacheth not a man to pray, but teacheth him that he must not pray. But behold, I say unto you that ye must pray always, and not faint; that ye must not perform any thing unto the Lord save in the first place ye shall pray unto the Father in the name of Christ, that he will consecrate thy performance unto thee, that thy performance may be for the welfare of thy soul."
(2 Nephi 32:8-9).

Long ago, the Psalmist wrote: "Evening, and morning, and at noon, will I pray, and cry aloud: and he shall hear my voice." (Psalms 55:17). In the Garden of Gethsemane, the Savior counseled Peter to "Watch and pray, that ye enter not into temptation: the spirit indeed is willing, but the flesh is weak." (Matthew 26:41). To his brethren, Nephi provided the additional insight that it is the evil one who teaches that we must not pray. With this knowledge, the practice of the church to consistently pray makes sense, since its members need regular reinforcement against encroachments by Satan and the tendency to be carnal, sensual, and devilish.

Brigham Young once observed that it does not matter if a man feels like praying or not; he should nevertheless pray. He said if men waited until they felt like praying, there would not be much prayer in this world. ("Discourses of Brigham Young," p. 44). Instead, we should be like "the builder who first bridged Niagara's gorge. Before he swung his cable, shore to shore, (he) sent out across the gulf his venturing kite, bearing a slender cord for unseen hands to grasp upon the further cliff and draw a greater cord, and then a greater yet; 'til at last across the chasm swung The Cable - then the mighty bridge in air! So may we send our little timid thoughts, across the void, out to God's reaching hands. Send our love, and faith, to thread the deep, thought afterthought, until the little cord, and we, are anchored to the Infinite! (Edwin Markham). The Lord requires His people to bow the knee before Him every night and morning, and to remember Him in their secret prayers. Every Latter-day Saint who neglects this requirement has not that supply of oil which is necessary to prepare him for the Coming of The Son of Man." (Francis S. Lyman, C.R., 4/1901). "For behold, verily, verily, I say unto you, that I come quickly." (V. 18).

The Lord numbers His children by their willingness to embrace The Book of Mormon, and the missionary objectives of His missionary army are really quite simple. Just find those who are willing to be taught by the Spirit. "And ye are called to bring to pass the gathering of mine elect," declared the Lord, "for mine elect hear my voice, and harden not their hearts."
(D&C 29:7).

(The) Sons of Mosiah

> Mormon was happy to report that the "sons of Mosiah were with Alma at the time the angel first appeared unto him; therefore Alma did rejoice exceedingly to see his brethren; and what added more to his joy, they were still his brethren in the Lord; yea, and they had waxed strong in the knowledge of the truth; for they were men of a sound understanding and they had searched the scriptures diligently, that they might know the word of God. But this is not all; they had given themselves to much prayer, and fasting; therefore, they had the spirit of prophecy, and the spirit of revelation, and when they taught, they taught with the power and authority of God."
> (Alma 17:2-3).

When Alma met the Sons of Mosiah on the road leading from the land of Gideon, fourteen years after they had bid each other farewell at the commencement of their missions, it must have seemed altogether remarkable that his highest and best hopes for the welfare of his brethren had been confirmed. As he learned the details of their experiences during those eventful years, he surely recognized and appreciated the unchangeable formula for success that had guided them so unerringly. Ammon, Aaron, Omner, and Himni "had waxed strong in the knowledge of the truth; for they were men of a sound understanding and they had searched the scriptures diligently, that they might know the word of God." (Alma 17:2).

"Who shall ascend into the hill of the Lord?" David had asked. "Or who shall stand in his holy place?. He that hath clean hands, and a pure heart; who hath not lifted up his soul unto vanity, nor sworn deceitfully. He shall receive the blessing from the Lord, and righteousness from the God of his salvation." (Psalm 24:3-5). The Sons of Mosiah precisely fit this description.

The scriptures had become their message and were the tools of their trade. Their confidence, we shall see, was directly related to their knowledge of holy writ. "But," Mormon explained, "this is not all. They had given themselves to much prayer, and fasting; therefore, they had the spirit of prophecy, and the spirit of revelation, and when they taught, they taught with the power and authority of God." (Alma 17:3). They were missionaries who had endured and overcome every obstacle that had been thrown in the path of their progress.

What was it that set these remarkable young men apart from the rest of the crowd? They had waxed strong in the knowledge of the truth. They were men of a sound understanding. They had searched the scriptures diligently. They had given themselves to much prayer and fasting. Therefore, they had the spirit of prophecy and the spirit of revelation, and when they taught, they taught with power and authority. "God help all honest men," said Marion G. Romney, "to be born again, to be of sound understanding, to know the word of God, and to maintain the spirit thereof by study, fasting, prayer, and work." (C.R., 10/1941).

The challenges we face are part of life, and the example of the Sons of Mosiah gives each of us courage to carry on. We shouldn't be so concerned about winning or losing. What is important is to carry the struggle further. In our pursuit of excellence, we know that we will face our share of trials, all tailored by Heavenly Father to meet our individual needs. We view these not as stumbling blocks to our progression, but as stepping-stones to greater heights of achievement. We carry the struggle as far as need be, relying on His strength to sustain us when we feel we can go no further by ourselves.

We have spiritual challenges, but recognize chastisement from the Lord as an invitation to repent. Throughout the week, we prepare ourselves to receive the Sacrament each Sunday. We strengthen our testimonies through fasting and prayer. To reinforce our understanding of gospel principles, we undertake a consistent program of scripture study. We make the sweetness of the temple a regular part of our experience. We resist temptation by recognizing and avoiding compromising situations. We learn to act upon spiritual promptings. We exercise our agency wisely.

We have intellectual challenges, and deal with them by reading uplifting literature and by exercising our minds with stimulating thoughts and meaningful conversation with others. We speak with purpose. We avoid the media when it focuses attention on trivial matters but maintain a working knowledge of current affairs that shape the world around us. We constantly challenge ourselves by developing new interests in creative fields and are mentors to those who show interest in developing expertise in those areas in which we excel.

We face emotional challenges head-on. When we have time on our hands, we remember to ponder and pray rather than wander and play. When things do not seem to go our way, we maintain an eternal perspective. We use a cosmic yardstick to measure our progress. Our only recreational drug of choice is endorphins. We respond to the casual greetings of others ("How are you?") with "If I were any better, I'd have to be twins," and we try to mean it. We make extraordinary efforts to influence for good those situations that are under our control. We learn to accept that which we cannot change, but at the same time we create reservoirs of positive energy upon which we may draw in time of need.

We make every effort to avoid the pitfall expressed in the poem "The Excess Express." "He worked out for years to reduce all his fat. His muscles were firm, and his stomach was flat. He jogged day and night to keep himself trim, and still found time to play tennis and swim. He drank protein drinks, and ate health food galore. Then lifted, stair-climbed, and lifted some more. He told family and friends that it gave him a 'high,' They encouraged him on as he waved them good-bye. 'If things work out,' he yelled back from afar, 'I'll be a great athlete, I'll be a big star!' But how could he miss the big truck up ahead? One thud, and his beautiful body lay dead. And then, he saw something that filled him with fright. His spiritual body was one sorry sight! No more than a skeleton, covered with skin. He got up to heaven, but didn't get in! 'Another soul's mine!' Satan started to scream. 'Give man something nice, and he'll take the extreme!' OK, I'll admit it; I'll outright confess. For the fast way to hell, take the excess express." (Anonymous).

As the years pass, we will have physical challenges. In anticipation of these, we establish fitness programs tailored to our individual needs and designed to help us maintain higher levels of health. We view physical limitations positively as opportunities to develop perspective. We regularly re-evaluate our adherence to the spirit of the Word of Wisdom, and commit to goals of improvement based upon adherence to its principles.

Our time is always at a premium and so there will be service challenges. We consistently discipline ourselves so that there will be time to be of service to our own families, to individuals outside our families, and to the church. We trust in the Lord's protection when we consciously and deliberately put ourselves at risk as we venture out into the world to reclaim lost sheep. We commit to regular and sustained efforts to contribute in positive ways to the welfare of our communities, state, nation, and the world.

Along the way, we may face character challenges. To guard against compromise, we learn to appreciate experiences that teach us humility, and look forward with anticipation to those that challenge our paradigm. We attempt to so live our lives that we would be happy to give our parrot to the town gossip. We commit the 13 Articles of Faith to life as well as to memory, and make them the tangible particles of our faith. We are honest, true, chaste, benevolent, virtuous, and do good to all men. As our faith increases, so does our capacity to see God's influence over all aspects of our lives. We learn to recognize and accept the suffering that is a part of life, and strive to see adversity as a necessary and beneficial aspect of our experience. In times of trial, we remember the Savior, Who descended beneath all things, and Who is our Exemplar. We shun the shadows and are drawn to His light. As we are immersed in the Spirit as a tangible element, we exult in His glorious influence. It becomes part of our nature to relate comfortably with all that is virtuous, lovely, of good report and praiseworthy. We seek after that which creates an atmosphere conducive to improvement.

As Joseph Smith exhorted the church, so we say, "Brethren, shall we not go on in so great a cause? Go forward and not backward. Courage, brethren, and on, on to the victory! Let your hearts rejoice and be exceedingly glad. Let the earth break forth into singing … and let all the sons of God shout for joy!." (D&C 128:22-23).

The scriptures were the
message of the Sons of Mosiah,
and they were the tools of their trade.
Their confidence was directly related to
their knowledge of holy writ. "But this is
not all. They had given themselves to much
prayer, and fasting; therefore, they had the
spirit of prophecy, and the spirit of revelation,
and when they taught, they taught with the
power and authority of God." (Alma 17:3).
They were missionaries who had endured
and overcome every obstacle that
had been thrown in the path
of their progress.

Speak Kind Words to Each Other

"And after this manner of language did my brethren murmur and complain against us." (1 Nephi 17:22).

Murmuring is the subdued and continually repeated expression of indistinct or inarticulate complaint or grumbling. Like an earthquake, murmuring can build into harmonic waves with the power to undermine the foundation of relationships and institutions. Because those who murmur expect results without responsibility, it is a cowardly act. While it is so often conducted anonymously or in the cloak of secrecy, its effect is felt publicly. Those who murmur want a tangible return without having made a legitimate initial investment.

Perhaps those who murmur do so because they are as "children, tossed to and fro, and carried about with every wind of doctrine, by the sleight of men, and cunning craftiness." (Ephesians 4:14). Those who stand for nothing will typically fall for anything. Those who murmur curse the darkness, without ever thinking to light a candle. They lack a strong will, but make up for it with an even stronger won't. They do not understand that "fame is a vapor, and popularity is an accident, and that those who cheer you today may curse you tomorrow. In the end, the only thing that endures is character." (Anonymous).

Those who murmur against the church often have only a weak foundation of doctrinal understanding of the gospel, and risk falling into transgression in consequence of their shallow comprehension of principles. Picking apart the scriptures, or the words of those who preach the gospel, can distort the doctrines into meaningless fragments without any coherent connection. As Alma declared to the inhabitants of Ammonihah, "Behold, the scriptures are before you; if ye will wrest them it shall be to your own destruction." (Alma 13:20).

Murmuring can distract us from completing the labor to which we have been called. Until our actions reflect our commitment, we cannot make sustained progress. Isaiah knew that, in the Last Days, the gospel would be as a healing balm for all the Father's children, and that they who "erred in spirit (would) come to understanding, and they that murmured (would) learn doctrine." (Isaiah 29:24).

Gossiping is a kindred spirit of murmuring, but is more focused on mindless chatter and speaking without real purpose. It is just as damaging, however, because it feeds voraciously on rumor, hearsay, second-hand information, innuendo, and vanity. Left unchecked, it may build into a self-perpetuating chain reaction leading to a cascade of unfortunate, yet inevitable, consequences. In its many forms, gossip has one common characteristic. The words so loosely spoken cannot be gathered up later on. Like feathers left on the doorstep of those with whom one engages in idle conversation, they will have drifted to the four winds, and they cannot be recalled. Words so carelessly scattered about in gossip suggest that the mouth has been brought on-line before the brain.

In the Book of Helaman, Mormon wrote of the many thoughtless words that the people did "imagine up in their hearts, which were foolish and vain; and they were much disturbed, for Satan did stir them up to do iniquity continually; yea, he did go about spreading rumors and contentions upon all the face of the land, that he might harden the hearts of the people against that which was good and against that which should come." (Helaman 16:22).

The Lord understands the power of gossip, and so He has cautioned the Saints: "Thou shalt not speak evil of thy neighbor, nor do him any harm." (D&C 42:27). Expressions of courtesy, support, and appreciation, on the other hand, are "never wasted, because, at a minimum, (they) enlarge the capacity of the giver." (Neal A. Maxwell).

Mark Twain said that we should so live that we would be willing to sell our parrot to the town gossip. In fact, "there is so much good in the worst of us, and so much bad in the best of us, that it hardly behooves any of us to talk about the rest of us." (Anonymous). How much better to live our lives as an exclamation, and not an explanation. Truly did Elder Neal A. Maxwell predict that in the Last Days, discipleship would be lived in crescendo, as the positions of adversaries gathered in diametrically opposed camps snap into sharp focus. Our words will reveal our allegiance to one Master, or betray the capitulation of our agency to the other.

On the one hand, the father of lies encourages us to bend and stretch the truth, react to rumors, give in to gossip, and murmur in all its mutated forms. His disciples habitually speak out of both sides of their mouths at the same time, suffering, in the process, from the confusion of languages. Their distorted words reflect a vacuum of values, a paucity of principles, and a divine center deficiency. Satan's disciples use the tools of vague and inconsistent language to build on the shifting sands of moral relativism situational ethics, and secular humanism, that are favorite playgrounds of those with golden tongues. Frequently, it is far too easy to quiet our consciences with the soothing and false counsel of "foolish and blind guides," illogical though they may be. (Helaman 13:29). "In all too many ways," when we ignorantly enlist in his army, we are actually substituting "human sophistry for the Almighty." (Gordon B. Hinckley, "Church News," 7/2/1988). No matter that the promises of the devil are a deception and an illusion. He panders to an audience that is only too eager to trade celestial sureties for telestial trinkets and to sell its divine birthright for a mess of pottage.

On the other hand, The Lord asks us to ground ourselves in the bedrock of gospel principles, and to express ourselves with words that are building blocks, and not bullets. His disciples use words as tools and not as weapons. They ponder and pray, rather than plunder and play. They avoid assumptions, speculation, and second-guessing. They plumb the depths of issues, rather than skim the shallows. They prefer substance to superficiality. They are good listeners, and when they do speak, it is with purpose. They value trust in relationships, and then act in good faith, and with confidence.

Many in the church find it easy to follow the leadership of the priesthood as long as it takes them on to well-traveled avenues dotted with conveniently located rest stops, and to brightly lighted world stages filled with the appreciative applause and laudatory comments of fawning followers. But placed in challenging settings with no-one looking, when there have been no preparatory fortifying experiences, and when there is no positive peer pressure to sustain correct choices, it is far easier to falter.

"You tell on yourself by the friends you seek, by the very manner in which you speak, by the way you enjoy your leisure time, by the use you make of dollar and dime. You tell who you are by the things you wear and in the way you wear your hair; by the kinds of things that make you laugh, by the records you play on your phonograph (or iPod). You tell who you are by the way you walk, by the things in which you delight to talk; by the books you choose from a well filled shelf. In these ways and more, you tell on yourself." (Anonymous).

Before we find fault with others, we should remember that when we throw dirt, we lose ground. With revulsion, we have all witnessed flies passing over healthy parts of the body to feed only at open sores. At the dedication of the Kirtland Temple, Joseph Smith referred to those predatory individuals who sought to tear down the Latter-day work through fault finding. "We ask thee," he prayed, "to confound, and astonish, and to bring to shame and confusion, all those who have spread lying reports abroad, over the world, against thy servant or servants, if they will not repent." (D&C 109:29).

Too often, people forget that when they point their finger at someone there are three other fingers pointing right back at them. On the other hand, when we seek to discover the best in others, we somehow bring out the finest in ourselves. The sobering reality is that we don't see things as they are; we see them as we are. How refreshing if our appraisals suggest a nobler estimate of man and his potential. Even if but little good is known, we can still speak in glowing terms of that which we do know to be true. If we are the first to discover a fault in others, let us not be the first to make it known to the world. Let us, instead, practice forbearance.

We should always be ready to give courage and hope, and to speak kind words that come from the heart to awaken the soul to cheerfulness, "til heart meets with heart and rejoices in friendship that ever is true." ("Let Us Oft Speak Kind Words," L.D.S. Hymns).

Part of the challenge of life is to successfully make an on-going series of righteous judgments. If we are to do so, however, we must investigate first, and then proceed cautiously, speaking only in moderation. Those who throw stones at windows to let in fresh air don't like fresh air as much as they like the sound of breaking glass. It is warranted to err on the side of tolerance, if need be, because when all is said and done, "a brother offended is harder to be won than a strong city." (Proverbs 18:19).

In our judgment, we would do well to praise loudly, but blame softly. After all, when straightening a bent nail, a pat on the back is better than a bump on the head. Before being critical of another, we should remember that others might not have had the same advantages we have had. Let us not forget that the uplifting spiritual experiences that members of the church learn to rely upon can be incredibly supportive and sustaining blessings.

In fact, after individuals go down into the waters of baptism and come out of the world, negative thoughts and damaging conversation are foreign to their nature. Their vision of world peace and order is not one of development, but of generation. Born again, they enjoy a unity and completeness with the faithful, and "are no more strangers and foreigners, but [are instead] fellowcitizens with the saints, and of the household of God." (Ephesians 2:19).

The Savior told His Saints, "Except ye are one, ye are not mine." (D&C 38:27). In His household, His disciples learn that 'kind words can be short and easy to speak, but their echoes are truly endless." (Mother Teresa). Their charity is defined by action, and is reflected in respect, appreciation, tolerance, acceptance, and forgiveness. It is the pure love of the Savior, for in Him "there should come every good thing." (Moroni 7:22).

Our goal should be to be the kind of person our dog thinks we are, to extend ourselves in our efforts to treat others as we would have them treat us. For when we go the second mile, when it becomes our nature to speak kind words to each other, we receive "a gift of spiritual independence that removes the veil of insensitivity from a destiny." (Richard L. Gunn, "A Search for Sensitivity and Spirit," p. 197). We discover that the key to theology is found in the kind and thoughtful words that unlock the door leading to the riches of eternity.

Alma asked the people of Zarahemla: "Have ye spiritually been born of God?" (Alma 5:14). He wanted to know if these baptized members of the church had experienced the pure and unconditional love of Christ and if they had charity for all men. He knew they had been converted to the church. What he really wanted to find out was: Had they also been converted to the Savior and His gospel?

(The) Spirit of Revelation

"We search the prophets, and we have many revelations and the spirit of prophecy; and having all these witnesses, we obtain a hope, and our faith becometh unshaken." (Jacob 4:6).

We learn how to invite the Spirit, as we are taught correct principles and learn to govern ourselves. (Attributed to Joseph Smith, cited by John Taylor, "Millennial Star," 13:22, p. 339). Ezra Taft Benson said: Our "preparation must consist of more than just casual membership in the church. We must be guided by personal revelation and the counsel of the living prophet so we will not be deceived." ("B.Y.U. Devotional," 4/14/1981).

"Sometimes during solitude," said Hugh B. Brown, "I hear truth spoken with clarity and freshness; uncolored and untranslated, it speaks from within myself in a language original but inarticulate, heard only with the soul." ("Eternal Quest," p. 435). The Holy Ghost teaches us about eternal truths; about things that we can learn in no other way. "Hearken unto me," urged King Benjamin, "and open your ears that ye may hear, and your hearts that ye may understand; and your minds that the mysteries of God may be unfolded to your view." (Mosiah 2:9).

What are these mysteries of God of which the Lord speaks, for He encouraged us: "Open your mouths in proclaiming my gospel, the things of the kingdom, expounding the mysteries thereof out of the scriptures, according to that portion of Spirit and power which shall be given unto you." (D&C 71:1). "I command you that you need not suppose that you are called to preach, until you are called," the Lord counseled Hyrum Smith. "Wait a little longer, until you shall have my word, my rock, my church, and my gospel, that you may know of a surety my doctrine." (D&C 11:15-16).

"But unto him that keepeth my commandments I will give the mysteries of my kingdom, and the same shall be in him a well of living water, springing up unto everlasting life." (D&C 63:23). "The preaching of the cross is to them that perish foolishness," wrote Paul, "but unto us which are saved it is the power of God." (1 Corinthians 1:18). He continued: "The natural man receiveth not the things of the Spirit of God: for they are foolishness unto him: neither can he know them, because they are spiritually discerned." (1 Corinthians 2:14).

On the Day of Pentecost, the mysteries of the kingdom were unfolded to the view of a multitude that had just been taught gospel principles by the Apostles. "Now when they heard this, they were pricked in their heart, and said unto Peter and to the rest of the apostles, Men and brethren, what shall we do? Then Peter said unto them, Repent, and be baptized every one of you in the name of Jesus Christ for the remission of sins, and ye shall receive the gift of the Holy Ghost." (Acts 2:37-38).

The mysteries of the kingdom, then, include, but are not limited to, prayer, revelation, priesthood authority, baptism, living prophets, the Godhead, the Atonement, repentance, forgiveness, the Sacrament, the endowment, celestial marriage, eternal progression, and exaltation. The Lord provided the answer to the question "How can we understand these mysteries?" when He said: "They shall know of a surety that these things are true, for from heaven will I declare it unto them." (D&C 5:12).

There are a number of elements that are key to a revelatory understanding of the mysteries, including the following:

Study the matter in your mind. Martin Luther once said: "I have so much to do today, that I must spend more time in prayer." In D&C 9, the Lord explained to Oliver Cowdery why he had been unable to translate the records: "I say unto you, that you must study it out in your mind; then you must ask me if it be right." (D&C 9:8). We need to ask ourselves: "Have I articulated a question in my mind, pondered it, and then taken it to the Lord for clarification and understanding? What do I first need to do to discover the answer for myself? Have I exhausted all the resources available to me? Have I wrestled with the question and then tried to identify some preliminary answers?. Have I perspired enough to justify being inspired?"

There are different ways of asking. Some require more effort and more mental calisthenics on our part than others: Where should I go to school? / Should I go to Eastern? Who should I marry? / Should I marry Heber? Should I buy the red VW Beetle, or the blue VW Beetle? / Is now the best time to go into debt and buy a car? Should I wear the red dress or the blue dress? / I thank thee for my clothing, my shelter, and my good fortune. Please bless me with a heart full of gratitude for the things that I so often take for granted. Please bless me with missionary opportunities. / Please bless me with the courage to express my feelings to my friend Eliza when I feel the spirit prompting me to do so. My financial state is pathetic. Please bless me. / Please bless me as I approach this interview. I really need this job, and I'd like thy help to get it. The big game is Friday night. Please bless our team. We just have to win! / The big game is Friday night. Please bless our team to remember its preparation, to work as one, to play fair, and to do its best. Please bless the Krispy Krème Donuts, the triple fudge brownies, and the fruit punch, to nourish and strengthen our bodies. / We thank thee for the refreshments. Bless us with a good spirit as we enjoy them in fellowship. Please bless us as we drive home from this meeting, that no harm or accident may befall us. / Please bless us as we travel to our various destinations, to use good judgment and caution on the highway, and to be protected from influences that might cause us harm. The election is Tuesday. Please bless me to know who to vote for. / The election is Tuesday. Please confirm my decisions regarding the candidates and issues. Please bless those who could not be here this time, that they may be able to be here next time. / Please bless each member of our ward with the desire to fellowship with the Saints. Please bless me that I might do really, really well on this test. An "A" would be nice. / Please bless me that my test score will be an accurate reflection of my preparation, and with a calm spirit, so I might more easily recall the material I have studied. We thank thee for our blessings, and ask thee for whatever we might stand in need of. / We thank thee for blessing us with the health, vigor, and strength to meet the challenges of the week. Help me to overcome my weaknesses. / Help me to make scripture study more of a daily habit, and with the strength to get up 15 minutes earlier each day. I'm confused. Please bless me with wisdom. / "I've thought this out pretty carefully, and I think I've reached an intelligent decision, so please bless me with confirmation if it is right."

Fervent prayer is often independent of circumstances. One morning, as a family began to eat breakfast, it was Tommy's turn to ask the blessing. He asked Father in Heaven to bless the food, and then he thanked Him for the beautiful day. When the prayer was finished, his mother reminded him that it was 33° outside and freezing rain was falling. To which he responded: "You don't judge the day by the weather."

Ponder and meditate on the scriptures and the teachings of latter-day prophets. Seek the influence of the Holy Ghost. "The still small voice … whispereth through and pierceth all things, and often times it maketh my bones to quake while it maketh manifest." (D&C 85:6 – in a letter from Joseph Smith to W.W. Phelps, incorporated into the D&C by the direction of Brigham Young, in the 1876 edition). Joseph Smith told the Saints: "And now, brethren, after your tribulations, if you do these things, and exercise fervent prayer and faith in the sight of God always, He shall give unto you knowledge by His Holy Spirit, yea by the unspeakable gift of the Holy Ghost." ("Teachings," p. 138).

Search for scriptures that might help you to reach a decision. "We do not overstate the point when we say that the scriptures can be a Urim and Thummim to assist each of us to receive personal revelation. Because we believe that scripture reading can help us receive revelation, we are encouraged to read them again and again. By this means, we obtain access to direction from our Heavenly Father. That is one reason Latter-day Saints believe in daily scripture study." (Dallin Oaks, "Ensign," 1/1995).

Immerse yourself in the scriptures. Completely engulf yourself with undivided attention and without diversion, deviation, distraction, disruption, digression, or disturbance. When we consciously immerse ourselves in the scriptures as a problem-solving strategy, principles that may have otherwise been difficult to comprehend snap into sharp focus! Harold B. Lee, when asked how he had resolved challenging issues, often responded by saying: "In the early hours of the morning, while I was meditating upon the scriptures…"

Look for Conference addresses or counsel from church leaders that might shed light on the problem. After his baptism, Joseph Smith recorded: "Our minds being now enlightened, (because we'd done our homework) we began to have the scriptures laid open to our understanding, and the true meaning and intention of their more mysterious passages revealed unto us in a manner which we never could attain to previously, nor ever before had thought of." (J.S.H. 1:74). This is akin to Neal A. Maxwell's description of "sudden sunbursts of spiritual sensitivity."

Ask for a priesthood blessing to help clarify your thoughts. Of our day, Moroni wrote: "I am mindful of you always in my prayers, continually praying unto God the Father in the name of his Holy Child, Jesus, that he, through his infinite goodness and grace, will keep you through the endurance of faith on his name to the end." (Moroni 8:3). We are always in the thoughts and prayers of our priesthood leaders.

Review your patriarchal blessing. The promises contained therein are catalysts that can release the powers of heaven in our behalf. The spirit of God expressed in blessings is the spirit of hope and not of gloom or pessimism. Negative feelings initiated by the adversary are conspicuously absent from the patriarchal blessings. Each time we ponder our blessing, the Spirit invites us to read between the lines and to have a fresh revelatory experience as we plumb the depths of meaning of its inspired counsel.

Sit in the Celestial Room of the temple and quietly invite the Spirit to help you to better understand your situation. The temple is like a celestial observatory where we go to get our bearings, not only on the universe, but also on eternity. "Organize yourselves," the Lord commanded, and "prepare every needful thing" in order to tap into the universal consciousness. "Establish a house, even a house of prayer, a house of fasting, a house of faith, a house of learning, a house of glory, a house of order, a house of God." (D&C 88:119).

Orson Pratt witnessed Joseph Smith receiving revelation. "No great noise or physical manifestation was made," he said. "Joseph was as calm as the morning sun. But I noticed a change in his countenance that I had never seen before, when a revelation was given to him. Joseph's face was exceedingly white, and seemed to shine. I had been present many times when he was translating the New Testament, and wondered why he did not use the Urim and Thummim, as in translating The Book of Mormon. While this thought passed through my mind, Joseph, as if he read my thoughts, looked up and explained that the Lord gave him the Urim and Thummim when he was inexperienced in the spirit of inspiration. But now he had advanced (in his understanding of) the operations of that Spirit, and did not need the assistance of that instrument." ("Millennial Star," 8/11/1874, p. 498-499).

Inquire of the Lord in faith with an honest heart, believing that you will receive. Faith is fear that has said its prayers. It is incompatible with fear. Dozens of times, the scriptures admonish us: "Ask, and ye shall receive." The Lord said: "Now after I have spoken these words, if ye cannot understand them it will be because ye ask not, neither do ye knock, wherefore, ye are not brought into the light, but must perish in the dark." (2 Nephi 32:5). We must persistently, insistently, and actively solicit the attention of the Lord. But we cannot hope to receive a ten-thousand-dollar answer after offering a ten-cent prayer.

Joseph Smith followed the admonition of James with spectacular results: "If any of you lack wisdom, let him ask of God, that giveth to all men liberally, and upbraideth not; and it shall be given him. But let him ask in faith, nothing wavering." (James 1:5-6). Nephi confidently wrote: "Yea, I know that God will give liberally to him that asketh. Yea, my God will give me, if I ask not amiss." (2 Nephi 4:35). How do we avoid "asking amiss?" Benjamin assured us: "God ... doth grant unto you whatsoever ye ask that is right, in faith, believing that ye shall receive." (Mosiah 4:10). There was once a little boy who, before going to bed, was saying his prayers in a very low voice. His mother gently chided him: "I can't hear what you're saying, son." "I wasn't talking to you, Mom," said the small child. We must be as little children, and prepare as Benjamin rejoined us: "Repent of your sins and forsake them, and humble yourselves before God, and ask in sincerity of heart."

Be obedient and serve God. Speaking of those who had been driven out of Jackson County, the Lord said: "They were slow to hearken unto the voice of the Lord their God; therefore, the Lord their God is slow to hearken unto their prayers, to answer them in the day of their trouble. In the day of their peace, they esteemed lightly my counsel; but, in the day of their trouble, of necessity they feel after me." (D&C 101:7-8).

We need to make regular deposits to our spiritual bank account so that when we need to make withdrawals, there will be sufficient reserves to do so. Dallin H. Oaks said: "We cannot have the companionship of the Holy Ghost, the medium of individual revelation, if we are in transgression or if we are angry or if we are in rebellion against God's chosen authorities." ("Ensign," 5/1997). "Wo unto him that shall deny the revelations of the Lord, and that shall say the Lord no longer worketh by revelation, or by prophecy, or by gifts, or by tongues, or by healings, or by the power of the Holy Ghost." (2 Nephi 29:6). "When the Spirit is withdrawn, darkness supersedes the light and apostasy follows. This is one of the greatest evidences of the divinity of the latter-day work. In other organizations, men may commit all manner of sin and still retain their membership, because they have no companionship with the Holy Ghost to lose, but in the church, when a man sins and continues without repentance, the Spirit is withdrawn, and when he is left to himself the adversary takes possession of his mind and he denies the faith." (Joseph F. Smith, Jr., "Doctrines of Salvation," 3:309).

Mormon recorded a revealing commentary on the state of affairs in Zarahemla, around 90 B.C. "And thus, we can plainly discern, that after a people have been once enlightened by the Spirit of God, and have had great knowledge of things pertaining to righteousness, and then have fallen away into sin and transgression, they become more hardened, and thus their state becomes worse than though they had never known these things." (Alma 24:30).

Be meek and humble. Martin Harris had a great desire to see the plates when Joseph was engaged in the work of translation. The Lord said to him through Joseph, "Behold, I say unto him, he exalts himself and does not humble himself sufficiently before me; but if he will bow down before me, and humble himself in mighty prayer and faith, in the sincerity of his heart, then will I grant unto him a view of the things which he desires to see" (D&C 5:24).

David Whitmer recalled that one morning when Joseph Smith was getting ready to resume translating The Book of Mormon, "something went wrong about the house, and he was put out about it. Something that Emma, his wife, had done. Oliver and I went upstairs, and Joseph came up soon after to continue the translation, but he could not do anything. He could not translate a single syllable. He went downstairs, out into the orchard, and made supplication to the Lord. He was gone about an hour, came back to the house, and asked Emma's forgiveness and then came upstairs where we were and then the translation went on all right. He could do nothing save he was humble and faithful." (B.H. Roberts, "A Comprehensive History of the Church," 1:131).

We are like "the builder who first bridged Niagara's gorge. Before he swung his cable, shore to shore sent out across the gulf his venturing kite bearing a slender cord for unseen hands to grasp upon the further cliff and draw a greater cord, and then a greater yet, 'til at last across the chasm swung The Cable - then the mighty bridge in air. So may we send our little timid thoughts across the void, out to God's reaching hands, send our love and faith to thread the deep, thought after thought until the little cord has greatened to a chain no chance can break, and we are anchored to the infinite!." (Edwin Markham).

Pray when things are going well, as well as when they are not. A man was walking along the edge of a steep cliff when he lost his footing and tumbled off into space. On the way down, he cried to God: "Save me, save me!" Just then, his pant leg snagged a root sticking out of the face of the cliff, and he was jerked to a stop. As he looked around himself, he muttered: "Never mind, God. I'm all right now." We must "pray always, and not faint (and He will) consecrate (our) performance unto (us), that (our) performance may be for the welfare of (our) soul." (2 Nephi 32:9).

Make sure your prayers are well intentioned. We should avoid vain repetition that is not so much saying the same thing, as it is not praying from the heart. A man drowning sputters the word "Help!" once, twice, and even a third time. The word that he uses is the same, but it's coming from his heart.

John Taylor said: "There are some Christian people in this world who, if a man were poor or hungry, would say, let us pray for him. I would suggest a little different regimen for a person in this condition. Rather, take him a bag of flour and a little beef or pork, and a little sugar and butter. A few such comforts will do him more good than your prayers." (J.D. 19:340).

Avoid slipping into "Mormonisms" when you pray. For example, a visitor was once invited to offer the invocation for a congregation of L.D.S. inmates at the Utah State Prison. As he was praying, he asked: "Bless all those who could not be here, that they may be able to be here next time."

A member of the ward brought their non-member neighbors to several church meetings and activities. At the conclusion of each, in the benediction, supplication was made that "no harm or accident might befall us." Finally, the neighbors asked, "Do a lot of Mormons die on the way home from meetings?"

When gooey, sticky, glistening pastries are brought out at the end of an activity, to complement the red punch and finger Jell-O, and an obese participant is asked to give thanks, he might supplicate: "And bless these refreshments, that they may be nourishing and strengthening for our bodies, and do us the good that we need."

At the conclusion of our church meetings, we sometimes hear: "And bless us with all those blessings that we stand in need of. This is a reminder of the legal jargon that goes: "Incorporate by reference," the act of including a second document within another document by only mentioning the second document.

Focus on the things of God rather than on the things of the world. Wealth is not measured by the quantity, or even the quality, of our possessions, but by our attitude toward our possessions. "Seek not for riches but for wisdom, and behold, the mysteries of God shall be unfolded unto you, and then shall you be made rich." (D&C 6:7). Generally, we obtain those things upon which we focus our attention, for "the soul attracts that which it secretly harbors; that which it loves." (James Allen, "As a Man Thinketh"). Of those who harden their hearts, the Lord said: "And even so, will I cause the wicked to be kept, that will not hear my voice but harden their hearts, and wo, wo, wo, is their doom." (D&C 38:6).

Find your own Sacred Grove, and go there often. "Inspiration comes more easily in peaceful settings," said Boyd K. Packer. "Such words as quiet, still, peaceable, and Comforter abound in the scriptures." These impressions were characterized by Mormon as "a pleasant voice, as if it were a whisper." (Helaman 5:46). Elder Packer went on: "The world grows increasingly noisy. Clothing and grooming and conduct are looser and sloppier and more disheveled. Raucous music, with obscene lyrics blasted through amplifiers while lights flash psychedelic colors, characterizes the drug culture. Variations of these things are gaining wide acceptance and influence over our youth. This trend to more noise, more excitement, more contention, less restraint, less dignity, less formality is not coincidental nor innocent nor harmless. The first order issued by a commander mounting a military invasion is the jamming of the channels of communication of those he intends to conquer. Irreverence suits the purposes of the adversary by obstructing the delicate channels of revelation in both mind and spirit." ("Ensign," 11/1991).

Unfortunately, in the Twenty-First Century, we "tend to fill space, as if what we have, what we are, is not enough. Being affluent, we strangle ourselves with what we can buy, things whose opacity obstructs our ability see what is really there." (Gretel Erlich, "Under Wyoming Skies," "Atlantic Magazine"). On the other hand, getting our priorities straight clarifies our understanding of our divine potential, illuminates the channels between mind and spirit, and brings us a little closer to heaven.

Observations

As it coherently
stitches together the foundation
principles of faith and repentance into a
usable pattern, The Book of Mormon makes
it possible for the power of the word and the
witness of truth of those principles to be
recognized and acted upon without
the need for external
warrant.

We
who have
the faith to
be born again
are set free to reach
our potential by the
Atonement of Christ,
that is so dramatically
described by the prophets
of The Book of Mormon. We
are as the acorns of mighty
oaks and we bask within the
nurturing influence of our
God to grow to the full
stature of our
spirits.

Only after the Nephites had cleared their heads, were they able to zoom in, as it were, with their mind's eye, to give their most important objectives clarity that was crystal clear. Then, enlightenment thru the Spirit flowed in one of the most pure forms of focus. It allowed input from the five somatic senses to be transformed by a spiritual sixth sense to structure an appropriate hierarchy of value. After they had been conditioned by their diligence, patience, and faith, information of the highest precedence automatically was granted immediate attention. They then drew upon both their spiritual and natural resources to address the concerns that, as Winston Churchill said, demanded their blood toil, sweat and tears.

The rock-solid steadiness of The Book of Mormon stands as the polar opposite, or contrary, of the intellectual instability and spiritual schizophrenia that characterizes so many in today's world.

As soon as the Nephites reached the Promised Land, they gripped their faith tightly and hung on for the ride. They listened closely, and could almost hear the Spirit whisper: "These things shall give thee experience." Then, they let their love for the Lord cast out all fear and doubt, and they moved forward, trusting that God's perspective was clearer than any caricature of reality that had been fashioned by the distortions and manipulations of their Lamanite brethren.

What the Nephites ultimately allowed to happen to themselves clearly illustrates that when hearts are hardened and minds are closed to the message of salvation, the light of truth is diminished as the Spirit is withdrawn. The point is finally reached when those wretched souls, concentered all in self, are left without defense against the relentlessly aggressive tactics of the Devil. Because they rely solely upon their own resources, they are influenced more by the lies of the deceiver than by the illuminating truths of the Spirit and they are dragged by the heavy weight of the chains of darkness down to a living hell manifest by ignorance, misunderstanding, and confusion, that sow the seeds of despair and are oppressively, inexorably, and ruthlessly self-destructive.

During our study, as we gain a testimony of The Book of Mormon and a mastery of its principles and doctrine, we are taught that the two most important milestones in our lives are the day we were born and the day we find out why. After we've come to understand life's purpose, we will never again be the same, up until the day we die, when we'll discover why it is that we lived.

As late as one hundred and fifty years after the organization of the church, missionaries were actively proselyting in fewer than half the nations of the earth. By 2016, missionaries were present in roughly 162 countries in the world. But also, the gospel had not yet been introduced in 57 countries, among them Afghanistan, Algeria, Burma, China, Cuba, Egypt, Greenland, Iraq, Kuwait, Libya, Monaco, Nepal, North Korea, Sudan, United Arab Emirates, and the Vatican City. One gets the idea. Between 1830 and 1970, The Book of Mormon had been translated into 25 languages, but in the next 11 years, there were an additional 25 language translations. Much work remains to be done, but currently (2016) The Book of Mormon has been translated in its entirety into 94 languages, with portions available in 20 additional languages.

Adversity, that is often a defining condition of our lives, can be either a diamond dust polishing us to a high luster, or it can be the abrasive that wears us down as it grinds us to pieces. However, we cannot hope to effectively deal with our difficulties without having first focused our lives on Jesus Christ. As He taught: "If men come unto me, I will show unto them their weakness. I give unto men weakness that they may be humble; and my grace is sufficient for all men that humble themselves before me; for if they humble themselves before me, and have faith in me, then will I make weak things strong unto them." (Ether 12:27).

We can do nothing that would ever put God in our debt. The more obedient we are, the more He blesses us, and the more indebted to Him we become. Finally, even as we see thru the clear lens of faith our "nothingness" before God, our hope is perfected "through the atonement of Christ and the power of his resurrection." We have a perfect assurance that we will be "raised up unto life eternal, and this because of (our) faith in him according to the promise." (Moroni 7:41). This assurance is the inevitable result of well-founded faith, when we are "meek and lowly of heart." (Moroni 7:43).

The posterity of
Lehi who chronically suffered
from weakness in their character were
defined by their temporal trappings, weaving
needless ecclesiastical embroidery into the coats
of many colors that were envisioned by God to be their
foundation garments of a heavenly wardrobe. Theirs were
simply improvised accouterments, and nothing more than
doctrinal decorations that they had hastily designed to prop up
their faltering faith. Self-actualized Nephites, on the other hand,
took their cues from the inside. The source of their power lay, not just
within their dreams, ideals, and values, but also in their core operating
principles. These were not readily influenced by external pressures and
so they were not easily subject to change. Their healthy reliance upon the
tender mercies of the Savior provided just the balance they needed, and
offered them an exhilarating vision of their potential to become self-
directed, self-managed, and self-motivated within the parameters
of the perfect Plan of Salvation wherein they could be guided
and mentored by their Heavenly Father.

The blind who lead the blind
adhere to the standard of "seeing
is believing," but that is irrelevant to
the acquisition of faith and sends them
the wrong message. Those who question the
faith and testimonies of the Saints are living
proof of the Great Apostasy. For them, it didn't
end with the Restoration of the gospel and the
gift of The Book of Mormon. They can't see
that faith is a spiritual strong searchlight
allowing disciples of Christ to fearlessly
step into the darkness to exercise their
trust in God by petitioning Him
to illuminate the path that
lies before them.

When the Nephites
violated the laws of God, which
they did with frustrating frequency,
in the best of times their conscience would
lead them to be broken down in humility and
inspire them to recognize the error of their ways,
that they might repent of their delinquent behavior,
experience remorse after having committed the sin in
the first place, right the wrong if it were in their power
to do so, refrain from repeating it, receive forgiveness,
and then move along in their lives. In the Atonement
of Christ their stumbling blocks were miraculously
transformed into stepping-stones. Only after they
had gone through this process would mortality,
with its potholes, pitfalls, and personality
precipices make any sense and become
the growth experience that God, in
His wisdom, had designed
it to be.

Every society on the face of the
earth that has lacked vision has always
paid a heavy price for its spiritual myopia, and
following the last great battle between the Nephites
and the Lamanites near Cumorah, those who survived
the conflict similarly closed their minds and hearts to an
expansion by the Spirit. Only the Dark Ages in Europe can
compare, but in many respects we are once again living in
that stifling era. Every time that a culture has lost its
spiritual equilibrium, it attempts to re-adjust its
values by conveniently realigning them with
worldly coordinates, but that approach
never seems to end well.

Mormon clearly saw our day,
when the worship of gods of wood and stone
would be justified as multiculturalism. Perversions
of every description are now embraced and are celebrated
as alternative lifestyles. The poor are exploited under the guise of
programs sponsored by government. Unborn children are torn from
mother's wombs, and the collective conscience is assuaged by calling it
pro-choice. The gross abuse of power is justified as the means to an end.
Obscenities pollutes the media, but new-speak characterizes it as the
freedom of speech. The target has been moved so many times that
self-congratulatory pundits actually believe that they are
scoring bulls-eyes when they are actually far from the
mark. The prophet Isaiah saw our day, and thus he
warned Israel: "Wo unto them that call evil good,
and good evil; that put darkness for light,
and light for darkness; that put bitter
for sweet, and sweet for bitter."
(2 Nephi 15:20).

It is in The Book of Mormon where
we find a powerful reiteration of the innocence of
little children, which was an integral element of a Plan
that was ordained in the Grand Council in Heaven before
the world was. "At the first organization in heaven, we were all
present and saw the Savior chosen and appointed, and the plan
of salvation made, and we sanctioned it." (Joseph Smith, quoted
by William Clayton, reporting on an undated discourse that
was delivered in Nauvoo, Illinois). The prophet's statement,
and The Book of Mormon, confirm that little ones who
have died before reaching the age of accountability
will be saved in God's Kingdom because, by the
power of the infinite and eternal Atonement
of Jesus Christ, they are blameless from
the beginning.

"If ye have procrastinated the day of your repentance even until death, behold, ye have become subjected to the spirit of the devil, and he doth seal you his; therefore, the Spirit of the Lord hath withdrawn from you, and hath no place in you, and the devil hath all power over you." (Alma 34:35). It may be no coincidence that, following the last great battle at Cumorah, the mind-numbing tedium and monotony of the unrelenting stretch of years between 400 and 1,000 A.D. has been characterized as the Dark Ages, a time that was stark in every dimension. Intellectual life vanished from Europe. Even Charlemagne, the first Holy Roman Emperor and the greatest of all medieval rulers, was illiterate. In all those static centuries, absolutely nothing of real consequence had either improved or declined. With the exception of the introduction of waterwheels in the 800s, there were no inventions of note. A creative vacuum existed, where everything remained as it had been for as long as anyone could remember.

To paraphrase Paul in 2 Corinthians 13:7-8, thanks be to God that The Book of Mormon has given us the opportunity to lead quiet and peaceful lives in all godliness and honesty.

The seraphs who surrounded God's throne cried one "unto another, and said: Holy, holy, holy is the Lord of Hosts; and the whole earth is full of his glory." (2 Nephi 16:2). In the Hebrew, to repeat something three times makes it superlative, as in "good," "better," and "best." These fiery beings, in support of a celestial Superstar, desired to make the brave statement that in all of creation there can be no Being that is more holy than the Firstborn of the Father, "a lamb without blemish and without spot." (1 Peter 1:19).

During the Millennium, those who dwell upon the earth will not be focused on a competition for scarce spiritual resources. Scriptural descriptions of millennial conditions paint a portrait where righteousness prevails; where "the earth is full of the knowledge of the Lord, as the waters cover the sea." (2 Nephi 21:9).

Prior to the millennial reign of the Savior, it will be as it was just before His birth, when great signs were given to the Zarahemla Saints, "to the intent that there should be no cause for unbelief," and also "to the intent that whosoever" would have faith to "believe might be saved." (Helaman 14:18-19). Finally, at His Second Coming, He will reveal Himself "from heaven with power and great glory" to those who have faithfully waited for the dawn of that millennial day. He will dwell with the Saints on the earth, in righteousness, for a thousand years. (D&C 29:11).

In these latter days, we are witnessing the phenomenon of those who have embraced The Book of Mormon, who have been transfigured by revelation and stare in wide-eyed wonder at the fire and smoke, and thunder and lightning of the Lord, while at the same time slit-eyed sceptics squint at every sunburst that would have, in more generous circumstances, foreshadowed their spiritual awakening. These are the naysayers, the doubters, and the cynics, who would rather wear designer sunglasses than adjust their eyes to the increased illumination radiating from the light of truth.

The Book of Mormon places a great emphasis on agency, which Jacob suggested to the people of Nephi is the guiding principle of heaven. (See 2 Nephi 10:23). God gives every one of us the opportunity to recommit ourselves to covenants of action. Free-will allows us to enjoy all of the privileges related to church membership, it empowers us to remain active, and it is the principle that sanctions our commitment to our covenant of baptism. All of these are essential if we're to nourish our spiritual wellbeing. Only the righteous exercise of agency will give us the tools we need to gyroscopically maintain spiritual equilibrium and manage the mercurial fluidity of a world where its only constant seems to be its harsh and unrelenting proclivity to continually reinvent itself on a stormy sea that is awash in moral and ethical equivocation.

The Nephites' obedience to the revealed word of God did not obviate the need to make periodic withdrawals from their spiritual savings accounts. Therefore, proper prior preparation required them to make dependable and recurring faith-based deposits in anticipation of unavoidable runs on the bank. They avoided writing checks that couldn't be cashed, and tried to live to be worthy of the cornucopia of comfort and cushion of confidence that were consistently created by a courageous criterion of conduct that eschewed cowardice in matters that pertained to faith.

Our certain and
unwavering comprehension
of the truthfulness of The Book
of Mormon is rendered possible by
the irreproachable influence wrought
upon us by the Spirit. Our knowledge
expedites the implementation of moral
agency that is but properly channeled
free will. It gives us the power to work
out our salvation with both fear and
trembling before the Lord. Gaining
wisdom is critical to the successful
execution of God's Plan. Thus, it
is another of the spiritual gifts
that has been providentially
provided by the Source of
all wisdom, Who is our
Father in Heaven.

Torah dictated the outward observances
of the Jews at Jerusalem. This body of wisdom
was as a phylactery and a reminder to keep God's law.
Among the Nephites, real justification came only through
saving faith in the principles and ordinances of the gospel.
Yet, in both cases, there were always two distinctly different
paths to follow, "one leading to an ever lower and lower plane,
where were heard the cries of despair and the curses of the poor,
where manhood shriveled and possessions wore down the
possessor; while the other led to the highlands of the
morning where were heard the glad shouts of
humanity, and where honest effort was
rewarded with immortality."
(John P. Altgeld).

Being prudent as we initially become accustomed to the revelation of God found in The Book of Mormon means that we have become adept in following the most politic and profitable course. But that practicality can also lead us to be circumspect, or cautious. In contrast, if we approach life's questions with an attitude of prayerful investigation, the qualities of worldly wisdom and erudition will lose their value. If we ever try to hide our counsel from the Lord, we will find that our private purpose has only diminished the potency of our inquiry. Only after the façade of our artificial veneers has been stripped away, can our spirits become prominently vulnerable to the undeniable whisperings, the urgent promptings, and the unmistakable calls to action, that come from the Holy Ghost.

Those Nephites and Lamanites who determined to follow in the footsteps of the Savior were like "brave Horatius, the Captain of the Gate," who declared: "To each of us upon this earth, death cometh soon or late. And how can we die better than facing fearful odds, for the ashes of our fathers, and the temples of our gods?" ("Lays of Ancient Rome," Thomas Babbington Macaulay).

Modern-day Nephites who follow the teachings of The Book of Mormon will abase the wealthy in order to exalt the poor, while Latter-day Lamanites will emphasize the treasures of the earth, worship the almighty dollar, trade in counterfeit currency, destroy initiative through a misguided sense of entitlement, allow ambition to replace righteous desire, and suppress upward mobility and progress by maintaining the status-quo and subjugating the interests of those who are no less deserving, but who, through no fault of their own, find themselves in much less fortunate circumstances.

The Book of Mormon was given to the world, the Lord emphasized, so that the inhabitants of the earth "might "see my face and know that I am."(D&C 93:1). "The veil shall be rent and you shall see me, not with the carnal neither natural mind, but with the spiritual." (D&C 67:10). We have been given this clarity "to the intent that there should be no cause for unbelief," and also "to the intent that whosoever will believe might be saved, and that whosoever will not believe, a righteous judgment might come upon them; and also if they are condemned, they bring upon themselves their own condemnation." (Helaman 14:28-29).

The Saints need to
begin right now to think about
making room in their assemblies for
the Children of the Covenant, whomever
they may be and wherever they may live, as
the gathering of Israel gains momentum. "For
Zion must increase in beauty, and in holiness.
Her borders must be enlarged. Her stakes must
be strengthened. Yea, verily I say unto you ...
arise and put on (your) beautiful garments."
(D&C 82:14). The Lord our God shall set up
the ensign of the church in the Last Days
"for the nations." (2 Nephi 21:12). As He
told Joseph Smith: "I have sent mine
everlasting covenant into the world
to be a light to the world, and to
be a standard for my people,
for the Gentiles to seek to
it; to be a messenger
before my face."
(D&C 45:9).

The example of Samuel
the Lamanite reminds us that
even though "The Church of Jesus
Christ of Latter-day Saints has earned
a prominent part in the great drama of the
Last Days, it is not the only force, nor the
only means, that the Lord has employed
in order to bring to pass the things of
which His prophets, in ancient
times, have testified."
(B.H. Roberts).

If those who
have only tentatively decided to
considered the merits of The Book of
Mormon later decline the invitation that
is extended to them by the Holy Ghost to sit
and sup with the Saints, perhaps it is because
their stiff necks have prevented them from looking
up to Heavenly Father for guidance, over to men and
women of God for counsel, around to find answers to
life's profound questions, and down in an attitude of
humility. The challenge for those who have found the
joy of the gospel is to soften the telestial tendencies
of these friends and neighbors, and find the keys
that will open their hearts, that they might
become as pliable clay in the creative
hands of the Master Potter.

The example of both Nephites
and Lamanites shows us that seeds
that have been lovingly sown and then
carefully nurtured in fertile gospel soil have
an excellent chance of blossoming into strong,
healthy plants with deep roots. These 'seeds' are the
covenants we make with God. They derive germinative
powers from their association with the firm foundation of
His holy character. When we are at our very best, we are like
the good seeds that have matured into a forest of trees that are
secure in numbers. When the winds of adversity blow hard, we
are unified and strengthened by our solidarity. But if we try
to stand alone, no matter how great the girth of our trunks,
no matter how securely planted we think our roots are, we
risk toppling over. We become as solitary 'widow-maker'
trees that have been left in the forest, to stand alone,
after it has been carelessly clear-cut.

In language that is unique in the scriptures, Mormon recorded that as the resurrected Lord ministered among His Nephite disciples in the land of Bountiful, "he did smile upon them, and behold they were as white as the countenance and also the garments of Jesus; and behold the whiteness thereof did exceed all the whiteness, yea, even there could be nothing upon earth so white as the whiteness thereof." (3 Nephi 19:25). They had been sanctified by Christ's redeeming blood and by His grace had been saved. They enjoyed the companionship of the Second Comforter and so their faces reflected His light. In our day, the Lord has re-affirmed that if our eyes are single to His glory, our whole bodies shall be filled with light, and there shall be no darkness in us. (See D&C 88:67).

Nothing that was short of the very best that the Nephites could provide was good enough for the Lord, and so their tithes were really only tokens. (See 3 Nephi 24:8-10). He asked them to consecrate that which they were, for He required more than just their tentative gesture of faith. As it turns out, their offerings could be found within themselves; they were in their hearts. It was not only a tenth part, for it consisted of their complete devotion to the will of their Father, Who was the Benefactor and Provider of everything they ever hoped to be, and not just of what they ever hoped to have.

Nephite prophets had unbridled
confidence in our Father's pledge that
His people would find joy by living lives that
were gospel-centered. Their happiness would be the
result of neither wishful thinking nor a misguided
reliance upon promises with no reasonable expectation
of fulfillment. Rather, it would be the inevitable result
of faith in God, harmonizing with their mastery of the
discipline to control their desires and emotions within
boundaries that He'd established, when their priorities
synchronized with gospel principles and doctrines of
the kingdom. Their actions, that were a reflection
of His noble character, would speak louder than
words and paint a portrait of a God-centered
earth that would be the shared sensory
experience of all those who would
commit by covenant to live
their lives in obedience to
the laws of heaven.

As Amulek, the faithful missionary companion of
Alma, gained spiritual fluency in the grammar of the
gospel, (see Alma 14:10-13), he saw, as Neal A. Maxwell has
more recently observed, that "death is a mere comma, and not
an exclamation point!" The intrinsic light radiating from the
martyred women and children of Ammonihah who had been
consumed by fire had not been extinguished. Instead, the
lamp that had illuminated their mortal lives had been
put out because a new dawn had arrived. Their
deaths only memorialized an artificial
horizon that would no longer
limit their sight.

Gossiping is a kindred spirit
of murmuring, but it is more focused on
mindless chatter and speaking without real purpose. It
is just as damaging, however, because it feeds voraciously on
rumor, hearsay, second-hand information, innuendo, and vanity.
Left unchecked, it may build into a self-perpetuating chain reaction
that leads to a whole cascade of unfortunate, yet inevitable, consequences.
In its many forms, gossip has one common characteristic. The words so loosely
spoken can't be gathered up later on. Like feathers left on the doorstep of those with
whom one engages in idle conversation, they will have drifted to the four winds, and
they cannot be recalled. Words so carelessly scattered about in gossip suggest that the
mouth has been engaged before the brain has been brought on-line. In Helaman 16:22,
Mormon wrote of the many thoughtless words that the people did "imagine up in their
hearts, which were foolish and vain; and they were much disturbed, for Satan did
stir them up to do iniquity continually (and he went) about spreading rumors
and contentions upon all the face of the land, that he might harden the
hearts of the people against that which was good and against that
which should come."

At the dawning
of the millennial day,
the confidence of the people in
priesthood-driven government will be
restored, for it will be righteous. The word
of the Lord will flow, from not one, but from
two capitals, "for out of Zion shall go forth the
law, and the word of the Lord from Jerusalem." (2
Nephi 12:3). There will exist neither disease nor
death, and when people have lived to an old age,
they will not die in the classical sense, but
will be changed in the twinkling of an
eye, from mortality to immortality,
in a process of translation.

In vision, Moroni saw uncommitted souls in the Last Days, and asked: "Why are ye ashamed to take upon you the name of Christ?" (Mormon 8:38). The world doesn't seem to be able to understand why dedicated disciples desire to carry out their study of the scriptures with an exclamation, and with no need for an explanation! But that is the case, and it remains one of the hardest things for the unconverted to understand, that when we are diligent in our Book of Mormon study, our free will enjoys its greatest expression. Unprincipled character is easily swayed by the siren song so seductively sent by Satan, and undisciplined minds crumble in the face of telestial temptations that are so tantalizing and yet so traumatizing, when they divert our attention from what really matters. The more we focus on the idols of the day, the less will we recognize the legitimate rule of heaven that guides our understanding of the revealed word of God.

"Without faith, we are free to do as we like, and that can be a pleasant feeling at first, because there are few questions relating to conscience, and no constraints except for custom, convention, and law, and these will accommodate most situations. It's only later that the terror comes. We're free, but only in the chaos of a baffling and inexplicable world. We are free in a desert from which there is no retreat but inexorably inward toward the hollow core of ourselves." (Morris West). As Jarom exhorted us in the 4th verse of his brief record: "Have faith, (and enjoy a) communion with the Holy Spirit.

Not only the Land of Canaan, but also sundry other locations throughout the world could be legitimately characterized as Lands of Promise. Many groups over the years left Jerusalem in search of these lands. The Dead Sea Covenanters who lived at Qumran near the shores of the Salt Sea have become the most conspicuous in our day. But there certainly were many other righteous individuals who, over the course of millennia, were inspired by the Holy Ghost amid deteriorating conditions in Israel to flee into the wilderness, where the Lord Jehovah could freely love them, and where His anger would be turned away. (See Hosea 14:4). They would be liberated from doubt and fear to pledge to each other and to Him their lives, their fortunes, and their sacred honor. The Lord would be as a dew, and Israel would grow as a "lily and cast forth her roots as Lebanon." (Hosea 14:5).

The great and terrible example of faithful Nephite disciples remind us that, in the Last Days "little people, like you and me, if our prayers are sometimes granted beyond all hope and probability, had better not draw hasty conclusions to our own advantage. If we were stronger, we might be less tenderly treated. If we were braver, we might be sent, with far less help, to defend far more desperate posts in the last great battle." (C.S. Lewis).

The Lord shows us how to become the architects of our own fate. He said to His "disciples, If any man will come after me, let him deny himself, and take up his cross, and follow me." (Matthew 16:24). He shows us how to gain eternal life, by denying ourselves "all ungodliness, and every worldly lust, and keep(ing the) commandments." (J.S.T. Matthew 16:26). He has reiterated: "I, the Lord, will show unto you what I will concerning you." (D&C 66:4). But He goes a step further, promising: "If men come unto me I will show unto them their weakness … then will I make weak things become strong unto them." (Ether 12:27). It is far better to have Him on our side and not the adversary, who would instead capitalize on our weaknesses and use them to his own advantage.

The gospel of Jesus Christ was the law of liberty for the Nephites, setting them free to make intelligent choices, free to receive all the blessings of the priesthood, free to enjoy unrestrained opportunity for improvement, and free to serve others more meaningfully, as they committed themselves to the observance of proven principles. With the gift of the freedom to act independently, they were welcomed to follow a path of progress, while they were discouraged from following another path leading to ruin.

Even as we confront
withering opposition, our
election to righteously exercise
our agency seals our longing to
yield our hearts to the Savior, to ponder
the consequences of Gethsemane, to travel
with Him to Calvary, and to enjoy the sweetly
redeeming power of His Atonement. When we keep
His law, we experience the "happiness which is prepared
for the Saints." (2 Nephi 9:43). That expression of joy
transcends all of our temporal insecurities and our
discomforts. It is the manifestation of a higher
power whose capacity can neutralize our
pathetic passion for pleasure that is
always jockeying for our
attention.

The Spirit desires
to quietly infuse each one
of us with confidence that the
Savior's ministry will continue
for as "long as time shall last, or the
earth shall stand, or there shall be
one man upon the face thereof
(who is yet) to be saved."
(Moroni 7:36).

For many, the gospel
has become almost dream-like, as if
it were a fairy tale attempting to convey
power and knowledge without the assistance
of continuing guidance from above. Moroni saw
that there would be many in the Last Days who had
"transfigured the holy word of God" or who had changed
its appearance and substance. (Mormon 8:33). It is no
wonder that Another Testament of Jesus Christ became
necessary in order to confirm the faith of a people
who were conversant with the four Gospels, but
who were, at the same time, in ignorance of
additional scriptural knowledge that
would illuminate the truth, and
not just multiply mirrors
without increasing
the light.

It has been the heartfelt
prayer of those who have read The
Book of Mormon that God would treat the
Saints gently when He comes in "glory, and
in his power, and in his might, majesty, and
dominion," and tramples out the vintage
where the grapes of wrath have for so
long been stored, as the Day of
Judgment draws nigh.
(Alma 12:15).

The Savior taught that we should be perfect, even as He is perfect, for otherwise we cannot inherit the kingdom of God. (See 3 Nephi 12:48). Perhaps He meant that we can become as He is by being perfect in our repentance, so that we might become holy and without spot. After Jacob taught the Plan of Redemption to his people, which solved the dilemma created by God's demand for perfection coupled with our inability to lead sinless lives, he simply stated: "What can I say more?" (Jacob 6:12). Moroni offered similar counsel to those living in the Last Days, when he urged: "Be wise in the days of your probation; strip yourselves of all uncleanness. Ask with a firmness unshaken, that ye will yield to no temptation, but that ye will serve the true and living God." (Mormon 9:28).

The prophets of The Book of Mormon have encouraged us to adopt the stimulating lifestyle of Zion, in contrast to the subsistence level of existence that is characteristic of the boring routines of Babylon. We emulate the listening ear of Zion, even as Babylon speaks in a confusion of tongues. We appreciate Zion's grip on reality, as Babylon grasps at straws in confusion. We admire Zion's dedication to spiritual absolutes, but pity Babylon's vacillation in the vacuum of moral and spiritual relativism. We witness the focus of Zion, as well as Babylon's congenital spiritual short-sightedness. We are comforted that Zion is grounded on the bedrock of truth, whereas Babylon basks in a false sense of security, confuses principles for values, and promotes the unsupportable lie that "all is well in Zion." (2 Nephi 28:21).

Justice Oliver Wendell Holmes taught: "Once a mind has been stretched by a new idea, it can never return to its original dimension." The Book of Mormon casts our afflictions, trials, and tribulations in a new light. We determine to discover for ourselves how the Savior's suffering in Gethsemane wasn't in vain, but was for our salvation. We resolve to embark upon a ministry of reconciliation with both heaven and earth. (See 2 Corinthians 5:18).

Guidance from above that is received in the forms of spiritual promptings and subtle impressions are more common that many would suspect. Powerful intuitive communicators strongly influence us to push forward in the direction of our dreams, toward a faith to believe that blesses us with a greater revelatory appreciation of The Book of Mormon, Another Testament of Jesus Christ.

If we ever hope to venture forth out of the shadows of sin, we must rely upon the guidance that is received from the Light of Christ and the ministering of angels. If we want to experience the special familiarity that the faithful enjoy with the Savior of the world, we must come unto Christ ourselves, and a good way to do that is by reading The Book of Mormon.

The Book of Mormon makes it simpler to have backs that have become sturdy enough to brace us against the fierce winds of adversity and the wiles of the adversary, and hearts that are receptacles of pure and virtuous thoughts and principles from which we may draw strength in our times of need.

Pride is motivated
by our own resolve, while
The Book of Mormon inspires
us to seek to know the will of God.
Pride is driven by fear of man, but
repentance is nurtured by our love of
the Savior. The applause of the world
rings in the ears of the prideful, but
it is the accolades of heaven which
we hear that warm our hearts even
as our faith convicts us of our
sins. On our journey to the
truth, the Spirit guides
us along the pathway
to repentance.

The arrogant,
boastful, conceited,
haughty, and self-centered
nature of the prideful is easily
conquered by altruistic, modest,
deferential, and self-effacing
behavior. Those with a firm
testimony of The Book
of Mormon confirm
their faith by the
power of the
Spirit.

In stark contrast to the faithful, who have prayed for confirmation that the doctrine contained within The Book of Mormon is true, and who learn to rely upon the merits of Christ, the proud are more comfortable with their own interpretation of truth than they are with His omniscience. They pit their own abilities against His mighty priesthood power, their stubborn will against His quiet counsel, and their own paltry overtures against His mighty works.

Unlike the repentant, who rely upon the merits of Christ, the prideful seek after signs. Because they are past feeling, they require greater and greater intensities of stimulation to entertain the same degree of gratification. What they've received is never enough to satisfy their adulterous craving for pleasure. (See 2 Nephi 31:19).

In The Book of
Mormon, we read
the accounts of both
Nephites and Lamanites
who sank to new lows after
having committed terrible sins
that were nigh unto unforgivable.
But as long as these long-suffering
Saints were unhesitant in their faith,
and as long as they drew upon the power
of the Atonement of Christ to bind up and
heal their wounds, they were particularly
sensitive to the comfort that came thru
the whisperings of the Spirit. When it
seemed that things couldn't get
any worse, they were at
their best.

Alma's counsel in Mosiah
18:9 strengthens our hands to
lift those who need our support. It
galvanizes our courage to allow our
feet to take us to those who've been
imprisoned by poor choices or by
bad habits, or who are hobbled
by ruinous circumstances
that may or may not
have been of their
own doing.

When
our spirits
are permeated
with the knowledge
of God, of Whom The
Book of Mormon so boldly
testifies, our "bodies shall be
filled with light, and there shall
be no darkness in (us); and that
body which is filled with light
comprehendeth all things."
(D&C 88:67).

Free will
and opposition are
ever before us, and The
Book of Mormon stands as
a sacred sentinel, beckoning us
to enter in at heaven's gate, to find
God's Rest. Its opposite is the road
to self-indulgence; the opposite of
submission to the will of God is
our self-gratification, and the
opposite of faith is idolatry.
It is really that plain
and simple.

We are
admonished to
follow The Book of
Mormon's counsel that
leads us to the strait and
narrow gate of baptism. In
fact, "few there be that find
it." (Matthew 7:14). We persist
in our efforts because we know
that the Lord's spiritual fitness
program was designed to help
us to achieve symmetry. its
discipline gives our lives
stability, coherence,
and meaning.

When we walk in the
light of life and we go out of
our way to grasp the principles of
truth that are found in The Book of
Mormon, we brim over with gratitude
as we discover how our Redeemer has
provided luxurious accommodations
for us in the household of faith by
reserving for us a room that has
an unobstructed view of
eternity.

In the Land of Zarahemla around 120 – 100 B.C., there were many young people who were sorely tempted, yielded themselves to Satan's influences, and who then fell into apostasy. (See Mosiah 26:1-5). As Brigham Young said: "Though our children are begotten in righteousness, and brought forth in holiness, they must be tried and tempted, for they are agents before our Father, the same as you or I." It is inevitable that many will, at the very least, stumble, as they make their way along the path leading to the Tree of Life.

"This much I can tell you, that if ye do not watch yourselves, and your thoughts, and your words, and your deeds, and observe the commandments of God, and continue in the faith of what ye have heard concerning the coming of our Lord, even unto the end of your lives, ye must perish."
(Mosiah 4:30).

Our engagement with The Book of Mormon can introduce us to a spotlight coming from above that quickens our minds and opens our hearts to the spiritual realities at the core of our existence. It invites us to move beyond a three-dimensional mortal experience. We look before us, behind us, and to both sides, but we also experience an upward reach that takes us into an other-worldly spiritual dimension. We look up to God, and, perhaps for the very first time, as we break through the cloud cover of mortality into eternity, we really live. (See Alma 37:47).

When we sit down to read The Book of Mormon, we will sink or swim largely on our own. But as we persevere in our study of the book, and particularly when we look introspectively, we hope and pray for the courage to change the things we can, the serenity to accept the things we cannot, and the wisdom to know the difference. But it is always nice to get a little help from our friends, including our Savior, who led the way with His life-saving counsel that has been preserved for us in the book of 3 Nephi.

An understanding of
our pre-mortal existence, as
it unfolds in 2 Nephi Chapter 2,
sanctifies life, dignifies individual
effort, and rewards achievement. But
more importantly, it recognizes the
Atonement as the pivotal center
of God's perfect Plan of
Salvation.

The Holy Spirit
bears a sacred witness of the
promises of The Book of Mormon,
as we repent with broken hearts. His
unimpeachable witness is as a baptism
of fire that puts the finishing touches on
the Atonement of Jesus Christ. When Mercy
intervenes to satisfy the demands of Justice
and cancels the penalties that are associated
with our sins, we are blessed to become holy
and without spot, in a rite of purification.
Though our "sins be as scarlet, they shall
be as white as snow. Though they be
red like crimson, they shall be
as wool." (Isaiah 1:18).

Our
abiding faith
in the divine Plan
of our Father in Heaven
is confirmed in The Book of
Mormon, and especially by Alma,
from whom we learn that its design
was to bring us back into His presence
after we had grown up unto the Lord, had
spiritually matured, and had received the
witness of the Spirit that the foundation
of our hope of salvation lies in our
Rock, Who is His Son Jesus
Christ.

The
demands
placed upon us
by the Lord to gain
a testimony of The Book
of Mormon have the capacity
to generate relationship capital,
when we feel ourselves being carried
to heaven's gate, as upon the wings of
eagles. At the same time, we understand
that the insolvency of Satan's seduction
cannot be mitigated by any third-party
bailout. The only financially feasible
solution to his nepotism is to utilize
the supernal bargaining chip of the
Atonement of the Savior, which is
doctrine that is clearly taught
by each of the authors
of the book.

The great Plan that was created by our Father envisions a utopian society, but it's also pragmatic, anticipating our weaknesses, and so it provided us with The Book of Mormon to offer practical advice for those of us (read: 'all of us') whose exercise of agency would create pressure with the potential to lead us ever so subtly away from the Rod of Iron.

Our refusal to repent, urged by prophets in The Book of Mormon, is an example of rebellion against the Atonement of the Savior. In the wake of the insurgency by Lucifer that resulted in war in heaven, the consequences for the losers were both excruciating and eternally damaging. For those of us who prevailed at the conclusion of that conflict, we were able to continue to grow in grace, that we might progress in stature until we could move on to yet another estate where we would reach a pinnacle of progression. By following the nurturing Plan of God, we would at last have internalized into our nature not only His image, but also His likeness.

In simple terms, The Book of
Mormon exposes us to the process
by which we progress. Our Father in
Heaven has designed our instruction to
test the depth of our determination. This is
why the book illustrates that righteousness
is intimately tied to the courage to be true to
our convictions. Only if we act on the basis
of faith will we receive a confirmation of the
power behind the ordinances of the gospel,
together with their related covenants, as
feelings of self-confidence grow and
purposeful action replaces our
tentative overtures.

As we
develop our own
independent witnesses
of The Book of Mormon, we
are easily entreated, and we try
to be firm in our obedience to every
one of the commandments of God. For
the conflagration of sin to be initiated, we
realize that all that is needed is combustible
fuel, an ignition temperature, and oxygen.
We live in the world, but we don't have to
be of the world. We can't allow the heat
of the moment to get the better of us.
Our faith introduces us to a strait
and narrow way that avoids the
Devil's ammunition dumps,
as well as the open flames
of rebellion. After our
baptism, we learn
not to play with
matches.

The Book of Mormon shows each of us how to break free from our limiting beliefs, which are those stories we tell ourselves that sabotage our best efforts. The book has the energy to unleash the awesome power of our potential. Its magic is waiting for our wits to grow sharper, so that we can be taught to be more easily inspired by the Holy Ghost.

The Book of Mormon is a palpable expression of the Doctrine of Christ. (See 2 Nephi 31:21). In it, Nephi clearly explains that all who have faith in the Savior and truly repent of their sins, entering into a baptismal covenant with Him, will receive the Holy Ghost, Who will then direct their way, showing them the things they must do to merit the grace of God and inherit salvation and exaltation.

In the Last Days, the tumultuous events that we experience on an almost daily basis mirror those of Mormon's time. He reported that "there were sorceries, and witchcrafts, and magics, and the power of the evil one was wrought upon all the face of the land" because of the lack of faith of the people. (Mormon 1:19). For those who will read it, The Book of Mormon can be the spiritual equivalent of ingesting a power bar or an energy drink 30 minutes prior to our engaging in potentially traumatic physical or spectral activity.

During the moments of our deepest reflection, such as when we've immersed ourselves in Book of Mormon study, we imagine that we've "stepped on a shore, and have found it heaven! We visualize taking hold of a hand, and finding it God's hand. We dream of passing from a storm and a tempest to an unbroken calm, and of waking up, and finding it home." (Anonymous).

Modern scribes and Pharisees who have little or no understanding of the Plan of God tend to omit the weightier matters relating to His laws. They strain at a gnat and swallow a camel. They appear to be honorable, but inside they are "full of extortion and excess." (Matthew 23:25). Our righteous desire to choose The Book of Mormon thru the discipline of faith brings us closer to the Savior and to our divine center, leaving no room for hypocrisy to creep into our lives.

In The Book of Mormon, and in frustratingly few other places, we are provided with the stellar examples of men and women to whom we can relate. (See 1 Nephi 5:8-9 & 18:19, & Alma 19:16-17). They are nothing like those chameleon-like creatures who'd peddle their birthrights for a mess of pottage, compromise their standards for a shot at stardom, and dilute the potency of their discipleship by embracing the values of vulgarity as well as the dress code of debauchery.

The first use of the name of Christ in The Book of Mormon only occurs in 2 Nephi 10:3, arriving when we are 32 chapters into the book. It reads: "Wherefore, as I said unto you, it must needs be expedient that Christ - for in the last night the angel spake unto me that this should be his name - should come among the Jews."

This initial use of the Savior's name invites an interesting question: Since Christ is the central figure in The Book of Mormon, why is it that His name wasn't used until its 78th page? The obvious answer is that it wasn't until then that the angel disclosed His name to Jacob. But that simple explanation, although it is supported by scripture (2 Nephi 10:3), begs another question: Why, then, didn't the angel reveal His name earlier in the narrative to Lehi, Nephi, or Jacob? The answer may seem surprising at first, but it corroborates the declaration that the book is what it claims to be, which is authentic ancient scripture.

The word "Christ" is Greek. The same term in Hebrew is "Messiah," which Nephi used 28 times prior to 2 Nephi 10:3 (excluding quotations from Isaiah). Neither he nor his family knew Greek, coming as they had, from a culture that spoke Hebrew. Instead, they used a name that was familiar to them and that was drawn from their own language and society. Consistent with this explanation, Nephi used the term 'Messiah' until Jacob received a revelation about the name of 'Christ.' After that time, 'Messiah' fell out of favor. Nephi used it only 10 times subsequent to Jacob's revelation, and 'Christ' became the primary term that was thereafter employed to identify the Savior.

Our takeaway lesson from 2 Nephi 10:3 is that Nephi had the humility to listen to his younger brother, and to learn from him. He wasn't blinded by his own position, authority, influence, experience, or even by his access to revelation, and by characteristically and consistently using the title of Christ as Jacob had just received it by revelation, Nephi unconsciously provides us with provocative evidence that The Book of Mormon is what it claims to be: ancient scripture.

During the post-mortal ministry
of Jesus Christ in the New World, the Nephite Saints
in the land Bountiful brought their children to Him, that
He might minister to them. After taking them "one by one"
in His arms, He "blessed them, and prayed unto the Father for
them." (3 Nephi 17:21). The Spirit was overwhelming. As the
multitude raised its eyes to the heavens, the veil itself parted,
"and they saw angels descending out of heaven as it were in
the midst of fire; and they came down and encircled those
little ones ... with fire. And the angels did minister
unto them." (3 Nephi 17:24). Truly, they were
"one, the children of Christ, and heirs
to the kingdom of God."
(4 Nephi 1:17).

3 Nephi Chapter 8 describes the destruction
that occurred in Book of Mormon lands. It appears
to have been one of the greatest natural disasters in the
history of the world. It was the physical manifestation of the
earth's revolt against the crucifixion of its Creator. Perhaps the
record of the experience of the Nephites is as close as any of
us will come to understanding just how overwhelming
will be the spiritual darkness that is going to prevail
among those who are resurrected to a kingdom
without glory, which is as a "lake which
burneth with fire and brimstone,
which is the second death."
(D&C 63:17).

Lamanites of any generation who haven't received forgiveness of their sins through repentance cannot dwell where Christ is. But if they are able to make behavioral changes, and if they can modify their nature so that as they mature their character more fully reflects that of their Father, perhaps they will then be invited to enjoy His hearth and home, on earth and in heaven. Surely, the story of the Prodigal Son, set against the backdrop of the infinite and eternal Atonement of Jesus Christ, lends support to this thesis.

The awesome spiritual gift of the interpretation of tongues includes our capacity to comprehend the words of the scriptures, including those in The Book of Mormon, as well as the inspired counsel that flows from the lips of those who sit in the presiding councils of the church. Clearly and unambiguously, the Plan has been designed to perfectly meet our needs.

As active
cast members in
life's Three Act Play,
we can better understand
our roles if we have engaged
others in the scenes we play. We
need to be on familiar terms with
those who participate in the drama,
and share the stage with them as we
rehearse, thru our study of The Book
of Mormon, the challenges we face
that are related to mastering the
assignments that are, in turn,
associated with each of our
individual parts.

The Book
of Mormon will
contest the merits of
our sincerity and our
candor with ourselves. It
is only with our acceptance
of its doctrine, that we place
our bets on the Savior. But we
haven't any proof or a return on
our investment, until we act on
the basis of trust. Then, comes
the confirmation of the reality
as feelings of self-confidence
grow and purposeful actions
replace tentative overtures.
We are all in; we let go
and let God.

If we ignore the
tandem influences of
the Light of Christ and
the Holy Ghost that nurture
our innate yearning to follow our
spiritual promptings to participate
in Book of Mormon study, and if we
allow ourselves to become preoccupied by
trifling concerns, we sin by omission and
by commission, and we risk settling for a
marshland of mediocrity that can very
easily degenerate into a quicksand
of sin, from which there can be
no easy escape.

"The ancient
record thus brought
forth out of the earth as
the voice of a people speaking
from the dust, and translated
into modern speech by the gift
and power of God as attested by
Divine affirmation, was first
published to the world in the
year 1830 as The Book of
Mormon." (Testimony
of the Prophet Joseph
Smith).

Timorous and fragile souls who are cautiously hesitant and tentatively faithful don't consciously intend to lose the desire to seek truth. Their undecided faith simply fades away, like the slow leak in an automobile tire, and not as a blowout. But it may often be traced back to the tendency to mischief that may have taken root during a time of particularly intense vulnerability to the wiles of the Devil.

Although it has been only briefly alluded to in The Book of Mormon (see Alma 46:23), Joseph's coat of many colors can serve as a metaphor for our faith in the Atonement of Jesus Christ. If we look closely at its fabric, it teaches us that even the most menacing clouds have silver linings, and we will realize that the bright dawning of a new day will follow on the heels of even the darkest of nights.

Thanks be unto our Heavenly Father for the penetrating clarity of the teachings of every Book of Mormon prophet, to help us get thru each day, and to comfort us during every long night of darkness. Truly, He will stay up late, and He leaves a light burning for us, to guide us back to our Home.

There is nothing else on earth that can make up for the revelatory rewards that are such prominent features of The Book of Mormon. Cheap thrills won't replace its originality. Neither novelty nor spectacle can defeat, but can only delay, implementation of its principles. The universal influence of the Light of Christ encourages us to set our sights on the brightly burning beacon of the the Savior of the world, as well as on the Holy Ghost, Who is waiting to guide us, in the company of God, angels, and witnesses, across an ocean of light to a new world that only awaits our discovery.

If God
did not make
covenants with His
children, or if there were
no law given, or if men and
women could sin with impunity,
"what could justice do, or mercy either,
for they would have no claim upon the
creature? The works of justice would
be destroyed, and God would
(simply) cease to be God."
(Alma 42:21-22).

Our Father
in Heaven envisions
that one day we might be
like His Son, and He has offered
us 3 Nephi to help us get a taste
of what He has, as well as
of what He is.

As Alma saw
it, baptism energizes God's grace,
allowing the repentant faithful to receive
blessings by binding them to Him thru
revelation by the means of a covenant
of action. Because Heavenly Father
will always honor the principle
of free will, the progression
of his people patiently
waits upon their
initiative.

As we embrace the power
of The Book of Mormon, we are
blessed with visions of glory that
dance before our eyes. It's our faith
in the Lord that will move us closer
to heaven's gate, if we first seek the
kingdom and His righteousness.
We have learned that when our
priorities are guided by the
Spirit, we need not fear
for want of our most
basic needs.

Those who have
declined the offer of the riches
of eternity that might have been
unfolded to their view by The Book
of Mormon are doomed to scratch out a
subsistence level of existence that is in
scarcity of their basic spiritual needs.
With the smorgasbord of life spread
out before them, they settle for the
processed factory food that is
dished out by the automats
of the world. They exist
beneath the poverty
level, but are not
even aware
of it.

If we
could be
participants
in the spiritual
equivalent of Weight
Watchers, we would have
less trouble sleeping, less
difficulty focusing, and less
of a problem bearing testimony
of the truthfulness of The
Book of Mormon.

When we
accept Moroni's promise
(see Moroni 10:4), the doctrines
of the kingdom, or the solemnities
of eternity, are positioned right in the
crosshairs of our conscious awareness. It
takes our understanding as far as our
capacity allows us to go, because it
is tailored to suit our individual
circumstances, and yet it is
collectively understood
and is universally
applicable.

If we have done as
the Lord has commanded,
our comprehension of the grand
themes that run throughout The Book
of Mormon will flow easily and poetically to
our minds. Our persistence and our participation
will lead us to a practiced fluency in the language of
the Spirit that is the result of the inspiration that will
come as we approach our study with faith, fasting,
and prayer. As our minds are enlightened, we
will be cast off into a stream of revelation
and carried along in the quickening
currents of direct experience
with the mind and
will of God.

If we want to receive the blessing of a testimony of The Book of Mormon, we will first need to experience how the Holy Ghost manifests personal revelation. "For God speaketh once, yea twice, yet man perceiveth it not. In a dream, in a vision of the night, when deep sleep falleth upon men, in slumberings upon the bed; then he openeth the ears of men, and sealeth their instruction." (Job 33:4-16).

From a gospel perspective, our discipline involves the consistent exercise of agency as we embrace ennobling eternal principles with action that is simply the right thing to do, although it may not be easy or convenient. If we desire a positive outcome, our free will needs to be accompanied by the courage to exercise the moral discipline that finds its expression in righteous behavior. That leads to The Book of Mormon, and then to baptism, to the Sacrament, and to the house of the Lord.

As we read The Book of Mormon, we are fortunate if we have also been blessed to have moments of quiet reflection when we can think of the Savior in new and symbolic ways. He is, after all, the rudder of our ship, guiding us past unseen rocks and reefs. He is our helm, holding steady when winds of adversity blow. He is our telltale, alerting us to impending storms. He is our keel, helping us to move against the current and the wind. He is our mainsheet, holding firmly with just enough pressure to prevent us from capsizing when we are dangerously heeled over.

Our ownership of a testimony of The Book of Mormon is all-encompassing in its scope. There are no height or weight restrictions, no social, economic, cultural, intellectual, or emotional prerequisites, but only an ecclesiastical endorsement that energizes our sincere desire to know the will of God.

Our sincerity, as we embark
upon the study of The Book of Mormon,
encourages us to be faithful, with an emphasis
on the "ful." In its abundance, we find there is more
than enough, even a surplus, a surfeit, brimming over
with possibilities, and overflowing with options that we
may have never before considered. If our cup seems to
run over, it is because that is how Heavenly Father
designed our discovery of truth to be, to allow
the Holy Ghost to overwhelm our telestial
tendencies and shepherd us right into
the embrace of eternity.

Every member of the church has
been foreordained by God our Father to
evolve into a second-miler. (See Abraham
2:22-23, Jeremiah 1:5, & Luke 1:13-17).
We do this, not so much by maturation,
but by generation, as we are born of
Him. We are encouraged to run,
and not walk, as we wend
our way to and thru The
Book of Mormon.

Some people see things as they are, and ask "Why? In The Book of Mormon, our attention is focused on things that never were, that we might ask while we are under the influence of the Holy Ghost, "Why not?" It prepares us for a rendezvous with destiny. It carries us above and beyond the shattered dreams of lost souls, to a sanctuary where we may "flourish in immortal youth, unhurt amidst the war of elements, the wreck of matter, and the crash of worlds." (Joseph Addison).

Just as water from the spring of Gihon was vital to the physical survival of King Hezekiah's subjects during the Assyrian siege of Jerusalem, living water is essential for our spiritual survival as we struggle with Satan. We are under siege throughout our lives, and constant access to living water, such as is found in The Book of Mormon, is our only hope of salvation.

If we really desire to
have God's Spirit to be with us
during the week, we might want to
put away our tablets, and turn off our
cell phones even if we have them on vibrate.
Instead of answering email, we might instead
quietly use our time seeking answers to our
prayers. Instead of searching for a strong
Wi-Fi signal, we could quietly turn to
The Book of Mormon, and let the Holy
Ghost introduce us to the analog
messages of Ne-Fi and his
companion prophets.

The gentle
Spirit that is nurtured
by our Book of Mormon study
quietly prompts us to ease off the gas
pedal and ratchet down the hectic pace of
our lives. It calms our souls and carries us
away, far from the madding crowd. The Lord
knows how busy we are. He knows how it feels
to be neglected, to be trivialized, and to be in a
fierce competition with sounding brass and
tinkling cymbals. In fact, He may have
been thinking about how The Book of
Mormon could influence our lives,
when He said: "Be still and
know that I am God."
(Psalms 46:10).

When Book of
Mormon study takes
us far from the tumult of the
teeming multitudes and telestial
crowds that so frequently characterize
the lifestyle of the rich and the famous, the
Holy Ghost will invite us to let His influence
iron out the wrinkles in our own spirits, to be
rejuvenated by a full facial and whole body
massage, that we might more comfortably
reflect both the image and the likeness
of God in our countenances.

All of us have a whole lot to
learn, and hopefully, we have the
gift of time on our side. If we do, perhaps
we should think about what we would like to
discover in the next twelve months. How would
we like to be different then, from what we are
now? How can reading The Book of Mormon
in the coming year help us to make positive
changes in our lives? As we consider that
challenge, we recall the familiar adage:
Some men see things as they are, and
ask why? Others dream things that
never were, and ask why not? Can
you give me one good reason
why you shouldn't let the
Spirit guide you as
never before?

By expanding
upon our vision, The
Book of Mormon brings us
close enough to heaven's gate to
view its riches. We'll move beyond
physical laws that pertain only to the
temporal world, toward an appreciation
of the gospel principles that relate to the
eternities. It explains what we must do
if we wish to reach through its bars to
touch the face of God. The path that
lies before us is clear. If we choose
to embark upon it, during our
exertion there can be neither
variability nor a shadow
of turning.

The Book
of Mormon encourages
us to step back and take a deep
breath, momentarily pause, and
ponder the next important moves
in our busy lives. Its covenants
powerfully familiarize us with
the intimate embrace of daily
spiritual experiences that are
divinely designed to help
us to keep our priorities
straight.

The Book of Mormon
schools us in an appreciation
of how all three members of the
Godhead can work in our behalf to
provide the blessings of immortality
and eternal life. By our baptism, we keep
the commandment of God; the Holy Ghost
will justify us before His throne; and the
blood of Jesus Christ will sanctify us
that we might be able to endure
their holy presence in the
eternities.

The Book
of Mormon will open
up windows of opportunity
to better understand the principles
of the gospel that remain as mysteries
to those who have not spiritually prepared
themselves for personal revelation from God.
The Lord has assured us that we "shall know
of a surety that these things are true,
for from heaven will (He) declare
it" unto us. (D&C 5:12).

After our exposure to The Book of Mormon, we will no longer be as children, to be tossed to and fro on the sea of life. Within its pages is God's promise that He will never leave us to fight our battles alone. Instead, we will always have His Spirit to be with us.

The Book of Mormon moves us from dependency, through independency, and then, surprisingly, to a healthy and established condition of interdependency with both man and God. It gives us the tools with which we might fashion harmony without sacrificing the very qualities that contribute to our individuality. The Spirit whispers to us that as we are, God once was, and that as He is, we may become.

When we read The
Book of Mormon, we feel
God's peace which surpasses
all understanding. But we are
given the opportunity to enjoy
the best of both worlds; to live on
earth, but still have a place where
we can retreat from the telestial
turmoil surrounding us. We
sit in a holy place when we
turn to that book, and to
the Holy Ghost, for our
enlightenment.

The Book of Mormon
affirms the eternal nature of our
spirits, because within ourselves, we
can feel immortal longings. When we
turn its pages, we sense a gentle breeze
as we brush up against the veil. We feel
inner stirrings that are the harmonic
vibrations of the music of heavenly
choirs, and we hear the indistinct
whisperings that, as the Spirit
confirms, are the voices of
angelic messengers.

As the battle rages on in their hearts, those who have chosen to defend The Book of Mormon live their lives in crescendo. The deafening roar of righteousness commands the attention of the angels who wield the sword of Justice and who only wait upon God's command to let it fall on an unrepentant world. Maybe it is only that marvelous work and a wonder that stays their hand. (For the time being, at least).

The Book of Mormon guides us to think less in terms of self sufficiency, and more about Christ dependency. We realize that His doctrine is intended to change not only our behavior, but also our nature. We are as malleable clay in His hands.

The Book of Mormon stands in opposition to the "evils and designs which do and will exist in the hearts of conspiring men (and women) in the last days." (D&C 89:4). Angels will attend us as we incorporate its teachings in our lives. They will go before our faces, and will be on our right hand and on our left hand, and the Spirit of the Lord will be in our hearts, as heavenly angels gather around us, to guard the way and bear us up. (See D&C 84:88).

The Book of Mormon was given to the world that it might be perfected in its Savior, Jesus Christ. its spiritual awakening progresses for only as long as it is learning. We take solace in the scriptures where, although we are admonished 154 times to be perfect, we are also encouraged 129 times to "learn" and 995 times simply to "begin." As D&C 29:22 suggests, in this life we only "begin to be redeemed." Our perfection is a process and not a point.

When we read
The Book of Mormon, it is
through God's infinite goodness
and the manifestations of the Spirit
that we have great views of that which is to
come. The comforting emanation of familiar
oscillations of energy resonating from within
the limitless reserves that are selflessly shared
by the Holy Ghost carry us along on rolling
waves of the Spirit toward a more sure
personal witness of the Savior's
divinity and of His
sacrifice.

As we learn life
lessons from The Book of
Mormon, we're struck by the
realization that when the Lord
gives us commandments, He also
prepares ways for us to accomplish
the tasks that are set before us. We see
what might be best for ourselves and for
the Kingdom of God, develop testimonies
that it should be, and then work with all our
capacity to make it happen, whatever the cost
may be. Then, when we are so richly blessed
far beyond the measure that we deserve, the
price, once paid so painfully, is recalled in
gladness. We receive full value. As D&C
82:10 suggests: "I the Lord am bound
when ye do as I say, but when ye
do not what I say, ye have
no promise."

An early leader of
the Reformation, Roger
Williams, declared: "There is
no regularly constituted church
on earth, nor any person authorized
to administer any church ordinance, nor
can there be until new apostles are sent by the
Great Head of the church, for Whose Coming
I am seeking." Thank God for the restoration
of the gospel, for The Book of Mormon, and
for all those who faithfully petitioned the
heavens to restore the church with His
authority to officiate in all of the
rites and ordinances to which
the Reformers referred.

We read The
Book of Mormon
because we desire to
become more observant
followers of righteousness,
to possess greater knowledge,
to be the progenitors of nations
and ambassadors of peace, and
to receive instruction, and to
keep the commandments.

The key
to liberation from
our bondage to sin, that
we might enjoy a freedom
to become, is an adjustment
in attitude that is reflected in
our desire to incorporate Book of
Mormon teachings into our lives.
To paraphrase Helen Keller, the real
tragedy is not those of us who were
born without sight, but those of us
who have sight, but lack vision.

The golden
cobblestones of the
stairway to the stars are
illuminated by the principles
of The Book of Mormon. These point
us in the direction of the recognition
of our iniquity, and then to a deep godly
sorrow for our sins. Next comes inescapable
suffering and torment stimulating an appeal
to the Savior, with awakening understanding
of His Atonement. After our baptism, comes the
remission of our sins, spiritual enlightenment,
and great joy. This motivates us to pursue a
lifestyle of righteousness and service that
is punctuated by our weekly observance
of the Sacrament of the Lord's Supper.
Each time this occurs, the endless
loop cycles one more time, but,
praise the God of miracles,
it is calibrated to an
ever higher plane
of existence.

We partake of the Sacrament, determined to follow the Savior "with full purpose of heart, acting no hypocrisy and no deception before God." (2 Nephi 31:13). As we do so, a long night of darkness will be followed by a renaissance, or a spiritual rebirth that paves the way for our enlightenment. Our world will blossom with new ideas and unbridled optimism as we realize that Isaiah was referring to our day when he prophesied: Although we "walked in darkness, (we) have seen a great light. They that dwell in the land of the shadow of death, upon them hath the light shined." (Isaiah 9:2).

Those who stand as witnesses to the world of the divine authenticity of The Book of Mormon in obedience to God's commandment, "shall receive health in their navel and marrow to their bones; and shall find wisdom and great treasures of knowledge, even hidden treasures; and shall run and not be weary, and shall walk and not faint."(D&C 89:18).

The
Nephites
participated
in the Sacrament
unto the confounding
of false doctrines and the
laying down of contentions.
(See 2 Nephi 3:12). They relied
upon the ordinance to neutralize
the sulfuric acid of sin and to
restore the normal alkaline
pH of 7.4 to their
bodies.

The Book of
Mormon is special in the
sense that it introduces our
souls to rhythms of nature that
can only be felt when our behavior
is in harmony with eternal principles.
Thus, heaven always holds its breath as
the children of God are invited to accept
a copy of a book of scripture that will
reveal the mysteries of where they
came from, why they are here,
and where they are
going.

The Book
of Mormon will
always be waiting in
the wings, to be applied
as a balm to repair bruised
egos, battered birthrights, and
bitter feelings. It asks us to show
kindness to strangers that we meet,
and, because we are the children of
God, to refrain from kicking
puppies or mistreating
kittens.

The Book
of Mormon is
an antidote for those
of us whose hearts are too
easily set upon the things
of the world. Without it, our
spirituality may be weakened
until we no longer look forward
to worship as a routine. We settle
for an economy hotel room with no
view, dirty carpeting, and broken air
conditioning, having dismissed from
our minds the vision of a four-star all
inclusive world class accommodation
that extends its invitation from just
beyond the parted veil thru which we
can see the covenant of baptism.
The only resort fee that must be
paid in advance, in order to
reclaim its delights, is to
have clean hands and
a pure heart.

There will be a day for each one of us when we will come face to face with eternity, and the spiritual element in which we are then immersed will transform our mortal clay. Until that time arrives, while we yet tarry upon the earth, we take care to remain obedient to the conditions under which that element might quicken us, so the wisdom of God that flows from it might be vitalized. At that day, our countenances will shine, and the boldness of our faces will be changed. (See Ecclesiastes 8:1). Even now, these miracles have begun to occur as the mighty wind of revelation that blows out of the East from each page of The Book of Mormon stirs our hearts.

We learn from The Book of Mormon and in other scriptures that it is only those who passionately embrace the gospel with its divine tutorial training, who will go to the highest degrees of glory to live in the presence of the Gods. "These are they who are priests and kings, who have received of his fullness, and of his glory; and are priests of the Most High, after the order of Melchizedek, which was after the order of Enoch, which was after the order of the Only Begotten Son. Wherefore, as it is written, they are (as the) gods, even the sons of God." (D&C 76:56-58).

Our worship on the
Sabbath day germinates
creativity. Our innovation can
be incremental or revolutionary,
but its end result is always revelatory.
The trickle-down economics of originality
during Sabbath day services increases value.
The focus of our attention is not only on the end
point, but also on the process. We are invited to
enjoy the journey as much as we are prepared
to anticipate the destination. The puzzle is
that all good things come only to those
who patiently wait upon the Lord.
This is especially true of those
who wish to receive a sure
witness of the Book
of Mormon.

The
day is not
far off when our
mortal bodies must
put on immortality. This
may be accomplished as our
Heavenly Father carries us into
the greater dawn of heaven. Just as
ultraviolet light is used in sterilization,
(ultraviolet germicidal irradiation – UVGI),
could it be that it is the physical phenomenon
of the unearthly light that is intrinsic to God
that purifies and renews our sin-stained souls?
The revelatory power of God that is manifest in
The Book of Mormon has something to do with
the change that will come over us when we
become new creatures and old things
are passed away.

Those of God's children who are growing into His spiritual stature will enjoy His revelatory gifts to behold the glory of the Celestial Kingdom, and in particular "the transcendent beauty of the gate through which the heirs of that kingdom will enter, which (is) like unto circling flames of fire; Also the blazing throne of God, wherein (shall be) seated the Father and the Son." And the "beautiful streets of that kingdom" will appear to be paved with gold. (D&C 137: 2-4). This moving imagery describes the power inherent in the spirit of revelation, and in The Book of Mormon, that can make our lives sublime, as we leave behind our footprints on the sands of time.

No matter how wide the net has been cast, only in religious experience such as is found in The Book of Mormon are we able to explain the flickering shadows of eternity that dance all around us, as the familiar features of mortality are illuminated for all of the children of God to see, by the brightly burning lamp of revelation.

It is in The Book
of Mormon where we learn
quite a bit about heaven and
its contrary that is hell. The latter
is a reformatory that has been designed
to improve the quality of our moral nature. It
is a penitentiary where faith can still convict us
of our sins. It was designed to help disobedient
spirits recognize that Christ is the Mediator of the
Covenant thru His infinite Atonement. In D&C 76,
we learn that the gospel was taught to those kept in
that prison. If, while there, they exercise free will to
accept not only Christ, but also the fulness of His
gospel, is it within the realm of possibility that
they might one day also inherit celestial glory
with the Saints. This is one of the reasons
why the Lord's church builds temples,
where vicarious work is performed,
not for just a select few, but
for all of our kindred
dead.

We think we can be
happy if we wander and
play. But we forget the key
message of The Book of Mormon
that compels us to ponder and pray,
and to take advantage of the revelation
that our Father in Heaven is so anxious to
give us, which thing leads us to appreciate
the Atonement as we speedily repent of
our sins. Only then, will we discover
the happiness that has been
prepared for us.

The Book of Mormon makes it perfectly clear that Heavenly Father has determined to keep open the lines of communication between heaven and earth, and to reveal His will to all of His children, because, in a sense, each of us is confined to a world our own making, and most of us are trapped within a narrowly defined perceptual prison that we created for ourselves. Its walls are reinforced by the razor-wire of limiting beliefs, those stories we tell on ourselves that sabotage our own best efforts. Without the revelatory power of God that is manifest by the power of the Holy Ghost, they can damage or cripple our lives as they diminish our abilities and prevent us from reaching our potential.

It is The Book of Mormon that fosters harmony with eternity. If our eye is single to God's glory, it can liberate us from confinement to the inexorable immutability of the laws governing our temporal world, as we find ourselves up and about and busily involved with our Father in His work and glory.

It is
the revelation of
The Book of Mormon,
flowing from the bedrock
of heaven, that transforms our
timidity into powerful presence of
mind. Thus, God creates a platform
for our assertive action. On the other
hand, if we seek to avoid the demands
that are placed upon us by the Word, we
will be swallowed up by a leviathan that
is no less tangible than that which was
encountered by Jonah, and we will be
likewise eventually spit out upon
the rocky shoreline of our
obligations.

Scribes and
Pharisees who have
little or no faith in the
power of The Book of Mormon
tend to omit the weightier matters
relating to God's law. They strain at
gnats and swallow camels. Although
they may appear to be righteous, on the
inside they're all "extortion and excess."
(Matthew 23:25). Our righteous desire to
choose to believe revealed truth with the
wisdom of faith brings us closer to
our Savior, the Lord Jesus Christ,
leaving little room for such
hypocrisy to creep into
our lives.

We determine to follow a yellow brick road with all of our heart, might, mind, and strength, until we arrive at the Emerald City of Oz. The Book of Mormon compels us to trust in God's revealed will, rather than in devilish doctrines that have been concocted by the world's apologists. He is more than a wizard, and His buoyant messages in that book invite us to believe that our lives can be "fairy tales waiting to be written" upon the rock of ages (see Isaiah 26:4), by His benevolent hand. (Hans Christian Anderson).

Book of Mormon scrutiny points us in the direction of its doctrine, so that when we come across the doctrine of God's Plan, we will all experience religious recognition, or a re-knowing of principles we'd previously been taught. We will respond to the truth with actions that have the form and substance of a godly walk, and that are bold testaments to the power of the Word.

Revelation coming from The Book of Mormon is a lynchpin that waits for those moments in time to figuratively tap us on the shoulder and offer us opportunities to accomplish great things that are unique to us and fitted to our talents. It would be a tragedy of cosmic proportion and eternal significance if we allowed ourselves to remain unprepared or unqualified to receive communication from the heavens that could have defined our finest hour. (Sir Winston Churchill, paraphrased).

As soon as we've opened our hearts to The Book of Mormon, we're consumed by God's divine fire. We're full of faith as we engage in His business. Idleness, on the other hand, is the workshop of the Devil, and our refusal to embrace the book is sin, for it wastes our precious resources in futile pursuits, when we should have been engaged in other and more worthwhile activities for which we would have been blessed by wisdom and understanding. Revelation would have flowed unto us, and it would have been wet with the dew of heaven. (See Daniel 4:15).

Our spiritual welfare is dependent upon a consistent diet of continuing revelation that comes from The Book of Mormon. We wouldn't think of consciously postponing our matriculation in a curriculum that's patterned after heaven, nor would we deliberately defer our gospel study in favor of worldly pursuits that ask for pitifully little in terms of commitment, but offer precious little by way of reward.

If we let nature caper, we'll use The Book of Mormon to visualize life in spatial dimensions, with it assuming the shape of an hourglass, and the strait gate representing its narrow midsection. Passing thru that constriction will be like a revelatory awakening that has been initialized by the Holy Ghost. We'll suddenly experience the dawn of a new day, as amazing vistas of unparalleled opportunity open up before our eyes.

If we have
donned the life vest
of The Book of Mormon,
and it remains securely
in place, we'll be prepared to
deal with whatever challenges
the rapids of life might choose
to throw our way. High water
can even be our friend, as it
propels us down the river
of experience, carrying
us in the direction
of our dreams.

The Holy Ghost certainly knows how; but
He patiently shows us how. Even though the devil has
street smarts, the Lord has reassured us that His delegation
of responsibility and priesthood-directed training and in-service
is a better way. He said of those who sought to destroy the work of the
publication and distribution of The Book of Mormon: "I will show unto
them that my wisdom is greater than the cunning of the devil." (D&C
10:43). In fact, He has a perfect formula to detect the fingerprints
of Satan: "I show unto you the way to judge; for every thing
which inviteth to do good, and to persuade to believe in
Christ, is sent forth by the power and gift of Christ;
wherefore ye may know with a perfect
knowledge it is of God."
(Moroni 7:16).

The Book of Mormon and its biblical companion reassure us that we are not as flotsam and jetsam that has been unceremoniously cast upon the sea of life. Nor are we "children, tossed to and fro, and carried about with every wind of doctrine, by the sleight of men, and cunning craftiness, whereby they lie in wait to deceive." (Ephesians 4:4). When we live "without Christ and God in the world ... (we) are driven about as chaff before the wind." (Mormon 5:16). Instead, we are reassured that wherever Jesus preached, "a great multitude followed him." (Matthew 20:29). When His sheep hear His voice, they will go wherever He might lead them.

As we read and study The Book of Mormon, a healthy measure of the Spirit protects us from the worldly contaminants of material prosperity; We recognize these accouterments as "tinkling ornaments, and cauls, and round tires like the moon" (2 Nephi 13:18), that manifest themselves as the temptation to fill space with telestial trinkets that will only canker our souls if they are viewed or used unwisely.

Paul preached to
the men of Athens (see Acts
Chapter 17), who were oblivious
to revelation that could have been a
positive influence in their lives. They
hadn't been blessed with the scriptural
equivalent of The Book of Mormon, and
they were inclined to bow down before the
unknown gods whom they worshipped in
ignorance. They had no idea that when it
would be their turn to come face to face
with eternity, the experience would be
revelatory, and that they would go
thru the mighty transformation
of their mortal clay into a more
enduring substance, leaving
no room for doubt or for
spiritual illiteracy.

As we faithfully persist
in our quest to receive revelation
in The Book of Mormon, the Spirit will
teach us how to become better at fashioning
defensive weapons in the armory of thought.
It is with these tools that the Holy Ghost
will show us how to put together a vast
arsenal of heavenly munitions,
such as faith, hope, and
charity, strength,
peace, and
joy.

In The Book of Mormon, presidents, magistrates, potentates, powers, and principalities pale in comparison to the government of God that will one day be led by the Newborn King.

The Book of Mormon shows us how to govern ourselves so that we can be up and about, and moving forward on the path leading to God's kingdom. Then, when we ultimately stand before Him and render an accounting, we will realize that He was always on our side, while Satan, the great detractor, was always in opposition. At that moment, we will realize that ours had always been the deciding vote in an election held to determine where we would spend eternity. Maybe the Kingdom of God can be both a theocracy and a democracy, after all.

The Book
of Mormon is "a tale as
old as time, and as true as
it can be." ("Beauty and The
Beast"). It speaks to us from
out of the dust.

The Book of Mormon joins the Old
and the New Testaments of the Bible
in a warning that negotiators may sue
for peace even as antagonists attempt to
gain the advantage, but there will be no
peace in the world until every faction
acknowledges the supremacy of the
Prince of Peace Who has the power
to provide us with well-ordered
and balanced lives and heal
our broken relationships.
(See Ephesians 2:19,
& Isaiah 9:6).

The utopia that
is described in The
Book of Mormon as the
Land of Promise reminds
us that the earth "was once a
garden place, with all her glories
common, and men and women
lived a holy race and worshiped
Jesus face to face, in Adam-
ondi- Ahman." ("Adam-
ondi-Ahman").

Whenever the vulgar
and profane appetites of the Nephites and the
Lamanites spun wildly out of control, it was their
passions that forged their fetters. At that very moment,
their birthright was sold for a mess of pottage, for they had
made a compact with the devil. The Savior came to break these
bands. (See Mosiah 15:9). Even though there may now be almost
universal commotion from ocean to ocean, the events that surround
the history of Lehi's descendants in the Americas will herald the
awakening of a beautiful, bright new day, when the world will
be stirred from its long sleep by The Book of Mormon, and
the mists of darkness that had for so long plagued it
will flee away as a wil-o-the-wisp in the brilliant
light of a rising sun.

In the Last Days, we pray "that we might toil, and not seek for rest; that we might give and not count the cost; that we might fight, and not heed the wounds; and that we might labor, and not ask for any reward, save that of knowing that we do God's will." (Ignatius Loyola). The Book of Mormon promises that men and women who have been inspired from heaven will stand "among the people in all the land" (3 Nephi 6:20). The Spirit will awaken in their hearts a firm determination to testify of the resurrection of our Savior, and of the divine authenticity of The Book of Mormon.

There is a pathway that leads beyond the stars to the Kingdom of Heaven. On its way, it passes not only through Bethlehem, but also through the Garden of Gethsemane, Calvary, and past an empty tomb. When we finally arrive at heaven's gate, its keeper will not be Saint Peter, but the Lord Himself, for "he employeth no servant there." (2 Nephi 9:41).

The Book of Mormon
encourages the Saints to wear,
not "stiff necks and high heads"
(2 Nephi 28:14), on the Sabbath, but
their Sunday best, and also to remember
to put on their best behavior. In essence, to
think celestial. They realize their outward
appearance is but a mirror of their inner
selves. It dawns on them that the acorn
might yet grow into a mighty oak,
and so they act in accordance
with their high and noble
calling.

The Book of Mormon encourages stewardship and
consecration to come together to enjoy symmetry. John
K. Edmunds enjoyed a distinguished legal career. One
day a widow came to him for advice, and when they were
finished, she apprehensively asked him, "How much do I
owe you?" Gently, he replied, "Why don't you just pay
me what you think it is worth." Relieved, she got out
her coin purse, produced a quarter, and pressed it
into his palm. He looked at the quarter, looked
at her, and then got out his own coin purse,
and gave her ten cents change.

There was always a perpetual battle
raging in the hearts of the Nephites, pitting their
desire to serve their Master against telestial tendencies
that twisted their focus inward. "Two ways lay before them,
one leading to an ever-lower plane, where were heard the cries of
despair and the curses of the poor; and the other leading to the
highlands of the morning, where were heard the glad
shouts of humanity, and where honest effort
was rewarded with immortality."
(John P. Altgeld).

The Sons of Mosiah knew that if they
would "hinder a very infidel from the right
of the law, they would sin against God." (William
Tyndall, "Obedience" p. 61). With profound gratitude
for His generosity, they extended the hand of fellowship
to the Lamanites, without regard to their circumstances in
life. "And it shall come to pass that ye shall divide (the land)
by lot for an inheritance unto you, and to the strangers
that sojourn among you, which shall beget children
among you; and they shall be unto you as born
in the country among the children of Israel;
they shall have inheritance with you
among the tribes of Israel."
(Ezekiel 47:22).

The thesis that is behind Moroni's 'promise (see Moroni 10:4-5) is that the Holy Ghost creates confidence. God has not "given us the spirit of fear, but of power, and of love, and of a sound mind." (2 Timothy 1:7). As the Savior asked: "Why are ye fearful, O ye of little faith?" (Matthew 8:26). Nephi was "full of the Spirit of God" when he urged us to awaken "from a deep sleep, yea, even from the sleep of hell, and shake off the awful chains by which ye are bound, which are the chains which bind the children of men, that they are carried away captive down to the eternal gulf of misery and woe." (2 Nephi 17:47).

Among the Nephites and the Lamanites, unresolved sin was "like an unquenchable fire" leaving their hope for happiness in ashes. (Mosiah 2:38). David O. McKay taught: "The first condition of happiness is a clear conscience." In physical terms, a wound cannot heal if it is unclean. The same principle applies to character development. There were no festering sores or skeletons that were lurking in their closets as long as recurring repentance released them from bondage to sin. It unleashed the powers of heaven in their behalf, and qualified them by worthiness to enjoy the blessings reserved for the faithful. Our Heavenly Father's Only Begotten Son made it possible for them to overcome their limitations and reach their potential. It was only by conforming their lives to His celestial law that the bands of death were broken and that their spiritual transformation was first initiated, and then consummated. (See 3 Nephi 2:14-15).

Numerous Nephite prophets of old "brought forth the key of the sweet promises, saying, repent, and be baptized every one of you in the name of Jesus Christ for the remission of sins, and ye shall receive the gift of the Holy Ghost." (William Tyndall). Many find it easy to follow their counsel so long as it takes them on to sprawling boulevards that are dotted with conveniently located rest stops, and to brightly lighted world stages filled with the appreciative applause and the laudatory comments of supportive audiences. But placed in challenging situations with no-one looking, when there have been no preparatory fortifying experiences and there are no positive peer pressures to sustain correct choices, it is far easier for Nephites, Lamanites, and Latter-day Saints to falter.

Reading
The Book of Mormon
prepares us to meet God, even
as we perform our labors, as the
soul scars of mortality are healed
thru our exercise of repentance, and
as we await our resurrection and our
reunion with our loved ones in the
Celestial Kingdom, thanks to the
Atonement of our Lord and
Savior Jesus Christ. (See
Alma 34:32).

Mormon knew what it was like to be the Savior's junior partner (see Moroni 7:31), and today we likewise know how it feels to be in business with Him. When we work hard and the sweat drips off the ends of our noses, we thank God for whatever talents and energy we may have been given to apply to our capacity to work. When we survey the fruits of our labor, we try to envision the greater purpose for which our blessings have come. We try to be good stewards, and if our talents are multiplied, our greatest enjoyment comes when they are put to good use for the benefit of others.

Shortly after we have undertaken our study of The Book of Mormon, "the first enemy we oftentimes will find is within ourselves. It is a good thing to overcome that enemy first, and bring ourselves into strict obedience to the principles of life and salvation." (Joseph F. Smith). The apostle Paul's formula for ridding ourselves of the limitations of the past was "forgetting those things which are behind, and reaching forth unto those things which are before" us. (Philippians 3:13-14). When we heed that advice, we find ourselves anticipating a spiritual feast as we devour the scriptures with new-found enthusiasm.

When we read and study The
Book of Mormon, our "delight is in the law of
the Lord; and in (it we) mediate day and night."
(Psalms 1:2). With developing maturity, we follow
general principles and scriptural guidelines, and
we listen to the promptings of the Spirit. We ask:
"Are my actions holy and of service to God? Am I
doing good? Am I using my agency to keep
myself unspotted from the world? Am
I honoring the Lord as one of His
true disciples?"

The gospel is designed to penetrate our hearts,
heal our deafness and blindness, and ease the tension and
inelasticity that so often characterizes our minds, so that "when
we are dead, others will seek our tomb, not in the earth, but in the
hearts of men." (Jalal al Din al Rumi, the 14th century Sufi poet
who founded the Order of Dervishes). The sweet fragrance of the
gospel should smell like bread that is fresh out of the oven.
We try to appreciate the supremacy of spiritual ideals
without experiencing the limitations of material
trivia, and so, the time we spend studying
The Book of Mormon is work without
pay, behind the scenes, and far
from media attention - but
the retirement benefits
are out of this
world.

Someone once said that time is a predator stalking us all our lives, and is the fire in which we burn. When we are reading The Book of Mormon, however, we prefer to think of time as a companion that accompanies us on our journey through mortality, reminding us to cherish every moment. The Savior teaches us how to manipulate time; to give it, make it, take it, find it, and buy it, while hopefully not killing it. God gave us the gift of the commodity of time in the hope and expectation that we would spend it on worthwhile activities, and not fritter it away, or waste it on trivial pursuits.

When we recall how the Savior scattered the tables of the money changers in the temple, we are struck by how cheaply "all virtue is sold, and almost any vice – almighty gold!" (Ben Jonson). The irony is that it is all for nothing, and even worse, the passion for what is nothing but telestial trash sometimes results in fratricidal bickering and "the destruction of nearly all the people of the kingdom." (Ether 9:12).

"For what praise is it, when ye be buffeted for your faults, ye take it patiently? But when ye do well, and ye suffer wrong and take it patiently, then is there thanks with God. Hereunto were ye called." (William Tyndall). The Savior taught: "Blessed are ye when men shall revile you and persecute, and shall say all manner of evil against you falsely, for my sake, for ye shall have great joy and be exceedingly glad, for great shall be your reward in heaven; for so persecuted they the prophets who were before you." (3 Nephi 12:11-12). Ultimately, "we can never be injured by any mortals, except ourselves." (Heber J. Grant).

"When thou hurtest not thy neighbours, then art thou sure that God's Spirit worketh in thee, and that thy faith is neither a dream nor any false imagination." (William Tyndall). By the temple in Bountiful, the Savior taught: "Blessed are the merciful, for they shall obtain mercy." (3 Nephi 12:7). "For with what judgment ye judge, ye shall be judged: and with what measure ye mete, it shall be measured to you again." (Matthew 7:2). What goes around comes around, and if we cast our bread upon the waters, after many days it shall return unto us. (See Ecclesiastes 11:1).

We choose the Savior in an act of free will that yields our hearts to Him. We ponder the great and terrible consequences of Gethsemane, travel with Him to Calvary, and enjoy the sweetness of the Atonement's redeeming power. When we keep His laws, we experience the "happiness which is prepared for the saints" that will transcend temporal insecurity and discomfort, and neutralize the pathetic passion for pleasure that is the worldly counterfeit to joy. (2 Nephi 9:43).
"Lo, saith he, I am with you always, even unto the end of the world." (William Tyndall). We are not alone, now or ever.
"Adam fell that men might be, and men are that they might have joy," not only in the comfortable environment of our heavenly home, but also in the here and now.
(2 Nephi 2:25).

Too often, the Nephites were hypocritical, pretending to be virtuous when they were only going thru the motions. They concentrated on public demonstrations of blind obedience to outward ordinances and observances. Their basic instability was associated with hypocrisy, and each time that they crossed the line between right and wrong they risked suffering eternally damaging consequences. They were faced with a conundrum of cosmic proportion. Free will itself was preserved as the crown jewel of mortality in order to avoid this dilemma. They were free to follow one lifestyle or the other, but not both. That desire runs counter to the laws of nature and is fatally flawed. Today, The Book of Mormon remains as God's prescription of deliverance for those who find themselves in the uncomfortable position of traveling down a one-way road leading to a personality precipice overlooking the gates of hell.

Benjamin taught that God "overcame us
with kindness and to make us to do of very love that thing
which the law compels us to do. For love only and to do service unto
our neighbors is the fulfilling of the law in the sight of God." (William
Tyndall). When their altruistic sensitivities predominated, as during
the reign of the kings in Zarahemla, the Nephites labored in behalf
of others and lost themselves in their service. (See Mosiah 2:17).
When they caught the vision, they gave themselves to the
Savior, yielding to Him their agency because of
their implicit trust in His power to save
them from their own follies.

After the separation of his people from the
Lamanites, and following the construction of a temple
in what was thereafter called the land of Nephi, Nephi mused:
"And it came to pass that we lived after the manner of happiness."
(2 Nephi 27:5). He understood that when we feel happy, we smile with
all our hearts, and if we're down and out, we smile with all our might. If
we do nothing else, we can still be the smile on the faces of those that mourn,
or stand in need of comfort. Our smiles are a daily exercise that we can easily
do without even breaking a sweat. The smiles that we wear on the outside tell
others what's happening on the inside. Sometimes, our joy is the source of
our smile, but sometimes, our smile may be the source of our joy. As we
smile with a determined effort to fight our way through brimming
tears, we can take comfort in the fact that at least the corners of
our mouths point toward heaven. When we get up in the
morning, we are only half-dressed until we put on
our smiles. We realize that, when it comes to
smiling, one size fits all. Our smiles
are fashion accessories that never
go out of style.

The Lord knew that in the world
of the Nephites, the vital distinctions
between good and evil would often be blurred.
Spiritual Babylon, personified by the wicked and
apostate Lamanites, was all around them, and so
they needed to be vigilant because, in every age,
"vice is a monster of so frightful mien, as to be
hated needs but to be seen. Yet seen too oft,
familiar with her face, we first endure,
then pity, then embrace."
(Alexander Pope).

Unlike indulgent parents in these
latter days, our Father in Heaven would never
give the Nephites that which they didn't deserve,
nor would He respond to their pressure to give them
what they didn't need. He allowed their agency to act
as a tool to deliver them from evil. Free will became
one of their greatest benefactors, especially when
it re-enthroned the Savior, together with His
Atonement, as their Mentor and
their Exemplar.

"The dark threads are as needful in the weaver's skillful hand as the threads of gold and silver, in the pattern God has planned." (Benjamin M. Franklin). But when we accept the invitation to try the virtue of His word (see Alma 31:5), we are exposed to the fruit of the Tree of Life and we open our senses to the matchless realm of joy that is available only through obedience to gospel principles.

When we tend to be a bit self-righteous and we think that we are worthy of our chattel, let us recall the example of the Nephites, who have taught us that fame "is a vapor, and popularity is an accident, and those who cheer you on today may curse you tomorrow. In the end, only our character endures." (Horace Greely). The Book of Mormon reestablishes our determination to concentrate our thoughts, words, and deeds on the unlimited potential of the divine model.

The Book of Mormon touches the mystic chords of memory so that we might recognize both the brotherhood of mankind and the fatherhood of God. We accept His Firstborn Son as our Exemplar, Advocate, and the Good Shepherd. He is our well of Living Water and the Bread of Life.

The Book of Mormon is a cosmological constant teaching us that the star that shined in the night sky above Bethlehem blessed the world with a heavenly beacon for all to follow without regard to their station in life. It reminds us that wise men still seek Him that was born King of the Jews.

The Book of Mormon is a safe haven that remains untainted from the blood and sins of our generation. It identifies the refuge where we may flee from spiritual Babylon to shelter our spirits, quiet our racing hearts, ease the tensions that build up when we spend too much time in the fast lane of life, grasp the horns of sanctuary, and quietly reflect on the quality of our preparation to live with Heavenly Father for eternity.

We have all heard that blood is thicker than water. This well known aphorism conveys the belief that, as a result of genetics, blood relations are more important than friendships. However, after some basic research, I found that the earliest form of "Blood is thicker than water" grew out of the phrase: "The blood of the covenant is thicker than the water of the womb." The meaning of this earlier phrase is actually the complete opposite of the way it is used today. In other words, the bonds that we have consciously chosen to make with God by covenant are more important than the ones that we find ourselves in through genetics and by chance, or as the saying goes, by the "water of the womb." As the prophet Isaiah put it: "Surely your turning of things upside down shall be esteemed as the potter's clay." (Isaiah 29:16). Blood is thicker than water. However, a blood covenant is thicker than the water of the womb. Bonding with those of like "mind" and "spirit" can be so much more meaningful and deeper than bonding by blood, which can turn on the roll of the dice. No greater bond can be formed than when we live under covenant with God.

The Greek Stoic philosopher Epictetus, writing in Rome at about the same time as the birth of the Savior, observed: "The universe is but one great city, full of beloved ones, divine and human, by nature endeared to each other." Later, after the ministry of the Savior among the Nephites, their love was so great that Mormon was moved to observe: "Surely there could not be a happier people among all the people who had been created by the hand of God." (4 Nephi 1:15-16).

In a bold move that has become the centerpiece of The Book of Mormon narrative, our Heavenly Father placed His Son squarely in the cross-hairs, with the intention that the account of His post-mortal ministry among the Nephites in the Americas might capture the world's attention. The story has persisted, that we might once again come to adore Him. However, there is also an element of vulnerability, always a risk of the chance that the miracle will be relegated to that of a tall tale, a fable, or a myth; or that it will be ridiculed, neglected, or worse yet, it will be treated with indifference. In His omniscience, God has placed the burden of responsibility for testimony just where it should be, and that is squarely on our shoulders.

Looking back on a
lifetime of devotion to his Heavenly
Father and of service to his family, Jacob
cried; "O how great (is) the holiness of our God!"
"For he knoweth all things, and there is not anything
save he knows it." (2 Nephi 9:20). He knows when we've
been sleeping and He knows when we're awake. He knows
when we've been good or bad, so does it not then make
perfect sense to do our best and to be our best,
if for no other reason than to be true to
the One Whose mission it was
to light the world?

We already have enough
on our plates to deal with without
adding to the burden by fretting about
what the future has in store for us. Worry, after
all, is interest on a debt that may never come due.
There are, after all, only three types of control in life.
First, are those circumstances over which we have absolute
control. Then, are those things over which we have indirect
control, and finally those things over which we have no
control. The Book of Mormon shows us where to most
profitably direct our energies and resources that
relate to the last category. By following the
counsel that is given in the book, we
get more bang for our buck.

The great deceiver and the father
of lies encourages us to stretch the truth,
react to rumors, give in to gossip, and murmur in
all its mutated forms. His disciples will habitually try
to speak out of both sides of their mouths at the same time,
but in the process, they'll suffer from the confusion of tongues.
Their distorted words reflect a divine center deficiency, a vacuum
of values, and a paucity of principles. Satan's disciples use the tools
of vague and inconsistent language to build on the shifting sands of
moral relativism, situational ethics, and secular humanism, that are
the favored playgrounds of those with golden tongues. Frequently, it
is far too easy to quiet their conscience with the soothing and false
counsel of "foolish and blind guides," illogical though they may
be. (Helaman 13:29). By enlisting in his army, we substitute
human sophistry for the Almighty God. The promises of
the devil are a deception and a snare, and he panders to
an audience that is all too eager to trade celestial
sureties for telestial trinkets and to sell its
divine birthright for nothing but a
mess of pottage.

As we read and study The Book of
Mormon, we recall Dag Hammarskjöld's
observation that "the longest journey is the
journey inward, for he who has chosen
his destiny has started upon a
quest for the source of
his being."

Our Father could give us everything He has, but what He is, we must earn for ourselves, as we struggle to overcome adversity and gain self-mastery. We learn in The Book of Mormon that it is covenants that help us to focus our efforts to become as He is. This is their purpose. If it were not possible to become as God is, they would be unnecessary. Thus it is, that in the final chapters of the book, Moroni emphasized the ordinance of the Sacrament to send home the message that by making covenants with God, we may clothe ourselves in the Spirit, as we take upon ourselves the name of Jesus Christ.

Mortality is, for each of us, a probationary state, a time in which we will be individually tried to see if we will put to the proof those things that we have been taught we must do if we are to inherit eternal life. In short, we are tested and tempted so that God can see if we are willing to go the second mile, particularly as it relates to our study of The Book of Mormon.

Our Father could give us everything He has, but what He is, we must earn for ourselves, as we struggle to overcome adversity and gain self-mastery. We learn in The Book of Mormon that it is covenants that help us to focus our efforts to become as He is. This is their purpose. If it were not possible to become as God is, they would be unnecessary. Thus it is, that in the final chapters of the book, Moroni emphasized the ordinance of the Sacrament to send home the message that by making covenants with God, we may clothe ourselves in the Spirit, as we take upon ourselves the name of Jesus Christ.

Mortality is, for each of us, a probationary state, a time in which we will be individually tried to see if we will put to the proof those things that we have been taught we must do if we are to inherit eternal life. In short, we are tested and tempted so that God can see if we are willing to go the second mile, particularly as it relates to our study of The Book of Mormon.

Following
the introduction of The Book of
Mormon to the emerging societies who
benefitted from the wonders that were introduced
by the Industrial Revolution, there could have been
unleashed a joyous celebration and continuation of the
Age of Enlightenment. But in its place we are witnessing a
conceptual free-for-all, with precious few regulations, rules, or
restrictions to temper moral or ethical depravity. The better angels
of our nature respond to righteousness, because the positive energy of
foundation principles is immune to the capricious character quirks of
those who have compromised their standards in a capitulation to the
telestial trauma of secular humanism. Those of weak will cannot
deny their noble birthright for too long before that disavowal will
begin to strangle their spontaneity as rapidly evolving children
of God. Obedience to our covenants, on the other hand, will
bless our lives with vitality that quickens our spirits in
ways that nothing else can. The gospel is a living,
breathing entity that is nourished by active
involvement with the Lord's disciples,
who are very much like you!

Even faithful Nephites
sometimes thoughtlessly exercised
unrighteous dominion, meaning that
they took strength unto themselves, rather
than giving God the credit and the glory for
their good deeds. For example, when Moses asked
Israel at Horeb: "Must we fetch you water out
of this rock?" (Numbers 20:10), he had a
pronoun problem of cosmic
proportion!" (Neal A.
Maxwell).

The Great and Eternal
Plan of Deliverance from Death
has also been called the Plan of Mercy,
Redemption, and Happiness, because it makes
possible the resurrection of otherwise imperfect souls
to heavenly glory and endless joy. These "great and
eternal purposes were prepared from the foundation of
the world." (Alma 42:26). "To the Son is given the
power of the resurrection, the power of redemption,
the power of salvation, the power to enact laws
for the carrying out and accomplishment of
His design. Both life and immortality
are brought to light as the gospel is
introduced, and He becomes
the Author of eternal life
and exaltation."
(John Taylor).

The
Apostle Paul
told us that "faith
is the substance of things
hoped for, the evidence of things
not seen." (Hebrews 11:1). Faith is not
to receive a sign from heaven. As Alma told
the Zoramites: "If a man knoweth a thing he hath
no cause to believe, for he knoweth it." (Alma 32:18). In
this context, if a sign is given before faith has transformed
us, we might have a sure knowledge of the event, but there has
been no expenditure of faith to create it. However, under proper
circumstances, by doing our duty, our faith can increase
until it has blossomed into perfect knowledge. Initially,
then, faith is to believe what we do not see, but its
indescribable reward is to clearly see what we
believe. (See 2 Corinthians 5:7).

In vision, Mormon saw our day, where in most Western societies, the rising generation faces unprecedented challenges as Satan makes a full-frontal assault on virtue and chastity. The new morality is intolerant, exploitative, and oriented toward intercourse and not life. The unity that couples seek cannot be accomplished at the pelvic level. The most basic of virtues, such as honesty, is no longer held in high esteem. "Now we are a people of contention with strident and accusatory voices heard in argument across the nation. We spend millions of our resources in litigation against one another. Our spiritual power is sapped by a storm surge of pornography, by a debilitating epidemic of the use of drugs that destroy body, mind, and soul. In all too many ways, we have substituted human sophistry for the Almighty." (Gordon B. Hinckley).

As we read The Book of Mormon, we discover that during the Nephites' eye-opening journey thru mortality, they often brushed up against the inviting portals of heaven without even realizing that they had done so. Helen Keller "asked a friend who had just returned from a long walk in the woods what she had observed. She replied, 'Nothing in particular.' How was that possible, I asked myself? I, who cannot see or hear, find hundreds of things that interest me through mere touch. I feel the delicate symmetry of a leaf. I pass my hands lovingly across the rough shaggy bark of a pine. Occasionally, if I am especially fortunate, I place my hand gently on a small tree and feel the happy quiver of a bird in full song."

The Lord told Moroni: "I am the light, and the life, and truth of the world." (Ether 4:12). Helen Keller wrote: "Keep your face to the sunshine, and you cannot see the shadow." It will still exist, but if we are oriented toward the light, it will always be behind us, out of sight, and out of mind. Light gives us courage to transforms timidity and temerity into powerful presence of mind. Light becomes a platform for assertive action, empowering us with boldness. It charges us with an intense and compellingly positive energy to meet challenge. In the fight or flight scenario, it is light that energizes the launch pad in preparation for the adrenalin rush that propels us beyond the threat. It provides the physical foundation upon which is built our character, and its luminescent trajectory can be traced to an unfailing source that is a celestial dynamo.

The Nephites were only following precedent when they engraved their history upon plates of ore. Not long after the death of her soul-mate, Eve is reported to have exhorted her children: "Hearken unto me, and make tables of stone and others of clay, to write on them about my life and your father's that ye have heard and seen from us. If, by water, the Lord judge our race, the tables of clay will be dissolved and the tables of stone will remain; but if, by fire, the tables of clay will be baked hard, and the tables of stone will be broken up." (Book of Adam and Eve – the Pseudepigrapha).

Like so many
of us, the Nephites felt no
desire to partake of the delicious
fruit of everlasting life when they
had not first accepted the proposition
that perspiration precedes inspiration.
Yielding to mediocrity, and choosing
placation, the world's profane baubles,
selfish pleasure, the honors of men, or
disobedience to God, illustrates that
our priorities are out of order. As
long as we remain in this state,
we cannot generate the power
that is necessary to progress
along the path that leads
beyond that great and
spacious building all
the way to the Tree
of Life.

that we have
been converted to
The Book of Mormon
when we begin to hear it
calling to us, inviting us to
come in out of the cold and
out of the darkness into
the marvelous light
of day.

In addition to an apple a day, we need to have regular doses of The Book of Mormon, so that as we enjoy experiences that are palpable, it will be as though the veil before our eyes has become transparent, and we feel clear, whole, and at peace with ourselves and our environment. Truth will permit us to reach out and touch eternity. We will hold certainty in our hands. Guiding principles will resonate with reality, allowing us to move along an illuminated pathway to our dreams. It is no wonder that Satan tries to cloud our vision with the glitz and glamour of carnal counterfeits that are really nothing more than optical and spiritual illusions. His foolish fire, or will-o-the-wisp fictions, cannot stand the heat of the mid-day sun; they wither and die when they are confronted by doctrine and principles that have been so vigorously activated by our agency.

With the guidance that's provided by Book of Mormon prophets, it becomes easier to negotiate the strait and narrow path all the way to the Tree of Life, there to partake of its delicious fruit, which represents eternal life in the Celestial Kingdom of God.

Out of the mists of the distant past in ancient America, and the not-so-distant past of mid-Nineteenth Century America, warnings from Mormon and Daniel Webster ominously echo in our ears: "If we and our posterity shall be true to the Christian religion, and if we and they shall live always in the fear of God and shall respect his commandments, we may have the highest hopes for the future fortunes of our country. It will have no decline or fall, but it will go on prospering. But, if we or our posterity shall reject religious instructions and authority, violate the rules of morality and recklessly destroy the political constitution which holds us together, no man or woman can predict how sudden a catastrophe may overwhelm us, that shall bury all of our glory in profound obscurity."

The Book of Mormon teaches us that "this life is the time to prepare to meet God, yea, behold the day of this life is the day for (us) to perform (our) labors," and to initiate the process of healing the soul scars of sin thru purposeful repentance, and by relying upon the power of Christ's Atonement and the grace of God. Thereby, we attend to every needful thing, and all done is in anticipation of resurrection to glory and of a wonderful reunion that will incude all of our loved ones in the Celestial Kingdom of God. (Alma 34:32).
.

Alma taught that, during its genesis, our "faith is not to have a perfect knowledge of things; therefore, if (we would) have faith, (we will) hope for things which are not seen, which are true." (Alma 30: 21). Faith is unnecessary, if its object is demonstrable to our physical senses. Faith, then, is not to have a perfect knowledge of things gained through our own experiences. Korihor's demand for a sign was a condition of his faith, since he trusted only his physical senses. This rational approach is the enemy of faith. Thus, secular humanism and other similarly corrupted ideologies destroy faith and are devilish doctrines, subtle though they may be. They are abominable to God because they thwart the successful execution of His Plan, by denying the efficacy of saving faith which is a commendable thing in the sight of God.

Each time we "press forward with a steadfastness in Christ, having a perfect brightness of hope, and a love of God and of all men," we are "feasting upon" His words and hear His voice. Our experience is then validated by an unimpeachable witness and a spiritual re-confirmation that we receive from the Holy Ghost. (2 Nephi 31:20)

Latter-day Nephites who "wait upon the Lord will "renew their strength (and) shall mount up with wings as eagles; they shall run, and not be weary, and they shall walk, and not faint." (Isaiah 40:31, see Mosiah 4:27). Long ago, it was recognized that there is a direct relationship between obedience to the commandments and our physical and spiritual well-being; that if we consciously and deliberately adopt lifestyles that lead to poor health, "wisdom cannot reveal itself, culture cannot become manifest, strength cannot fight, wealth becomes useless, and intelligence cannot be applied." (Heraclitus).

The Nephites' inability to consistently concentrate on eternal principles created a conundrum of cosmic proportion. They could not simultaneously focus their attention on two things that were of contrasting value. In prayer, their faith competed with timidity; first blessing, and later cursing, escaped the same tongue, and their devotion to God clashed with allegiance to Babylon. They tried to be grounded on a bedrock of standards, but sometimes they confused values for principles. Their vanity and pride projected a false sense of carnal security, and they told each other that all was well in Zion, even as the world came crashing down around them.

One message of
The Book of Mormon is
that it is possible for each
of us not just to resist evil, but
also to live abundantly by tapping
into unlimited reserves of living water
that are waiting for us in an inexhaustible
aquifer. "These currents and many more are
part of the flowing fountain of the church. If
we do not drink, but instead die of thirst while
only inches away from that fountain, the fault
comes down to us because the free, full, flowing,
living water is there." (Truman Madsen). We
discover the source of David's strength from
a careful study of his 23rd psalm. It was
his cup of living water, we learn, that
"runneth over." (Psalms
23:5).

If we haven't
yet enrolled in our
Savior's spiritual fitness
program, illustrated in The
Book of Mormon, and that has
been designed to help us achieve
the symmetry of optimal muscle
tone through repentance, living in
the lone and dreary world will lack
both coherence and stability. Even
worse, our weigh-in at the day of
Judgment will find that, as out
of shape couch potatoes, we've
remained in our fallen
state as 97-pound
weaklings.

As long as
the Nephites internalized
the quality of charity, their lives
enjoyed an expansion of opportunity into
new dimensions. They saw things differently.
All of a sudden, good outweighed evil, love overcame
jealousy, hate, and prejudice, light drove out darkness,
knowledge banished ignorance, humility displaced pride,
courtesy overwhelmed rudeness, appreciation overpowered
thanklessness, abundance superseded poverty, well-being
replaced weakness, simplicity overshadowed perplexity,
harmony supplanted discord, faith subdued fear, hope
cast out despair, charity ousted selfishness, joy
deposed unhappiness, sadness, dejection,
and misery, confidence was substituted
for timidity, certainty dethroned
bewilderment, and assurance
unseated discouragement
and even despair.

The Book of Mormon
unmistakably warns that
a deadly threat to our temporal
and spiritual welfare exists, hidden
in an improvised explosive device called
pride, ready to explode and scatter its lethal
contents among the people in a deadly deluge of
deception. The warning applies especially to those
who are trying to move beyond an outward law of
carnal commandments to the internalization of a
higher standard of behavior that is powered by
the Holy Ghost, Whose presence demands of
true disciples a celestial criterion, where
humility quietly reigns supreme.

One of the
inherent dangers
that is associated with
a shallow understanding of
doctrine is that we risk being
blind-sided, then falling into
transgression, finally suffering
the inevitable consequences of our
poor choices. We have all witnessed
how picking apart the scriptures can
distort the doctrines into nonsensical
fragments with little or no coherent
connection. The wicked inhabitants
of Ammonihah were counseled by
Alma: "Behold, the scriptures are
before you. If ye will wrest
them, it shall be to your
own destruction."
(Alma 13:20).

Every one of
God's equitable laws has
been perfectly crafted with
His children in mind, to have
both blessings and punishment
affixed to it. Our obedience brings
happiness, while disobedience always
ends badly. "Despair cometh because of
iniquity." (Moroni 10:22). That is the
feeling of helplessness which is one
of the natural consequences of
our violation of the hallowed
covenants that govern the
conduct of heaven.

Commentary, Compendia, & Observations Index

Without The Book of Mormon's influence, we tend to seek after signs to fill the voids in our lives. When we are past feeling, we require a greater and greater intensity of stimulation to receive the same level of temporal or theological gratification. What we have been given is never enough.

Commentary Volume One
Born in The Wilderness

- 1 Nephi
- 2 Nephi
- Jacob
- Enos
- Jarom
- Omni
- Words of Mormon
- Observations
- Author's Note
- Addendum – A Sampling of Scriptures

Commentary Volume Two
Voices From The Dust

- Mosiah
- Alma
- Observations
- Author's Note
- Addendum – A Sampling of Scriptures

Commentary Volume Three
Journey to Cumorah

- Helaman
- 3 Nephi
- 4 Nephi
- Mormon
- Ether
- Moroni
- Observations
- Author's Note
- Addendum – A Sampling of Scriptures

Revelation from God necessarily co-exists with The Book of Mormon, and is as a nursemaid to the nations. Its influence reaches out to lift up the downtrodden and those who are poor in spirit, as well as to help those who are firm in the faith but continue to struggle.

Compendium
Volume One

- Introduction
- Questions Answered by The Book of Mormon
- Topical Index
- Observations
- A few of my favorite things
- Familiar Scriptures
- Commentary & Compendium Index

Compendium
Volume Two

- Introduction
- Questions Answered by The Book of Mormon
- Topical Index
- Without The Book of Mormon
- Observations
- Introduction to the Isaiah Chapters
- "And it came to pass in The Book of Mormon
- "Ad thus we see" in The Book of Mormon
- "Behold" in The Book of Mormon
- "Wherefore" and "Therefore in The Book of Mormon
- The Appearance of Gold
- The Use of The Name of Christ
- Pragmatism in The Book of Mormon
- Dry Humor in The Book of Mormon
- A Book of Mormon Timeline
- Commentary and Compendium Index

Compendium
Volume Three

- Compendia Index
- Essays That Relate to Teachings in The Book of Mormon
- Observations
- Commentary, Compendium, & Observations Index

Compendium
Volume Four

- Compendia Index
- Essays That Relate to Teachings in The Book of Mormon
- Observations
- Commentary, Compendium, & Observations Index

Compendium
Volume Five

- Compendia Index
- Essays That Relate to Teachings in The Book of Mormon
- Observations
- Commentary, Compendium, & Observations Index

Joseph's
coat of many colors is a symbol of
our faith in the positive and uplifting
messages of The Book of Mormon; that
every cloud has a silver lining and
that even the darkest night is
followed by promise at
the dawning of a
new day.

Compendium
Volume Six

- Compendia Index
- Essays That Relate to Teachings in The Book of Mormon
- Observations
- Commentary, Compendium, & Observations Index

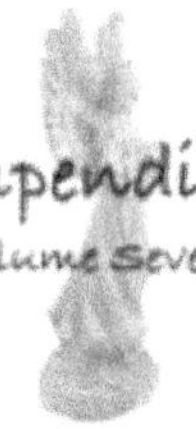

Compendium
Volume Seven

- Compendia Index
- Essays That Relate to Teachings in The Book of Mormon
- Observations
- Commentary, Compendium, & Observation Index

Compendium
Volume Eight

- Introduction
- Hebrew Poetry in The Book of Mormon
- Synonymous Parallelism
- Antithetical Parallelism
- Synthetic Parallelism
- Climactic Parallelism
- Chiasmus
- Book of Mormon Scriptures Illustrating

Observations
Volume One

- 550 Observations

Observations
Volume Two

- 550 Observations

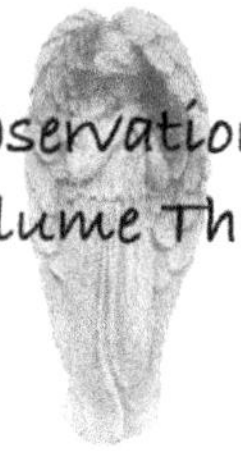

Observations
Volume Three

- 550 Observations

Observations
Volume Four

- 550 Observations

By using specifically authorized and sanctioned words that have been received by revelation, we exercise the faith to perform a variety of ordinances ranging from baptisms to the sealing ordinances of the temple. (See Mosiah 18:13 & Moroni Chapters 2 – 5).

Observations Volume 5

- 550 Observations
- Commentary, Compendium, & Observations Index

Observations Volume 6

- 550 Observations
- Commentary, Compendium, & Observations Index

Regarding our testimonies of The Book of Mormon, our attitude will always determine our altitude. We must raise our sights and always look upward, in the direction of our hopes and our dreams.

A Book of Mormon Commentary
Volumes One - Three

Compendia
Volumes One - Eight

Observations
Volumes One - Six

www.ingramcontent.com/pod-product-compliance
Lightning Source LLC
Chambersburg PA
CBHW061400010526
44107CB00012B/1002